OXFORD MEDICAL PUBLICATIONS

Studies in Psychiatry

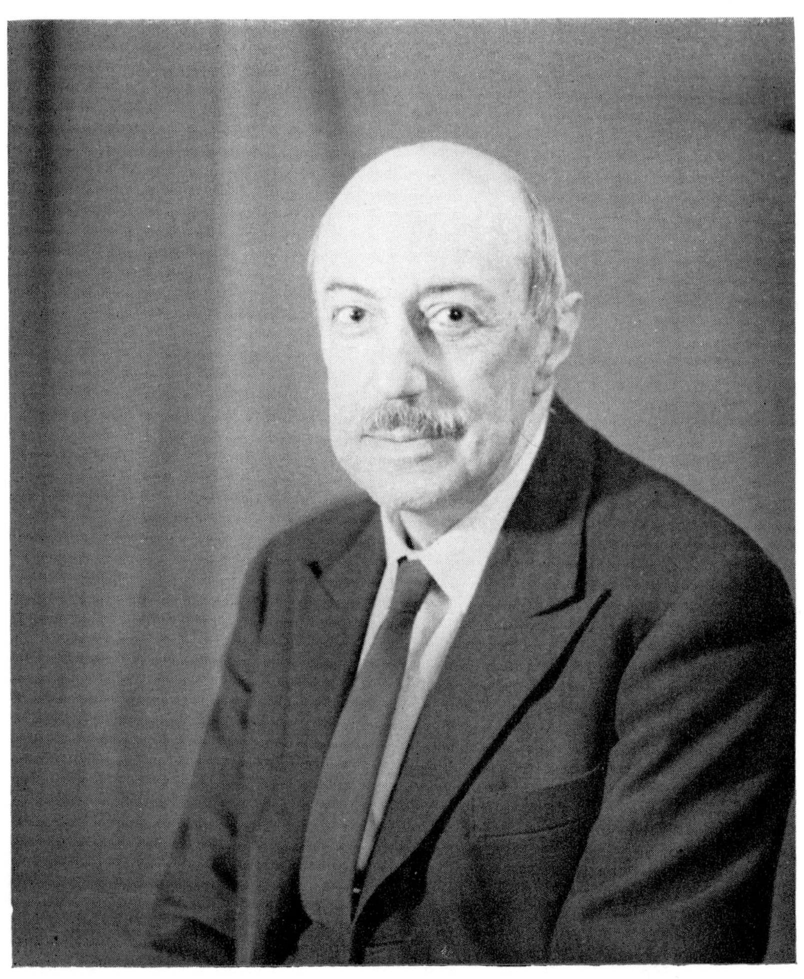

Sir Aubrey Lewis

Frontispiece]

Studies in Psychiatry

A SURVEY OF WORK CARRIED OUT IN THE DEPARTMENT OF PSYCHIATRY OF THE INSTITUTE OF PSYCHIATRY, UNDER THE CHAIRMANSHIP OF SIR AUBREY LEWIS, 1945–66

Edited by

MICHAEL SHEPHERD

D.M., M.R.C.P., D.P.M.

Professor of Epidemiological Psychiatry
Institute of Psychiatry, University of London

and

D. L. DAVIES

D.M., M.R.C.P., D.P.M.

Physician, The Bethlem Royal and Maudsley Hospitals

LONDON

OXFORD UNIVERSITY PRESS

NEW YORK TORONTO

1968

Oxford University Press, Ely House, London W. 1

GLASGOW NEW YORK TORONTO MELBOURNE WELLINGTON
CAPE TOWN SALISBURY IBADAN NAIROBI LUSAKA ADDIS ABABA
BOMBAY CALCUTTA MADRAS KARACHI LAHORE DACCA
KUALA LUMPUR HONG KONG TOKYO

PRINTED AND BOUND IN ENGLAND BY
HAZELL WATSON AND VINEY LTD
AYLESBURY, BUCKS

Contents

List of Contributors vii

Preface ix

INTRODUCTION

Sir Aubrey Lewis and the Institute of Psychiatry 3
SEYMOUR S. KETY

Sir Aubrey Lewis and the Institute of Psychiatry 6
P. BAAN

The Origins of the Medical Research Council Social Psychiatry Research Unit 11
NEIL O'CONNOR

PART I. PSYCHOSOCIAL STUDIES

1. Social Treatments of Mental Illness 17
J. K. WING

2. Social Attitudes and Psychiatric Epidemiology 32
K. RAWNSLEY

3. Social Psychiatry and Mental Subnormality 50
JACK TIZARD

4. Psychology and Intelligence 65
NEIL O'CONNOR

5. Experimental Psychological Studies of Chronic Schizophrenia 83
P. H. VENABLES

6. Psychological Treatments 106
MICHAEL G. GELDER

7. Forensic Psychiatry 122
T. C. N. GIBBENS

PART II. CHILD PSYCHIATRY, GENETICS, AND EDUCATION

8. Child Psychiatry 147
MICHAEL RUTTER

9. Psychiatric Genetics 168
JAMES SHIELDS

10. Psychiatric Education and Training 192
D. L. DAVIES

PART III. BIOLOGICAL STUDIES

11. Sensorimotor Physiology 209
CYRIL RASHBASS

12. Research Conducted in the Metabolic Unit, 1956–66 225
G. F. M. RUSSELL

13. Pharmacological Studies 253
E. MARLEY

14. Cerebral Amine Functions in Health and Disease 289
W. G. DEWHURST

15. Neuroendocrine Studies on Instinctual Behaviour 318
RICHARD P. MICHAEL

Index of Names 337

Index of Subjects 339

List of Contributors

P. Baan
Chief, Mental Health Unit, World Health Organization, Geneva.

D. L. Davies, D.M. (Oxon.), M.R.C.P., D.P.M.
Physician, The Maudsley Hospital.

W. G. Dewhurst, M.A., B.M., B.Ch. (Oxon.), M.R.C.P., D.P.M. (London)
Senior Lecturer, Institute of Psychiatry, University of London; Honorary Physician, The Maudsley Hospital.

Michael G. Gelder, M.A., D.M., M.R.C.P., D.P.M.
Physician, The Bethlem Royal Hospital and The Maudsley Hospital.

T. C. N. Gibbens, M.B.E., M.D., M.R.C.P., D.P.M.
Professor of Forensic Psychiatry, Institute of Psychiatry, University of London.

Seymour S. Kety, A.B., M.D., D.Sc. (Hon.)
Professor of Psychiatry, Harvard Medical School; Director of the Psychiatric Research Laboratories, Massachusetts General Hospital, Boston, U.S.A.

E. Marley, M.A., M.D., F.R.C.P.E., D.P.M.
Reader in Pharmacology, Institute of Psychiatry, University of London.

Richard P. Michael, Ph.D., M.B., B.S., D.P.M.
Senior Lecturer in Psychiatry, Institute of Psychiatry, University of London; Director, Primate Behaviour Research Unit; Honorary Physician, The Bethlem Royal Hospital and The Maudsley Hospital.

Neil O'Connor, M.A., Ph.D.
Medical Research Council, External Staff, The Maudsley Hospital.

Cyril Rashbass, M.A., M.D.
Senior Lecturer, Institute of Psychiatry, University of London.

K. Rawnsley, M.B., F.R.C.P., D.P.M.
Professor of Psychological Medicine, Welsh National School of Medicine, Whitchurch Hospital, Cardiff.

G. F. M. Russell, M.D., M.R.C.P., F.R.C.P.Ed., D.P.M.
Senior Lecturer and Dean, Institute of Psychiatry, University of London.

Michael Rutter, M.D., M.R.C.P., D.P.M.
Senior Lecturer in Psychiatry, Institute of Psychiatry, University of London; Honorary Physician, The Maudsley Hospital.

James Shields, B.A.
Lecturer, Institute of Psychiatry, University of London, attached to the Medical Research Council Psychiatric Genetics Research Unit, The Maudsley Hospital.

Jack Tizard, M.A., B.Litt., Ph.D.
Professor of Child Development, University of London Institute of Education.

Peter H. Venables, B.A., Ph.D.
Professor of Psychology, Birkbeck College, University of London.

J. K. Wing, M.D., Ph.D., D.P.M.
Director, Medical Research Council Social Psychiatry Research Unit, Institute of Psychiatry, University of London.

Preface

VISITORS to the Institute of Psychiatry of the University of London now have no difficulty in finding the department of psychiatry. Since early 1967 it has occupied two floors of the Institute's new building in the grounds of The Maudsley Hospital. Before this time, however, the department had no geographical identity. Its members were scattered widely over the rooms, huts and basements of the hospital site; its unity was principally dependent on the force and vision of its progenitor, Sir Aubrey Lewis, who was Professor of Psychiatry from 1945 to 1966.

From 1948, when the Maudsley Hospital Medical School became the Institute of Psychiatry within the British Postgraduate Medical Federation, this department came rapidly to occupy a central position in the development of psychological medicine in the United Kingdom. As an academic centre it has been the seed-bed for many university teachers in Britain, the Commonwealth and elsewhere. Under Aubrey Lewis' direction the professorial unit ensured that their early clinical training and experience were acquired in what Alan Gregg has referred to as the 'atmosphere of expectancy' which characterizes an active, living institution.

A modern academic department must be judged by its achievements in research as well as in teaching. In 1948 the Institute of Psychiatry comprised only two departments. One was concerned with laboratory investigations, the other with clinical psychiatry in its broadest sense. The former developed by fission into separate departments concerned with such conventional fields of endeavour as biochemistry and neuropathology. Lewis' department fostered the growth of psychology until it was able to stand independently. It also ramified in many directions, bringing several fields of inquiry to the stage of embodiment as independent departments when financial resources permitted. Within the department there was no division into laboratory and clinical studies: on the contrary, there was a deliberate effort to unite both lines of approach within each field of study.

The value of Lewis' personal contribution to psychiatric research is attested by his many publications [1, 2]. But over and above his own work he initiated, stimulated and guided a large number of studies by the many members of his department, always with a clear-sighted awareness of the real obstacles to scientific progress in the branch of medicine: 'The barrier to conspicuous advance in psychiatry has not been stinginess and prejudice on the part of those who decide whether a research project submitted to them should live or die; nor has it been lack of ability among those who are engaged in psychiatric research: it lies in the inherent toughness of the problems' [3]. Tackling these problems as the proponent of a broad, undogmatic standpoint Lewis has consistently argued that '. . . no single approach can be recognized in the process of psychiatric research' [4]; it followed naturally that the '. . . fields within which psychiatric research is carried on are so wide that there is scope for many kinds of interest and ability' [5].

The logical results of this view were amply demonstrated during Lewis' occupancy of the chair of psychiatry at the Institute. One of the fundamental activities regarded by Claude Bernard as necessary for scientific inquiry is the capacity to create conditions favouring research. To sustain a continuous flow of research into the biological, psychological and social aspects of psychiatry over a twenty-year period represents a considerable achievement. Yet the very breadth of the spectrum of this activity has partly obstructed a rounded view of its dimensions since the numerous scientific reports have appeared in so many widely disparate vehicles of publication. To try and reveal something of the nature and extent of these research activities within the compass of one book is the primary objective of this collection of essays. Most of them have been contributed by senior members of the department of psychiatry at the time of Lewis' retirement. Together they span the principal fields of investigation which have been cultivated in the department over two decades, though references to several individual studies have had to be omitted.

Each area of psychiatric research within the department is covered by the man who has made it his particular concern. Workers in the psychosocial sciences include five present and past members of the Medical Research Council Social Psychiatry Unit which Lewis founded and directed until 1965. Dr. John Wing, the present director, describes the work on the social treatments of mental illness; Professor Jack Tizard and Dr. Neil O'Connor cover the research into the social and psychological aspects of mental subnormality; Professor Peter Venables summarizes a sequence of experiments on the psychophysiology of schizophrenia; and Professor Kenneth Rawnsley collates a series of epidemiological studies linking social attitudes and mental disorder. In addition, Dr. Michael Gelder reviews a variety of investigations into the psychological treatment of mental illness and Professor Trevor Gibbens outlines the studies on forensic psychiatry. The biological sciences are represented by chapters on both animal and human research: thus laboratory programmes of neurophysiology, neuropharmacology and neuroendocrinology are covered by Drs. Cyril Rashbass, Edward Marley and Richard Michael respectively, while Drs. Gerald Russell and William Dewhurst deal with a group of metabolic and biochemical studies on human subjects.

Three other topics of major academic importance each receive separate chapters. Child psychiatry is surveyed by Dr. Michael Rutter, genetics by Mr. James Shields. The evolution of psychiatric education is traced by Dr. D. L. Davies, the only contributor who has not been a full-time member of the department. However, as Dean of the Institute for 16 years he has been a central figure in matters of policy and one whose role in the growth and development of the Institution has still to be fully appreciated. No one is better qualified to delineate the history of this massive and successful exercise in postgraduate education.

Finally, to help provide a more detached perspective, there are two short essays by distinguished foreign workers, both of them former professors of psychiatry. The American assessment is by Dr. Seymour Kety, until recently Chief of the Laboratory of Clinical Science at the National Institute of Mental Health. A European view comes from Dr. Peter Baan, now Chief of the Mental Health Unit of the World Health Organization.

These chapters, then, bring together in one place an impressive volume of scientific activity conducted over many years and owing its inspiration in large measure to one man. If they constitute a *Festschrift* they do so not only as a scattered collection of essays by former pupils: rather, they put on record the scope and diversity of research which was organized and developed in a single department. It is now apparent that at the Institute of Psychiatry Sir Aubrey Lewis played the major role in the laying of the foundations of academic psychiatry in Great Britain. Some measure of the quality of his achievement may be gauged from this book.

Institute of Psychiatry
University of London — Michael Shepherd
June 1967

REFERENCES

1. Lewis A. (1967) *The State of Psychiatry*, London.
2. Lewis A. (1967) *Inquiries in Psychiatry*, London.
3. Lewis A. (1963) Medicine and the affections of the mind, *Brit. med. J.*, ii, 1549–57.
4. Lewis A. (1963) *Research and its Application in Psychiatry*, Glasgow University Publications.
5. Lewis A. (1961) Psychiatric education and training, in *Psychiatrie der Gegenwart*, Band III, pp. 111–29, Berlin.

INTRODUCTION

Sir Aubrey Lewis and the Institute of Psychiatry

SEYMOUR S. KETY

MUCH of the perspective of modern medicine has come to it by way of psychiatry. Whatever tendency there is to reconstruct the patient and his feelings from the multitude of radiographic and electronic dissections, the counts and clearances and indices of this increasingly exact science, is quite probably attributable to a generation of psychiatrists who made the consideration and treatment of 'the whole patient' an important desideratum. The now firmly established psychosomatic branch of medicine has drawn its strength from the thinking and writings of men like Henry Maudsley, Morton Prince, Adolf Meyer and Stanley Cobb—to suggest only a few—who brought the ancient contemplations of metaphysics into modern medicine, tempering them in clinical observation.

From psychiatry, too, there appears to have come the realization that there was an environment of more than micro-organisms which affected man's well being: a dense jungle of interpersonal relationships which influenced the growth of his personality; a host of nutritional, cultural and motivational factors lumped into various social and economic classes which modified his intellectual and emotional development with perhaps as great a weight as have the genetic determinants.

It is noteworthy that this impact of psychiatry on medicine has occurred only minimally by virtue of substantive contributions which psychiatry has made to the body of knowledge, but very largely and characteristically through a broadening of viewpoints, a posing of questions which entertain new possibilities, an elaboration of new hypotheses. Before a science has matured to the point where it can confidently offer answers and establish its explanations it must develop a dissatisfaction with its present state of knowledge, the humility to question, the open-mindedness to seek answers wherever they may lie, the willingness to entertain them even though they may threaten long established prejudices. That is the status and those are the necessary qualities of psychiatric research in the present context of psychiatric knowledge.

Those, too, are the qualities which, for me, the Institute of Psychiatry of The Maudsley Hospital has exemplified on the basis of its intellectual endowments from Henry Maudsley, its founder, and from Professor Sir Aubrey Lewis, who for more than twenty years has been its leader.

In 1900, with remarkable insight, Henry Maudsley described in a sense the work of the yet unborn Institute which was to be associated with his name: 'I conclude that man as a whole is a larger affair . . . than any single method of minute inquiry—be it chemical, physical, pathological, microscopical, or psycho-physical—will ever unfold. . . . There is work enough for as many methods of study of mind as are rationally based: have the definite aim of a concrete mental organization to be studied, and work definitely and progressively for it by observation of facts, exclude not one another, but know that in the end they must bring, and, knowing, strive to bring their results into harmony.' The wisdom of that statement is borne out in the productivity of the many branches of the Institute whose design it anticipated. Any single observer, especially one from afar, cannot fairly describe all of the scientific contributions of the Institute; he must be satisfied to see it and describe it in terms of the work of which he has some knowledge. I have been privileged to know a number of its staff and to have learned a little of their work.

I remember being impressed more than fifteen years ago with Professor George Dawson's system of condensers for differentiating cortical-evoked potentials from noise which was the first computer of average transients I know of and heralded a new era of clinical neurophysiology, and with J. B. Brierley's studies in Professor Meyer's department of neuropathology on the migration of radioactive phosphorus along motor axons. The contributions of Professor Henry McIlwain to the important problem of the coupling of neural metabolism to activity are widely appreciated and the ability of R. Rodnight to move comfortably between rigorous clinical biochemical studies and fundamental research on phosphoproteins is indicative of the breadth and freedom which the Institute fosters. In the many years he spent there, Professor Geoffrey Harris added more than one landmark to neuro-endocrinology, not the least of which was the exciting demonstration with Richard Michael of steroid-sensitive chemoreceptors in the hypothalamus capable of activating sexual behaviour. The work of Professor John Eayrs on the neuro-embryological and behavioural effects of thyroid hormone represents an important contribution to the understanding of the role of this hormone in normal development and the means by which its absence leads to intellectual retardation. The studies on psychiatric genetics by Eliot Slater and James Shields are among the most definitive in that important area. I will not readily forget Michael Shepherd's penetrating examination of American psychiatry and I have had occasion to consult his Maudsley Monograph as well as that of Vera Norris in psychiatric epidemiology and P. H. Connell's illuminating dissertation on amphetamine psychosis.

The mere listing of the impact which work at the Institute of Psychiatry and The Maudsley Hospital has had upon a single observer speaks for the quality, versatility and breadth of what is regarded as psychiatric research there. It also explains why, when my country decided to establish a programme of psychiatric research in the National Institute of Mental Health, it was developed along similar lines and with a comparable scientific philosophy. Its research achievements alone, but also the 2,000 postgraduate students from abroad and the substantially larger number from the British Isles, would serve to justify the prediction made in 1944 by the Committee which recommended the establishment of the postgraduate Institute of Psychiatry: '. . . There is no reason why . . . the London mental health service should not develop as the European centre of progress in psychological medicine. . . .'

As if to insure the fulfilment of that prediction, just one year later, Aubrey Lewis was appointed to the Chair of Psychiatry. His name is inextricably woven into the Institute, its philosophy of research fettered only by the rigors of scientific excellence, its outstanding success. One hundred years ago Henry Maudsley described the type of creative men for whom he had the greatest respect—'. . . men of wide intellectual grasp, vast wisdom and serene energy'. How aptly and succinctly was he describing Sir Aubrey Lewis, whose broad erudition and wisdom give him a rightful place among the world's leaders in psychiatry. His inspiration, judgement and indefatigable but unassuming energy have made the Institute of Psychiatry at The Maudsley Hospital a bulwark of sound and scientific psychiatry.

Sir Aubrey Lewis and the Institute of Psychiatry

P. BAAN

FIVE years ago Professor Sir Aubrey Lewis, in his inaugural speech for the Scientific Session of the First Pan-African Conference on Mental Health in Abeokuta, Nigeria, stated: 'Fortunately, it is now the practice of all countries with an enlightened health policy to pay due regard to mental as well as physical needs. The World Health Organization has given a notable lead in this direction.' [1]

I should like to return this praise and affirm that in its mental health work WHO owes an immense debt of gratitude to this great and scholarly man.

During the few years I have had the privilege of learning about world problems in psychiatry and mental health, I have seldom tackled a problem, visited a country, held a conference or consulted an expert without finding that Sir Aubrey, the Institute of Psychiatry and The Maudsley Hospital had exercised a direct or indirect influence. This is no small praise, as we know that the position of psychiatry and mental health is still obscure and insecure in most countries. In a world where far more than half the inhabitants live under the menace of hunger, serious diseases and early death, where smallpox, malaria, plague, cholera and undernutrition affect many hundreds of millions, the situation of psychiatry is not unlike that of public health in the pre-Pasteur period of our part of the world: and it might be better compared with a situation many centuries earlier.

In developed countries, in the best cases, psychiatry has followed the rapid development of public health with some delay; but now it mostly runs parallel, no real integration being achieved. The great discoveries in the field of physical health must have challenged and stimulated those working in the field of psychiatry, but in recent decades psychiatry has tended to develop an empire of its own. There are few countries where psychiatry has an adequate place within the context of preventive and curative health administration. It is understandable that, when control of serious physical diseases makes such heavy demands on all possible manpower and available funds, psychiatric problems are not counted as priorities for attention. We all know, however, that when a country has managed to overcome many of the threats to physical health and some of the welfare problems have been incorporated into the socio-economic structure, then psychiatry and mental health, together with control of cancer, cardiovascular disease and degenerative disease, emerge as first priorities.

Will there ever be an integrated structure for both physical and mental health care? The U.S.S.R., the United Kingdom—especially since the nationalization of health services—and one or two of the European continental countries seem to be moving in that direction. It is clear, however, that the future prospects will depend largely on a system of medical education where the best of our psychiatric knowledge (preventive and curative) can be incorporated in medical courses from the first year to the last, in order to inculcate a more balanced approach to man and his health and illness. Much also depends on the kind and quality of the future psychiatrist and the delimitation of his proper sphere. I concur with Sir Aubrey's statement in his Harveian oration [2] that: 'We can, however, agree that the practice of psychiatry should be limited to illness and its prevention, and that illness occurs broadly when there is *disabling or distressing interference with normal function.*' Apart from the problems implicit in this definition (the precise meaning of disabling, distressing, normality, etc.) I agree that this is the sphere for which up till now the psychiatrist has been trained. Sir Aubrey goes on to denounce the fallacy of the syllogism: 'Psychiatrists are expert in mental disorder. Mental disorder is a form of abnormal behaviour. Therefore psychiatrists are experts in abnormal behaviour of every sort.' Psychiatric training gives little or no preparation for understanding or dealing with abnormal behaviour as distinct from mental illness. Yet psychiatrists often feel constrained to comply with demands upon them as experts in this field: and are censured when their lack of competence becomes apparent.

If we feel that psychiatrists should play a more responsible, more adequate role in the very much wider field of mental health, then the question arises of whether we should radically change the postgraduate training in psychiatry or keep to a modern, solid psychiatric training in which more room is given to contact with many other disciplines. In the latter case the psychiatrist has to be trained from the first day on to become a devoted, tolerant, open-minded, modest and skilled member of a team, in which he will have to cooperate with psychologists, sociologists, nurses, social workers, educationalists, etc., all of whom would also receive a specific training for their share of the mental health task. In order to communicate adequately with these groups, the psychiatrist will need to become acquainted during his training with the elements of psychology, sociology, educational theory and so on. Personally, I consider that such improvement of psychiatric training is more feasible than a radical change.

It is, in my opinion, the very great achievement of Sir Aubrey that, in a time of rapid social change, of overwhelming changes even in our medical and psychiatric knowledge, he built a stronghold from which he and his co-workers served practically the whole world. When I visited a developing country on a WHO mission, I almost always found one, if not more, Maudsley-trained psychiatrists doing the job of advising the government, educating medical students, training co-workers, treating patients and trying to do something in the field of prevention. They all spoke with deep respect and immense gratitude about 'their' Sir Aubrey in London. They have been key men for WHO activities. The same holds good for the many consultants, without whose help it would not have been possible for WHO to convene meetings of the Expert Committee on Mental Health, or design its mental health research programme or field projects in the various countries. All these psychiatrists were trained at a time when it still seemed to be possible to develop psychiatry apart from or only slightly integrated with public health activities.

In the turmoil of the present day I think it is becoming increasingly clear that now psychiatric and mental health activities, but especially psychiatry proper, have to become integral parts of public health, just as public health will have to be an integral part of the cultural and socio-economic structure of a country or even of a region of the world. Again, this calls for a new or changed type of medical education, and also an attuning of psychiatric training to this new requirement.

In both developed countries and those in the process of development, the psychiatrist requires a training where psychiatry proper will remain as the motive force but will be better geared to a public health practice that meets the demands of modern society. That is not easy to accomplish in a training far from the home country. Many of Sir Aubrey's pupils whom I have met all over the world have agreed with this but felt they would not have had the opportunity to obtain their knowledge and skill elsewhere. On many occasions these psychiatrists, in addition to admitting their recent awareness that they often could not meet the demands of public health adequately, made the following three points:

1. In most cases, on return to their own country they were submerged by mental hospital activities without finding the means or

knowing the way to shift the main accent sufficiently from the mental hospital to general hospital, out-patient and community facilities.

2. Some were aware that, for a variety of reasons, they had not been able to take full advantage of the range of opportunities open to them during their training. Of course, they realized that they were not being trained for a professorial post in Great Britain and, apart from that, they also saw very well that a first-class training such as they perhaps would have liked to receive would have required many more years in England than they and their governments would have desired.

3. As expatriates during their training they often felt terribly 'displaced' and alone, a suffering which was balanced only by the enormous gain of having a Maudsley training and of course by all the friendships, hospitality and guidance they got there.

Personally, I feel that just as the place of public health in the cultural and socio-economic structure of a country has now changed, so the place of psychiatry in that field also suddenly seems to have changed considerably. Therefore, I believe that the time has come for us to try to reverse the stream; I mean that an overseas training should perhaps more and more be restricted to those who, on the basis of a solid medical and psychiatric training at home, need some specific additional training (child psychiatry, community mental health, forensic psychiatry, psychotherapy, electroencephalography, etc.) The basic training of psychiatrists should be acquired, if possible, in the home country or at least in the region. Since, however, most developing countries do not have nearly as many people as they would need to perform the preventive and curative work and the teaching of medical and paramedical students, it will be necessary for well trained people from the so-called 'developed' countries to go to the developing ones. Here again, a new pattern is needed: it should not be the more experienced, older consultant, who has already obtained all the honours in his own country, who goes to a developing country for some weeks or some months to advise. This pattern also worked for several years after the war, but for some reason or other it seems not to work well now.

What we need is a group of young, gifted, well balanced and well trained, devoted and modest psychiatrists who are willing to go with their families for at least three years, but better for five or more, to a country developing its mental health services. First they would have to be there as pupils, learning about the cultural background, the socio-economic climate and what is going on in the field of public health and mental health. Perhaps they could be of some help already in the beginning by communicating some of their knowledge, if pertinent, in teaching and training courses, conveying techniques, and so on. Only after a longer stay of a year or more would they slowly begin to understand and to appreciate their role in providing service in a different community, and only then, knowing more of the language, the habits and the customs, would they achieve some skill and knowledge enabling them to work with the psychiatrists and 'paramedical' helpers of the country in the common tasks of developing preventive measures, assisting in curative processes, helping in the medical education and the training of the psychiatric team, and in the designing of adequate, appropriate and modest research schemes, without which the former tasks would lack efficacy.

If it were possible that in many years to come of *otium cum dignitate* Sir Aubrey could address himself to these new tasks as I see them, I feel that psychiatry and mental health, which already owe him so much, would incur an even greater debt.

I hope Sir Aubrey will continue to help and guide us in the world and in the World Health Organization so that in the future we may profit from his exceptional human and scholarly gifts as we have in the past. On behalf of the World Health Organization, I should like to express deep gratitude to this great and remarkable man.

REFERENCES

1. Lewis, A. (1962) Inaugural speech of the scientific session, in *First Pan-African Psychiatric Conference*, 1961, ed. Nambo, T.A., Ibadan, Government Printer.
2. Lewis, A. (1963) Medicine and the affections of the mind, *Brit. med. J.*, ii, 1549–57.

The Origins of the Medical Research Council Social Psychiatry Research Unit

NEIL O'CONNOR

In 1942 Sir Aubrey (then Dr.) Lewis was associated with a study carried out by Dr. Russell Fraser, on the prevalence of neurosis in industry and its cost to the nation. The work raised many problems of scientific interest, and led to the setting up of a Medical Research Council Unit under Lewis' honorary direction in the summer of 1948. The Unit had three aims: (1) to examine the conditions under which the mentally handicapped and disturbed could do productive work in institutions and the community; (2) to describe and measure the mental and emotional characteristics of industrial workers; and (3) to study the conditions of the psychiatric interview and its use as a means of appraising personality and mental health.

Originally there were seven professional workers—a psychiatrist, five psychologists and an economist—to begin investigation of these areas. By early 1949 an initial survey of their respective fields had been conducted and investigations and experiments had already begun. The Unit was first called the Occupational Psychiatry Research Unit. Two sections were centred on the newly-formed Institute of Psychiatry in The Maudsley Hospital where Dr. Frieda Goldman-Eisler and Miss M. Withers studied the interview in London, and Dr. (now Professor) Tizard and Dr. N. O'Connor began studies of the occupational skills of the subnormal. The third section began its activities in Manchester where Dr. M. Markowe, Dr. A. Heron and Mr. L. Barber formed a team. In 1950 the first report to the Medical Research Council listed four publications and described the lines of work being pursued. The subnormal were being trained in industrial tasks in workshops set up in a hospital. The effects of supervision on their output was being studied, and the work record of a hundred backward boys who had just left school was being investigated. The Manchester team was studying the productivity of neurotic workers in a factory, and was beginning more intensive studies of the occupational effects of mental instability. Basic theoretical work on the interview, using a technique devised by E. D.

Chapple of Harvard, was being pursued by Dr. Goldman Eisler, studying the psychiatric interview.

During the next 3 years the name of the Unit was changed to the Unit for Research in Occupational Adaptation. This change was made to prevent misconceptions arising among industrial workers and supervisors, but the work continued essentially along the same lines with many of the same investigators, although one additional psychiatrist and another psychologist joined the staff of the Unit. Publications rose beyond thirty during the first 5 years of the Unit's existence, and Lewis wrote two articles which were to be especially important for the future direction of the Unit's work. These articles were entitled 'Social Aspects of Psychiatry' [1] and 'Health as a Social Concept' [2]. In these he reviewed the whole field of social psychiatry and the role of empirical research in providing answers to theoretical and practical problems.

During the next period, from 1954 to 1958, the Unit extended its work to an investigation of the social and clinical problems of chronic psychosis. The Manchester team returned to London to take part in these studies and a series of field investigations into attitudes towards both minor and major mental illness was begun, under the leadership of Dr. (now Professor) Rawnsley, in South Wales. At the same time, a number of changes in personnel took place which reflected both the extension of the investigations into the community, and the transfer of lessons learned with the subnormal to work with chronic schizophrenics. This trend, which occurred about 1955, had been already foreshadowed in Lewis' original memorandum to the Medical Research Council in 1947. New members of the Unit included Dr. (now Professor) G. M. Carstairs as Assistant Director, and Dr. G. W. Brown and Dr. J. B. Loudon. The Unit's report to the Medical Research Council in 1958 was presented also under a new title, that of the Social Psychiatry Research Unit, its current designation. Dr. J. K. Wing, who joined the Unit towards the end of this period, subsequently became Unit Director on Lewis' retirement.

By 1958, when the Unit had been in existence for nearly 10 years, the publication list had risen to over eighty titles.

The work of the Unit at the end of this period begins to overlap with the current work reported in this volume. There has been a movement away from occupational workshop studies, which were the basis of much of the work with defectives and industrial workers, and towards an examination of the effect of social pressures on the mentally ill. At the same time, experimental and physiological studies of both chronic schizophrenics and severely subnormal children were undertaken.

It would be possible to analyse this more recent material on the basis of the Unit's reports to the Medical Research Council in 1961 and 1964, but it is better to leave the reader to find its more vivid expression in subsequent chapters.

REFERENCES

1. LEWIS, A. (1951) Social aspects of psychiatry, *Edinb. med. J.*, **58**, 214–47.
2. LEWIS, A. (1953) Health as a social concept, *Brit. J. Sociol.*, **4**, 109–24.

PART I
PSYCHOSOCIAL STUDIES

1

Social Treatments of Mental Illness

J. K. WING

THE work described in this chapter is concerned with the revolution which has overtaken the practice of psychiatry during the past twenty years. In 1954 the number of beds in English mental hospitals, which had been steadily rising throughout the century, reached a peak and thereafter, against all expectation, declined. The chief contribution to this dramatic turn of events was made by the group of patients which had hitherto resisted all efforts at treatment, which had given to folk-lore its ideas on madness, and which represented to lay and professional minds alike the ultimate in hopelessness and incurability. This group was composed of patients suffering from schizophrenia. The decrease in bed-occupancy of mental hospitals which is now evident could not have occurred unless schizophrenic patients (who accounted for more than two-thirds of the long-stay population) had ceased to accumulate at the old rate.

The new watchwords for mental hospitals became 'socialization', 'rehabilitation' and 'therapeutic milieu'. In the community, the new terms were 'after-care' and 'family therapy'. It is, in fact, convenient to divide investigations of these techniques of treatment into two main parts, one dealing with patients who had stayed for more than 2 years in a mental hospital, the other dealing with patients discharged after a short stay, who now spend most of their time in the community. This dichotomy is seriously misleading in several respects which will be discussed later, but it does allow the demonstration of many of the principles which underlie a rational social psychiatry. Most attention will be concentrated upon studies of schizophrenia, which have close parallels with (and were in part derived from) the investigations into mental subnormality described by Professor Tizard in Chapter 3.

INSTITUTIONALISM

The long-stay schizophrenic patient was the hallmark of the old-fashioned mental hospital. Even today, the simplest way to discover the quality of a hospital is to look for the shambling gait, the bent, posture, the stereotyped movements, the eternal mumbling, the inactivity, the apathetic conformity, the distaste for company, the dull and vacant look of the well-institutionalized patient. The more often this picture is seen, the poorer the social environment of the hospital is likely to be, though no hospital is without its quota of such patients. Nevertheless, 'well-institutionalized' was once a term of approbation—this end-state was actually desired by the staff. It is not the patients, and certainly not the patients' relatives who have initiated the new policies. There has been a change of attitude on the part of doctors, nurses and social workers.

The processes of institutionalization were studied in two mental hospitals near London. It was found that the longer a schizophrenic patient had been in hospital, the more likely was he to be socially withdrawn, to speak with monotony and a startling poverty of vocabulary, to have no knowledge of the outside world and to be able to produce no plans for the future. The longer he had been in hospital, the more likely he was to want to stay. This gradual adoption of a way of life which automatically excludes ordinary community living is at the very heart of institutionalism—a condition to which schizophrenic patients, perhaps above all others, are prone. It is much more difficult to show a similar gradual progression of florid clinical symptoms. Delusions, incoherence of speech or catatonic mannerisms do not seem to be related to length of stay in the same way. It is, of course, true that some schizophrenic symptoms, particularly the negative ones—muteness, withdrawal, poverty of speech and affect—may be seen in severe form in patients who have never been in an institution in their lives. The 'end-state' shown by schizophrenic patients in mental hospitals has a primary component due to the disease, and a secondary component due partly to *specific vulnerability* to an understimulating environment and partly to institutionalism, that is, to a gradual acquiescence in the institutional mode of life. Old-fashioned mental hospitals are members of the class of 'total institutions': refugee camps, Dickensian orphanages, and high-security prisons are other examples [31].

It is the secondary components which vary most with the social environment of the hospital. In 1960, there were sufficient differences between hospitals to allow natural experiments to be undertaken. Three hospitals were chosen on their reputations, and a series of social measurements confirmed the justice of report. The hospitals provided different social environments for their patients to live in, varying in the liberality of ward regimes and the therapeutic enthusiasm of staff, in the degree to which the patients were encouraged to be constructively active, rather than being allowed to sit for hours doing nothing, and in the extent to which they were 'stripped' of personal possessions. The hospital which provided the most barren and understimulating environment contained the patients who were most withdrawn, most silent and most affectively blunted [10, 43]. Subsequent studies on the same lines, 2 years and 4 years after the first, have demonstrated that certain changes in the social environment are accompanied by changes in the clinical condition of the patients. At the time of the last survey there was much less difference between the hospitals, so far as the gross indices used could be taken as a measure.

REHABILITATION OF LONG-STAY IN-PATIENTS

One of the major factors correlated with morbidity in these studies was inactivity. Patients who spent large parts of the day doing nothing (not even watching television) tended to be most severely disturbed in ward behaviour and showed most deficits in conversation at interview. In a series of experiments, Unit workers showed that one of the most convenient, economical and clinically helpful ways to activate a chronic schizophrenic patient was to set up hospital workshops where the rehabilitation process could begin. Some of the general problems of the rehabilitation process were considered by Lewis [14]. Carstairs, Clark and O'Connor [11] had visited centres abroad, particularly in Holland, where mentally ill and handicapped patients had been employed, and a small workshop was set up in Banstead Hospital in which long-stay patients could do simple assembly work for a wage [12]. Numerous studies of motivating factors were made possible by this workshop since the patients' output was also a useful measure of behaviour. In several experiments it was shown that additional social incentives, such as encouragement, goal-setting and knowledge of results, which improve the performance of most subjects, failed to make any impact on that of the schizophrenic patients and, indeed, might even lead to a fall-off in performance in paranoid patients. However, a steady linear improvement in performance with practice *was* found, though it did not take the negatively accelerated form of the usual learning curve [18, 19, 20, 26].

Wing and Freudenberg [45] followed these experiments with another in which controlled social pressure was brought to bear by familiar staff-nurse supervisors in two workshops. Industrial performance improved under these natural conditions when patients were encouraged, but the increment only continued while social stimulation was maintained. Time-sampling of workshop behaviour during each of five consecutive fortnightly periods showed that the increase in output during periods of active encouragement was accompanied by a significant decrease in the patient's abnormal behaviour—immobility, mannerisms, laughing and talking to themselves, and restlessness. Improvement in workshop behaviour was not, however, necessarily reflected in improvement in the ward.

These studies provided the background for an experimental assessment of the value of the Industrial Rehabilitation Units run by the Ministry of Labour, principally for physically-handicapped, but also for psychiatric patients. Any effort at rehabilitation of long-stay schizophrenic patients needs to take into account the various components of the final condition of disability—those due to pre-existing deficiencies of personality, education, social competence or occupational skill; those due to illness itself; and those acquired secondarily because the patient has become institutionalized or has otherwise acquired maladaptive attitudes or habits. The most severely ill patients are unlikely to be discharged unless the clinical condition improves. Those who are moderately ill can be discharged only if their attitudes to living and working outside hospital are satisfactory, or can be changed.

A group of 20 chronic schizophrenic men from Long Grove Hospital was admitted to a course at an Industrial Rehabilitation Unit. Ten equivalent patients remained in hospital as controls. All patients were aged 25 to 45 years and had been occupied in the hospital without close supervision. Half were severely, and half moderately, ill. The 10 moderately ill men who went to the I.R.U. showed a considerable improvement in attitude to work, and this was thought to be at least partly responsible for the fact that seven of them were employed and self-supporting 1 year later. There was also an improvement in attitude to discharge. The 10 severely ill men who went to the I.R.U. improved in symptoms but not markedly in attitudes. They demonstrated an ability to work at a low level, but they were not considered acceptable in open industry. A recommendation of sheltered work for some of them could not be implemented because of lack of facilities. The 10 control patients, who received no special rehabilitation, showed no improvement at all [28, 29, 46].

This experiment indicated that severely ill patients (over half of the long-stay schizophrenic group) were unlikely to be able to benefit unless more prolonged industrial rehabilitation were made available, but that attitudes to work could be influenced in the moderately ill patients. It also showed that an I.R.U. presents three features which could hardly be reproduced in a special unit in a mental hospital: demonstration of working ability in a realistic setting; presence of a large majority of non-schizophrenics and non-institutionalized workers; and deliberate inculcation of good working habits—time-keeping, workshop behaviour, standard of finish, and so on.

These findings were extended and consolidated in a further study. Forty-five moderately handicapped male long-stay schizophrenic patients from two mental hospitals, aged between 45 and 60 years, who had all been resident for many years, went to an I.R.U. while continuing to live in hospital. Almost half the patients were employed a year later, 10 of them in sheltered work (mainly in Remploy factories). Seventeen patients were living outside hospital. Even among the successful patients, however, many continued to require medical and social supervision throughout the follow-up period, and very keen and skilled staff were necessary to achieve a good result. Patients who had special preparation in industrial workshops and a rehabilitation villa before they went to the I.R.U. were less likely to break down again while there, and more likely to obtain work after completing the course. The patients who worked in Remploy factories proved just as satisfactory (if not more so) as physically handicapped people who started work at the same time [41]. Less research work has been carried out on the domestic aspects of resettlement, but Wing [27] has discussed the advantages of the Norwegian and Dutch systems of family care.

Some of the practical consequences of this and other work were considered by Bennett and Wing [1]. A more general theory of rehabilitation was based on a study of physically and psychiatrically handicapped individuals passing through an I.R.U. [34].

THE LONG-STAY PATIENT AFTER DISCHARGE

Rawnsley, Loudon and Miles [23] showed that there was often a discrepancy between the attitudes that mental hospital staff and the relatives of patients in the hospitals attributed to each other. In about 6 per cent. of cases, for example, the staff thought the patient could be discharged if only the relatives would accept him, while the relatives said that he could come home if only the doctor would say he was well enough. It is clear that at that time (and perhaps to some extent still) there was a group of long-stay patients who could relatively easily be discharged, although the rehabilitation experiments just described indicate that a 'hard core' is eventually reached which presents difficult resettlement problems, only soluble by a planned and skilled approach to rehabilitation.

What the outcome might be if rehabilitation procedures were not applied was shown by Brown, Carstairs and Topping [6] and Brown [2] who followed up 240 men discharged from seven metropolitan mental hospitals between 1950 and 1956. About two-thirds remained out of hospital for at least 1 year and, of these, two-thirds attained a fairly satisfactory social adjustment: that is, about one half were readmitted or failed to adjust satisfactorily. Success appeared to be related to severity of clinical condition at discharge, ability to obtain work, and type of domestic environment lived in. Patients fared best if they went to lodgings or lived with siblings, and much less well when they returned to wives or parents.

This study was carried out while the flow of discharges from mental hospitals still showed only a moderate increase. It is convenient, at this stage, to consider some statistics describing the enormous changes which were about to take place in admission and discharge practice.

STATISTICAL STUDIES OF MENTAL HOSPITAL PRACTICE

In 1954 a survey was carried out of all the patients resident in four metropolitan mental hospitals, which showed that by far the largest diagnostic group among the long-stay patients was that of the schizophrenias [13]. Analysis of the Registrar General's admission and discharge statistics for the years 1949–53 indicated that admissions and discharges were increasing, and length of stay decreasing, at a time well before the introduction of phenothiazine drugs. This might have been due to the admission of a new type of patient and it was not clear that chronic schizophrenic patients were sharing in the general reduction of length of hospital stay. In order to clarify this point Wing, Denham and Monro [44] analysed the outcome of all schizophrenic patients admitted to Long Grove Hospital in 1950 and in 1955. Of the former cohort, 38 per cent. remained in hospital continuously for over 2 years, of the latter cohort only 20 per cent. did so. If first admissions alone were considered, the proportions of patients in the two cohorts who became long-stay were 29 per cent. and 12 per cent. respectively.

Brown, Parkes and Wing [8] then made a more detailed study of patients admitted to Banstead, Springfield and West Park Hospitals in 1951 and in 1956, in order to study readmission rates. Each cohort was followed for 3 years. There was an increase in the number of schizophrenic patients in the second cohort (800 compared with 500), and a decrease (from 17 months to 10 months) in total length of stay, including readmissions, during a 3-year follow-up period. However, there was a threefold increase in the number of occasions on which patients were readmitted to London hospitals.

These two statistical studies illustrate the new state of affairs in psychiatry. The London hospitals studied were ahead of the national trend, which has now caught up: fewer than 10 per cent. of schizophrenic patients now admitted for the first time remain in hospital for 2 years. The influence of social factors on length of stay, which used to be so important [4], is therefore now less relevant. This was neatly shown by Brown [3] who found that patients admitted to hospital in 1951 were significantly more likely to leave within the subsequent 2 years if they were visited during the first 8 weeks. In 1956, when most patients were discharged in any event, no such relationship could be demonstrated. Thus part of the decrease that has occurred in mean length of stay is due to the earlier discharge of socially isolated individuals who previously would have remained in hospital.

These statistical investigations pointed to the need for more intensive study of the social and clinical progress of patients after they left hospital.

THE SCHIZOPHRENIC PATIENT IN FAMILY AND COMMUNITY

One of the main findings of the study by Brown, Carstairs and Topping was that long-stay schizophrenic men were best adjusted when they returned to live in lodgings or with siblings rather than with parents or wives. In part this finding could be attributed to the greater readiness of mothers than siblings or landladies to accept more disturbed patients in their homes.

A further study was therefore carried out, in which the clinical condition of schizophrenic patients was assessed before discharge and the relationship between them and their relatives also evaluated before and immediately after discharge. The family was visited again 1 year after discharge and at the time of any readmission. Of 50 patients who were rated as having a high level of emotional involvement with their relatives, 38 deteriorated substantially in clinical condition or social behaviour during the follow-up year; on the other hand, only 13 of 47 patients who returned to low-involvement homes showed deterioration. This result held true when clinical condition at discharge was controlled. It supported the inference drawn from the earlier study that intimate emotional involvement with another person is sometimes deterimental to the mental health of a schizophrenic patient.

At the time of discharge from hospital, 46 per cent. of the schizophrenic patients were rated as showing mental symptoms of moderate severity, and 13 per cent. were thought to show severe symptoms. At the time about one-third of them were still actively deluded but the rest denied delusions or hallucinations. Nearly all strongly wanted to leave hospital, in marked contrast to long-stay patients; in effect, they were not 'institutionalized'. Most were confident that things would go well after they left hospital—they would find work, their relatives would welcome them and they would not be readmitted. Only 20 per cent. thought that they had been mentally ill.

During the subsequent year 43 per cent. were readmitted to hospital and a further 19 per cent. showed severely disturbed behaviour which did not lead to admission. In at least 40 per cent. of cases where a patient was living with relatives, there was considerable behaviour disorder, lasting for a month or more, such as violence or threats of violence, shouting at night, abnormal sexual behaviour, or involvement of the relative in delusions. Eighty per cent. of the patients had attended an out-patient clinic or seen their family doctor and 40 per cent. had been to an employment exchange, usually to the disabled persons section. Many of those who found work through the employment exchange did not retain it and no sheltered workshop facilities were available to them. There was very little domiciliary visiting even when patients failed to keep their clinic appointments. Many patients did not take the drugs they were advised to continue with [7, 17, 22, 47].

These findings partly reflected the lack of services available in London at that time, partly the fact that more severely ill patients are likely to be admitted to hospitals in large conurbations, and partly sampling problems. However, they did provide a baseline against which to measure the success of any new community care services which might be introduced. In a further study, 339 schizophrenic patients admitted to three mental hospitals in Surrey, Nottingham, and Essex were followed over a 5-year period. The process of admission or readmission to hospital was closely studied. About 70 per cent. of admissions followed a 'social crisis' in which it seemed that patients' violent, threatening, or other seriously disturbed behaviour could no longer be contained within the family or domestic circle, and emergency help had been called in. In Nottingham, where there was an integrated mental health service (between hospital and local authority) more detailed information was available, and it was found that at least as many social crises occurred which were *not* followed by admission. It was not possible to see any differences between the crises that immediately led to admission and those that were managed without in-patient hospital treatment.

However, 'institutionalism'—in the sense of a condition brought about by a long stay in a mental hospital—was almost completely prevented during the 5 years after first admission. It could not, therefore, be regarded as an important factor determining outcome in the community. Several measures of outcome gave a consistent picture of the 5-year prognosis. The most clear-cut operational criterion was the proportion of patients who spent some time in hospital during the fourth or fifth year of the follow-up period: this was 28 per cent. A similar proportion of patients was either in hospital throughout the final 6 months (11 per cent.) or had been severely disturbed in behaviour during that time (17 per cent.). In addition, 16 per cent. were unemployed throughout the final 6 months though they had not been severely disturbed, and a further 7 per cent. had been moderately disturbed but were working. The remaining 49 per cent. were functioning well. According to a categorization of clinical course over the 5 years, 28 per cent. of patients had shown symptoms of at least moderate severity throughout the whole period, 27 per cent. had been episodically disturbed, 11 per cent. had shown disturbed behaviour during the first half of the follow-up period but not the second, and 35 per cent. had not been disturbed except during the first year after admission. In summary, just over one quarter of schizophrenic patients were still severely ill 5 years after first admission, and another quarter were still handicapped by less severe symptoms. The results were not greatly different in the three areas studied. One of the hospitals was justly famous for its integrated community care services and another for its rehabilitation facilities so that the services available were, if anything, better than elsewhere. None of the areas was in the centre of a conurbation, where there is probably a concentration of patients with particularly difficult problems. It seems safe to assume that the results do not overestimate the problem found in early schizophrenia.

Two-thirds of the patients studied had been admitted before 1956 and the indices of outcome for this group showed a similar consistency of result. Fifty-three per cent. of such patients spent some time in hospital during the fourth and fifth year of the follow-up period. Twenty per cent. were in-patients throughout the final 6 months and 24 per cent. were severely disturbed in behaviour during that time. A further 16 per cent. were unemployed for the whole of the final 6 months but were not severely disturbed, and 10 per cent. had been moderately disturbed but were working. Thirty per cent. were functioning well. Again there was very little difference in any of the indices between the three cohorts of patients.

It can be concluded that a prolonged stay in hospital causes certain disadvantages which are avoided by early discharge but that, so long as patients are not completely cured, they remain liable to accumulate other types of secondary handicap. At the moment rehabilitation efforts are mainly concentrated in hospital and tend to cease altogether at discharge. 'After-care', where it exists, is generally supervision rather than treatment or rehabilitation in the sense discussed earlier and, when it is decided that action must be taken, the policy is still to admit the patient to hospital or day hospital. The current early discharge practices can continue even if extra services are not provided, without undue complaint from four-fifths of relatives. Relatives are not in a strong position to complain—they are not experts, they may be ashamed to talk about their problems, and may have come to the conclusion that no help can be offered which will substantially reduce their difficulties. At the same time a strong feeling of duty and humanity makes many relatives accept the burden of caring for a handicapped patient. It is not necessarily good clinical practice to accept the situation as a justification of 'community care'. There was very little complaint from relatives in the days when schizophrenic patients remained in hospital for long periods but this would not now be regarded as a justification for that more traditional practice. The key relatives of 29 per cent. of first-admitted patients, and 60 per cent. of previously-admitted patients who were not in hospital at the time, mentioned at the follow-up interview that they had one or more current problems which they thought were due to having the patient at home. A frequently mentioned problem concerned the health of the informant. In households where there were children at home, 16 per cent. of informants mentioned a current problem about the child's health where a first-admitted patient was involved, and 29 per cent. concerning a previously-admitted patient.

Two problems require special mention. One concerns the age of parents. If the age of the younger parent was used as an index when both were alive, 34 per cent. were aged 61–70 and 40 per cent. were 71 or older, at the end of the follow-up period. Half the mothers were widows. The second problem concerns the 124 patients (37 per cent.) who were living with their marital partners at the time of key admission. Twenty-four patients separated during the follow-up period because of abnormal behaviour. By the end of the period 44 per cent. of the male patients and 27 per cent. of the female patients who had ever been married were divorced or separated. The figures of Rowntree [24] suggest that the rate for a sample of the general population who married between 1930 and 1949 was less than 10 per cent. [5, 33, 35].

The principles underlying the provision of specialized environments which can be used for handicapped schizophrenic patients, whether they are in the hospital or in the community, have been discussed in several papers [32, 36, 39, 40].

METHODOLOGICAL PROBLEMS

One of the difficulties in interpreting the findings in the studies summarized above is that, like most intensive work in social psychiatry, they have had to be based on hospital or clinic populations, with an inevitable bias due to defects of selection. A cumulative disease register has therefore been set up, with the support of the Ministry of Health, which acts as a sampling frame for future studies. In this register the data from many different psychiatric agencies, including local authority services, in-patients, day hospitals, out-patient clinics, emergency clinics, etc., are collated so that duplication is avoided. Data are collected about all patients receiving any psychiatric service from the given geographical area, so that selection bias is avoided. The characteristics of the community are known through census and other data and provide a context for the register material. The register is cumulative so that the progress of patients can be followed through time, or as they move from one agency to another, or as new services are introduced. The data are comparable with those derived from other registers in Aberdeen, Rochester (New York), and Maryland. Studies of prevalence and other epidemiological problems are therefore relatively simply undertaken [49, 50, 51].

With the aid of the register further studies are being carried out to investigate more intensively than hitherto the precipitants of schizophrenic illnesses and their clinical and social course. Factors determining the course, the problems of relatives and the effects of various types of service and treatment are also being investigated. The techniques and problems described in connexion with schizophrenia apply to other psychiatric conditions, particularly those which run a chronic course, with severe residual handicaps. A study of these other conditions is likely to prove very fruitful. An epidemiological study of early childhood autism, for example, has provided an estimate of prevalence and data which may be of relevance to the aetiology [15, 16, 48]. The condition, which must be differentiated both from schizophrenia and from mental subnormality, provides a paradigm for looking at the problems of social psychiatry and community care, since the handicaps can be described in detail and methods for overcoming them or compensating for them are now beginning to be available [38].

The area which has so far proved most difficult to quantify has been that of domestic and family functioning. Much more attention has been paid to working capacity which can be more readily measured. New methods of measuring the warmth of feeling, hostility, tension, and amount of criticism between marital partners and between parent and child have been developed. The division of labour at home, child care and discipline, housework, leisure activities, communication between family members, and their dissatisfactions can also be quantified. The indices are reliable as between interviewers, and techniques have been developed which enable the reliability to be maintained throughout a long research programme [9, 25]. If these methods prove satisfactory it will be possible to describe the social outcome of psychiatric illnesses in much greater detail, and to examine more rigorously some of the hypotheses about family relationships and clinical course which arose from the earlier work of the Unit.

The third area of measurement which has received considerable attention is that of clinical phenomenology. Parkes [21] showed that it was possible to make a reliable diagnosis even from criteria available in mental hospital case notes, which has been confirmed [5]. A simple and reliable technique for subcategorizing chronic schizophrenic conditions was used throughout much of the early work [28, 30]. More recently a standardized diagnostic present state interview has been developed which covers most of the symptoms likely to be encountered during an ordinary diagnostic interview. The information is available as ratings of specific symptoms, as scores of sections of symptoms such as worrying, anxiety, depression, varieties of delusions and hallucinations, etc., and as profiles of section scores. All these indices have been shown to be reasonably reliable in practice, at least between psychiatrists who have been educated in the same clinical school. A simple diagnostic classification based on this material has also been shown to be very reliable. The interview is being used in current research and also in the international pilot study of schizophrenia in which the Unit is taking part [37, 42]. Finally, since such detailed information on the psychiatric services available to Camberwell residents is being accumulated, there is an excellent baseline against which to measure any progress made in future. Teaching hospitals are taking on district responsibilities and Camberwell, served by a postgraduate and undergraduate teaching hospital, should be in a favourable position for development. If so, new opportunities for studying the effects of social measures of prevention, treatment, rehabilitation and management will occur, and the Unit will be well placed to take advantage of them.

REFERENCES

1. Bennett, D. H., and Wing, J. K. (1963) Sheltered workshops for the psychiatrically handicapped, in *Trends in the Mental Health Services*, ed. Freeman, H., and Farndale, J., Oxford.
2. Brown, G. W. (1959) Experiences of discharged chronic schizophrenic mental hospital patients in various types of living group, *Milbank mem. Fd Quart.*, **37**, 105–31.
3. Brown, G. W. (1959) Social factors influencing the length of hospital stay of schizophrenic patients, *Brit. med. J.*, ii, 1300–2.
4. Brown, G. W. (1960) Length of hospital stay and schizophrenia: a review of statistical studies, *Acta psychiat. scand.*, **34**, 414–30.
5. Brown, G. W., Bone, M., Dalison, B., and Wing, J. K. (1966) *Schizophrenia and Social Care*, Maudsley Monographs Series, No. 17, London.
6. Brown, G. W., Carstairs, G. M., and Topping, G. G. (1958) The post-hospital adjustment of chronic mental patients, *Lancet*, ii, 685–9.
7. Brown, G. W., Monck, Elizabeth, Carstairs, G. M., and Wing,

J. K. (1962) The influence of family life on the course of schizophrenic illness, *Brit. J. prev. soc. Med.*, **16**, 55–68.

8. BROWN, G. W., PARKES, C. M., and WING, J. K. (1961) Admissions and readmissions to three London mental hospitals, *J. ment. Sci.*, **107**, 1070–7.
9. BROWN, G. W., and RUTTER, M. L. (1966) The measurement of family activities and relationships, *Hum. Relat.*, **19**, 241–63.
10. BROWN, G. W., and WING, J. K. (1962) A comparative clinical and social survey of three mental hospitals, 'The Sociological Review' Monograph No. 5: 'Sociological Studies in the British National Health Service', Keele University.
11. CARSTAIRS, G. M., CLARK, D. H., and O'CONNOR, N. (1955) The occupational treatment of chronic psychotics: observations in Holland, Belgium and France, *Lancet*, ii, 1025–30.
12. CARSTAIRS, G. M., O'CONNOR, N., and RAWNSLEY, K. (1956) The organization of a hospital workshop for chronic psychotic patients, *Brit. J. prev. soc. Med.*, **10**, 136–40.
13. CARSTAIRS, G. M., TONGE, W. L., O'CONNOR, N., and BARBER, L. E. D. (1955) Changing population of mental hospitals, *Brit. J. prev. soc. Med.*, **9**, 187–90.
14. LEWIS, A. J. (1955) Rehabilitation programs in England, in *The Elements of a Community Mental Health Program*, New York.
15. LOTTER, V. (1966) Epidemiology of autistic conditions in young children, I. Prevalence, *Soc. Psychiat.*, **1**, 124–37.
16. LOTTER, V. (1966) Epidemiology of autistic conditions in young children, II. Some characteristics of the parents, *Soc. Psychiat.*, **1**, 163–73.
17. MONCK, ELIZABETH M. (1963) Employment experiences of 127 discharged schizophrenic men in London, *Brit. J. prev. soc. Med.*, **17**, 101–10.
18. O'CONNOR, N., HERON, A., and CARSTAIRS, G. M. (1956) Work performance of chronic schizophrenics, *Occup. Psychol.*, **30**, 153–64.
19. O'CONNOR, N., and RAWNSLEY, K. (1959) Incentives with paranoid and non-paranoid schizophrenics in a workshop, *Brit. J. med. Psychol.*, **32**, 133–43.
20. O'CONNOR, N., and RAWNSLEY, K. (1959) Two types of conditioning in psychotics and normals, *J. abnorm. soc. Psychol.*, **58**, 157–61.
21. PARKES, C. M. (1963) Interhospital and intrahospital variations in the diagnosis and severity of schizophrenia, *Brit. J. prev. soc. Med.*, **17**, 85.
22. PARKES, C. M., BROWN, G. W., and MONCK, ELIZABETH (1962) The general practitioner and the schizophrenic patient, *Brit. med. J.*, i, 972–6.
23. RAWNSLEY, K., LOUDON, J., and MILES, H. L. (1962) Attitudes of relatives to patients in mental hospitals, *Brit. J. prev. soc. Med.*, **16**, 1–15.
24. ROWNTREE, G. (1964) Some aspects of marriage breakdown in Britain during the last thirty years, *Population Studies*, **18**, 147–63.

25. RUTTER, M. L., and BROWN, G. W. (1966) The reliability and validity of measures of family life and relationships in families containing a psychiatric patient, *Soc. Psychiat.*, **1**, 38–53.
26. TOPPING, G. G., and O'CONNOR, N. (1960) The response of chronic schizophrenics to incentives, *Brit. J. med. Psychol.*, **33**, 211–14.
27. WING, J. K. (1957) The family care systems in Norway and Holland, *Lancet*, ii, 884–6.
28. WING, J. K. (1959) The measurement of behaviour in chronic schizophrenia, *Acta Psychiat. et Neurol.*, **35**, 245–54.
29. WING, J. K. (1961) Attitudes to the employability of chronic schizophrenic patient, *Occup. Psychol.*, **35**, 58–64.
30. WING, J. K. (1961) A simple and reliable subclassification of chronic schizophrenia, *J. ment. Sci.*, **107**, 862–75.
31. WING., J. K. (1962) Institutionalism in mental hospitals, *J. soc. clin. Psychol.*, **1**, 38–51.
32. WING, J. K. (1963) Rehabilitation of psychiatric patients, *Brit. J. Psychiat.*, **109**, 635–41.
33. WING, J. K. (1965) Community services for schizophrenic patients, Proceedings of the Leeds Symposium on Behavioural Disorders, Chapter 19, May and Baker Ltd.
34. WING, J. K. (1966) Social and psychological changes in a Rehabilitation Unit, *Soc. Psychiat.*, **1**, 21–28.
35. WING, J. K. (1966) Five-year outcome in early schizophrenia, *Proc. roy. Soc. Med.*, **59**, 17–18.
36. WING., J. K. (1966) Evaluating community care for schizophrenic patients in the United Kingdom, in *Community Psychiatry*, ed. Roberts, L. M., Halleck, S. L., and Loeb, M., Madison.
37. WING, J. K. (1966) The measurement of psychiatric diagnosis, *Proc. roy. Soc. Med.*, **59**, 1030–2.
38. WING, J. K., ed. (1966) *Early Childhood Autism*, Oxford.
39. WING, J. K. (1967) The modern management of schizophrenia, in *New Aspects of the Mental Health Services*, ed. Freeman, H., London.
40. WING, J. K. (1967) Social treatment, rehabilitation and management of schizophrenia, in *Recent Developments in Schizophrenia*, ed. Coppen, A., *Brit. J. Psychiat.* Monograph.
41. WING, J. K., BENNETT, D. H., and DENHAM, J. (1964) The industrial rehabilitation of long-stay schizophrenic patients, *Memor. med. Res. Coun.(Lond.)*, No. 42, H.M.S.O.
42. WING, J. K., BIRLEY, J. L. T., COOPER, J. E., GRAHAM, P., and ISAACS, A. (1967) Reliability of a procedure for measuring and classifying 'Present Psychiatric State', *Brit. J. Psychiat.*, **113**, 499–515.
43. WING, J. K., and BROWN, G. W. (1961) Social treatment of chronic schizophrenia: a comparative survey in three mental hospitals, *J. ment. Sci.*, **107**, 847–61.
44. WING, J. K., DENHAM, J., and MONRO, A. B. (1959) The duration of stay in hospital of patients suffering from schizophrenia, *Brit. J. prev. soc. Med.*, **13**, 145–8.
45. WING, J. K., and FREUDENBERG, R. K. (1961) The response of severely

ill chronic schizophrenic patients to social stimulation, *Amer. J. Psychiat.*, **118**, 311–22.

46. WING, J. K., and GIDDENS, R. G. T. (1959) Industrial rehabilitation of male chronic schizophrenics, *Lancet*, ii, 505–7.
47. WING, J. K., MONCK, ELIZABETH, CARSTAIRS, G. M., and BROWN, G. W. (1964) Morbidity in the community of schizophrenic patients discharged from London mental hospitals in 1959, *Brit. J. Psychiat.*, **110**, 10–21.
48. WING, J. K., O'CONNOR, N., and LOTTER, V. (1967) Autistic conditions in early childhood: a survey in Middlesex, *Brit. med. J.*, ii, 389–92.
49. WING, J. K., and WING, LORNA (1965) First Report of the Camberwell Psychiatric Disease Register.
50. WING, J. K., and WING, LORNA (1966) Second Report of the Camberwell Psychiatric Disease Register.
51. WING, LORNA, WING, J. K., HAILEY, ANTHEA, BAHN, ANITA K., SMITH, HELEN A., and BALDWIN, J. A. (1967) The use of psychiatric services in three urban areas: an international Case Register study, *Soc. Psychiat.*, **2**, 158–67.

2

Social Attitudes and Psychiatric Epidemiology

K. RAWNSLEY

CONTACT between a patient and the specialist mental health services represents a relatively late stage in the social process which begins with the earliest recognition by the individual patient (or by his relatives) that something is wrong. The process continues when the abnormality is reckoned by the patient, or by his family, to have medical significance and when a decision is made to seek advice, usually from the general practitioner. Further stages are encountered in the appraisal of the case by the general practitioner and in his decision whether to handle matters himself or whether to refer the patient for a psychiatric opinion. Other agencies, for example, mental welfare officers of the local health authority may be involved at this stage in the evaluation and in the process of decision-making.

Part of the work of the Medical Research Council Social Psychiatry Research Unit (South Wales detachment) has been to examine certain aspects of the elaborate social process whereby psychiatric cases are defined in the community, recognized by community members and by medical and social agencies, and dealt with by one means or other. Studies of this kind are very relevant to the epidemiology of mental disorder since, by the nature of such illness, the detection and enumeration of cases is intimately linked with prevailing social 'yardsticks' pertaining to the acceptable bounds of 'normal' behaviour and experience and also to the categorization of deviant behaviour as falling within the doctors' province.

A preliminary inquiry indicated differences between a coal-mining valley and a rural area in South Wales in the prevalence of psychiatric cases attending specialist services [3] and gave encouragement to the planning of more detailed and extensive investigations.

A person's readiness to seek or to accept psychiatric treatment will depend, in part, upon his own attitudes to mental illness and to psychiatric institutions, and upon those of his relatives. Such attitudes may also influence the willingness of subjects to declare symptoms in the course of surveys of psychiatric disorders in samples of the general population. Declaration will also be affected by prevailing concepts of mental disorders in society and by the resulting interpretation and evaluation of anomalies of behaviour and/or experience.

Before embarking on direct estimations of psychiatric morbidity in the local populations it was therefore decided to carry out a series of preliminary attitude studies. The most intimate and searching of these inquiries formed part of a detailed investigation of the social organization of a rural population using the method of social anthropology [9, 10].

Apart from the anthropological work, a series of relatively structured surveys was made of the attitudes and behaviour of particular categories of persons generally considered to have special duties, responsibilities or functions in relation to psychiatric cases. These studies focused attention upon critical stages in the social process whereby mental disorders are defined, recognized and dealt with.

ATTITUDES TO THE PSYCHIATRIC IN-PATIENT

A feature of post-war British psychiatry has been the mobilization and rehabilitation of many long-stay patients in mental hospitals. The increasing number of cases with residual symptoms living either with their families, or at institutions in closer proximity to the local population than traditional mental hospitals, demands much tolerance and sympathy from relatives, friends, neighbours and members of the general public. The Mental Health Act of 1959 emphasized the desirability of developing a comprehensive scheme of care and treatment in the community. The success of this policy will depend, in part, on the attitudes which prevail towards mental disorder in the community.

An inquiry was carried out in South Wales to examine the attitudes of relatives to a family member in a mental hospital and especially those attitudes which may influence family behaviour if and when the time comes for the patient to leave hospital [16]. The survey was based upon all patients, 230 in number, who were in mental hospitals at the time of the inquiry and those whose home addresses on admission lay in one of three defined areas in South-east Wales—a mining valley, a rural area, and a small town.

Patients were assessed by the hospital staff in terms of their social capabilities and potentialities. Attitudes of relatives were studied principally by home interviews conducted with a sample of relatives from each family and by the examination of records of contacts—visits, letters, parcels—between relatives and patients.

Twenty per cent. of the patients, many of them with very long hospital stay, were found to lack any contact with their families for the past year or more. It was a little surprising, therefore, to discover relatives of these patients—usually close relatives—living locally. Furthermore, offers of accommodation in the event of discharge were forthcoming in a quarter of the cases where contact had been lost for so long.

Of the patient sample, 6·1 per cent. had been continuously in hospital for a year or more, were fit to live at home (according to the hospital staff) and had a home waiting for them (according to the family). Although on the face of it these patients would appear to be promising candidates for rehabilitation, certain reservations must be entered. There is evidence that contact with close relatives at home may have a deleterious effect upon schizophrenics [2]. Disquieting reports have also been published of the disrupting effects on the family of the returning patient with residual disability [23].

In the South Wales investigation, analysis of frequency of visits by relatives and of their willingness to accommodate patients in the event of discharge by age of patient and by duration of stay in hospital indicates that although interest expressed through visiting is sustained in the elderly group of patients, this is not matched by willingness to house them. Judging by the response of relatives, it is clear that a policy which seeks to discharge long-stay elderly patients of either sex must look for accommodation outside the family. The provision of special hostels for the elderly long-stay patient with mild symptoms is an obvious solution. Social work with families would be best reserved for the younger group whatever their length of stay in hospital.

Married schizophrenics of less than two-years' stay command a higher level of active interest (as judged by visiting frequency) and better prospects of accommodation on discharge than do single schizophrenics. This finding illuminates earlier statistical inquiries into the differential probability of discharge for single and married patients. Thus Norris [12] showed that amongst schizophrenic admissions in 1947–49 to some London hospitals, single patients had the greatest chance of remaining in hospital for 2 years or more and that the married had least, with the widowed and divorced occupying an intermediate position. Brooke [1] showed that 19 per cent. of single schizophrenic first admissions in England and Wales in 1954–56 were still alive and in hospital 2 years later, while 12 per cent. of the patients who had been married at some time were likewise retained. Wing, Denham and Monro [22] found that single schizophrenic patients in two cohorts of admission to Long Grove Hospital had a worse prognosis for discharge within 2 years than married patients.

Comparison of the attitudes of relatives to patients from the three geographical areas in South Wales indicates that despite equivalence of 'active interest' revealed through visiting, patients from the town have a substantially lower proportion of relatives willing to house them on discharge than have patients from the rural area. Patients from the mining valley are intermediate in this respect.

One important factor not systematically examined in this study is the attitude of the patients themselves to their future and, in particular, to the prospect of leaving hospital. Although many patients would undoubtedly prefer an early discharge, others are too apprehensive or too settled to want it. Folkard [6] found that the expectations of a group of selected chronic patients regarding prospects of discharge and level of performance after discharge, were more optimistic than those expressed by their relatives. Wing, Bennett and Denham [21] have shown that the desire of some chronic male schizophrenics to leave hospital can be substantially sharpened by exposing them to an Industrial Rehabilitation Course at a Ministry of Labour Unit.

ATTITUDES OF GENERAL PRACTITIONERS

An interesting opportunity occurred in South Wales to make a close comparison of the factors influencing referral of patients to psychiatric services from six general practices, including eight practitioners, situated in the same mining valley [13, 14]. Information about cases referred during the period 1951–59 was gathered from hospital and clinic records. This included clinical data, name of general practitioner and a statement as to whether the patient was referred directly by the general practitioner to a psychiatrist or came by way of another specialty, e.g. the general medical clinic. Data about the practice populations was gathered principally from a private census taken throughout a defined area in the mining valley by Professor A. L. Cochrane of the Medical Research Council Epidemiological Research Unit. One of the items on the census schedule requested the name of the general practitioner. The populations of the six practices were found to be closely similar in their distributions by sex, age, occupation, number in household, place of birth, and education.

Despite this homogeneity, the rate of referral of patients directly to psychiatric services shows a substantial variation among the practices, so that, for females, the highest rate (36·8)[1] is almost twice the total average (19·4) and more than three times the lowest (10·8). One reason for this diversity of rates could be the selective recruitment of psychiatric cases to those general practitioners regarded by the population as being especially competent or sympathetic in handling such problems. This hypothesis is not supported by evidence available from the material. It may be supposed that doctors differ in the

[1] Average annual rate of direct referrals per 10,000 population at risk.

criterion of clinical severity which they apply in deciding to refer a patient, or in the relative proportions of diagnostic categories referred. The findings, however, show no significant difference between the six practices in either of these factors, nor in the distribution of referrals by age, civil state or occupation.

A clue to the factors which may influence referral came from interviews conducted with the practitioners themselves. The commonest reported factor was the failure to respond to treatment provided by the practitioner. However, a medley of 'non-clinical' factors was also mentioned, each of which appeared to weigh in varying degree with individual doctors. Examples are: (1) pressure from relatives for something else to be done; (2) request by patient to see a specialist; (3) serious impairment of patient's working capacity; (4) lack of emotional support for patient from members of the family; (5) the doctor's opinion that the patient may find it more acceptable to be told he has nervous trouble by a specialist, rather than by his own doctor.

It was not possible to make a quantitative estimate of the influence of each of these factors separately upon referral practice. Their diversity, however, even among the eight practitioners studied, was noteworthy. The varying weight accorded to these non-clinical factors by different practitioners could perhaps account, in part, for the variation in direct referral rates.

The variation in rates of referral to psychiatric services shown in the above study has implications for epidemiological research in psychiatry based on specialist-treated cases. Since the general practitioner is the principal agent by whom patients are passed to the mental health services, he must exercise a powerful influence on mental hospital and clinic morbidity statistics. The habits of practitioners in referring cases may well be determined, in part, by the nature of the training in psychiatry received at the medical school. The psychiatric morbidity statistics for a large population might be influenced by the teaching policy in psychiatry in the medical school which produces a substantial proportion of the doctors for the area.

ATTITUDES OF MEDICAL AND OTHER UNIVERSITY STUDENTS

Medical students are of special interest since many of them are destined to spend a substantial fraction of their eventual professional lives coping with psychiatric problems. An attempt has been made to examine the evolution of their concepts of psychiatric disorder during the medical course and also to study their appreciation of their own potential role *vis-à-vis* psychiatric illness. An inquiry into student attitudes was carried out by Dr. J. B. Loudon and the author in collaboration with Professor M. Shepherd and Dr. Graham Grant.

Students in the Welsh National School of Medicine and in University College of South Wales and Monmouthshire were involved. The aims were:

1. To examine variations in students' concepts of abnormal behaviour.

2. To examine students' views on the *nature* of abnormal behaviour in terms of the kind of agencies which they believe should properly be concerned.

3. To study the medical student's concept of his own potential role in coping professionally with certain common psychiatric disorders as against physical disorders.

A two-part questionnaire was devised. The first part consisted of 29 very brief sketches of behaviour, some of which might be regarded as of interest, professionally, to a psychiatrist; some to a physician; some to the police; some to a social worker; others might be interpreted as essentially normal. All words which might provide a lead, such as neurosis, mental illness, psychiatry, delinquency, were carefully avoided. In each instance the sex, age and social status of the actor was mentioned. Respondents were asked to say for each of the examples whether, in their view, anything was amiss, and if so, whether help, advice or action from a person or organization outside the family or circle of intimate friends, was desirable. In the latter event, respondents were asked to mention the person or organization which they regarded as appropriate.

This section of the questionnaire was completed by 428 students, including 190 medical, 60 social science, 90 education, 19 Anglican theological, 22 Baptist theological and 47 engineering students in the University of Wales.

The second part, completed by the medical students only, presented brief summaries of four clinical problems, two with an organic and two with a psychiatric aspect. Students were asked to imagine themselves working in general practice and, through their responses to a series of questions, to indicate their level of interest in each of the four cases; their opinion of their competence in diagnosing and treating the problems; their judgement as to the propriety of general medical care, specialist treatment or other forms of professional, non-medical intervention in each case.

In the majority of the 29 sketches of behaviour making up part I of the questionnaire there was considerable diversity of view about whether or not anything was amiss and as to the most appropriate source of help, action or advice.

Students of engineering were more disposed than students in other courses to say that problems should be handled by the individual concerned or by family and friends. They were the group least ready to call in a psychiatrist. By contrast, social science students envisaged that 'outside' assistance or intervention would be required in a relatively high proportion of problems, and, of all groups, they were the most ready to see problems as requiring psychiatric treatment. Baptist theological students were the group recording the highest number of abnormalities ('something amiss') in the 29 sketches and, together with the Anglican students, they had recourse to help from religious quarters in a comparatively high proportion of instances.

Comparing medical students in the early part of their course with those in later years, the results indicate that, as the course proceeds, students become less inclined to see problems handled within the family and readier to call upon medical aid in general and psychiatry in particular.

The two psychiatric cases in part II of the questionnaire (with symptoms suggestive of anxiety neurosis in one case and depression in the other) were regarded as inappropriate objects of medical care by comparison with the two cases with physical symptoms (cough and fever in one case; dyspnoea and ankle oedema in the other). Medical students believed they would be relatively ill-equipped to diagnose and treat the psychiatric cases.

Although a third of the students thought medical training was essential in providing the means to help the psychiatric cases, half regarded it as helpful but not essential. When asked to specify other kinds of professional skill which might be equally effective as medicine, the medical students most commonly singled out the priesthood in one form or another.

Senior medical students accepted the psychiatric cases as falling within the medical ambit to a greater extent than did the juniors.

The results of this survey are of interest both from the standpoint of the psychiatric education of medical students, and also in regard to the assessment of psychiatric morbidity in epidemiological inquiries.

Students in their later years of medical training are more inclusive in their notions of what constitutes a 'medical' problem and are more ready than their juniors to utilize psychiatric facilities. If it may be tentatively assumed that this difference represents a change in the attitudes of students the question arises as to how much this may be attributed to specific psychiatric teaching, to other medical teaching or to factors unrelated to formal instruction. Despite this trend, many senior medical students relegate the psychiatric problems to the borderland of medicine or beyond, regarding them as a matter for the clergy or other non-medical professions.

Assessment of psychiatric morbidity in populations where case finding is not restricted to patients identified through medical care records depends to a degree upon interpretation and evaluation of behaviour by members of the community. The student attitude inquiry provides some indication of the considerable variation in judgements of this kind shown by university students, despite the fact that as a population they have a good deal in common. The corresponding variations in attitudes in the general population may be substantially greater.

ATTITUDES OF THE GENERAL PUBLIC

Carstairs and Wing [4] working in the Social Psychiatry Research Unit (Maudsley) obtained some information about attitudes of the general public to mental illness through a survey conducted by the British Broadcasting Corporation. Groups of television viewers were asked to complete questionnaires in order to assess their reaction to a series of five programmes under the general title of the 'Hurt Mind' which dealt with various aspects of mental illness.

At the onset of the inquiry and before seeing the programmes, 167 viewers were asked to write as fully as possible what they understood by the expression, 'a person who is mentally ill'. They seemed to think primarily of the traditional 'madman' who could not think logically and was unpredictable, deluded and withdrawn. Depressive, neurotic and personality disorders were much less frequently mentioned. Aetiology was conceived mainly in terms of general or specific life stresses beginning in the recent past with little mention of physical or hereditary causation. Therapy, similarly, was thought to consist of unspecific measures such as rest and kindness; the nature of psychotherapy was almost certainly not understood and physical treatments were hardly mentioned.

ATTITUDES OF MENTAL WELFARE OFFICERS

Mental Welfare Officers were chosen for study because it was thought they might exercise an important function in the recognition as well as in the disposal of psychiatric cases.

An inquiry involving thirty-two Mental Welfare Officers from the local authorities of Glamorgan, Bedfordshire and London County was carried out between April and November 1959. The aims were to examine attitudes and practice of these officers in respect of compulsory and of voluntary admissions to psychiatric hospitals. Their reactions to changes of role envisaged in the Mental Health Act, 1959 were noted.

The differences in attitudes and practice discovered were due, in part, to variations in attitudes of general practitioners, or in policies of psychiatric hospitals, or in the policies of the various local authorities.

In general it was found that Mental Welfare Officers did not identify or determine a psychiatric case. This appeared to be a function of the medical practitioner. Mental Welfare Officers occasionally exercised this function in the London County area where they were called out by non-medical referrers to deal with emergency cases. This identifying function seemed likely to diminish with the progressive implementing of the Mental Health Act [11].

ATTITUDES, VALUES AND SYMPTOM PATTERNS

The study of the relationship between the prevalence of mental disorder measured by direct survey of a population and the complex web of social attitudes, values and standards which also prevail in the same population raises difficult theoretical, methodological and technical issues.

Detection of the common pyschiatric ailments—neuroses and personality disorders, for example—depends upon reports of behavioural anomalies or of changes in inner experience which will, in turn, be governed by the standards of 'normal' behaviour and experience of patients themselves, or subscribed to by their relatives or by other members of their social world. Quite apart from the awareness of the existence of abnormality, attitudes of diffidence arising from the possibility of stigmatization may lead to concealment of such disorder even during special inquiry. Beliefs concerning depression or morbid anxiety may cause a denial of such phenomena. Potent in this regard may be the notion that these manifestations are not of medical importance but rather indicate moral defect or a weak character. The neurotic may be held personally responsible for his symptoms which are seen, in the last analysis, to be susceptible of voluntary control in a way which does not apply to manifestly 'organic' symptoms.

An opportunity to study the influence of the social climate upon the pattern of psychiatric symptomatology arose when the entire population of the South Atlantic island of Tristan da Cunha was evacuated to England in 1961 following a volcanic eruption [15].

Although there has usually been fairly regular contact between Tristan and the rest of the world, the community may be regarded as closed in that, for half a century before the volcano erupted, there had been virtually no permanent migration into or out of the island. The nature and circumstances of life on Tristan—close proximity of residence in a corner of an inhospitable island mountain; universal interrelatedness through blood or marriage; an economic life requiring much co-operation in certain processes—had led to a remarkable homogeneity in social values and attitudes and a low tolerance for departures from generally accepted standards.

In 1937 the population was subject to an epidemic of major

hysteria which was extremely well documented by the doctors of a Norwegian expedition which arrived shortly after the epidemic began [5]. Twenty-one islanders were affected, 11 per cent. of the population. It was possible to identify these cases by name from the details provided in the Norwegian report and 19 of them came to England as evacuees almost 25 years later.

The hysteria took a variety of forms—faints, convulsions, 'sleeping spells', 'fighting spells' and 'choking spells'. The epidemic gradually subsided over a period of several months and although sporadic cases have occurred since, the condition has never recurred on the same scale. It is difficult, in retrospect, to say what factors may have precipitated this outbreak. Strained relationships between families; sexual rivalries and jealousies; the isolated monotonous life, are among the causes mentioned both by the Norwegian investigators and by members of the community. In the early stages, at least, this series of dramatic exhibitions attracted a great deal of attention and evoked much interest in the population.

In a socio-medical survey conducted in 1962 by a social anthropologist (J. B. Loudon) and a psychiatrist (K. Rawnsley), the investigators were impressed early in the course of the inquiry by the high frequency of headaches (59 per cent. of adult population) and by the remarkably stereotyped manner in which these were described. They were bifrontal in distribution, the position often being indicated by a characteristic gesture. They were common both on Tristan and in England and sufferers were accustomed to have them every week or two. Sometimes they were disabling, causing the patient to cease work for a while, but usually they were said not to interfere with life activities. They were not associated with eye symptoms or vomiting and were relieved by aspirin. The commonest provoking factors were exposure to strong winds or bright sunshine, menses, and worry.

An association was found between the occurrence of headache, especially of worry-provoked headache, and a history (from the Norwegian report) of previous hysterical attacks. Thus, of the 19 individuals known to have had hysteria 25 years previously, 16 now stated they were subject to headaches associated with worry. Only 3 members of a control group of 19, matched for sex and age, had headaches of this kind.

Sixty per cent. of the islanders who reported headaches denied the influence of anxiety or worry in provoking attacks. In considering the physiogenic as well as the psychogenic basis of the Tristan headaches one is reminded of the experimental work by Holmes, Goodell, Wolf and Wolff [7] on responses of the nasal mucosa to a variety of stimuli in normal subjects. Swelling of the turbinates, hyperaemia, increased secretion, obstruction, lowered pain threshold, and sometimes the development of a rather characteristic headache occurred in response to the following: pain elsewhere in the body; cold; bright lights; menses; allergens and certain emotional states, notably anxiety, resentment, anger, guilt, humiliation, frustration. To recapitulate: the precipitating causes of headache reported by the islanders were worry; bright sunshine, strong winds; and menses.

Two hypotheses may be advanced but cannot be resolved on the evidence provided by this survey:

1. A high proportion of the population is liable to nasal congestion with consequent headache in response to a number of provoking agents. Those of neurotic disposition may find that their undue load of anxiety or other morbid affect is especially potent in producing the response.

2. There is a nucleus of people, perhaps quite a small one, with headache due to nasal congestion. In addition, however, there are islanders who, without a physiogenic mechanism of this kind, have adopted the headache response to anxiety as a convenient, socially acceptable, commonplace symbolic reaction. The homogeneous nature of Tristan society, together with the high degree of social interaction, may have powerfully influenced the establishment and spread of this symptom. If one accepts the Norwegian figures for prevalence of headache in 1937, it must be concluded that this malady has become much more extensive in recent years. Headache may now have become, in part, an endemic neurotic symptom modelled on a physiogenic disorder, but spreading through the community in a less dramatic though more enduring fashion than the convulsive hysteria of 1937.

The association between certain social attitudes and the prevalence of symptoms has been studied in the much more complex, much less homogeneous society of a rural area in South Wales. By the methods of social anthropology a number of social groupings were identified and were regarded as important structural features of the local community [9, 10]. These groupings are made up of relatively homogeneous aggregates of individuals who interact on a level of felt equality of status and who tend to share similar attitudes, values, and expectations. An association was noted between membership of these groupings, established on the basis of the social networks of individuals and the possession by members of varying combinations of such elementary social characteristics as occupation, occupation of father, and place of birth.

These simple social data were available for every inhabitant, about 14,000, through a private population census made by the Medical Research Council Epidemiological Research Unit and Social Psychiatry Research Unit. It was therefore possible to assign each resident to one or other of six social sections which may be regarded as corresponding roughly to extensions of the social groupings defined by anthropological inquiry.

A summary description of the constitution of these sections is as follows:

Section A. Individuals in professional and high administrative occupations, together with members of their households.

Section B. Farmers and members of their households, together with certain other individuals with kinship connexions with local farmers.

Section C. Individuals in managerial and 'white-collar' occupations who are of local origin or who have kinship connexions with such individuals, and members of their households.

Section D. Individuals in managerial and 'white-collar' occupations without local connexions, together with members of their households.

Section E. Individuals in manual occupations (skilled, semi-skilled and unskilled) who have local connexions or who are themselves of local origin, and members of their households.

Section F. The remainder of the population, consisting mainly of manual workers and their families who have no local connexions.

The assessment of symptoms and of associated attitudes was carried out on a random sample of the rural population confined to the age range 26–45 and stratified in such a way as to include equal numbers of males and females and equal numbers of representatives of the six social sections. This sampling procedure was made possible only through the existence of the private population census. The members of this sample were approached individually and as many as possible were assessed in their homes using a standard interview procedure. Special techniques were devised for application in home interviews for the assessment of symptoms and of associated attitudes. The attitudes measured were: (1) level of sympathy manifested towards certain symptoms; and (2) extent to which the same symptoms are regarded as proper objects of medical care.

Symptoms were assessed using techniques designed to minimize the observer's active participation with the consequent distortion due to prejudice and bias in the observer. For comparative purposes, main reliance was placed on two 'objective' procedures—a modification of the Cornell Medical Index Health Questionnaire which, in its original form comprises some 200 questions (to be answered 'Yes' or 'No') about physical and psychological symptoms; and specially designed scales for a limited number of symptoms [8]. The scales had an advantage over conventional questionnaire forms in providing a method of grading the severity of the symptom. They also, by their design and method of presentation, served to reduce the influence of certain spurious response 'sets', e.g. a tendency to answer 'Yes' to questions whatever the content, which might otherwise yield spurious variations between social categories.

Other measures of morbidity were also employed, including re-interview of a subsample by a psychiatrist who was ignorant of the performance on the first interview; special observation by general practitioners for a period of 3 months; records of attendance at psychiatric hospitals or clinics in recent years.

The interrelation between these independent measures of morbidity is of interest. On the basis of a clinical interview, the psychiatrist categorized respondents as predominantly psychiatric cases; cases with predominantly physical pathology, or as healthy individuals. The large majority of psychiatric cases could be classified as neuroses or personality disorders. For both sexes, respondents in the psychiatric category have high mean symptom frequencies on the modified Cornell questionnaire by comparison with the healthy respondents. The mean frequencies for physically sick respondents are intermediate but are closer to the healthy than to the psychiatric means.

It might be expected that the physically ill cases would tend to have 'physical' symptoms, and the psychiatric cases to have 'psychological' symptoms. In each of these groups, however, both physical and psychological mean symptom frequencies were raised.

A positive and highly significant association was also found between the judgement of the psychiatrist about the presence of current psychiatric disorder and that of the general practitioner, formed independently, regarding the occurrence of psychiatric disorder during the past 12 months.

Respondents believed by general practitioners to have current or recent psychiatric disorder have a higher mean number of positive Cornell questionnaire symptoms than individuals regarded as free from psychiatric ailments.

To summarize, positive associations are found between three independent measures of psychiatric morbidity (taken as pairs) when the analysis is at the level of individual respondents.

A lack of congruence between these measures is to be found, however, when the variation in morbidity between social sections is examined. Data for this purpose are available for respondents in all social sections from the Cornell questionnaire and from general practitioners. The mean number of positive Cornell symptoms varies significantly by sex and by social section. Females have higher mean symptom frequencies than males in each social section.

The proportion of respondents in each social section regarded by general practitioners as manifesting current or recent psychiatric disorder shows a significant variation between sections for females but not for males.

Females, therefore, show significant variation in morbidity between social sections according both to general practitioners and to the Cornell measures. However, comparative ranking of the sections in these terms shows striking differences in rank order. The females of section E, for example, show the highest mean symptom frequency according to the Cornell questionnaire, but have the lowest proportion of psychiatric cases according to the general practitioners' assessment.

This lack of congruence cannot be accounted for by variation between sections in the frequency of contact with general practitioners, nor by variation in declared readiness to consult general practitioners for certain 'physical' and 'psychological' symptoms. It might depend upon differential perception of psychiatric disorders by general practitioners among members of the various social sections.

It was noticed during the course of interviewing general practitioners that they would occasionally volunteer beliefs and expectations about the health, behaviour and qualities of character of members of particular groups. Thus farmers were said by some to be healthy individuals who were not likely to trouble the doctor for trifling complaints. Attitudes of this nature, whether well-founded or not, could conceivably exert an influence upon the doctor's assessment of an individual member of the group with putative neurotic symptoms.

This lack of correspondence between morbidity estimates at various levels of declaration in population subgroups which are socially dissimilar is not confined to the present study. In the survey of psychiatric disorder in a new town [19] the prevalence of nervous conditions as assessed by the home interview showed a variation by social class. The prevalence according to general practitioner estimates also varied by social class but in a way which was not congruent with the home interview variation. The rate of admission of psychoneurotics to psychiatric hospitals in England and Wales from the Registrar General's five social classes shows a gradient from high in Class V to low in Class I [17]. This gradient was found to be reversed in a national study of morbidity in general practice in England and Wales [20].

It may be argued that the most sensitive, flexible and 'valid' technique available for estimating psychiatric disorder is the clinical interview conducted by an experienced psychiatrist. This therefore should constitute the final court of appeal in determining the differential prevalence of such disorders in population subgroups. Counter to this runs the view that, while conceding the virtue of the psychiatric interview, the inevitable bias which operates to an unknown extent in the field situation where the observer must know something of the respondent's social background vitiates objective assessment.

This being so, the appropriate question to ask is not 'Which measure of differential prevalence is the true one?' but rather, 'For any given measure of differential prevalence, what factors, including those inherent to the instrument used, influence the results?'

Thus, for general practitioners, simultaneous assessment of their attitudes and beliefs regarding individuals in various social categories might be relevant. For questionnaires and symptom inventories, measures of non-specific acquiescence 'sets', or of attitudes to health surveys might contribute to the interpretation of findings.

In this way, due regard is paid to the nature of the transaction which takes place between observer and observed—itself a variable influenced by social and other factors—in drawing up the epidemiological balance sheet.

In relating symptoms to attitudes measured in the survey of the rural population it was found that the presence of a specific symptom was positively associated with a relatively high degree of sympathy towards others who have the same symptom. The variation between social sections in expressed sympathy for specific symptoms was not significant.

From this survey it is not possible to draw firm conclusions as to the functional relationship between sympathetic attitudes and symptoms. The positive association may reflect the influence of a common factor related, possibly, to traits of character. Personal suffering may engender sympathetic attitudes to like troubles in others. Alternatively, the presence of a sympathetic outlook in respect of a particular symptom may generate a climate which favours the emergence and expression of the symptom. It was suggested earlier that the epidemic hysteria and the endemic headache of the Tristan da Cunha people might constitute examples of this process.

PERSONALITY AND THE DECLARATION OF ILLNESS

Many inquiries in the past have purported to show positive associations between disorders such as hypertension, asthma, peptic ulcer, ulcerative colitis and aspects of personality. Most of these studies have been confined to patients attending clinics or hospitals. Epidemiological surveys of the general population raise doubts as to the universal validity of earlier studies.

Dr. Robinson [18] examined the relationship between personality and blood pressure in collaboration with Dr. Miall of the Medical Research Council Pneumoconiosis Research Unit.

Miall had measured the blood pressure of a random sample of the population of a mining valley. Robinson administered a battery of tests designed to assess emotional instability or neuroticism to the members of the sample. The battery was also applied to a group of neurotics attending a psychiatric clinic and to a group of hypertensives attending a medical clinic.

For the random sample, no association between blood pressure level and emotional instability was found. The clinic neurotics had high ratings of emotional instability and the clinic hypertensives were intermediate in this respect.

A group of individuals with high blood pressure selected from the random sample did not differ significantly in emotional instability from the random sample as a whole.

One possible explanation for these findings is that the patients who find themselves attending medical clinics for hypertension have been self-selected in terms of personality traits of neuroticism. Such individuals may attend their doctor relatively frequently with a variety of complaints and thus be at greater risk of having their hypertension detected.

Further evidence on this score comes from the Tristan da Cunha survey. Individuals who had manifested hysteria during the epidemic of 1937 were found to have relatively high consultation rates with their doctor 25 years later. According to his records they showed a higher than average frequency for a variety of ailments including infective hepatitis, cough, diarrhoea, injuries, burns, and strains. This may indicate a relatively high predisposition of the 1937 hysterics to a variety of disorders; or it may merely reflect a greater readiness on their part to seek medical advice.

CONCLUSION

Progress in the epidemiology of mental disorders hinges in the first place upon the sharpening of methods for the reliable and valid estimation of psychiatric morbidity. Attempts to design such methods quickly evoke fundamental questions concerning the nature and definition of psychiatric disorder. The answers involve, *inter alia*, consideration of social values and attitudes pertaining to human behaviour. In addition to influencing the recognition and disposal of the psychiatric case by the general practitioner and affecting the fate of the patient in hospital, social attitudes may make a powerful contribution to determining the occurrence and content of psychopathology.

REFERENCES

1. Brooke, E. M. (1959) A longitudinal study of patients first admitted to mental hospitals, *Proc. roy. Soc. Med.*, **52**, 280–3.
2. Brown, G. W., Carstairs, G. M., and Topping, G. (1958) Post-hospital adjustment of chronic mental patients, *Lancet*, ii, 685–9.
3. Carstairs, G. M., and Brown, G. W. (1958) A census of psychiatric cases in two contrasting communities, *J. ment. Sci.*, **104**, No. 434, 72–81.
4. Carstairs, G. M., and Wing, J. K. (1958) Attitudes of the general public to mental illness, *Brit. med. J.*, ii, 594–7.
5. Christophersen, E., ed. (1946) *Results of the Norwegian Scientific Expedition to Tristan da Cunha, 1937–38*, Det Norske Videnskaps-Akademi, Oslo.
6. Folkard, S. (1960) Comparative study of attitudes to the rehabilitation of psychiatric patients, *Brit. J. prev. soc. Med.*, **14**, 23–27.
7. Holmes, T. H., Goodell, H., Wolf, S., and Wolff, H. G. (1950) *The Nose*, Springfield, Ill.
8. Ingham, J. G. (1965) A method for observing symptoms and attitudes, *Brit. J. soc. clin. Psychol.*, **4**, 131–40.
9. Loudon, J. B. (1961) Kinship and crisis in S. Wales, *Brit. J. Sociol.*, **12**, No. 4, 333–50.
10. Loudon, J. B. (1966) Religious order and mental disorder: A study in a rural community in S. Wales, in *The Social Anthropology of Complex Societies*, A.S.A. Monograph No. 4, London.
11. Miles, H. L., Loudon, J. B., and Rawnsley, K. (1961) Attitudes and practice of mental welfare officers, *Publ. Hlth (Lond.)*, **76**, No. 1, 32–47.
12. Norris, V. (1956) A statistical study of the influence of marriage on the hospital care of the mentally sick, *J. ment. Sci.*, **102**, 467–86.
13. Rawnsley, K., and Loudon, J. B. (1962) Factors influencing the referral of patients to psychiatrists by general practitioners, *Brit. J. prev. soc. Med.*, **16**, 174–82.
14. Rawnsley, K., and Loudon, J. B. (1962) *The Attitudes of General Practitioners to Psychiatry*, Sociological Review Monograph No. 5, University of Keele.
15. Rawnsley, K., and Loudon, J. B. (1964) Epidemiology of mental disorder in a closed community, *Brit. J. Psychiat.*, **110**, 830–9.
16. Rawnsley, K., Loudon, J. B., and Miles, H. L. (1962) Attitudes of relatives to patients in mental hospital, *Brit. J. prev. soc. Med.*, **16**, 1–15.
17. Registrar General's Statistical Review of England and Wales 1954–56, Supplement on Mental Health (1960), London, H.M.S.O.
18. Robinson, J. O. (1963) A study of neuroticism and casual arterial blood pressure, *Brit. J. soc. clin. Psychol.*, **2**, 56–64.
19. Taylor, Lord, and Chave, S. (1964) *Mental Health and Environment*, London.
20. Watts, C. A. H. (1962) Psychiatric Disorders, Chapter 3, in *Morbidity Statistics from General Practice*, Vol. III, Disease in General

Practice. Studies on Medical and Population Subjects No. 14, General Register Office, London, H.M.S.O.

21. WING, J. K., BENNETT, D. H., and DENHAM, J. (1964) *The Industrial Rehabilitation of Long-stay Schizophrenic Patients*, Medical Research Council Memorandum No. 42, London, H.M.S.O.
22. WING, J. K., DENHAM, J., and MONRO, A. B. (1959) Duration of stay in hospital of patients suffering from schizophrenia, *Brit. J. prev. soc. Med.*, **13**, 145–8.
23. WING, J. K., MONCK, E., BROWN, G. W., and CARSTAIRS, G. M. (1964) Morbidity in the community of schizophrenic patients discharged from London mental hospitals in 1959, *Brit. J. Psychiat.*, **110**, 10–21.

3

Social Psychiatry and Mental Subnormality

JACK TIZARD

IN psychiatry, as in general medicine, little research has until recently been undertaken on problems of patients with chronic illnesses or handicaps. Clinical medicine is naturally concerned first with the cure of disease, just as social medicine and public health have been concerned first with its prevention. In consequence, the needs of chronically ill and disabled persons—those who do not respond to treatment, or for whom medical treatment seems to be ruled out—have been neglected by research workers and, perhaps in consequence, by medical administrators.

Just as the needs of chronically handicapped patients have been thought uninteresting by research workers, so also the services themselves have received little empirical study. During the last half-century services for the handicapped have grown out of all recognition; but changes in public policy have followed Reports by Royal Commissions or Departmental inquiries, rather than surveys and experimental evaluation.

Sir Aubrey Lewis' interest in the neglected problems of patients with chronic disabilities was already a long-standing one [11] when in 1948 the establishment of the Medical Research Council Unit at the newly-created Institute of Psychiatry provided the opportunity to investigate these problems in a series of long-term inquiries. There were good reasons for beginning with the social psychiatry of mental deficiency. Though traditionally a branch of psychiatry, mental defect in 1948 still received little attention in most psychiatric textbooks, and few general psychiatrists were interested in it. Four-fifths of the mentally retarded were regarded as suffering from 'primary' amentia, so that although remarkably little was known about causation there appeared to be little which required explanation. Treatment, even for what was often thought to be a well-established clinical condition such as cretinism, was of dubious efficacy [13]. Medical and surgical treatment was in any case considered to have such a small part in mental deficiency that it occupied only three pages out of more than five hundred in the only standard English textbook [27]. In this respect it compared unfavourably with 'education and training', which warranted six pages, and with 'moral training' which was given four. The rest of the book was taken up largely with clinical and pathological descriptions and with administrative and legal matters.

A substantial amount of research in mental deficiency had been carried out by educational psychologists, notably, in this country, Sir Cyril Burt [1], but their work was mainly concerned with educable children of school age. The needs of severely handicapped children, and of subnormal adults, had received much less study.

Mental deficiency is, as Lewis insisted, none the less 'a rewarding field for systematic inquiry. It has the advantages that its salient phenomena are less diverse and elusive, and lend themselves rather more readily to measurement, than those of most other branches of psychiatry. Our knowledge of it has been furthered by methods drawn, on the one hand, from clinical medicine and pathology and, on the other, from the social sciences and genetics. The work of psychologists, in particular, has been indispensable: it has been most striking in cognitive studies through which Binet and others made their outstanding contributions to the subject' [12].

THE SETTING FOR THE RESEARCH

The mental deficiency services were, at the end of the war, very much in need of review. Though long established they had never been very adequate, and they had suffered greatly from the effects first of the economic depression of the thirties, and then the war. Changes were still awaiting the implementation of the National Health Service Act which came into force in 1948. The local authorities had the task of replanning domiciliary services for defectives living in their own homes, but the residential services which they had formerly administered now passed into the hands of the Regional Hospital Boards which became responsible for the hospitals. In the hospitals themselves little had been done for nearly a decade. There was a shortage of medical staff and nurses. There were practically no psychologists. The teachers and instructors were nearly all untrained. Many of the senior nursing staff, who had the main responsibility for the day-to-day care and management of the patients, were about to retire, and there were few trained staff to replace them. The hospitals were grossly overcrowded, yet few patients were discharged from them.[1]

[1] An exception among London institutions was the Fountain Hospital, to which was attached an 80-bed hostel for feeble-minded women who were transferred there from other hospitals to work in the wards and laundry. Dr. L. T. Hilliard, Physician-Superintendent of the Fountain Hospital says [6] of his feeble-minded patients that he 'often disagreed with those who certified them on the

The first tasks of the new Unit were two-fold: as there were few data describing the institutional population, detailed surveys were carried out of the behavioural and social characteristics of institutional retardates; then, on the basis of this information, experiments and pilot studies were undertaken of ways of utilizing the potentialities of the patients.

The first inquiries were concerned largely with the feeble-minded (retardates with I.Q.'s mostly above 50) rather than with trainable imbeciles (with I.Q.'s between about 20 and 50) or idiots (I.Q.'s of less than 20). The feeble-minded were in some ways the least well provided for. They were also those likely to be most easily rehabilitated.

EPIDEMIOLOGICAL STUDIES

Between 1948 and 1951 extensive inquiries were carried out of institutional populations in the London area, and more detailed clinical and psychological studies were undertaken in particular hospitals. From these several conclusions were drawn:

1. The proportion of feeble-minded or high-grade patients in mental deficiency institutions was much larger than had been thought. Among patients over 16 years of age, who made up 88 per cent. of the total institutional population, the percentages by grade were as in TABLE I: [7].

2. The institutional feeble-minded were on average more intelligent than was generally thought. Criteria of grades of mental defect had been laid down by Dr. E. O. Lewis, whose survey formed the basis of the recommendations of the Wood Report (1929) [19]. For him, an I.Q. of 60 marked the upper limit of defective intelligence, though he thought that unstable adults with I.Q.'s of more than 60

necessity to invoke the Mental Deficiency Act. If one thinks of them as mentally defective one is naturally pessimistic as to their ability to manage in the community. If one believes that medical, social, or emotional factors are the main cause of their difficulties one is more likely to give them a chance in a different environment. . . . Every patient at the South Side Home was on parole immediately on arrival even if she had been in a locked ward at the previous hospital. Patients were allowed to work outside as soon as a job was available, and if a patient found herself a job instead of waiting to be placed in one she was always licensed to it, although it would be checked for suitability by the social worker.' Of 250 women so transferred to the Fountain Hospital between 1946 and 1955, 60 per cent. had been discharged from the Mental Deficiency Act by 1956 and a further 16 per cent. were in daily employment or residential jobs outside the Hospital. Thus three-quarters were living or working in the community, making a satisfactory adjustment.

Both to his hospital practice, and to the lectures and clinical demonstrations which he gave at the Institute of Psychiatry, Hilliard brought a fresh approach to the social psychiatry of mental deficiency.

TABLE I

PERCENTAGE OF ADULT PATIENTS IN MENTAL DEFICIENCY INSTITUTIONS IN GREATER LONDON, LISTED BY GRADE OF DEFECT (N = 11,840)

	GRADE			
AGE	IDIOT	IMBECILE	FEEBLE-MINDED	TOTAL
16–29	2	15	20	37
30–39	1	8	15	24
40–49	—	8	15	23
50+	—	8	8	16
	3	39	58	100

points might in rather rare instances be considered feeble-minded as 'hybrid' cases. However, in the London surveys of representative samples of feeble-minded adults in institutions, the *average* I.Q. was consistently found to be above 70 points, and similar findings were obtained when adult feeble-minded persons living under Statutory Supervision in their own homes were tested [18].

3. Though about 40 per cent. of the patients investigated appeared to be mildly unstable, only 6–12 per cent. were thought to be seriously neurotic. Moreover, the number of males who had been before the Courts, and of females who had been promiscuous, were both surprisingly small. Indeed, in reviewing the case histories of several hundred patients, the most consistent finding was that of poverty and neglect in the homes from which they came.

4. The living conditions of these patients in hospital were unsatisfactory. Exceedingly few patients were dangerous or violent, but about 20 per cent. were kept in locked wards. Of patients actually discharged from mental deficiency hospitals (about 2 per cent. per year) the median period of stay before discharge was nearly 9 years for men and more than 9½ years for women.

5. The occupations provided for these patients were not in general of a sort which seemed likely to equip them to find and keep jobs in the community. About a fifth worked in workshops which at the time were very run-down, and as many as a third were employed in the wards or as domestic servants to the staff. However, only 10 per cent. were regarded as 'unemployable'.

In summary, large numbers of persons who were called by the formidable term 'feeble-minded' turned out to be rather ordinary, dull adolescents and adults who had for the most part been badly brought up in unsatisfactory homes, and badly educated. To segregate them, and to lock them up when they ran away, did not appear to be a helpful way of dealing with their needs—especially since the environment of most hospitals was a bleak one. It was one in which most patients had few if any personal possessions or clothes of their own, and in which fewer than 10 per cent. of patients (including those who went out to paid work in the community but who slept in the hospital) had more than five shillings a week as 'pocket-money'. Most of the hospitals had no educational facilities or library to speak of; no properly structured occupational programme; little in the way of social work, e.g. only five social workers were available to meet the needs of five thousand patients in three London institutions, and their families; the patients had few incentives to strive for; few opportunities for meeting people of the opposite sex except clandestinely; little in the way of after-care. The vague concept of high-grade mental deficiency rested on shaky and crumbling foundations which had not been examined for decades.

It should perhaps be added that the situation has changed considerably since the Mental Health Act of 1959. Between 1954 and 1963 the numbers of feeble-minded patients in institutions dropped by one-third. One of the principal agents in bringing about this change was the National Council for Civil Liberties [17].

WORKSHOP STUDIES

While the surveys of institutional defectives were being carried out, plans were made for a series of studies to be undertaken both in training workshops, which were established in a hospital expressly for this purpose, and in the community where young mentally subnormal adults were sent on licence, i.e. daily work in open industry.

We were fortunate in being able to find in one hospital an excellent purpose-built workshop which at the time was being used for other purposes. Work was subcontracted from outside industry and about sixty feeble-minded lads were put to work on tasks which were economically useful to the community and socially meaningful to them. They were paid for the work they did. Many patients were quickly placed in work outside the hospital and the numbers rose by 240 per cent. in a single year, and most of these patients were later discharged.

Other studies were carried out to examine the suitability of different kinds of employment, and to investigate the effects of different types of supervision on the output and behaviour of these young people in their work environment. It was found that 20 per cent. of a hundred feeble-minded adolescents who were tested on Schonell's Mechanical Reading Test were unable to read at all, and that half of them had reading ages of less than 9 years. When given reading instruction for an hour a day over a period of 5 months the average gain in mechanical reading score on the Schonell Test was 1 year; on a reading comprehension test the gain was 10 months if the test was given on a timed basis but 2 years 7 months when the students were given their own time.

After a few years of working in mental subnormality hospitals with high-grade patients we came to think that the methods of social work and of education which have been developed to deal with ordinary children and young people in trouble could be applied with little modification to the subnormal. The main needs were, and remain, for extended welfare, education and social work services rather than psychiatric services, and the main *research* needs of importance appeared to be into the evaluation of different types of social programme and their efforts. The employment and rehabilitation of intellectually handicapped young people appeared not to be a major research problem [4].

STUDIES OF TRAINABLE IMBECILES

Investigations into the occupational adaptation of the feeble-minded and related problems were followed by studies of the psychological, social and occupational characteristics of imbeciles. A series of psychological studies of learning and maturation [4, 18] showed that even severely handicapped persons could in general respond to incentives, learn simple skills, and concentrate for long periods of time on problems they were interested in. It seemed a logical next step to see whether their work environment could be restructured also to provide socially meaningful and challenging experiences.

Studies were carried out of the learning ability of young adult imbeciles [15, 26] and a series of experiments in the laboratory was followed by a study of a number of simple industrial tasks that seemed likely to be within the capacity of these severely handicapped persons to perform. The work tasks were analysed into their elements, and teaching programmes were devised which would enable the defectives to master them. Clarke and his colleagues [2] continued and extended these investigations, studying both the learning ability of imbeciles and their work capacities. It was noted that whereas the initial ability of imbeciles on industrial as on other tasks tended to be exceedingly low, this had little relationship to the level achieved with training. Furthermore, as Clarke and Hermelin put it [3] 'The main distinction between the performance of imbeciles and others on simple tasks is not so much the end level as the time taken to achieve it'; and 'qualities such as manual dexterity and motor co-ordination are not static, but are capable of improvement within limits which are often ill understood and ill defined'.

These later investigations showed that the methods which had been earlier applied to the subnormal in the I.Q. 50–80 range could be applied to the severely subnormal in the I.Q. 20–50 range. Thus the work of the Unit had a practical outcome in so far as it was one influence among others which helped to bring about changes in mental health policy. But it also had a more general purpose—to examine afresh the psychological characteristics of the mentally retarded.

Later work in the social psychiatry of mental subnormality has been concerned with the prevalence of mental defect and with the factors that influence the functioning of a mental subnormality service.

PREVALENCE

Two surveys of the prevalence of mental subnormality were carried out in 1960 in the Metropolitan Counties of London (population 3,200,000) and Middlesex (population 2,250,000). One was a study of 'administrative' prevalence—that is, the numbers for whom services would be required in a community which made provision for all who needed them. The second, undertaken only in Middlesex, was a 'true' prevalence study of idiots and imbeciles aged 10–14 years [5, 21].

The London study of administrative prevalence will not be discussed here; it was used to provide estimates of the numbers of places and types of provision required to meet the needs of a population of 100,000 persons. The true prevalence study attempted to answer the epidemiological question of what changes in incidence and prevalence had occurred in the 30–35 years following E. O. Lewis' prevalence survey of mental subnormality in England and Wales [14].

Because high-grade mental subnormality is to an unknown extent culturally determined, and because it cannot be precisely defined or diagnosed, it is not possible to obtain a definitive prevalence rate [7, 23]. Severe mental subnormality is however largely a pathological, or at least a biologically determined phenomenon, and for children aged 10–14 years, in the last years of compulsory schooling in Britain, case finding is relatively easy. In a population of 158,978 children aged 10–14 years in Middlesex, 574 were classified as idiot or imbecile, a rate of 3·61 per thousand. This was the highest age-specific prevalence rate obtained in the survey, and it is thought that few children in that age group were missed. The rate for children aged 7–13, which could be compared with E. O. Lewis' findings—he does not give age-specific prevalence rates for children aged 10–14—was 3·45 per thousand. The corresponding rates in Lewis' survey were, for urban areas 3·71, and for rural areas 5·61.

It is known that the life expectancy of mongols, who constitute by far the largest clinical group, has increased considerably during the last generation. Lewis found only 0·34 per thousand mongols in his 7–13-year-old sample (urban and rural combined); the corresponding rate in Middlesex was 1·14. The data thus pointed to a substantial decline in the numbers of 'non-mongols' (3·71—0·34 = 3·37 in urban areas of England and Wales in 1929 as compared with 3·45—1·14 = 2·31 in Middlesex in 1960). The reasons for this decline are a matter for conjecture and for further research, but at the time it was suggested that if more than mere administrative changes were responsible, an even larger decline in prevalence would be found in rural areas.

Other studies carried out independently at about the same time as the London and Middlesex studies [9, 10] produced almost identical findings. Of particular interest is Kushlick's Wessex Survey. For defectives aged 15–19 years, who make up his peak prevalence group, he reports rates of 3·54, including 1·15 mongols, for urban areas (county boroughs); and 3·84, including 1·18 mongols, for largely rural areas (counties). The highest age-specific prevalence rate for non-mongol defectives in rural Wessex (2·66 per thousand) is thus approximately half the peak rural rate reported by Lewis (5·27).

The next steps are clearly to establish an on-going programme of case-finding by diagnostic categories as well as by grade of defect, and to follow cohorts over time in order to construct life tables and to monitor changes in prevalence and if possible incidence. A scheme on these lines is under way in the Wessex Region [9].

FACTORS AFFECTING SERVICES AND INSTITUTIONAL CARE

Three inquiries bearing on services have been carried out. The first was a survey of the mentally subnormal and their families; the second was concerned with the education and care of severely subnormal children; the third, which is still in progress, is investigating child management practices in residential institutions, and the relationship between child management practices and the social organization of institutions.

The Mentally Handicapped and their Families [24]

The families of 250 idiots and imbeciles 'on the books' of the London County Council were interviewed, and records describing the defectives and the family situation were scrutinized. The survey obtained information about: (1) the prevalence of mental and physical disabilities of the defectives; (2) the conditions of life of the families and the problems they had in bringing up mentally retarded children; and (3) the extent and adequacy of the social and medical services, the parents' opinions about them, and their role in determining whether the defectives went into institutional care or remained at home.

It emerged that among the mentally subnormal who were in institutions there were many who were severely handicapped. One-third (33 per cent.) had more than two major physical or mental disabilities such as epilepsy, severe behaviour disorders, cerebral palsy or sensory handicaps, as compared with only 12 per cent. of those living at home. On the other hand, 32 per cent. of institutional cases had no complicating disabilities as compared with 64 per cent. of those living at home. The remainder (35 per cent. and 24 per cent. respectively) had one or two major complicating disabilities.

The two sets of *families* presented very different patterns. Those with the children living at home were on the average worse off economically, more overcrowded, with poorer housing, and fewer social contacts than the families with a child in an institution. As far as could be determined, it was the presence of the defective in the family which accounted for these differences. Two-thirds of the families with the defective living at home had at least three severe family problems as compared with 45 per cent. of those with a similar child in an institution. The families who kept their mentally subnormal children at home were penalized by doing so.

In spite of this most families wished to keep their handicapped member at home and more would have been able to do so had the services been more adequate. The major factors leading to institutional placement (apart from problems of management which accounted for half the placements) were family problems such as broken homes, adverse housing, adverse effects of sibs (26 per cent. of cases); social or medical grounds (12 per cent.) and mother's ill health (11 per cent.).

At the time of the survey both the medical and social services gave grounds for criticism by families. When those families who still kept their mentally subnormal children at home were followed up again 7 years later in an independent survey carried out by Miss Jean Moncrieff [16] the main causes of concern (in an ageing group of parents) were the shortage of money among people who had retired or who would have retired had they been able to afford to, and the indifferent quality of the social work they were getting. It appeared that the quality of the social work services had deteriorated following the reorganization of London services on a Borough basis.

None of the problems brought to light in the social survey of London families was of course new. But the number, the severity and the range of problems had not been studied systematically before, and the purpose of the research was to make good this lack of information. The inquiry pointed to the need to provide better community services for patients living in their own homes and for their families, and to delineate the range of problems that they should be concerned with.

The Brooklands Experiment [22]

Between 1958 and 1960 a study of residential care and education for subnormal children was undertaken, with the help of a grant administered by the Mental Health Research Fund on behalf of the National Society for Mentally Handicapped Children. Over a period of 2 years a group of sixteen mentally handicapped children of imbecile grade were cared for and educated in a small residential nursery. Their progress was compared with that of a matched group of children who lived in a traditional institution, and with norms obtained about similar children who lived either in mental deficiency hospitsl or at home.

The pattern of care at Brooklands was modelled on the best child care practices available and the research had three objects: (1) to serve as a pilot scheme in which a particular technique of care and education could be studied; (2) to compare the development over a 2-year period of children in the small unit with that of a matched control of children living in the parent hospital; and (3) to explore the administrative and social implications of a system of care for the mentally subnormal based as far as possible on the type of care offered to deprived normal children.

The Brooklands children showed an acceleration of development as compared with matched controls who remained in the parent hospital. Their average scores on the verbal scale of the Minnesota Pre-School Intelligence Test increased until they approached those of comparable mentally subnormal children living in their own homes, rather than those of comparable children in the hospital. In social and personality development the Brooklands children appeared to benefit from living in a small family group. The control group of children who remained in the parent hospital showed no such gains.

Brooklands also provided an opportunity to develop a model for institutional care. Subsequent work, in part supported by the Medical Research Council and in part from other sources, has been much concerned with the problems of institutional care.

The Child Welfare Project

A question of sociological interest as well as of practical importance is how to account for differences in institutional care between mental subnormality hospitals and Children's Homes. This problem was examined in detail in an investigation made possible by a grant from the Association for the Aid of Crippled Children and administered by the Medical Research Council. Six residential institutions for children have been studied. Two of these were children's hospitals—one for mentally subnormal children and the other for children with chronic physical handicaps associated with conditions such as spina bifida, cerebral palsy and muscular dystrophy. Two large grouped cottage homes for ophans and other socially deprived children of normal ability have also been studied, while the remaining two establishments were homes for severely subnormal children which were organized on lines similar to those of the Children's Homes rather than the hospitals [25]. One purpose of the inquiry was to find objective ways of describing child management practices and to relate these to different patterns of social organization in the establishments.

Social organization was studied mainly at ward and cottage level, through observation and by interviews with the staff. Marked differences were found between the two hospitals on the one hand and the other four establishments on the other. The hospitals, like nearly all hospitals, had a highly centralized authority structure. Wards were inspected several times a day by senior nursing staff who signed the written reports prepared by the ward sisters or charge nurses. Many decisions, for example about deployment of staff, meals, clothing, hours of duty, were made centrally. Student nurses and domestics were moved frequently from one ward to another—the students to gain experience of 'types' of mental deficiency, the domestics because they were thought of as a pool of labour rather than as members of a staff team. Within the ward there was a fairly sharp division of labour among various cateogories of staff, namely sisters and charge nurses, staff nurses, student nurses, and domestics, each grade being clearly designated by a uniform which provided visual evidence of status. In many wards virtually all decisions were made by the ward sister. Staff neither ate with the children nor slept in the unit.

The cottages in the Children's Homes, including the two homes for mentally subnormal children, were on the contrary organized as households (this formulation is due to Mr. R. D. King). Many more decisions were made at cottage level rather than centrally. The few senior administrative staff had overall responsibility for all units in the establishment, but in the day to day affairs of the units they functioned as advisers rather than inspectors. Matters affecting clothing, meals, hours of duty, schooling, were settled largely at cottage level. Within each cottage decisions usually followed discussions among all staff members irrespective of grade. Each cottage had a budget to spend on clothes, food, holidays and amenities; and how the money was spent was left very much to the discretion of houseparents. Most staff slept on the unit and ate with the children.

In child management practices the establishments also differed. A scale of child management practices was drawn up [8]. This measured in an objective way salient characteristics of child management which could be scored numerically and summed to give an over-all score. Low scores characterized units which could be described as having 'child-centred' patterns of management, whereas high scores signified 'institution-oriented' patterns of management.

The hospitals were characterized by high scores on the child management scale. They showed block treatment or regimentation of the children, inflexibility of routine, restrictions in the use of social space in the unit, and a striking absence of things and activities which were personal to particular children. In the Children's Homes, child management practices were 'child-centred'. There was no overlap whatsoever between the scores of any unit in either of the two hospitals and any unit in either of the two large Children's Homes.

A matter of particular interest was to compare the two institutions for subnormal children which were run as Children's Homes with the mental subnormality hospital. The social organization of the residential hostels for the subnormal was, as far as staff were concerned, modelled on that of the other Children's Homes rather than the hospitals. The children in these two units were, however, like those in some of the wards in the hospitals. The question was therefore whether in child management practices these two units would resemble those having similar inmates or those having similar patterns of staff organization.

It was found that on the scale of child management practices the two homes for subnormal children resembled the Children's Homes rather than the hospitals. One unit, with very severely handicapped children, fell midway between the mental subnormality hospital and the Children's Homes. The second, with children who resembled those in a few of the mental subnormality wards in the hospital but which did not contain bedfast or seriously crippled children, scored as well as cottages characterized by highly child-centred patterns of child management.

It was noteworthy that in neither hospital was there an association between the numbers who were severely handicapped and the child management practices exhibited on the ward. That the proportion of children who are severely handicapped does influence child management practices is however suggested from the data collected from the Children's Homes for subnormal children.

The conclusion drawn from this study was that each type of child management practice appears to be associated with, and perhaps to depend upon, a corresponding pattern of social organization among staff in an establishment. In places characterized by institutionally oriented practices of child management, staff roles are circumscribed, hierarchically defined, and centrally determined. Staff at unit or ward level have to conform to rules laid down by administrative officers who are not themselves directly involved with children. In establishments characterized by child management practices which are child-oriented, staff have a much greater degree of autonomy, and organize and function on a household basis within each cottage rather than as parts of a larger total institution. There is a mixed pattern which falls between these extremes both in respect of staff organization and child management practices.

There are, of course, other variables which influence patterns of child management. The over-all size of the establishment is one such variable; others are the number of staff, the training given to staff and the handicaps of the children. All these have been shown to be important. But these factors cannot in themselves account for the differences found, and further work is in progress to attempt to refine and extend the tentative conclusions drawn from the comparative study of residential children's establishments.

FUTURE RESEARCH

A feature of a successful unit is that it is able to complete projects and to initiate others which arise from the knowledge gained through work carried out. The investigations described here have made possible further large scale studies which are now beginning. An epidemiological and experimental study of subnormality in Wessex, in which Dr. Albert Kushlick will be the principal investigator, is the first of these. The objects are to continue epidemiological studies of mental defect, the need for which was mentioned earlier, and to evaluate the advantages and disadvantages of different types of residential care for those subnormal persons who cannot live in their own homes. The Wessex Regional Hospital Board proposes to build seventeen hostels for mentally subnormal children and adults, and to run these on an experimental basis. The hostels are planned to vary in size and in the type of resident they cater for. Over a period of years, the functioning of existing hospitals in the region, and of the differing types of hostels, will be compared and evaluated. Factors to be considered are those bearing on the development of the residents, the effects on families, the social and administrative problems encountered, the costs and cost benefits of different forms of care. The study is envisaged as a large scale social experiment, comparable in some ways with a clinical trial in which the effects of different treatments upon individual patients are studied through a controlled experiment. In the present instance, 'treatment' is the service provided, and the 'cases' are demographically defined areas. Thus the problems of analysis and evaluation are likely to be complex, and the design to be less tidy than one in which randomization and, in principle, indefinite replications are possible. Experience obtained in small scale studies has however led us to believe that large scale experiment is feasible, and that generalizable results may accrue from it.

The other line of inquiry is also epidemiological and experimental. It concerns the whole range of children with mental and physical handicaps. Two surveys have been carried out on the Isle of Wight, of three age cohorts of children (Total N = 3,500). The numbers with mental and physical handicaps of educational concern have been found, and the implications for services are being considered [20]. Further work is planned which will involve the introduction on an experimental basis of differing patterns of service for those mentally and physically handicapped children who require it and for their families. As in the Wessex Subnormality Research, epidemiological studies will be linked with service trials.

REFERENCES

1. Burt, C. (1937) *The Backward Child*, London.
2. Clarke, A. D. B., and Clarke, A. M. (1965) The abilities and trainability of imbeciles, in *Mental Deficiency, the Changing Outlook*, ed. Clarke, A. M., and Clarke, A. D. B., 2nd ed., pp. 356–85, London.
3. Clarke, A. D. B., and Hermelin, B. F. (1955) Adult imbeciles: their abilities and trainability, *Lancet*, ii, 337–9.
4. Clarke, A. M., and Clarke, A. D. B. (1958, 1965) *Mental Deficiency: the Changing Outlook*, London.
5. Goodman, N., and Tizard, J. (1963) Prevalence of imbecility and idiocy among children, *Brit. med. J.*, i, 216–19.
6. Hilliard, L. T. (1956) Discussion on community care for the feeble-minded, *Proc. roy. Soc. Med.*, **49**, 837–41.
7. Gruenberg, E. (1964) Epidemiology of mental retardation, in *Mental Retardation: a Review of Research*, ed. Stevens, H. A., and Heber, R., Chicago. (Republished in *Int. J. Psychiat.*, **2**, 78–128.)
8. King, R. D., and Raynes, N. V. (1968) An operational measure of inmate management in residential institutions, *Amer. J. ment. Defic.*
9. Kushlick, A. (1964) Prevalence of mental subnormality of I.Q. under 50 in children in the South of England with reference to the demand for places for residential care, in *Proceedings of the International Copenhagen Conference for the Scientific Study of Mental Deficiency*, Vol. 2, 550–6.
10. Kushlick, A. (1966) Subnormality—the size of the problem, in *Mental Handicap*, Documenta Geigy, Basle.
11. Lewis, A. J. (1935) Neurosis and unemployment, *Lancet*, ii, 293–7.
12. Lewis, A. J. (1956) Foreword to *The Social Problem of Mental Deficiency*, ed. O'Connor, N., and Tizard, J., London.

13. Lewis, A. J., Samuel, N., and Galloway, J. (1937) A study of cretinism in London, *Lancet*, i, 1505–9, and ii, 5–9.
14. Lewis, E. O. (1929) See Report of the Mental Deficiency Committee [see Ref. 19], Part IV.
15. Loos, F. M., and Tizard, J. (1955) The employment of adult imbeciles in a hospital workshop, *Amer. J. ment. Defic.*, **59**, 395–403.
16. Moncrieff, J. (1966) *Mental Subnormality in London*, London.
17. National Council for Civil Liberties (1951) *50,000 Outside the Law*, London, and (1955) *Minutes of Evidence to Royal Commission on the Law Relating to Mental Illness and Mental Deficiency*, 22nd and 27th days, London, H.M.S.O.
18. O'Connor, N., and Tizard, J. (1956) *The Social Problem of Mental Deficiency*, London.
19. Report of the Mental Deficiency Committee (Wood Report) (1929) Parts I–IV, London, H.M.S.O.
20. Rutter, M. L., Tizard, J., and Whitmore, A. K. (1968) *Health, Education and Behaviour: the Isle of Wight Survey* [in press].
21. Tizard, J. (1964) *Community Services for the Mentally Handicapped*, London.
22. Tizard, J. (1964) *Community Services for the Mentally Handicapped*, Part IV, London.
23. Tizard, J. (1966) Discussion of Gruenberg, E. M. (1966), *Int. J. Psychiat.*, **2**, 131–4.
24. Tizard, J., and Grad, J. C. (1961) *The Mentally Handicapped and Their Families: a Social Survey*, Maudsley Monographs, No. 7, London.
25. Tizard, J., King, R. D., Raynes, N. V., and Yule, W. (1966) The care and treatment of subnormal children in residential institutions, in 'What is Special Education?', pp. 164–78, in *Proceedings of the First International Congress of the Association for Special Education*, Stanmore, Middlesex.
26. Tizard, J., and Loos, F. M. (1954) The learning of a spatial relations test by adult imbeciles, *Amer. J. ment. Defic.*, **59**, 85–90.
27. Tredgold, A. F. (1949) *A Textbook of Mental Deficiency*, 7th ed., London.

4

Psychology and Intelligence

NEIL O'CONNOR

INTRODUCTION

In his foreword to a research report called *The Social Problem of Mental Deficiency* which was published in 1956 [37] Sir Aubrey Lewis pointed out that 'Mental deficiency is a rewarding field for systematic inquiry'. It was his interest in this field which initiated the studies which Professor Tizard and I have set out in our respective contributions to this volume [24]. In what follows I have tried to present the laboratory and experimental studies which have been carried out by members of the Social Psychiatry Research Unit of the Medical Research Council. In doing this I will be re-evaluating existing reports such as that of O'Connor and Tizard [37] mentioned above or that of O'Connor and Hermelin [34]. However, in addition I will be indicating the lines of more recent studies concerned with extensions of previous work or with the behaviour of psychotic children, chiefly the work of Dr. Bryant and Dr. Hermelin respectively.

THE SCIENTIFIC STUDY OF THE PSYCHOLOGY OF MENTAL DEFECT

There is every reason to begin a chapter such as this with an acknowledgement to Binet, the founder not only of the scientific study of mental deficiency but also a very great figure in the development of psychology itself. Binet was noted for his studies of the intelligence of backward children which appeared either in *L'Année Psychologique* [1] or in such works as *Les Enfants Anormaux* [2]. Binet characteristically made two contributions to clinical psychology, namely measurement and method. At the time, his approach was invaluable in indicating the limitations of enthusiasm without measurement in the course of treatment. This lesson has not yet been learned by many investigators. His limitations were those of the school which his work has generated, lack of a dynamic approach. His achievements, however, gave rise to a social deficit. In search of answers in the field of education and training, educators and doctors seized on the concept of intelligence and used it to 'solve' their problems. It 'explained' the failure of so many patients and pupils. Combined with somewhat crudely extrapolated applied genetics it became a social standby. The failure of the educator to devise teaching methods for the severely handicapped and the failure of the medical profession to prevent the birth of mental defectives were both explained away and at the same time excused through the notion of the intelligence quotient.

The problems of disposal and training were in fact formidable ones. Even excluding considerations of low intelligence, society was neither economically nor socially prepared to accept large numbers of unskilled workers into its shops or factories, especially as they were socially as well as industrially unskilled.

Yet the problem of socialization and of training was humanly and historically ripe for solution and in 1948 the Unit for Research in Occupational Adaptation was created to look at just such questions. As few clinical psychologists existed in England immediately after the war, their function was a matter for experiment. As the nature of experimental psychology itself had not been intensively developed, the models for experimentation hardly existed. What work there was centred around studies of personality by Eysenck [15] and earlier work by Burt [8] on intelligence and his later work [9] on personality which Eysenck's studies have developed and extended. The most relevant work in the field was that of Burt and his applications of Binet's test to English conditions [7] is well known. The aim which we set ourselves at this time was that of analysing the nature of the handicap characteristic of the subnormal adolescent and the possibility of using residual skills to retain and rehabilitate such young men and women.

The results of the project in social terms are set out in Chapter 3. The project involved the examination of skills, intelligence, personality, social response and motivation. In each of these areas studies were designed and carried out. In each case the findings formed part of our justification for social experiment; this in turn eventually led to the policy of social care for the feeble-minded which characterizes our mental health services at present.

SKILLS AND MOTIVATION

The basic findings of the work which was instituted in this phase can be summarized as follows. Individual intelligence averaged at the supposed upper level of subnormality, i.e. 70 points of I.Q. Studies by Tizard [42] showed the mean for three commonly used tests of intelligence to be 71, 72 and 75 points. Scores ranged up to 120 points. A further study carried out later with two more recently introduced tests gave closely similar results. The findings encouraged us to anticipate that mechanical skills would be not too inadequate.

At this stage we carried out studies using factory contracted work as our laboratory tasks. Our aim was to investigate the output rate on factory type tasks and to relate this rate to different types of incentives. The common clinical assumption at this time was that mental defectives were likely to be slow in work and hard to motivate. The first study carried out into this question was that of Gordon, O'Connor and Tizard [18]. Subsequent work by the same authors and by O'Connor and Claridge [33] and Claridge and O'Connor [11] showed that financial rewards could materially improve the production output of subnormal adolescents and that self-competition or knowledge of results was an even more effective incentive. An incidental finding of this phase of the research was that the approval of a supervisor was of great importance to subnormal workers. Each of these findings was verified in workshop experience. Later the results were generalized and applied in a series of workshop studies with schizophrenics. As it turned out the studies with schizophrenics led to a more complex set of results and inferences, but these experiments were a direct historical consequence of the earlier studies with the educationally subnormal adolescents.

The success of these studies demonstrated that low initial scores did not predict low final scores; that the main distinguishing feature of subnormal workers was not a low final output level, but the relatively long time taken to achieve a normal output. Skills of the kind measured are relatively independent of the intelligence quotient and can be much improved with adequate incentives.

One example of the publications summarized in *The Social Problem of Mental Deficiency* [37] must serve to illustrate the type of work which we carried out to show that severely subnormal patients were capable of response to normal incentives. This was a later study in the sequence and was published by O'Connor [31]. The value of financial incentives had been established by this time and there was also enough evidence for the value of knowledge of results with a severely subnormal group from the work of Gordon, O'Connor, and Tizard [18]. The later study aimed at comparing the effect of incentives given earlier and later in a learning programme. The results can be assessed by consulting FIGURE 1.

Two groups, one an incentive group and one a control without incentive, were split after Trial 12 and half of each switched to the opposite condition, i.e. incentive to control or control to incentive, while the other halves continued as before.

It is clear from this figure that some delay in applying an incentive is not necessarily a disadvantage in achieving a high final level of performance. Somewhat surprisingly, little fall-off was found following the removal of the incentive. Human beings, unlike animals, seem to retain standards for some time after the termination of an incentive situation.

Other results in this field are also of interest. In later work Claridge [10] was able to show that active as opposed to inactive subnormals showed different responses to incentives. The active subject showed less responsiveness to incentives than the inactive, partly because he operated at an initially higher level of output. A striking difference was also found in a group of female subjects who

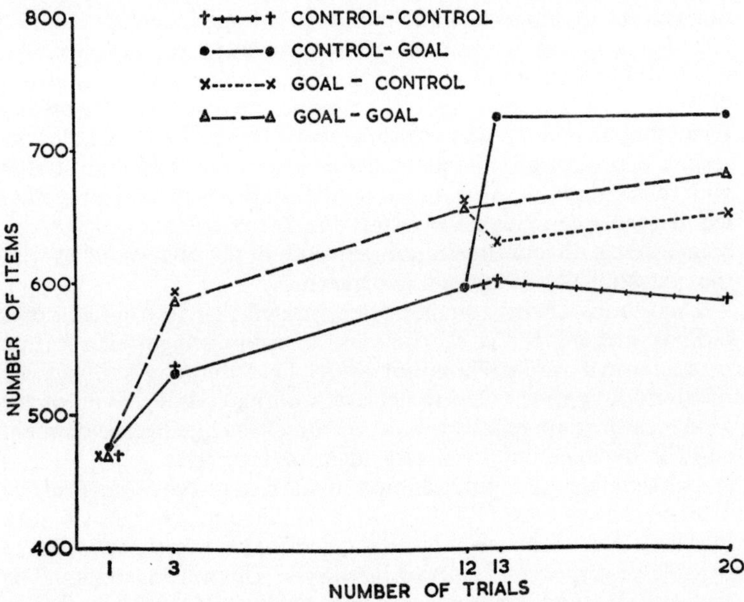

FIG. 1. The effect of incentives early and later in a learning process.

did not react to the incentives as had their male contemporaries. They were found to resemble the male hyperactive subjects who were operating at a high output level in the absence of incentives.

Perhaps one rather important aspect of this latter set of findings is that it shows the relative sensitivity of the 'personality' of severely subnormal adolescents to a variety of changes in the social environment. It has often been maintained that supportive therapy and personality tests would be inapplicable among such patients because they lack the range of manifestations of personality found in the normal person. As can be shown from the next and subsequent sections, this belief is not well founded any more than it would be in relation to children, even though in both cases differences of quality of response are to be expected because of the difference of mental age.

PERSONALITY AND WORK ADJUSTMENT

The second major set of studies attempted to assess the effects of personality disorders on success in job placement. Tests of personality, intelligence and ability and hospital records were all used. In addition, ratings of anxiety, aggressiveness and instability were made by clinicians, and measures of body build were taken. A technique of multiple regression was used to predict a criterion of work success using these variables. The criterion was based on work record. The basic correlation matrix was also used as the foundation of a factor analysis. Here we will simply refer to the multiple regression results. The relationship between some of the variables and the criterion are given in TABLE 2.

TABLE 2

RELATIONSHIPS BETWEEN TESTS AND CRITERION OF EMPLOYMENT SUCCESS AMONG SUBNORMAL PATIENTS

	PARTIAL CORRELATION WITH CRITERION	CUMULATIVE MULTIPLE R^2	FACTOR LOADINGS
1. Rating of anxiety	35	12	53
2. Manual dexterity	37	26	63
3. Finger dexterity	08	27	65
4. Matrices	11	28	56
5. Locomotor test	21	33	51
6. Persistence test I	−02	33	—
7. Persistence test II	−03	33	−10
8. Suggestibility test	−20	37	−43
9. Instability rating	−24	42	−54
10. Flexibility rating	17	45	—
11. Motor speed test	−01	45	−53
12. Aspiration test	06	45	—
13. Judgement test	02	45	−41
14. Responsiveness index	02	45	09

The table also shows the factor loadings. The best predictors of the work success criterion were ratings of past behaviour or the history of socially unacceptable behaviour. Measures which in other patients of higher intelligence were measures of personality variance became tied in this group to the dominant intelligence variables. It is therefore of great interest that none the less emotional instability emerged as the most serious cause of occupational disability among the feeble-minded or subnormal patients. A further investigation carried out subsequently confirmed this finding although other predictors were indicated, possibly because of the heterogeneity of the population in relation to the size of the two samples in these separate investigations.

An important indication for training was the relatively high proportion of emotional instability in subnormal patients: this condition was related to external circumstances and was relieved by amelioration of conditions. Age is related to improvement in stability and some improvements in this respect may be the result of the ultimate termination of the backward child's often long delayed adolescence. Rundle and his colleagues [39, 40 and 41] have recently presented more details of this delayed development. Only about 6 per cent. of the sample showed long-continued disablement of a neurotic kind. However, over 40 per cent. of the groups showed disturbance of a milder sort which yielded to changes of conditions or mild supportive therapy or guidance. Thus, whereas the proportions of neurosis were similar to those found by Russell Fraser [16] in the general population, a much smaller number showed hardcore neurosis. Productivity was temporarily but not permanently affected by emotional instability of a mild kind. In some instances work seemed to operate as a stabilizing force. In all cases it had a beneficial effect on the patient's social adjustment, whether he had a stable or labile temperament.

Several other experiments which could with some indulgence be regarded as connected with subnormal personality were carried out at this time. These included studies of the discipline appropriate to maximizing the involvement of adolescent subnormals in a work situation and experiments concerned with psychotherapy in subnormal adolescent disturbance.

The first group was concerned with situations similar to those studied by Lipsitt [25]. Groups of young men who were already working in the hospital workshops which we had established in a hospital in Kent were subjected to regimes of discipline which graded into three levels of permissiveness: these were defined as strict, friendly but firm, and *laissez faire*. Supervisors were instructed in their roles and carried them out on three separate groups of boys who were submitted to them in different orders. The results were judged in terms of both work output on jobs subcontracted from factories and also in terms of the items of good and bad behaviour reported from the workshop itself and from the ward where the subject lived.

The results could be summarized briefly, as Tizard [43] does, by saying that 'on the whole there were no great differences between the scores of groups working under strict, and those under friendly supervision, both of which contrasted strongly with the scores of those working under *laissez-faire* supervision . . . The experiment may be thought to exemplify some of the possibilities and limitations of research carried out with small groups in an institution. Small groups are convenient units for research in social psychology, because it is easy to modify or control certain features in the psychological environment of their members. Society as a whole, however, and more specifically the social organization in which the studies are carried out, greatly influences the behaviour of individuals in small groups.'

The study of psychotherapy and its effects was made in collaboration with Yonge [38, 45]. Over a period of 6 months, 2-hourly sessions per week were carried out by the psychiatrist and the groups' verbal and intrapersonal activities were recorded by the psychologist. The number of patients involved was 21 and their average age was 19 years. Over the period of treatment and observation, verbal behaviour was recorded and analysed, and gestures were interpreted as meaning either friendly or aggressive approaches to other members of the group or to authority figures. The trends were in the direction of encouraging an increase in aggression towards authority in the first few weeks, and criticism of each other within the group and increased self-criticism at later stages. The increase of what was called 'realistic ambition' was also notable but perhaps even more remarkable was the increase in measured verbal intelligence. Tests were used before and after treatment to help assess personality changes but these were ineffective in showing change. A test of verbal intelligence included in the pre- and post-test batteries did, however, show a significant 10 point average increase. It was assumed that this was part of a general increase in social responsiveness although part of the increase, perhaps as much as 5 points, might have been the result of doing the test twice.

Although the results were limited, they can be claimed to have been beneficial and might have been more so had the approach had less of a non-directional character.

It is not part of my task here to assess the social effects of these experiments or to indicate how they have affected the lives of the mentally retarded. The experiments showed, however, that work with adequate incentives, especially including payment, was beneficial to the retarded. They showed that the greatest barrier to the success of the retarded in regular work was not lack of intelligence, but emotional instability and frustration; and they showed also that regular work and occasional guidance and support and sometimes therapy, were valuable aids in alleviating emotional problems and problems of social maladjustment. In this respect subnormal patients differed from chronic schizophrenics whose increased industrial activity following occupational training was not accompanied by any improvement in their social and interpersonal contacts [32].

SOCIAL COMPETENCE AND INTELLECTUAL INCOMPETENCE

Many implications of these experiments were embodied in the 1959 Mental Health Act. Many subnormal patients who had been kept in mental deficiency hospitals until this time were released at about the time of the Act. Other provisions are now often made for them in the community where the industrial training experiments initiated by this work have been considerably extended.

At the time of the completion of these studies on rehabilitation, a number of questions were asked about the basis of the psychology of backwardness by those who had witnessed the relative success of our industrial training experiments. These questions often took the form of statements concerning the reasoning power of the backward. Typical statements of this kind were—routine repetitive tasks can be taught to the backward, but they cannot think or be taught to think. Such statements, however general and unexamined, contained some element of truth and needed careful examination.

Unquestionably the major feature of the performance of the retarded is their incapacity to succeed scholastically. Quite often their performance in other more physical or practical ways can be adequate or comparable with that of their more normal peers. Since Lewin [23], Goldstein [17], and Kounin [22] first set the pattern for analysing the intellectual function of the severely retarded, abstraction has been seen as the major question in this field. Incapacity to abstract may be the foundation for intellectual disability in scholastic achievement but the nature of thought is more complex than the one word 'abstraction' might suggest. It was in fact from the multiple operations involved in thinking that the second and more recent phase of our work began. Which, if any, aspect of intellectual function was missing or deficient in our group of patients? Was it simply the capacity to abstract or some other function or functions?

THE NATURE OF INTELLECTUAL DEFECT

This sub-heading is meant to emphasize the idea that defects can be 'mental' in the sense that some one function may be deficient and that this deficiency may have other psychological consequences. It in no way pretends to judge the relevance or irrelevance of physiological dysfunction. What functions are relevant to reasoning and scholastic skill? In a preliminary analysis of these possible factors [34] we listed conditioning, imitation, reasoning and judgement among others. However, even at this stage it was possible to delineate such operations as memory, association, attention and perception, all of them factors previously examined by Sir Cyril Burt [8] in relation to backwardness.

In subsequent work [20, 29] we analysed perception, inference, coding, cross-modal coding, attention and arousal, retention, input and speech. The nature of the experiments we carried out can only be illustrated in this chapter with one or two examples but they were intended to show to what extent the concept of the intelligence quotient could be re-analysed into its component parts and to find which of these components were most weakened by mental deficiency of whatever kind. For example, following the work of Luria [26] we were able to show that the connexion between thought and speech at some levels of operation was deficient. Thus, when trained to discriminate two squares of different area and choose one in order to gain a reward, defectives could do so nearly as well as control children of 5–6 years of age. When, after training, they were required to reverse this procedure and choose the other square, they did this readily. Normals, however, found this task nearly as hard as the first learning task. The normals could say why it was that they had made their choice in each case and which choice it was; the subnormals, however, could not present a verbalized rationale. For this reason, a new group of subnormals was introduced and trained on the first task. This time they were obliged to verbalize their behaviour. The effect of this linking of behaviour and speech was to stabilize the former in such a way that reversal was by no means as easy as it had been. This procedure of 'normalizing' the backward by associating their speech and visual-motor behaviour has practical implications for teaching at least some of them. Any instruction in motor skills should be carefully re-inforced by a verbal description of the process which they should be required to repeat.

Another example of the research concerns what came to be called cross-modal coding. This is a generalized form of the last example, i.e. it is the translation from one mode of representing the outer world in the mind, to another such mode. As an example, the world of vision could be represented in the world of touch so that a correspondence between the two methods of exploration could be arranged. Such an arrangement could be called 'integration' [3], which is virtually synonymous with cross-modal coding. Children have to learn to integrate their environments and the backward can do so only with difficulty. The reason why this is hard for some of them may be because of the deficiency of a connecting medium or nexus. Retention, for example, does not occur readily among the backward who do not verbalize the material presented to them. If, however, recognition is required of material presented in one modality which was initially presented in another, a connexion must be made. As the only connexion possible often involves the use of words, these are forced on the subject and the results are often unusually good. Thus, when a backward person is required to formulate his learning process verbally his retention is improved. This example emphasizes the need to develop verbal coding of perception in the backward. Clearly, the value of speech is emphasized as one of the major deficiencies in the defective mind and a deficiency which contributes considerably to scholastic inefficiency in many backward children.

There are, of course, other deficiencies which we can list as characterizing intellectual defect. These include a possible deficiency of arousal, a possible deficiency of input organization which may be what we mean by low arousal, and a possible deficiency of orientation or attention. What we can also say with some confidence is that some operations are relatively unimpaired in the subnormal. Examples of the latter might be some aspects of transfer and long term memory, especially long term memory.

It was with the intention of analysing the strengths and weaknesses of cortical function in the subnormal that we began a series of experiments which are described in the next section. Most of this work was carried out in collaboration with Hermelin, but some of the material reported in the later part of the section is the independent work of Bryant.

SPEECH AND THINKING PROCESSES IN THE SEVERELY SUBNORMAL

If one examines subnormality of problem solving, a number of possible sources of learning failure spring to mind. One can begin by looking for deficiencies in perceptual ability. If the external world is misperceived then adequate problem solving will be impossible. Perception could be deficient for a number of reasons but one of the most common is the failure to appreciate differences in shape or differences in direction or proportion. In an experiment carried out with groups of 16 mongol and 16 non-mongoloid severely subnormal adolescents, figures differing in the proportion of black and white and other figures differing in orientation were presented as part of a matching task. Patients of I.Q. about 36 and aged about 18 years were the subjects of the experimental groups and normal children aged between 4 and 6 were the controls. If the task was a matching one in which one shape was the prototype and one of the same kind had to be selected to match it from four figures, then no differences were found between normals, mongols and non-mongoloid severely subnormal subjects. If a delay were introduced then the recognition was relatively poor. However, there was no greater tendency in this study for reversal or rotation to take place in either of the severely subnormal groups as compared with the controls. Nor was there a tendency to mismatch because of such possible perceptual deficiencies. A similar inference was made as the result of a discrimination conditioning experiment with severely subnormal patients. The subjects were taught the difference between two points on a scale and then tested on three intermediate stimuli on the same scale. Normals proved to be no more refined than the subnormals in their capacity to respond appropriately to the intervening points.

In subsequent experiments we have found some problems about discrimination at this level of ability, although this may be for other reasons than perceptual disability. Thus the capacity of some severely disturbed and subnormal children to discriminate between one orientation and another may be because of difficulties in association rather than perception. At least in this series of experiments we were unable to find any obvious deficiency in the perceptual processes of the severely subnormal children. In fact some teaching devices which take account of the perception of minimal differences could be used with profit in instructing these patients.

If perception were adequate according to our studies, we would need to implicate other processes as part cause of difficulties in learning in the backward. One obvious possible deficiency was speech as a process accompanying learning. In early studies, as we noted above, problem solving could proceed without any verbal accompaniment and correct solutions could be reached in practice while the subject presented an incorrect verbal formulation of the solution.

The problem of formulation in words was tackled in three ways in our studies. First, we looked at the verbal accompaniments of voluntary motor functions and noted the discrepancy between them. This led us to the inference that learning was incomplete in the severely subnormal unless reinforced by an accompanying repeated verbal formulation. The second approach was to consider the need the subnormal have to integrate all processes in a unified picture or reflection of the external world. This process of 'cross-modal-coding' or integration occurs at a particular stage in the development of children and is part of the growth of the subnormal. In our experiments we tested the memory of severely subnormal subjects using material presented and recognized in one modality only. For example, sounds or words would be presented to be learnt; subsequently the same sounds or words could be presented for recognition along with others. The same procedure was followed with simply drawn outline pictures of objects or people. We found that auditory recognition of auditory data and visual recognition of visual data would result in chance recognition scores. If, however, an auditory test of visually learned material or a visual test of auditory data were made, the the scores would rise above chance.

Our theory concerning this finding was that integration had occurred to bridge the visual-auditory or auditory-visual gap in this kind of learning procedure. To our way of thinking, the bridging process was via verbal nomination of visually presented material or through visualization of the 'learning' of words in the case of auditory material. This coding or translation or integration process was not necessary in the uni-modal learning process which could proceed either on the basis of remembered sounds or remembered images, sound matching or image matching. The need for and value of cross-modal coding via verbal semantic formulation appeared to have been demonstrated by this series of experiments. The subnormal were shown to be able to profit from a process of coding which they could employ but which they generally found it hard to initiate.

A third approach to the examination of verbal inefficiency among the subnormal was the straightforward measurement of the number of words available for communication betwen the severely subnormal resident in a hospital. This study was reported by Mein [28, 29] and Mein and O'Connor [30] as a survey of the vocabularies in use among 80 imbeciles living in London mental deficiency hospitals. Based on ten 10-minute interviews with 80 subjects the study showed that the subnormal followed a normal pattern of development and learned to use nouns before introducing many verbs into their speech just as normal children do. Characteristic of this level of verbalization, the severely subnormal patients used an average of 359 different words in the experimental situation and altogether their speech contained 2,419 different words. The equivalent figures for normal six-year-olds would be 273 and 3,504 as based on Burroughs' study in Birmingham [6]. The structure of sentences, verb-adjective ratio and similar measures conformed to expectations for their mental age. The logical structure of their sentences was therefore in no way bizarre or different from that of normals of a similar mental age.

The foundation of vocabulary collected in this way has been used to show that words most often used are learned most easily in learning to read and that given a grasp of the vocabulary used the subnormal are as capable of semantic generalization as we are ourselves. In this respect our findings slightly modify those of some of our Soviet colleagues. Words of similar meanings interact in the subnormal mind as they would in ours providing these words are understood. Our experiments in teaching reading to severely subnormal subjects are reported in Hermelin and O'Connor [19]. The report shows that learning took place at the average rate of some three words per week over an 18-month period. Individual differences in the acquisition of learning skills were not explained by lack of visual discrimination or lack of auditory discrimination and memory. Rather they were accountable to the failure of some subjects to associate sounds and visual signs. Mair [27] showed this in her study of reading deficiencies and cross-modal coding.

If we reconsider our original question at this point we can note that whereas perceptual processes seemed relatively unimpaired in the severely subnormal, speech processes were severely limited. One other important aspect of learning was reported in our monograph: this was the question of memory.

Our earlier studies concerned long term memory. In two subsequent studies [20, 36] we have looked at short term memory. The first study of long term memory compared the success of normals and subnormals in retaining recorded verbal paired associates presented at different intensities and for different numbers of trials. We found that although learning conditions varied as expected by trials and intensities of sound in presentation, retention was independent of conditions of learning. This experiment is described in *Speech and Thought in Severe Subnormality* [34].

At this time we were investigating the hypothesis that one of the major deficiencies in the learning of the defectives was their poor memory. This experiment seemed to refute this theory. It might have been the case that even if long term memory were adequate immediate memory would have been inefficient; the memory trace over a few seconds may have decayed more rapidly in the case of the backward than the normals. Such a view implicating arousal and reverberating circuits was being promoted at this time by Ellis, Pryer and Barnett [14].

Our next two experiments were designed to test this theory of the rapid 'decay' of a memory trace, whether this was seen as a reverberating circuit, a biochemical process or the state of arousal due to an activating system. In the first we demonstrated the relatively rapid failure of retention in the severely subnormal when presentation time or delay was of the order of 1–2 seconds. The severely subnormal showed poor retention scores when compared with normals of the same mental age although after this period little further loss was recorded relative to normal scores. This finding gave us the impression that perhaps the loss was not in fact a memory loss at all, but an input weakness or failure of acquisition. We tested this notion in our second experiment concerned with this problem.

This experiment attempted to measure the retention of three digits presented either simultaneously or successively at different speeds. Long term successive presentations placed a 'strain' on recall and tested the trace decay hypothesis. Short term simultaneous presentations placed a strain on 'grasp' and hence tested adequacy of input. The experiment is presented in more detail elsewhere but the sum of the results shows that the major inadequacy in this group of subjects was due to input and not to trace decay in which the subnormals matched the controls. We have concluded from this work that we can reasonably suggest that the subnormal have deficiencies connected with coding and with input, and that these are related to speech deficiencies. We had not at this time made any studies of another major functional area, that of transfer of training which Tizard and Loos [44], Clarke and Blakemore [12], and Clarke and Cookson [13] had shown to be adequate in the severely mentally handicapped.

Bryant, however, has recently carried out certain experiments connected with this general problem which deserve notice both for the interest of their results and the ingenuity of the questions they ask and the methodology employed [4, 5]. These are briefly described in the next section.

LANGUAGE AND TRANSFER

Bryant began with the hypothesis that language in defectives may be less flexible than language in normal children. As a result perhaps the type of general instruction useful with normals might not be generalizable in the same way with defectives. Choosing the transfer situation Bryant [4] used a setting in which general instructions given in relation to one learning situation were tested in a similar transfer situation.

In a series of situations using both verbal and non-verbal instructions, Bryant showed that whereas general instructions aided learning in the subnormal, they did not aid transfer as they did in the normals. This turned out to be true of general instructions given both verbally and non-verbally. The failure of transfer could not therefore be attributed to the rigidity, inflexibility or lack of abstraction in the speech of subnormals, but perhaps indicated some deficiency of logic in the analysis of experience.

Bryant extended his experiments to analyse the problems involved and was able to show that the subnormal followed a different learning pattern from that followed by normal children. Instead of attempting to maximize a positive or rewarded cue, they seemed to attempt to eliminate negative or unrewarded cues one by one. As a result, this learning process in a transfer situation was not aided by a general instruction in a learning situation. The tendency of the subnormal to explore negative cues was tested by noting the relatively greater failure of this group in those transfer situations where more alternatives were involved. More recently Bryant [5] has shown a further apparent deficiency of the logical processes of imbeciles in so far as they appear to extend the process of individual cue analysis to the learning of discrimination problems. Such problems seen by normal children are learned in a relational fashion. The positive or rewarded cue is seen as 'correct' and the alternative is 'automatically' assumed to be incorrect. Bryant's data suggests that the severely subnormal have to learn each item of the two discriminanda as separate problems. This finding suggests a 'discontinuity' theory of learning. These and other similar findings have resulted from the analysis of the learning and perceptual problems of the severely subnormal following lines of research aimed at clarifying the learning processes of the mentally handicapped. It is hoped that further work of this kind will result in more knowledge concerning the handicapped and that it will also elucidate the developmental processes of normal children.

There have been other comparative studies using the material developed with the severely subnormal. One such extension of this work has been the recent attempts by Hermelin and O'Connor [21] and O'Connor and Hermelin [35] to establish the significant differences between severely disturbed and severely subnormal children. The aim of this series of studies was to indicate the degree to which symptoms regarded as due to autism or psychosis in children could be accounted for in terms of deficiencies in learning capacities or strategies of learning.

The general approach to the problem of descriptive diagnosis in autism and the analysis of patterns of psychological assets and deficit in the subnormal has been the guiding thread of our recent research. It is possible to see future work as the extension of this approach. Psychological problems which are of central significance in the study of the psychology of backwardness are those concerning the generality of intelligence and its effect on scholastic functions. Two antagonistic views are possible: the idea current in the first half of this century, namely that abilities were more or less equivalent from operation to operation in any one person, and the contrary view that patterns of abilities differ from person to person. Future work in the psychology of mental deficiency must inevitably bear on this question, and we hope to make a contribution to this and similar problems. The study of these issues would seem to be a logical extension of the work presented in this chapter.

REFERENCES

1. Binet, A., and Simon, T. (1908) Le dévelopment de l'intelligence, *Ann. psychol.*, **14**, 1–94.
2. Binet, A., and Simon, T. (1907) *Les Enfants Anormaux*, Paris.
3. Birch, H., and Belmont, L. (1966) Auditory-visual integration in brain-damaged and normal children, *Develop. Med. Child Neurol.*, **7**, 135–44.
4. Bryant, P. E. (1965) The transfer of positive and negative learning by normal and severely subnormal children, *Brit. J. Psychol.*, **56**, 81–86.
5. Bryant, P. E. (1965) The transfer of sorting concepts by moderately retarded children, *Amer. J. ment. Defic.*, **70**, 291–300.
6. Burroughs, G. E. R. (1957) *A Study of the Vocabulary of Young Children*, Birmingham University, Institute of Education, Educational Monographs No. 1, Edinburgh.
7. Burt, Sir Cyril (1923) *Handbook of Tests*, London.
8. Burt, Sir Cyril (1937) *The Backward Child*, 3rd ed., London.
9. Burt, Sir Cyril (1940) *The Factors of Mind*, London.
10. Claridge, G. (1959) A re-analysis of 'excitability' and its relationship with improvement in performance of imbeciles, *J. ment. Defic. Res.*, **3**, 116–21.
11. Claridge, G., and O'Connor, N. (1957) The relationship between incentives, personality type and improvement in performance of imbeciles, *J. ment. Defic. Res.*, **1**, 16–25.
12. Clarke, A. D. B., and Blakemore, C. (1961) Age and perceptual-motor transfer in imbeciles, *Brit. J. Psychol.*, **52**, 125–31.
13. Clarke, A. D. B., and Cookson, M. (1962) Perceptual-motor transfer in imbeciles: a second series of experiments, *Brit. J. Psychol.*, **53**, 321–30.
14. Ellis, N. R., Pryer, M., and Barnett, C. D. (1960) Motor learning and retention in normals and defectives, *Perceptual mot. Skills*, **10**, 83–91.
15. Eynsenck, H. J. (1947) *Dimensions of Personality*, London.
16. Frazer, Russell (1947) The Incidence of Neurosis among Factory Workers, *Report Indr. Health Res. Board* (*Pink Reports*). No. 90, H.M.S.O., London.
17. Goldstein, K. (1939) *The Organism*, New York.
18. Gordon, S., O'Connor, N., and Tizard, J. (1954) Some effects of incentives on the performance of imbeciles, *Brit. J. Psychol.*, **45**, 277–87.
19. Hermelin, B., and O'Connor, N. (1960) Reading ability of severely subnormal children, *J. ment. Defic. Res.*, **4**, 144–7.
20. Hermelin, B., and O'Connor, N. (1964) Short-term memory in normal and subnormal children, *Amer. J. ment. Defic.*, **69**, 121–5.
21. Hermelin, B., and O'Connor, N. (1965) Visual imperception in psychotic children, *Brit. J. Psychol.*, **56**, 455–60.
22. Kounin, J. S. (1941) Experimental studies of rigidity, I. The measure-

ment of rigidity in normal and feeble-minded persons, *Charact. and Pers.*, **9**, 251–72.

23. LEWIN, K. A. (1935) *A Dynamic Theory of Personality*, New York.
24. LEWIS, A. J. (1960) The study of defect, *Amer. J. Psychiat.*, **117**, 289–305.
25. LIPSITT, P. (1940) An analysis of group reactions to three types of experimentally created social climates, Unpublished Doctoral Thesis, State University of Iowa.
26. LURIA, A. R. (1961) *The Role of Speech in the Regulation of Normal and Abnormal Behaviour*, London.
27. MAIR, K. J. (1963) Coding and literacy in severely subnormal children, *J. ment. Defic. Res.*, **7**, 46–52.
28. MEIN, R. (1961) A study of the oral vocabularies of severely subnormal patients, II. Grammatical analysis of speech samples, *J. ment. Defic. Res.*, **5**, 52–59.
29. MEIN, R. (1962) The vocabularies of severely subnormal patients, Ph.D. Thesis, University of London.
30. MEIN, R., and O'CONNOR, N. (1960) A study of the oral vocabularies of severely subnormal patients, *J. ment. Defic. Res.*, **4**, 130–43.
31. O'CONNOR, N. (1957) The social effectiveness of the mentally handicapped, *Adv. Sci.*, **52**, 373–7.
32. O'CONNOR, N., CARSTAIRS, G. M., and RAWNSLEY, K. (1957) Communication in a mental hospital population, *Int. J. soc. Psychiat.*, **3**, 183–7.
33. O'CONNOR, N., and CLARIDGE, G. (1955) The effect of goal-setting and encouragement on the performance of imbecile men, *Quart J. exp. Psychol.*, **7**, 37–45.
34. O'CONNOR, N., and HERMELIN, B. (1963) *Speech and Thought in Severe Subnormality*, Oxford.
35. O'CONNOR, N., and HERMELIN, B. (1965) Visual analogies of verbal operations, *Language and Speech*, **8**, 197–207.
36. O'CONNOR, N., and HERMELIN, B. (1965) Input restriction and immediate memory decay in normal and subnormal children. *Quart. J. exp. Psychol.*, **17**, 323–8.
37. O'CONNOR, N., and TIZARD, J. (1956) *The Social Problem of Mental Deficiency*, Oxford.
38. O'CONNOR, N., and YONGE, K. A. (1955) Methods of evaluating the group psychotherapy of unstable defective delinquents, *J. genet. Psychol.*, **87**, 89–101.
39. RUNDLE, A. T., DUTTON, G., and GIBSON, J. (1959) Endocrinological aspects of mental deficiency, I. Testicular function in mongolism, *J. ment. Defic. Res.*, **3**, 108–15.
40. RUNDLE, A. T., and SYLVESTER, P. E. (1962) Endocrinological aspects of mental deficiency, II. Maturational status of adult males, *J. ment. Defic. Res.*, **6**, 87–93.
41. RUNDLE, A. T., and SYLVESTER, P. E. (1963) Endocrinological aspects of mental deficiency, III. Growth and development of young males, *J. ment. Defic. Res.*, **7**, 10–21.

42. Tizard, J. (1950) The abilities of adolescent and adult high-grade male defectives, *J. ment. Sci.*, **96**, 889–907.
43. Tizard, J. (1953) The effects of different types of supervision on the behaviour of mental defectives in a sheltered workshop, *Amer. J. ment. Defic.*, **58**, 143–61.
44. Tizard, J., and Loos, F. M. (1954) The learning of a spatial relations test by adult imbeciles, *Amer. J. ment. Defic.*, **59**, 85–90.
45. Yonge, K. A., and O'Connor, N. (1954) Measurable effects of group psychotherapy with defective delinquents, *J. ment. Sci.*, **100**, 944–52.

5

Experimental Psychological Studies of Chronic Schizophrenia

PETER H. VENABLES

UNTIL 1953 work in the Medical Research Council's Unit under Sir Aubrey Lewis' direction was mainly concerned on the one hand with studies on the occupational potentialities of mental defectives ([30] and Chapters 3 and 4), and on the other hand with studies aimed at the determination of the importance of the presence of neurotic tendencies among industrial workers [12, 28, 37] which had been reported by Russell Fraser [7]. The subsequent decision to undertake work on chronic schizophrenia was influenced by a number of factors. Undoubtedly the most important of these was the existence of a population of patients, with in some sense a defined disease, whose magnitude was such as to form a problem of social importance.

The method of approach to the study of the chronic schizophrenic followed from the principles which had been found successful with the earlier investigations and could be seen to fall under three headings. First, study of the influence of the family and hospital background on the patient; secondly, the empirical investigation of the employability of the patient; and thirdly, the experimental analysis of some of the behaviour leading to the deficits most clearly evident in his day to day performance.

It is with this last aspect of the work that this chapter is primarily concerned. The first series of experiments to be described may be seen as searches for a starting point and the second group of studies as attempts to analyse the implications of a tentative model that was formed as a basis of explanation for some of the earlier findings. The testing of this model led to its breakdown, and the subsequent experimental studies, which are still continuing, are concerned with finer grain analysis of some of the schizophrenic mechanisms which were suggested by the second phase of experimentation.

One of the most pervading deficits shown by the chronic schizophrenic, which is evident even to the lay observer in many cases, is his slowness. Consequently the initial series of studies were concerned with attempts to examine this handicap.

Rodnick and Shakow [32] pointed out that the finding of reaction time studies, that schizophrenics take longer to respond than normal persons, in itself makes little contribution to knowledge, and experiments are required which examine factors leading to increases or decreases in slowness. Rodnick and Shakow showed that by using a reaction time procedure with the stimulus for response preceded by a forewarning with regular and irregular series of foreperiods, an experiment could be carried out which gave more opportunity to expose the factors leading to slowness. The findings of their study pointed to a formulation of the schizophrenics' poor performance in the terms of their 'inability to maintain a set to respond', and a composite score or 'set index' was derived, of which Hunt and Cofer [15] said that it is 'the only score known to us that has differentiated any diagnostic group from a normal group without any overlapping'. Knehr [18] cast doubt on these findings and suggested that impairment of speed of response was related to a general deficit in intellectual functioning. Knehr's study could itself be criticized in that he had employed a much restricted range of foreperiods, thus distorting the subjects' expectancies and hence the 'set' which was the factor on which the experiment primarily rested. Examination of these conflicting findings seemed a useful starting point and a bridge from previous work on the subnormal, as the implication of Knehr's suggestions could best be studied by repeating Rodnick and Shakow's studies and extending them by the inclusion of a group of subnormal subjects to test the suggestion that deficit in general intellectual functioning was accompanied by an impairment of speed. The results of this first study [35] essentially confirmed those of Rodnick and Shakow [32], and showed that with two exceptions the subnormals performed in a similar way to normal persons. The two subnormals whose 'set' scores placed them within the schizophrenic range were noted in their case papers to be markedly schizoid.

While the outcome of this preliminary experiment could be considered successful, attempts to explain the data in terms of other hypotheses were unfruitful, and it was felt at the time that conclusions in terms of 'inability to maintain a set to respond' were more descriptive than explanatory. Alternative lines of investigation were thus explored. These involved the concept of inhibition to explain slowness; in two studies the use of the concept was clearly Pavlovian [31], while in two others the ideas were derived from Hullian concepts [13].

Pavlov [31] claimed that the withdrawal and negativism shown by schizophrenics are examples of 'paradoxical' and 'ultraparadoxical' phenomena. These he had demonstrated, in work with dogs, to occur in those animals described as having 'weak, inhibitory nervous systems'. Paradoxical effects are said to be exhibited when weak stimuli bring about larger responses than strong stimuli, and ultraparadoxical effects exist when excitatory stimuli are converted into inhibitory ones and vice versa. These ideas are related to the concept of 'protective inhibition', whose function is to protect the nervous system from the harmful consequences of prolonged or excessive stimulation. It was suggested that if paradoxical effects are to be found in schizophrenic patients they should be demonstrable in a reaction time experiment using different intensities of stimulation. A study [51] was carried out in which eight intensities of visual stimulation covering a 2 log unit range from 16 to 1,500 foot candles were used. Twenty responses to each of these stimulus intensities were made by 24 chronic schizophrenic patients. It was found that on the first occasion of testing that 22 out of the 24 showed an increase in reaction time (RT) from the moderate intensities of 135 and 275 foot candles to the high intensities of 800 and 1,500 foot candles. This paradoxical effect was only shown, however, on the first occasion of testing, and did not appear on a second occasion 24 hours later, when a uniformly slow RT (slower than that to the medium intensities on the first occasion) was given to all intensities. A group of less severely ill, short-stay schizophrenics and a group of normal subjects showed no evidence of the paradoxical effect on either occasion. The regression slope of increase in RT to stimuli from the moderate to the high intensities (i.e. the paradoxical effect) was calculated for each subject and related to his general speed of reaction for which the RT to the lowest stimulus intensity was used as an index. It was found on this basis that there was a correlation of 0·74 ($p < \cdot001$) between the extent of the paradoxical effect and the subject's general speed. Thus the slower, and probably the more ill the patient, the greater the extent of decrease in speed with increase in intensity of stimulation. Expressed in another way, the more ill the patient is the more he would appear to be responsive to his environment. This type of phenomenon is shown in an extreme form by those patients who were too ill to co-operate fully. In the reaction time experiment these patients appeared to be unable to release the key while an intense stimulus was present, and were only able to make a response when the stimulus was switched off. This might be considered to be an example of the ultraparadoxical effect.

Experimentation of this kind was extended to include stimulation in the auditory modality [53]. Preliminary experimentation suggested that no paradoxical effects were apparent in the auditory modality. In order to make sure that patients who were being tested were those in whom these phenomena might be present in the visual modality, both light and sound stimuli were used. One group was tested first on four visual and then on four auditory intensities, and a second group in the reverse order. Of the group of 16 patients tested first in the visual modality, 13 showed a paradoxical increase in RT with high intensity stimulation. The group of sixteen patients who were tested on a second occasion with visual stimuli showed no evidence of paradoxical effects. The findings of the earlier study were thus confirmed. No paradoxical effects whatsoever were shown to stimuli in the auditory modality, although the mean RT shown by the group who received auditory stimuli first was higher than those who received it second (who showed paradoxical effects in the visual modality) and, therefore, might be expected to show the effect in a more marked form. Further attempts were made to show the effect with more intense auditory stimuli, and also with white noise and lower frequencies than those originally used (200 cps instead of 1,000 cps), but no evidence of paradoxical phenomena were found. The finding of a greater RT to auditory than to visual stimuli among schizophrenics, which is a reversal of the normal pattern, is of significance and stimulated further work which is described by Venables [45] and Venables and O'Connor [48].

A further pair of experiments involved the use of the Hullian notion of reactive inhibition as an explanatory concept. In origin they stem from much earlier findings reported by Kraepelin [21], who had shown that on a simple addition task involving 10 minutes' continuous performance, schizophrenics showed rapid deterioration. When a pause was introduced in the fifth minute, performance was markedly improved on the sixth minute, but thereafter declined rapidly as before. This finding is readily explicable in terms of Hullian theory, by suggesting that the schizophrenic rapidly develops reactive inhibition in the performance of the arithmetic task, and performance deteriorates. If, however, a rest pause is allowed, reactive inhibition dissipates, and on a post-rest trial performance improves and the phenomenon of reminiscence is demonstrated.

Attempts to repeat Kraepelin's experiment directly did not prove possible, as marked practice effects obscured any signs of a progressive deterioration in performance.

A five choice repetitive reaction time task was used in two studies [39, 52]. Five lights and five keys alongside them were arranged round the circumference of a semicircle in the first study, and in two rows 2 inches apart in the second. Response to one light was instrumental in setting up the next light stimulus. In the first study patients worked for two 5-minute periods which were separated by a 1-minute rest pause. In the second experiment work periods were of 10 minutes, and rest pauses 5 minutes and 10 days' duration. The first experiment provided evidence that schizophrenics tended to show marked reminiscence during the rest periods. This, and a subsequent fall off in performance after rest, was taken to indicate that schizophrenics were particularly prone to develop reactive inhibition during the performance of a task and that this dissipated during the rest period to bring about a large reminiscence effect. In the second experiment no difference was shown between either the work decrement or the amount of reminiscence shown by schizophrenics or normals. In the form of the task used in the second experiment normal subjects worked much faster than the schizophrenics. The former were thus able to build up an amount of reactive inhibition which made their performance, with the exception of the over-all speed, indistinguishable from that of the schizophrenics. An hypothesis to explain the differences between the two sets of results was put forward and involved the suggestion that the speed at which reactive inhibition is dissipated is different in normals and schizophrenics. If the task is sufficiently easy for responses to be made rapidly then the responses may be so close together that the reactive inhibition generated by a single response is not dissipated before the next response is made; therefore, reactive inhibition accumulates. At high speeds even normal subjects are unable to dissipate reactive inhibition and the amounts accumulated by different groups tend to be similar. At slower speeds, as in the first experiment, normal subjects are able to dissipate the reactive inhibition that is generated by one response before the next occurs. However, if the schizophrenic dissipates reactive inhibition more slowly it will not be fully dissipated before the next response occurs and will accumulate. While this hypothesis explains some of the features of the performance found in the experiments described, the large differences in over-all response speed remain unexplained. This residue of slowness in the schizophrenics' performance despite situational manipulations will be examined in greater detail later on in the chapter.

The experiments described have suggested that the chronic schizophrenic is either prone to develop, or slow to dissipate, protective or reactive inhibition. It could be suggested that Hullian 'reactive inhibition' is operationally similar to the Pavlovian concept of 'internal inhibition' and therefore to be distinguished from protective inhibition. However, while it is possible to distinguish these two forms of inhibition as constructs, the underlying physiological mechanisms may be similar.

This line of thinking led to the next series of experiments. If it could be suggested that the slowness characteristic of the performance of many chronic schizophrenics is due to the excessive accumulation of 'inhibition' of some sort, it was thought that it might be possible to disinhibit this by the presentation of some distracting additional stimulus during the performance of a task.

An experiment was therefore carried out [36] in which the subject made 20 visual reaction time responses in quiet; 10 while 70 db white noise was presented, and then a further 20 in quiet. In a control session 50 responses were made without any extraneous noise. The over-all result was that of the 74 schizophrenic subjects who were tested, 35 were slower when the noise was present and 39 were faster. Thus, in general the hypothesis did not hold. Previous pilot studies had, however, led to the observation that those patients who speeded up with additional stimulation tended to give a clinical impression of withdrawal, while those who slowed down in the presence of noise were less withdrawn, more sociable and had wider interests.

A rating scale [38] to measure this clinical impression was constructed using some items from the M.S.R.P.P. Scale [26], and was used to divide the 74 patients into withdrawn and non-withdrawn groups. It was found that of the withdrawn patients 23 were faster during noise and 8 were slower, while in the non-withdrawn group 27 were slower and 16 were faster ($\chi^2 = 9{\cdot}89$ $p < 0{\cdot}01$). In order to extend this finding a second experiment was carried out on 30 withdrawn and 30 non-withdrawn schizophrenics. Reaction times to an auditory stimulus were measured in a room which could be brightly or dimly illuminated. The subject sat for 3 minute in each level of illumination before making 20 responses to a 1,000 cps tone 60 db above threshold. The findings of the previous experiment were replicated. Twenty-one of the 30 withdrawn patients were faster in the brightly lit room than when the room was dimly lit; 19 of the non-withdrawn patients were slower in the bright light and 11 slower in the dim light ($\chi^2 = 11{\cdot}84$ $p < 0{\cdot}001$).

As withdrawal, according to Pavlov [31], is a paradoxical phenomenon, it could be said that the withdrawn sub-group had more inhibition to dissipate, and therefore showed a greater effect of the disinhibiting stimuli. On the other hand, the fact that some at least of the withdrawn subjects showed a slowing down of responses in noise give rise to some uneasiness in using disinhibition as an explanatory concept.

These results could also be interpreted as being due to a non-specific facilitatory effect of additional stimulation in the case of the withdrawn patients, while in the case of the non-withdrawn patients additional stimulation might be considered to have been sufficiently distracting to worsen the performance of these patients.

In order to minimize factors of set or distractability a third experiment [40] was carried out where instead of a voluntary reaction, an involuntary reflex, the skin potential response, was used. A 1-second burst of 1,000 cps tone 90 db above threshold, or a 1-second illumination of a translucent screen at an intensity of 900 ft L were used to evoke the skin potential response. Background stimuli were either continuous 75 db white noise or continuous illumination of the screen with an intensity of 700 ft L. Thirty-two chronic schizophrenic patients, half of whom were rated as withdrawn and half as non-withdrawn, were allocated at random to each of four experimental treatments: (1) visual stimulus, no background; (2) visual stimulus, noise background; (3) tone stimulus, no background; (4) tone stimulus, light background. The results of this experiment showed that, as with the previous experiments using reaction time as the measure of response, the speed of the skin potential response was greater in the withdrawn patients when additional stimulation was present than when it was not, and that the reverse was the case with the non-withdrawn patients.

A further experiment on the effect of additional stimulation on the speed of response made use of the five choice repetitive reaction time task previously described. It was found as before that in a control period the performance of schizophrenics and normals tended to fall off over time. However, in an experimental session where 85 db white noise was introduced during part of the time that the subjects were performing on the task, the withdrawn, in contrast to non-withdrawn patients and normals, showed an improvement in speed while the noise was present.

At this point is seemed that a more economical explanation of the last four experiments could be made in terms of the inverted U relation between performance and level of activation or arousal proposed, for example, by Hebb [11] and Malmo [27]. It was suggested that withdrawn schizophrenics might be less aroused, and non-withdrawn patients more aroused than optimal. If additional stimulation can be thought of as raising the arousal level via collateral sensory input to the reticular system and thence by non-specific pathways to the cortex, then the increase of the withdrawn schizophrenics' arousal level will raise their performance to an optimal position, while a similar change in arousal will move the performance of the non-withdrawn patients further away from optimal. This model served the purpose of enabling the next steps in the investigation to be stated clearly. These may be listed as: (1) the measurement of arousal; (2) the measurement of withdrawal; (3) the examination of the relation between arousal and withdrawal; (4) the examination of whether arousal and performance are in fact related in an inverted U-shaped fashion; (5) the determination of the direction of change in arousal following stimulation.

Following Lindsley's [23] presentation to psychologists of the early findings of the role of the reticular activating system, the functioning of this system came to be identified under the name of 'arousal' with the intensive dimension of emotion in earlier ideas current in the psychological literature [5, 8]. Hebb [11] clearly related arousal on the abscissa of the inverted U-shaped curve diagram to the degree of diffuse non-specific cortical bombardment from the reticular system. Psychologists who wished at this stage to measure 'arousal' could on the one hand make use of the indices employed in the earlier 'pre-reticular' work, for instance the electrical activity of the skin or level of muscular tension. On the other hand, as arousal had become synonymous with the operation of the activating system, an index which reflected the functioning of this became desirable. As an index of the activity of the ascending reticular activating system, the EEG would initially seem to be the measure of choice. The quantification of EEG activity is not simple, although work such as that by Goldstein and his colleagues [9, 10] has recently shown that it can successfully be carried out. At the time another approach to the problem was made. Lindsley [24] had published evidence to show that the temporal resolution of the optic cortex of the cat was under reticular control. If two flashes of light 50 msec apart were presented, the visual cortex responded with only a single spike of evoked potential. If then the reticular formation were stimulated electrically the resolution of the cortex was improved and two flashes of light were represented by two evoked potential spikes. While it could not be assumed that because reticular stimulation produced a change in temporal resolution within the subject, measurement of temporal resolution could reflect the differences in degree of reticular activity between subjects; in the absence of better indices, when dealing with the intact human organism, it was decided to use the measurement of two-flash threshold as a tentative measure of arousal. In addition, as a more traditional type of measure of activation, one of the aspects of the electrical activity of the skin, namely skin potential level, was also measured by the techniques outlined in Venables and Sayer [50].

The first experiment of the series [42], designed to test the implications of the model outlined above, was concerned with the relation between the two different types of measures of arousal which have been described. Two-flash threshold was measured by presenting to each subject pairs of flashes, the interval between which could be varied. The subject reported whether he saw one flash or two by giving one or two presses on a key which he held in his hand. The threshold of fusion of the paired flashes was taken to be the longest interflash interval at which the subject always reported one flash. Skin potential was measured between two silver/silver chloride electrodes placed on the palm and an abraded site on the forearm. In the first experiment 30 male non-paranoid schizophrenics took part. The sub-diagnosis was made by the use of a rating scale developed for the purpose [49]. The correlation between threshold and potential was found to be $-0{\cdot}79$ ($p<0{\cdot}001$). This negative relation between the level of skin potential and two-flash threshold was that which had been initially expected on the assumption that both were measures of arousal: that is, that high skin potential in the same way as high skin conductance represented high arousal, and a low threshold of fusion of paired flashes was brought about by the presence of ascending reticular activity improving the temporal resolving power of the cortex. This study was, however, carried out using only non-paranoid schizophrenics as subjects; a further experiment was therefore conducted to extend the findings; in this, normals as well as schizophrenics served as subjects. As before the relation between two-flash threshold and skin potential was negative in the non-paranoid schizophrenic group ($r = -0{\cdot}72$ $p< 0{\cdot}001$, $N = 27$). In the case of the normal subjects, however, the relation between the two measures was positive ($r =+0{\cdot}45< 0{\cdot}02$, $N=27$). Twelve patients were available who were diagnosed [57] as paranoid with coherently expressed delusions. The correlation between skin potential and two-flash threshold was positive in this group, as had been found with the normal group. Because of the rather unexpected finding that the two measures of arousal did not correlate in the expected direction in the normal group it was thought worth while to replicate this part of the experiment on a further normal group, the findings with non-paranoid patients having already been confirmed. In the third experiment the correlation between skin potential and two-flash threshold was again positive ($r = +\ 0{\cdot}61$ $p < 0{\cdot}001$, $N = 25$). In no case in any of the three experiments just described did the mean levels of skin potential or two-flash threshold separate the normal from the schizophrenic group; it is only in the direction of the relation between the two measures of 'arousal' that the two classes of subject are distinguished.

More recent findings [14] have failed to repeat the positive relation between the two measures in normal subjects that was replicated in the experiments just outlined. Some explanation for this discrepancy must be sought. This may be done in terms of experiments carried out by Darrow and his colleagues [2, 3]. They found a relation between cortical and autonomic indices in normals in the same direction to that reported here when the measures were taken *in the resting state*. However, when the subject was activated the direction of the relation between cortical and autonomic measures was in the direction expected, i.e. both moved in the direction of arousal. In discussing the 1946 study Darrow suggests 'that levels of autonomic activity giving correlations with EEG in the resting state opposite in sign to correlations produced in conditions of cortical activation provide evidence of opposing cortical vs sub-cortical influences on cerebral function, and offer a means for studying phenomena of mutual cortical-sub-cortical regulation'.

It was the practice in all the experiments with schizophrenics which have so far been described, completely to familiarize the patient with the experimental set-up by having him perform pilot experiments before conducting the experiment proper. Thus it was hoped to be able to examine the patient's reaction to controllable changes in his environment rather than to experiment in the presence of idiosyncratic reactions to the unaccustomed experimental conditions. As this was necessary with patients, the process had to be gone through with normal subjects undertaking the same tasks. Thus all normals were very familiar, and even bored, with the experiment reported, and might justifiably be considered to be in a resting state in which Darrow's findings might apply. Given any other sort of testing situation where the normal subject was not so completely at ease, a correlation between cortical and autonomic measures in a direction similar to that found in schizophrenics might appear.

As a result of the three experiments described it became clear that the measurement of a unitary variable 'arousal' in terms of the two measures used was not possible, but rather one might speak of cortical and autonomic activation as two separate processes. For further understanding of the relations between the two variables as measures of cortical and autonomic activity a series of more dynamic studies was undertaken in which changes in the measures due to noise were examined.

In the next experiment to be described [43] changes in two-flash threshold which were due to exposure to 80 db white noise were analysed. Sixty-three schizophrenics and 47 normal subjects took part in the experiment. Thirty-eight patients were not receiving drugs (as had been the case with all patients so far tested), and 25 were on various dosages of chlorpromazine. A first measure of two-flash threshold was made, and 1 minute afterwards an 80 db white noise was presented from a loudspeaker directly in front of the patient. The noise remained on continuously until after the determination of the second threshold 4 minutes later. In the case of both the medicated and the non-medicated patients a plot of the data showed that with few exceptions the threshold of fusion was altered in the presence of noise, and that the amount and direction of this change was related to the original threshold about which this change took place. Those patients with the highest threshold levels in quiet showed a fall in threshold in noise, while those with low initial threshold showed a rise. This phenomenon was similar in degree whether or not the patients were on or off drugs, or whether or not their sub-diagnosis showed them to be paranoid or non-paranoid. In contrast, the normal subjects did not show a significant change in threshold due to noise. To make these findings clear both normal and schizophrenic groups were divided into three sub-groups on the basis of their initial thresholds. The changes in threshold shown by the schizophrenics were, for those with high initial threshold, −8·7 msec, mid −3·0 msec, low +3·6 msec; the results for the normals were correspondingly, high +1·5 msec, mid −1·0 msec, low +0·4 msec. The findings of this experiment make it possible to repeat the suggestion which was made earlier in the discussion of the 'paradoxical effect' experiments, namely that the schizophrenic appears to be more responsive than the normal to stimulation from the environement. If those subjects showing a threshold change of more than 3 msec are called 'unstable' and those showing a smaller change are called 'stable', then two-thirds of the normals and one-third of the schizophrenics remain cortically stable in noise of 80 db by this definition.

Further experiments were designed to examine the implications of this finding, and were concerned with concomitant changes in two-flash threshold and skin potential.

Preliminary experimentation with 25 normal subjects, on noise-induced changes in threshold and potential, confirmed the last finding of a small insignificant change in two-flash threshold (0·6 msec), but showed that this was accompanied by a 4·2 mV increase in skin potential ($t = 3·6 < 0·01$). This finding led to an experiment to compare changes in skin potential level in schizophrenics and normals during a period in which an 80 db white noise was presented continuously for 3 minutes. Twenty normal and 20 non-paranoid schizophrenic patients took part. Seven minutes of skin potential recording were made after a preliminary rest of 5 minutes in which the subject adapted to the experimental situation. In the experimental session, which was used with half the subjects first and half second, the noise was presented during minutes 2, 3, and 4 of the 7-minute recorded period. During a control session no noise was presented. Examination of the data showed that the record could be divided into sections with different characteristics. The first major change occurred at the onset of noise, and lasted for about a quarter of a minute. During the next 2¾ minutes there was a slow change in potential with an approximately linear trend. Other sections of the record are not important in the present analysis. The main significant differences shown by normals and schizophrenics were that in the first ¼ minute in noise the normals showed a 1·3 mV drop in skin potential, while the schizophrenics showed a 2·8 mV rise. In the subsequent 2¾ minute period the normal subjects showed a rise in potential of 2·3 mV, while the schizophrenics showed a fall of 2·4 mV. In both cases the normal and the schizophrenic performance differed significantly.

With these findings in mind, a final experiment was designed to examine concomitant changes in skin potential and two-flash threshold. As before two measures of two-flash threshold were taken, the first in quiet, and the second after exposure to 4 minutes of 80 db white noise. The noise was increased to its full intensity in 10 db steps in order to minimize startle. As the interest was mainly that of the observation of concomitant changes in the two variables the first measure of skin potential selected for analysis was that at the end of the first threshold measure in quiet. On this measure of potential pairs of normal and schizophrenic subjects were matched within a millivolt in practically every case. Thirty pairs of subjects were matched in this way from among 42 schizophrenics and 36 normal subjects who had been tested. FIGURE 2 shows the mean potential levels at five selected points taken from the total record. In addition to the changes in skin potential level, a record of the number of spontaneous fluctuations made by each subject was taken. Spontaneous fluctuations were defined as those alterations of skin potential which had the same form as induced responses and which showed an amplitude of not less than 0·5 mV in either the positive or negative component.

As with the previous experiment it may be seen from FIGURE 2 that on the onset of noise the potential level of the normals fell and subsequently rose, while that of the schizophrenics rose and subsequently fell during the time in which noise was present. In schizophrenics the range of threshold change due to noise was from −25 to +23 msec, while in normal subjects the range was from −10 to + 6 msec. Presenting this variablity in terms of a standard deviation the value for schizophrenics was 10·6 msec while that for the normals was 4·5 msec. These two figures are significantly different.

The crudest relation between changes in skin potential and changes in two-flash threshold, is that between the difference in the thresholds and changes in the potential level taken at the same time, regardless of more complicated intervening changes of skin potential shown in FIGURE 2. In schizophrenics the correlations between the changes in these two measures was found to be −0·49 ($p < 0·01$), while in normals the correlation was only +0·05(NS). Thus, while in schizophrenics an increase in skin potential is found alongside an increase in cortical activity measured by a decrease in two-flash threshold, this relation is not found in normal subjects.

In order to extend these findings and to establish whether there was any particular section of the total skin potential record which showed more relation to change in threshold than any other point, further analyses were carried out. The subjects in each diagnostic group were divided into two sub-groups. Those whose thresholds changed by 3 msec or less, due to the presence of noise, formed a 'cortically stable' group, while those whose thresholds changed by 4 msec or more formed a 'cortically unstable' group. The changes in skin potential level and number of spontaneous fluctuations in each section for each sub-group were analysed. It was found that the change in skin potential level during the first $\frac{1}{4}$ minute in noise

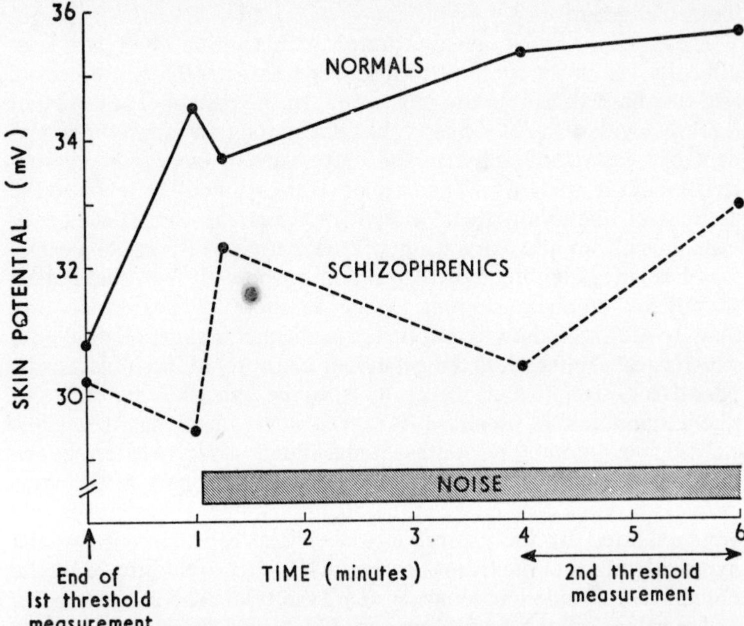

FIG. 2. Changes in skin potential level of normal and schizophrenic subjects brought about by the presence of noise.

was related to cortical stability within groups. In the case of the 'stable' normals the mean fall in potential during this period was 2·4 mV; on the other hand, in the 'unstable' normals there was a mean rise in potential over the same period of 1·2 mV. In the case of the 'stable' schizophrenics the mean rise in potential in the first $\frac{1}{4}$ minute in noise was only 0·42 mV, while in the 'unstable' schizophrenics, which formed the majority of this group, the mean rise in potential was 3·9 mV. In both normals and schizophrenics differences of about 3·5 mV between the 'stable' and the 'unstable' groups were significant. No other changes in skin potential level while noise was present distinguished one sub-group from another. However, the number of spontaneous fluctuations in potential during the period from the end of the first ¼ minute to the end of the third minute in noise distinguished the 'stable' from the 'unstable' normal groups. In the case of the normal 'stable' group the mean number of fluctuations of skin potential was 9·9, and in the 'unstable' group 4·1, figures which are different at the 1 per cent. level of significance. Among the schizophrenics the two groups did not differ, the mean number of fluctuations being 11·0 for the 'stable' and 10·0 for the 'unstable' group.

These results must be interpreted with caution. Not the least difficulty lies in the attempt to discover what exactly skin potential and two-flash threshold are measuring. In the case of skin potential level the evidence [29] suggests that this measure is largely independent of sweat gland activity, and may relate to membrane characteristics of the epidermis. The measure is thus difficult to relate to the activity of the sympathetic nervous system, as the existence of mechanisms for the alteration of the permeability of epidermal membranes is obscure. For the present purposes it is probably best to rely on empirical findings, such as those of Leiderman and Shapiro [22], who showed that there are changes in skin potential level which parallel changes in the behavioural arousal of the subject as he passes from sleep to alert wakefulness. In the case of the spontaneous fluctuations in skin potential, it is reasonably clear that these, like elicited skin potential responses, are mediated to a large extent by the sweat glands and are thus under the control of a part of the sympathetic nervous system. Wang [55, 56] has shown that these responses are facilitated by the rostral mesencephalic reticular system, the hypothalamus and the frontal cortex; while they are inhibited by the bulbar ventromedial reticular system, the cerebellar anterior lobe, and portions of the frontal cortex. Bloch and Bonvallet [1] have shown that skin potential responses may be elicited from the reticular formation which has a lower threshold for producing this response than other surrounding areas. These workers suggest that sensory input triggers electrodermal response by the direct mediation of this system. It is possible, therefore, that the operation of the reticular system as part of a regulatory system may be monitored by the electrodermal responses which it evokes concomitantly.

No less difficult to interpret clearly is the physiological background of two-flash threshold measurement. It has been shown [24] that the peripheral mechanisms and the visual pathways up to the cortex do not seem to be the limiting factors in the transmission of neural impulses resulting from paired light flashes within the range of inter-stimulus intervals used in the experiment described. There does seem to be some justification, therefore, in the suggestion made earlier that the threshold of fusion of paired flashes might be a reflection of cortical activation. It would seem reasonable to suggest that when two separate spikes of evoked potential are apparent in the optic cortex, there is the possibility of seeing two flashes of light, whereas when there is only a single spike, there is no likelihood of perceiving two flashes. Some evidence on the relation between cortical representation and perception is provided by an experiment reported by Lindsley [25], and carried out by himself and Schwartz. In cats trained to respond to the difference between a continuous or a flickering light, perception of flicker or fusion signalled by conditioned responses in general followed cortical events. That is, when the cortex ceased to follow the flashes of light with separate evoked responses the cat signalled fusion and vice versa. That the resolving power of the cortex, i.e. the ability to separate two stimuli appearing close together in time, is influenced by reticular activity seems to be fairly well established. Lindsley's experiment on the effect of reticular stimulation on the resolution of the optic cortex has already been cited. Similar results have been obtained for the auditory cortex by Steriade and Demetrescu [34], and for the somatosensory cortex by Schwartz and Shagass [33].

Additional support of a more direct kind is given in an experiment of Kopell, Noble and Silverman [19] who showed that the effect of an injection of amphetamine was to lower the mean threshold of a group of subjects, while the effect of barbiturate was to raise it.

The expected relation between two-flash threshold and level of skin potential on the basis of this discussion might therefore with some justification be considered to be negative. That is, a high skin potential level might be expected to be accompanied by a low two-flash threshold, both showing the activating influence of a subcortical arousal system. This, however, is only found with any degree of consistency in the case of the schizophrenic subject, and is more variable in the normal subject where there would appear to be great dependence on the conditions under which the experiment is carried out.

Jasper [16] has suggested 'that the function of the reticular system in normal adaptive or integrative behaviour may be more in the nature of the prevention of a general arousal action to all stimuli with a control of the selective responsiveness to significant stimuli. Indiscriminate arousal reactions to all stimuli could only result in chaotic behaviour, as may be the case in certain mental disorders. This implies that inhibitory rather than excitatory functions may be most important, either during sleep or wakefulness.'

Demetrescu and Demetrescu [4] have provided evidence for the existence of an ascending inhibitory system in the caudal part of the ventral region of the pontine reticular formation. They present data which suggest that the dorsal region of the reticular formation 'represents only a servo-mechanism of ascending activation which receives its driving input from the posterior hypothalamus—central gray complex'. These workers state 'the ascending inhibitory system including an area of the pontine R.F. and the caudate nucleus balances the ascending activating system, including the activating R.F., its hypothetical driving structures (posterior hypothalamus and central gray) and the thalamic unspecific system'.

An explanation for the results reported may be sought in terms of the regulatory system which has been described. If, as suggested by Jasper [16], it is the inhibitory function of a total regulatory system which is malfunctioning in the case of 'certain mental disorders', of which schizophrenia may be one, the observed correlations between cortical and autonomic indices may be expected. The state of the cortex is at the mercy of the amount of stimulation in the environment and the level of cortical activity may change due to noise input due to lack of adequate regulation. In the case of the normal, however, it may be hypothesized that there is clear signalling of overaction of the cortex by cortical-reticular fibres and the full retroaction of the inhibitory function of the reticular system upon the cortex may keep the latter at an optimal level.

It could further be speculated that the reason for the significance of the direction of the immediate change in skin potential level on the onset of noise in the final experiment described, is that here we have something akin to an orienting response. The function of this response is to alert the regulatory system to the existence of otherwise disturbing stimulation and to act as the first link in a chain of events which maintain optimal functioning of the cortex. An additional suggestion which can be made is that the significance of the relation of the number of spontaneous fluctuations of skin potential to the stability of the two-flash threshold measure in normal subjects is that this measure reflects the activity of the reticular system as part of a regulatory process. If we take the analogy of the simplest form of servo-mechanism, the thermostat, the greatest number of cycles of operation is likely to take place when the thermostat is efficiently controlling the temperature of a body whose environment is being subject to change. When the body is either too hot or too cold the thermostat will remain either in the 'on' or the 'off' position. In an analogous way it may be that if we view the spontaneous fluctuations of skin potential as evidence of the switching cycles of a cortico-reticular regulatory system we should expect that the greatest number of fluctuations would be made in the presence of noise by those subjects whose cortical level is most closely controlled. This is so in the case of normal subjects. In the case of schizophrenics, however, there is no relation between the number of fluctuations of skin potential and stability of the two-flash threshold. What would appear to be lacking is an adequate process signalling the state of overactivation of the cortex. It may be that it is the purpose of the mechanism whose outward manifestation of function is the 'orienting response' to bring into action the regulatory mechanism which has been suggested.

So far the experiments which have been described whose purpose was to test the model described on page 89 have shown this model either to be too simple or erroneous. A further aspect of the model which was tested at the same time as the experiments which have just been described was that of the relation between activation and withdrawal. It has already been shown that the unitary conception of activation must be modified to encompass a more complicated notion, and it should be borne in mind that the measures of skin potential and the threshold of paired stimuli which are used as experimental tools cannot be viewed as reflections of identical processes.

In the course of studies carried out on non-paranoid schizophrenics, primarily with the aim of accustoming the patients to the experimental situation and of perfecting the technique of skin potential measurement, withdrawal ratings were available for the patients which were used. In three separate studies the correlations between skin potential and withdrawal were +0·85, +0·67, and +0·75, that is the greater the degree of withdrawal shown by the patient the higher was his skin potential. When similar relations were examined for data which had been gathered using paranoid patients, mainly negative and insignificant results were obtained. Plotting the data from the paranoid patients showed that some of the patients showed the same direction of relations between withdrawal and skin potential as that for the non-paranoid patients, while in the case of others the reverse was true. To clarify the position a study was carried out [54] in which each patient was rated on the basis of a standardized clinical interview, on the symptoms of flatness of affect, poverty of speech, incoherence of speech and the presence of coherent delusions as described by Wing [57]. Nurses' ratings of withdrawal using the scales which were mentioned earlier were also used. In this study the previous correlations between skin potential and withdrawal for the non-paranoid patients were confirmed by a correlation of +0·70 ($p < 0{\cdot}001$, $N = 31$). The correlation between two-flash threshold and withdrawal in this group was −0·69 ($p < 0{\cdot}001$). The direction of this relation was to be expected from the negative relation between skin potential and two-flash threshold which had previously been found. The data for the patients with coherent delusions were then examined. The correlation between two-flash threshold and withdrawal was found to be +0·22 (NS), and that between skin potential and withdrawal −0·52 ($p < 0.05$, $N = 15$). This small group was further subdivided on the basis of the patients' ratings of incoherence of speech. It was found that those patients who had marked incoherence of speech showed a similar pattern of relation between two-flash threshold and skin potential as the non-paranoid subjects, whereas those patients without incoherence of speech did not. When the data from the deluded but incoherent patients were included with those of the non-paranoid patients, the correlations between withdrawal and two-flash threshold of skin potential did not change. In the case of the deluded patients who expressed themselves coherently, however, the correlation between skin potential and withdrawal was increased to −0·78 ($p < 0.1$, $N = 10$), while that between withdrawal and two-flash threshold remained insignificant.

These results were extended in a further study which differed from that just described in two ways. First, division of the patients into sub-groups was carried out entirely by the use of rating scales which were completed by nurses. Secondly, two-click as well as two-flash threshold was measured in order to extend the generality of the previous findings. In addition to the use of scales for rating withdrawal and paranoid tendency, a single item was used for rating incoherence of speech whose inter-rater reliability proved to be 0·83. The results of this study [46] essentially confirmed those of the earlier one. The correlation between withdrawal and two-flash threshold was −0·64, and between withdrawal and two-click threshold was −0·68 for the non-paranoid and the incoherent paranoid patients. Both these figures are significant at the 1 per cent. level. In the case of the coherent paranoid patients the correlation between two-flash threshold and withdrawal was +0·67, and between withdrawal and two-click threshold it was +0·68. While these results are very similar to those of the previous experiment for the non-paranoid and incoherent patients, in this instance there is a significant relation ($p < 0.01$) between two-flash and two-click threshold and withdrawal in the coherent paranoid patients in the opposite direction to that in the non-paranoid patients. The results of these two studies and that described earlier on the relation between two-flash threshold and skin potential support a general notion of the essential difference between the disorganized 'true' schizophrenic patient, and the intact paranoid patient whose inclusion within the schizophrenic ambit is debatable [6].

There is some evidence which can be provided to back the finding of these studies as far as non-paranoid schizophrenics are concerned: namely, that the more withdrawn the patient is the more he appears to be both cortically and subcortically overaroused. Perhaps the most direct piece of confirmatory evidence is that of Jasper, Fitzpatrick and Solomon [17]; these workers showed that patients who were rated as being in good contact with their environment had EEG measures which gave evidence of lower arousal than those patients whose ratings showed them to be in poor contact. More recently there have been a number of studies [10, 20], which suggest that the chronic schizophrenic population as a whole tend to be more 'aroused' than normal. Bearing in mind what has already been said in this chapter, some reservations must be felt about a global statement which uses the concept of arousal as unitary and which groups all schizophrenics together. Nevertheless, in so far as the majority of chronic schizophrenic patients would tend to be withdrawn, we may take it that most schizophrenic patients would give results indicating cortical overarousal. The reason for the inverse relation between cortical activation measures and withdrawal in the coherent paranoid group of patients is obscure. Probably the most likely reason for the disparity must be sought in the measure of withdrawal which, although giving an appearance of factorial purity, undoubtedly contains sub-elements such as deterioration, and lack of interests on the one hand, and active avoidance on the other. It is possible that the former attributes may be more characteristic of the non-paranoid patient, while the latter may more readily typify the paranoid.

The final aspect of experimental work which led from the model which was outlined on page 89 was the attempt to examine how far an inverted U-shaped relation existed between performance and activation. Experiments were carried out in which an attempt was made to relate the patients' level of cortical activation as measured by his threshold of fusion for paired flashes with his visual reaction time [44]. In an initial study the results showed that no simple relation of any kind existed between the two measures. However, purely *ad hoc* manipulation of the data showed that it was possible to encompass 86 per cent. of it with a series of equally spaced inverted Vs. As this procedure involved the arbitrary construction of a pattern imposed on the existing data, a second experiment was carried out to see how far a completely independent set of new data would fit the pattern of multiple Vs which had been imposed on the data from the first experiment. The fresh set of results from schizophrenic patients did in fact fit the pattern from the earlier experiment at an acceptable level of significance. Data from a group of normal subjects did not fit the pattern. These results, which receive some support from other experiments, are surprising, and need work from other investigators before they can be considered to be established. If a multiple V- or U-shaped relationship found between activation and performance can be found, it will at least explain why, in spite of the general acceptance of the notion of the inverted U relation in theory [11, 27], there is very little solid experimental evidence to support it. Some support for a multiple relationship comes from earlier work on simple reaction time in schizophrenia [41] where it was shown that there appeared a sense in which the gross slowness of many severely ill schizophrenics could be made up of quantal elements of delay in responding so that even reaction times as slow as 1 second could be thought of as explicable in terms of a lawful mechanism rather than as a result of the unwillingness and lack of co-operation of a sick patient. The relationship between this finding of periodicity in reaction time and the multiple V formation is extremely speculative and will not be outlined at this point. The rather simple model which prompted the bulk of the experiments described in this chapter has been shown to be altogether unable to cope with the complications of the mechanisms which have been exposed. The next step in this line of investigation necessarily involves a closer look at the measures which have been used rather loosely and speculatively. Work has already been undertaken [47] to examine in greater detail the peripheral mechanism determining the level of skin potential. More recently, work has suggested that differences in two-flash threshold result from differences in the control of the signal/noise ratio of the cortex. Further work is planned to follow up the suggestion of a faulty mechanism in the schizophrenic for regulating the level of cortical activity. This can probably be done most productively by the use of a continuous measure of cortical activity such as quantified index of the EEG, rather than by temporally discrete measurements using fusion thresholds. As a first step the relation between fusion thresholds and the EEG is being investigated. In these ways the programme of research continues to be very active.

REFERENCES

1. Bloch, V., and Bonvallet, M. (1960) Le déclenchement des réponses électrodermales à partir du système réticulaire facilitateur, *J. Physiol. (Paris)*, **52**, 25–26.
2. Darrow, C. W., Jost, H., Solomon, A. P., and Mergener, J. C. (1942) Autonomic indications of excitatory and homeostatic effects on the electroencephalogram, *J. Psychol.*, **14**, 115–30.

3. Darrow, C. W., Pathman, J., and Kronenberg, G. (1946) Level of autonomic activity and the EEG, *J. exp. Psychol.*, **36**, 355–65.
4. Demetrescu, M., and Demetrescu, M. (1962) Ascending inhibition and activation from the lower brain stem: the influence of pontine reticular stimulation on thalamo-cortical evoked potentials in cat, *Electroenceph. clin. Neurophysiol.*, **14**, 602–20.
5. Duffy, E. (1932) The relationship between muscular tension and quality of performance, *Amer. J Psychol.*, **44**, 535–46.
6. Foulds, G. A., and Owen, A. (1963) Are paranoids schizophrenic?, *Brit. J. Psychiat.*, **109**, 674–9.
7. Fraser, R. (1947) The incidence of neurosis among factory workers, *Rep. industr. Hlth Res. Bd, London, Report No. 90* London, H.M.S.O.
8. Freeman, G. L. (1948) *The Energetics of Human Behavior*, Ithaca, N.Y.
9. Goldstein, L., Murphree, H. B., Sugerman, A. A., Pfeiffer, C. C., and Jenney, E. H. (1963) Quantitative electroencephalographic analysis of naturally occurring (schizophrenic) and drug-induced psychotic states in human males, *Clin. Pharmacol. Ther.*, **4**, 10–21.
10. Goldstein, L., Sugerman, A. A., Stolberg, H., Murphree, H. B., and Pfeiffer, C. C. (1965) Electro-cerebral activity in schizophrenics and non-psychotic subjects: quantitative EEG amplitude analysis, *Electroenceph. clin. Neurophysiol.*, **19**, 350–61.
11. Hebb, D. O. (1955) Drives and the C.N.S. (Conceptual Nervous System), *Psychol. Rev.*, **62**, 243–54.
12. Heron, A. (1955) Four studies of the relation between psychological and occupational handicap among industrial workers, *Brit. J. industr. Med.*, **12**, 322–5.
13. Hull, C. L. (1943) *Principles of Behavior*, New York.
14. Hume, W. I., and Claridge, G. S. (1965) A comparison of two measures of arousal in normal subjects, *Life Science*, **4**, 545–53.
15. Hunt, J. McV., and Cofer, C. N. (1944) Psychological deficit, in *Personality and the Behavior Disorders*, ed. Hunt, J. McV., New York.
16. Jasper, H. H., Fitzpatrick, C. P., and Solomon, P. (1958) Recent advances in our understanding of ascending activities of the reticular system, in *Reticular Formation of the Brain*, ed., Jasper, H. H., *et al.*, London.
17. Jasper, H. H., Fitzpatrick, C. P., and Solomon, P. (1959) Analogies and opposites in schizophrenia and epilepsy. Electroencephalographic and clinical studies, *Amer. J. Psychiat.*, **95**, 835–51.
18. Knehr, C. A. (1954) Schizophrenic reaction time responses to variable preparatory intervals, *Amer. J. Psychiat.*, **110**, 585–8.
19. Kopell, B. S., Noble, E. P., and Silverman, J. (1965) The effect of triamylal and methamphetamine on the two-flash thresholds, *Life Science*, **4**, 2211–14.
20. Kornetsky, C., and Mursky, A. F. (1966) On certain psychopharmacological and physiological differences between schizophrenic and normal persons, *Psychopharmacologia* (*Berl.*), **8**, 309–18.

21. KRAEPELIN, E. (1913) *Psychiatrie*, Leipzig.
22. LEIDERMAN, P. H., and SHAPIRO, D. (1964) Studies on the galvanic skin potential level: some behavioural correlates, *J. psychosom. Res.*, **7**, 277–81.
23. LINDSLEY, D. B. (1951) Emotion, in *Handbook of Experimental Psychology*, ed. Stevens, S. S., New York.
24. LINDSLEY, D. B. (1958) The reticular formation and perceptual discrimination, in *Reticular Formation of the Brain*, ed. Jasper, H. H., *et al.*, London.
25. LINDSLEY, D. B. (1961) Chapter in *Brain and Behavior*, Vol. 1, ed. Brazier, M. A. B., American Institute of Biological Science, Washington.
26. LORR, M., SINGER, M., and ZOBEL, H. (1951) Development of a record for the description of psychiatric patients, *Psychol. Serv. Cent. J.*, **3**, No. 3.
27. MALMO, R. B. (1959) Activation: a neuropsychological dimension, *Psychol. Rev.*, **66**, 367–86.
28. MARKOWE, M. (1953) Occupatonal psychiatry: an historical survey and some recent researches, *J. ment. Sci.*, **99**, 92–102.
29. MARTIN, I., and VENABLES, P. H. (1966) Mechanisms of palmar skin resistance and skin potential, *Psychol. Bull.*, **65**, 347–57.
30. O'CONNOR, N., and TIZARD, J. (1956) *The Social Problem of Mental Deficiency*, London.
31. PAVLOV, I. P. (1941) *Conditioned Reflexes and Psychiatry*, trans. Gantt, W. H., London.
32. RODNICK, E. H., and SHAKOW, D. (1940) Set in the schizophrenic as measured by a composite reaction time index, *Amer. J. Psychol.*, **97**, 214–25.
33. SCHWARTZ, M., and SHAGASS, C. (1963) Reticular modification of somatosensory cortical recovery function, *Electroenceph. clin. Neurophysiol.*, **15**, 265–71.
34. STERIADE, M., and DEMETRESCU, M. (1962) Reticular facilitation of responses to acoustic stimuli, *Electroenceph. clin. Neurophysiol.*, **14**, 21–36.
35. TIZARD, J., and VENABLES, P. H. (1956) Reaction time response by schizophrenics, mental defectives and normal adults, *Amer. J. Psychiat.*, **112**, 803–7.
36. TIZARD, J., and VENABLES, P. H. (1957) The influence of extraneous stimulation on the reaction time of schizophrenics, *Brit. J. Psychol.*, **48**, 299–305.
37. VENABLES, P. H. (1955) Changes in motor response with increase and decrease in task difficulty in normal industrial and psychiatric patient subjects, *Brit. J. Psychol.*, **44**, 101–10.
38. VENABLES, P. H. (1957) A short scale for 'activity-withdrawal' in schizophrenics, *J. ment. Sci.*, **103**, 197–9.
39. VENABLES, P. H. (1959) Factors in the motor behaviour of functional psychotics, *J. abnorm. soc. Psychol.*, **58**, 153–6.

40. VENABLES, P. H. (1960) The effect of auditory and visual stimulation on the skin potential response of schizophrenics, *Brain*, **83**, 77–92.
41. VENABLES, P. H. (1960) Periodicity in reaction time, *Brit. J. Psychol.*, **51**, 37–43.
42. VENABLES, P. H. (1963) The relationship between level of skin potential and fusion of paired light flashes in schizophrenic and normal subjects, *J. psychiat. Res.*, **1**, 279–87.
43. VENABLES, P. H. (1963) Changes due to noise in the threshold of fusion of paired light flashes in the schizophrenics and normals, *Brit. J. soc. clin. Psychol.*, **2**, 94–99.
44. VENABLES, P. H. (1964) Performance and level of activation in schizophrenics and normals, *Brit. J. Psychol.*, **55**, 207–18.
45. VENABLES, P. H. (1966) A comparison of two-flash and two-click thresholds in schizophrenic and normal subjects, *Quart. J. exp. Psychol.*, **18**, 371–3.
46. VENABLES, P. H. (1967) The relation of two-flash and two-click thresholds to withdrawal in paranoid and non-paranoid schizophrenics, *Brit. J. soc. clin. Psychol.*, **4**, 60–62.
47. VENABLES, P. H., and MARTIN, I. (1967) The relation of palmar sweat gland activity to level of skin conductance and potential, *Psychophysiology*, **3**, 302–11.
48. VENABLES, P. H., and O'CONNOR, N. (1959) Reaction times to auditory and visual stimulation in schizophrenic and normal subjects, *Quart. J. exp. Psychol.*, **11**, 175–9.
49. VENABLES, P. H., and O'CONNOR, N. (1959) A short scale of rating paranoid schizophrenia, *J. ment. Sci.*, **105**, 815–18.
50. VENABLES, P. H., and SAYER, E. (1963) On the measurement of the level of skin potential, *Brit. J. Psychol.*, **54**, 251–60.
51. VENABLES, P. H., and TIZARD, J. (1956) Paradoxical effects in the reaction time of schizophrenics, *J. abnorm. soc. Psychol.*, **53**, 220–4.
52. VENABLES, P. H., and TIZARD, J. (1956) Performance and functional psychotics on a repetitive task, *J. abnorm. soc. Psychol.*, **53**, 23–26.
53. VENABLES, P. H., and TIZARD, J. (1958) The effect of auditory stimulus intensity on the reaction time of schizophrenics, *J. ment. Sci.*, **104**, 1160–4.
54. VENABLES, P. H., and WING, J. K. (1962) Level of arousal and the sub-classification of schizophrenia, *Arch. gen. Psychiat.*, **7**, 114–19.
55. WANG, G. H. (1957) The galvanic skin reflex. A review of old and recent works from a physiologic point of view, *Amer. J. phys. Med.*, **36**, 295–320.
56. WANG, G. H. (1958) The galvanic skin reflex. A review of old and recent works from a physiologic point of view, *Amer. J. phys. Med.*, **37**, 35–57.
57. WING, J. K. (1961) A simple and reliable sub-classification of schizophrenia, *J. ment. Sci.*, **107**, 862–75.

6

Psychological Treatments

MICHAEL G. GELDER

PSYCHIATRIC treatment now ranges so widely that it is impossible to consider every aspect in one short article. Of the three main divisions of treatment—physical, psychological and social—two are considered in other parts of this book. This chapter, therefore, will concentrate on psychological treatment, with a short digression into the use of psychological measurements in the investigation of physical treatment.

Investigations of psychological treatment fall into two groups: (1) those concerned with the process of treatment, that is the changes which take place during the treatment sessions and their relation to the techniques employed; and (2) investigations of the outcome of treatment and the selection of suitable patients. Each can be carried out in two ways, by traditional methods of clinical observation, or by the use of quantitative methods based on experimental psychology and statistics. Each field of investigation and each method of inquiry has its own value. Quantitative methods are only of value when preliminary descriptive studies have shown which variables are important and have led to the formulation of hypotheses which can be put to the test. Studies of process and outcome also complement each other. On the one hand it is valueless to investigate the process of a treatment in detail until outcome studies have given some reason for thinking it effective; on the other hand, it cannot necessarily be assumed that the results of a treatment arise directly from the specific techniques employed unless this has been shown by careful process studies.

Progress in psychotherapy research has been slow and quantitative studies have only become possible recently. When a subject is so vast and so complex, and when available techniques of investigation are so few and so inadequate, great skill and foresight are needed in selecting topics which are ripe for investigation. Even a cursory survey of the many investigations of psychotherapy which have been attempted in the last 15 years shows how many have proved fruitless because they were too ambitious in their aims and insufficiently rigorous in their design. Most progress has been made when discrete problems have been chosen, as Frank's [15] series of investigations of psychotherapy shows so well.

Sir Aubrey Lewis' particular contribution to research in this field has been his skill in selecting topics for research which, in the state of development of the subject at the time, were likely to succeed. The topics were deliberately limited in scope but they were capable of being brought to completion. Taken together, they begin to form a pattern into which more and more pieces of evidence can be fitted as better methods of investigation are developed.

These investigations have ranged widely. Some concerned the interview, the basis of all psychological treatment, exploring basic aspects of the interaction between patient and therapist. Others dealt with the outcome of certain forms of brief psychological treatment, chosen partly because they lent themselves most readily to investigation. We shall start with studies concerned with interviewing.

INVESTIGATIONS OF THE INTERVIEW

Goldman-Eisler's work on speech patterns in interviews is now well known. The early stages of this work were carried out when she was working in the Medical Research Council Unit for Occupational Adaptation [p. 12]. She investigated one of the simplest aspects of the interview: the pattern of the patient's speech and silences and the ways in which these change in response to the therapist. The interaction chronograph technique, originated by Chapple [4], was used and it was found that the pattern of conversational pauses of any one individual tends to be constant and independent both of the interviewer and the topic [20]. Psychiatrists also had rather constant speech patterns when interviewing but they were able to adjust their activity to some extent according to the speech patterns of the patient interviewed. This led to corresponding changes in the amount of the patient's conversational activity even though his basic patterns persisted. Experienced interviewers were more flexible than novices. These investigations were extended and elaborated by Goldman-Eisler after leaving the Occupational Adaptation Unit. They have formed the basis of a continuing programme of research which has contributed much to our understanding of this aspect of the interview.

Other measurable elements of patients' behaviour in interviews are the gestural movements made, which were investigated by Sainsbury [33, 34, 35] [p. 209], using electromyography.

The work of Goldman-Eisler and Sainsbury showed how patients' emotional responses are accompanied by changes in behaviour which can be measured precisely and reliably. The findings are of particular interest because they concern aspects of patients' behaviour of which they are themselves largely unaware. Goldman-Eisler's work also indicates something of the interplay of emotional changes between patient and therapist. This complicated interplay is one of many factors which make research in this field so difficult; not only do therapists differ in the way they conduct interviews but each therapist himself responds to the patient he interviews and thereby changes. Interviewers are unaware of these changes at first, but with training they come to recognize and control them to some extent. We shall consider next an investigation which further underlines this interplay between interviewer and patient.

A more complicated aspect of patients' response in interviews was chosen by Sakinofsky [36]. He studied emotional changes during structured interviews, measuring these both by clinical ratings and by galvanic skin responses (GSRs). Sakinofsky's experimental interviews included three degrees of 'discordant feedback' of communication. Neurotic and depressed patients took part. The interviewer induced 'discordant feedback' by failing to reply, or by replying in a way that was either at variance with the patients' statement or totally irrelevant to it. Discordant feedback led to emotional arousal as judged both clinically, by an independent rater, and by GSR changes. The interviewer himself was also found to show evidence of emotional arousal when conducting those interviews in which communication feedback was discordant. Emotional responses in both patient and interviewer subsided quickly when communication became concordant again. These experiments lend support to the clinical observation that inappropriate interpretations can lead to excessive emotional responses.

Another experimental study of the interview concerned simpler forms of communication between interviewer and patient [17]. This investigation followed the extensive experimental work on verbal conditioning carried out by experimental psychologists [22], who have shown that minimal verbal and gestural cues on the part of an interviewer can influence the content of conversation in an interview. These cues have been shown to behave as agents of reinforcement in precisely the same way that concrete rewards reinforce the behaviour of laboratory animals. They also follow the same rules of operant conditioning [22]. This experimental work helps to show why psychotherapists must control their own behaviour so carefully if they are to avoid influencing their patients. As Sakinofsky's investigation illustrated how the therapist must control *what* he says, so experiments on verbal conditioning indicate why the therapist must regulate *how* and *when* he says it.

Despite the obvious relevance of verbal conditioning to psychotherapy interviews, surprisingly little work has been carried out with patients interviewed in a clinical setting. Yet verbal conditioning is known to be highly sensitive to minor changes in the experimental situation so that it cannot be assumed that the experimental findings apply to clinical interviews. Gelder [17] therefore investigated verbal conditioning in clinical interviews and confirmed that neurotic patients can be conditioned. They are more susceptible than normal subjects who in turn respond more than schizophrenic patients.

It was also shown that when the content of a neurotic patient's conversation changed as a result of conditioning it did so without his awareness. The effect was enhanced when the interviewer first established a positive relationship with the patient by conducting a preliminary interview in which he expressed sympathy with the patient and interest in his problem. However, the clinical importance of verbal conditioning remained in some doubt because effects did not accumulate from interview to interview, nor did they occur equally with every kind of conversational content; for example it was easier to condition the patient to talk about himself favourably than it was to condition him to talk about himself unfavourably.

It is clear that verbal conditioning is only one of a number of influences which are at work in the interview and at present it is impossible to predict their combined outcome. It is, however, especially interesting that quite a small intensification of the patients' feelings about the interviewer increased their response to conditioning; the response of patients who have a strong positive transference to the interviewer may be very much greater than that found in these experiments, and correspondingly verbal conditioning may be more important in psychotherapy than the results suggest.

These experiments on the interview exemplify both the strength and the weakness of this kind of investigation. Their strength is to allow quantitative investigation of clinical observations culled from practical experience of psychotherapy. Their present weakness is that psychological methods are not yet far enough advanced to allow more than mere confirmation of these clinical insights: they have not been extended or improved upon, and an investigator must be prepared to be told that he is demonstrating the obvious. And so he is at present; but eventually this kind of inquiry will surely help us to understand and refine the procedures of psychotherapy and to lay a rational basis for the points of technique which have emerged from clinical observation and experience.

INVESTIGATIONS OF HYPNOSIS

Psychotherapeutic methods are so diverse and each is so complex that they can only be studied one part at a time. This piecemeal procedure is necessarily laborious, and psychotherapists are often impatient of the slow progress. Certain forms of psychotherapy lend themselves more readily than others to investigation because their procedures can be more clearly defined, and their aims can be specified with greater precision. One of these is hypnosis, especially when used as a suggestive therapy rather than hypnoanalysis. Though the method has throughout its history been dogged by the accusation that it is unscientific and imprecise, perhaps no other work carried out in the department of psychiatry in the field of psychological treatment better illustrates the value of careful planning and precise measurement than Edwards' work on hypnosis. It also shows clearly how clinical research and experimental investigation can reinforce one another, the results of each throwing further light on the other.

Edwards carried out a series of ingenious experiments on the process of hypnosis, using reaction time as the dependent variable and thus avoiding the pitfall of so many experiments on hypnosis—the lack of any precise measure of response. This simplified situation was used to study four problems concerned with the post-hypnotic effect: its duration, the effect upon it of contrary motivation, the importance of post-hypnotic amnesia and the degree to which it is specific. Deep trance subjects were studied and also controls who were not hypnotized, but were asked to play the role of deeply hypnotized subjects responding to the instructions received by the hypnotic group. In each experiment the results of this control group showed that the effects of hypnosis could not be attributed solely to role-playing. In the first experiment [7] the post-hypnotic suggestion was that reaction time would increase when the subject awoke. This took place and, by repeatedly retesting reaction times, the duration of the post-hypnotic effect could be measured. It was found to vary considerably—from 2 to 405 days—between subjects, even when the depth of hypnosis and the precise form of the original suggestion were carefully standardized. Edwards pointed out the clinical implications of this finding: hypnosis could be of little benefit to patients in whom its effects last only a day or two, but would be immensely valuable in others where it lasts more than a year. He then set out to determine some of the reasons for the variability, other than possible differences in personality.

He first studied the effect of contrary motivation [10]. Most experiments on the post-hypnotic effect have been carried out in situations in which the subject was highly motivated to please the hypnotist. In clinical practice motivation will nearly always be two sided and however strong the original desire to obey the therapist there will be many times when events in the patient's life induce contrary motivation. An accumulation of such factors might explain why the post-hypnotic effect is sometimes so very short. Deep trance subjects were hypnotized and given the suggestion that their reaction times would lengthen on waking. Subjects were then given faradic shocks whenever their reaction times were prolonged. In the final part of the experiment shocks were withdrawn, and reaction time again measured. Shocks did produce a little shortening of reaction time and this outlasted the shocks, but the post-hypnotic effect was by no means abolished even by quite strong shocks. Edwards suggested that these findings could be applied also to clinical practice where adverse social factors, rather than electric shocks, induce contrary motivation. He was careful to point out that the experiment examined only short-term effects and suggested the possibility that repeated contrary motivation over a longer period might have a greater adverse effect.

Further experiments [11, 12] examined the specificity of the response to a suggestion and the effect of breaching the post-hypnotic amnesia.

These experiments were complemented by two clinical trials of hypnotic treatment. The first concerned the treatment of alcoholism, the second the use of hypnosis in an anti-smoking clinic. Hypnosis was found to be of limited value in each [8, 9, 13], and Edwards has emphasized the gap which still separates experimental studies of the process of hypnosis and clinical studies of outcome. There is much to do before the two can be linked, but there is no doubt that a most fruitful way of achieving this is the kind of combined research which his own work exemplifies.

DECONDITIONING THERAPIES AND PSYCHOTHERAPY

Another form of psychological treatment which has both a clearly defined procedure and limited and specific aims is deconditioning therapy, or behaviour therapy. Work on deconditioning therapies began in the Institute's department of psychology: new methods of treatment were developed which were based on learning principles, and these were tested on an increasing number of patients under the general supervision of consultant psychiatrists.

Psychologists have made invaluable contributions in this field both by suggesting ways in which learning principles can help the understanding of certain psychiatric problems, and also by developing new treatments based upon these principles. However, all but a few psychologists lack the breadth of knowledge of clinical psychiatry and the experience of a wide range of psychiatric treatments, both of which are necessary for a balanced appraisal of these new techniques.

Lewis therefore encouraged the evaluation of these conditioning techniques in his own department at the same time as psychologists in the Institute of Psychiatry were making their contributions to the subject. Work in the department of psychiatry began with Cooper's

[5] important investigation in which he followed for a year the course of patients treated with behaviour therapy by members of the psychology department, comparing them by a method of 'blind' assessment with carefully matched patients who had received conventional treatments, usually a combination of brief psychotherapy and anxiety-reducing drugs. He found little to support the more extravagant claims which had been made for the new methods. Two-thirds of the behaviour therapy patients improved, a proportion that might at first appear highly satisfactory. However, Cooper's work showed clearly how essential it is to have control groups when studying neurotic patients. Control patients improved to almost exactly the same extent as those treated by deconditioning. Only in phobic disorders did deconditioning appear to achieve better results but even here the trend was not significant. However, the numbers were small and further work was clearly required.

Cooper's study was extended by Cooper, Gelder and Marks [6] who compared 77 patients who had received deconditioning treatment with matched controls. 'Blind' assessments of the outcome of treatment showed that desensitization had a clear advantage in only one group of patients, those with simple phobias. It tended to be somewhat, but not significantly, better for the patients with agoraphobia, and it had no advantage for patients with obsessional rituals. Avoidance conditioning for writer's cramp also had no clear advantage over conventional methods. Marks and Gelder [27] further examined the results with the phobic patients. They found no evidence that desensitization and psychotherapy helped different types of patient. Contrary to expectation, the severity of phobias and the length of the patient's history were unrelated to outcome. New symptoms and social difficulties did appear occasionally in patients whose phobias improved with direct symptomatic treatment, but appeared just as often in the controls who received psychotherapy.

The next inquiry [18] concerned patients with severe agoraphobia, a common clinical problem and one which is difficult to treat by other means. The results of desensitization in these patients was quite limited, although, of course, even a limited symptomatic improvement can contribute usefully to the rehabilitation of these patients. The previous findings were taken further in a prospective inquiry with phobic outpatients [19]. This is important because it was a *collaborative* study in which specialist psychotherapists took part, and allowed the results of psychotherapy carried out either by themselves or under their close supervision to be compared with the results of deconditioning therapy. Fears are often expressed that psychotherapy will be disturbed, and patients will suffer, if ratings are made of their progress. This did not happen; indeed, any doubts or anxieties which arose could always be analysed in the same way as other events in their lives. When this was done, ratings were never found to impede the patients' treatment; on the contrary, analysis of anxieties about them sometimes helped the understanding of other emotional problems.

The scheme of ratings was the same as that used in the previous investigation and patients were again allocated randomly, this time to three treatments: desensitization therapy, group psychotherapy carried out on analytic lines following the method developed by Foulkes [14], and brief analytically orientated individual psychotherapy. All were rated six weekly for 18 months whether treatment had been completed or not. The findings, in brief, were that phobic symptoms responded significantly faster to desensitization and that treated phobias changed faster than the others. Other symptoms of general anxiety, depression, obsessions and depersonalization did not change more quickly with one treatment than with the others. As before, social adjustment was rated. Only work and leisure adjustment changed faster with desensitization, and this was a direct consequence of the improvement in the patients' phobias, e.g. when a travel phobia improved the patient might be able to return to work. Sexual adjustment ratings changed little in any group. Ratings of interpersonal relations changed by the same amount with all three treatments, but detailed examination of the case records and ratings showed that with desensitization they changed only when phobias improved; with psychotherapy they improved in patients whose phobias were unchanged. Thus it seemed that, with desensitization, patients' interpersonal relationships improved only when their phobias abated, presumably because when this happened they gained self confidence. In psychotherapy, changes in this sphere were related to events in treatment and independent of changes in phobias which improved only slowly.

Did the same kind of patients respond to each treatment? On the whole they did, but a few important differences were found. Response to desensitization was particularly impaired if patients had many symptoms, and especially if they had intense obsessional symptoms, severe general anxiety or unexplained panic attacks. Rather surprisingly, there was no indication that older patients, or those who had their symptoms longer, did less well with desensitization—although such patients did far less well with psychotherapy. Patients who described certain anxious, depressive or hypochondriacal traits of personality also did less well with desensitization.

Will deconditioning relieve phobias of patients who receive psychotherapy without symptomatic improvement? Seven patients were studied who had taken part in group psychotherapy but failed to improve symptomatically 6 months after their treatment ended. They were then desensitized. Five of the seven improved, the mean rating of severity of their phobias of the group reaching a level of almost exactly that which had been reached by similar patients who had been desensitized from the start. The improvement was particularly striking because it took place in an average of 4 months among patients whose fears had hardly changed at all during the 2 years in which they had previously been under observation.

It was concluded that desensitization and pyschotherapy, far from being incompatible alternatives, each have a part in the treatment of phobic patients. When personality disorder is severe and symptoms widespread, psychotherapy is more likely to be helpful; if necessary it can be followed by desensitization should the phobias persist. When the personality is good and phobic symptoms are relatively isolated, patients can be treated quickly and effectively with desensitization. One result of this research was to draw attention to the many factors which behaviour therapy and psychotherapy have in common, and to the few essential points of difference [28]. Many different forms of treatment are needed for psychiatric patients, each one being capable of helping only a selected few. Similarly each theory of mental functioning can explain only a limited range of the problems met in psychiatric patients.

Generalized anxiety had been shown to impair the response to desensitization, presumably because this depends on the repetition of behaviour in the absence of anxiety and relaxation techniques can only neutralize a limited amount of anxiety. An obvious suggestion is that anxiety should be reduced with drugs, and these are effective when the anxiety is not too severe. But when it is severe, these drugs are of little help even when given in large doses, possibly because they themselves impair learning. The role of generalized anxiety in phobic patients was examined in two ways; first by investigating patients with severe phobias who underwent leucotomy, and secondly by the use of certain psychophysiological measures.

Patients with severe agoraphobia were studied who had been treated in earlier years with modified leucotomy.[1] A controlled comparative inquiry was carried out [30], the design of which resembled that of the retrospective investigation of desensitization already described. The immediate result of leucotomy was a sudden and marked reduction of generalized anxiety, but the immediate effect on phobias was much less. The patients were therefore left in a state in which severe phobias were still present but anxiety was very much reduced.

[1] Half had been treated at St. Thomas's Hospital and the investigation was only possible through the generous collaboration of Dr. William Sargant, Mr. Harvey Jackson and Mr. Wylie McKissock.

Would their phobias now subside with re-exposure to the feared situation? This did happen once patients started to practise going out, but it did not occur before this. Patients with sociable personalities improved faster than those with anxious depressive traits, and this appeared to be because they made more determined efforts to go out again. Formal desensitization treatment was not given to most, but one patient had desensitization both before and after modified leucotomy: before the operation it had no effect; afterwards, when there was very little anxiety, it was rapidly effective. The findings therefore supported the idea that patients with the most severe agoraphobia had failed to respond to desensitization because of the presence of severe generalized anxiety.

Another approach to the same problem was made by Lader [23], who studied the rate of habituation of the galvanic skin response (GSR) in phobic patients who subsequently received desensitization. Lader had already shown in a careful and systematic series of investigations that the galvanic skin response habituated less rapidly in anxious patients than in normal subjects [24]. There was a significant association between the rate of GSR habituation and outcome of desensitization. This confirmed the importance of anxiety and also suggested a possible mechanism whereby high anxiety may interfere with desensitization which may also be a habituation procedure.

A related study may be mentioned in this context. Sergeant [37] carried out a small series of interrelated single case studies which support the idea that the rate at which anxiety dies away is important in desensitization. He found that there is an optimal rate of presenting stimuli in desensitization therapy and that a fast rate can give rise to a smaller decrement of anxiety by the end of the session, even though each stimulus has been presented more often. There may well be an interaction between the rate of desensitization and the kind of individual differences of rate of habituation which Lader found.

Thus our understanding of the indications for desensitization treatment are increasing, our knowledge of the way in which anxiety is important is becoming clearer, and more is being discovered about the way in which desensitization and psychotherapy can be used together in clinical practice.

AVERSION THERAPY

A third and very different kind of brief psychological treatment is aversion therapy. Once again it is convenient to discuss research in terms both of the process of treatment and its outcome. In this case research has been particularly concerned with the process of treatment.

Pearce [32] has reported the results of treatment of transvestism. He used a modified form of apomorphine aversion therapy to treat thirteen transvestists and showed that treatment produced striking improvement. He identified important stages in the patient's psychological reaction to treatment which he showed were comparable to the stages which patients pass through in intensive psychotherapy.

Marks and Gelder [29] used a less drastic form of treatment in which mild electric shocks were substituted for apomorphine aversion. The method comprised a modification of techniques described by Blakemore [1] and by McGuire and Vallance [31] and consisted of giving the patients mild faradic stimuli usually to the forearm. This method is very much less unpleasant for the patient than apomorphine aversion, is not dangerous, and because it can be timed with precision, is a more potent way of producing conditioning. Photographs, coloured slides, and even moralizing talks on tape recordings have sometimes been used as part of a regime of aversion therapy. They were avoided in this research not only because they are often embarrassing for both patient and therapist, but also because they introduce elements other than simple aversive conditioning into the treatment. More than this, it was considered that these physical reminders of the patient's sexual deviation are less relevant than the fantasies which preoccupy him. These fantasies are the first link in the chain of behaviour which ends in the deviant sexual act and there is good reason for attemping to weaken this first link as well as later ones.

Several methods of assessment have been used in this research. One, which proved particularly valuable, was the semantic differential whose use in psychiatric patients had been studied extensively by Marks [25, 26]. It was used to study changes in patients attitudes to sexual and other concepts during the course of aversion therapy. Another measure was the time taken to imagine fantasies connected with the sexual deviation.

Two findings were of particular interest. Aversive conditioning often had a striking and specific effect on the patient's ability to imagine scenes connected with his deviation. When shocks were regularly associated with these imaginary scenes, patients found it increasingly hard to imagine them. In some patients this was accompanied by a progressive increase in the time taken to imagine the scenes (the latency) which rose more and more steeply in each new session until eventually they could not be imagined at all, however hard patients tried. The latency during the first trial of each session rose less than the latency of subsequent trials, suggesting a process of suppression rather than true extinction, an explanation which was supported by the finding that some patients continued to have vivid dreams about their sexual deviation at a time when they were quite unable to imagine the same scenes in their waking state. Other patients responded in a somewhat different way, showing no increase of latency but reporting a complete loss of the pleasure previously associated with the imaginary scenes. Again, however, the scenes might appear in dreams with full emotional force. It is tempting to draw an analogy between these changes and the defence mechanism of repression. However, these changes were observed when the mental content gradually disappeared from consciousness, while the clinical observations of repression describe the changes when a previously inaccessible mental content re-emerges into consciousness. It is therefore difficult to know how far the two can be equated.

The second important general finding was the very specific nature of the change in attitude which took place as aversion proceeded. Control periods were interpolated in which the treatment continued with the one exception that no shocks were given. In this way two kinds of specificity were shown. First, attitudes changed only slowly in the absence of shocks, much more quickly as soon as shocks were introduced. Secondly, only those attitudes changed which were connected with situations used in treatment: for example, if shocks were given to a transvestist when he was dressing in a single feminine garment, his attitude to this garment changed but attitudes to other female clothes were unaltered.

Changes in attitudes and fantasies were therefore quite specific. This has two consequences: first, treatment must be longer than many psychologists have predicted, for they anticipated a greater degree of generalization of learning; secondly there is little danger that the effects of this kind of aversion treatment will spread in unwanted ways. One is reminded of Edwards' demonstration of the specificity of the post-hypnotic effect which imposes similar limitations, but carries equivalent safeguards.

The long term results of this kind of treatment are still uncertain but further work is being undertaken both to this end and also to discover the indications for treatment. It is important to look for other methods which are equally effective but less unpleasant for patient and therapist. It is clear that aversion therapy will have definite indications and contra-indications, and that only a small proportion of patients with sexual deviations may be amenable. However, within this limited field it has great promise, not only as a method of treatment but also as a way of investigating the psychopathology not only of the sexual disorders but also of the patient's response to anxiety.

PSYCHOLOGICAL MEASUREMENTS DURING PHYSICAL TREATMENT

Psychological measurements can further our understanding of physical treatment as well as psychological treatments such as psychotherapy or aversion therapy, where we have seen the value of the semantic differential and studies of response latency. A single example must suffice: Brengelmann's work on the impairment of learning produced by electroconvulsive therapy (ECT) [2, 3]. Brengelmann [2] carried out a series of careful experiments in which depressed patients were tested on a simple non-verbal visual learning task which was given 30 minutes, 4 hours and 28 hours after repeated application of ECT. He showed that learning was severely impaired half an hour after each shock, but recovered partially after 4 hours and completely after 28 hours. He also tested a control group who received the entire ECT procedure, including thiopentone, a muscle relaxant and even the application of electrodes to the head, but with the one exception that no shock was given. These patients showed no impairment of learning, although when subsequently shocked they showed an impairment identical with that seen in the patients who were shocked from the start.

Progressive matrices I.Q. scores were impaired very much less than learning, so that the learning deficit could not be attributed to impairment 'intelligence' immediately after the shock. A further control group was given the learning materials but with new instructions which transformed the task into a test of perception with no component of memory. No perceptual impairment was found. Finally, because in animals the effects of electro-shock on learning have been shown to vary with the degree of difficulty of the task, a more difficult task was given. The same pattern of impairment was found with the harder task as had been found with the original easier one.

As shocks were repeated, learning capacity 48 hours after ECT improved after the first three treatments, then fell somewhat after the fifth, to improve again thereafter. To account for this, Brengelmann postulated three processes at work: the reversal of pathological depression which leads to better learning; a cumulative impairment due to the ECT itself which shows up after about five shocks; and an adaptation effect which accounts for the final improvement. Brengelmann's carefully controlled study provides an excellent example of the value of psychological method in quantifying and refining clinical observations, and relating these to particular aspects of the treatment process. And it shows how psychological tests and experimental designs can be applied as readily to the study of physical treatment as to psychotherapies.

FUTURE RESEARCH

Research into psychological treatment is one of the most difficult questions facing psychiatrists. Problems abound: treatment methods are hard to define and standardize; there are differences of opinion about the criteria which should be used for evaluation; there are very few simple and reliable methods of assessment; and patients who are treated do not fall readily in clearly defined groups whose natural history is known. Ambitious programmes of research into the outcome of psychotherapy have seldom produced results which justify the expenditure of time and money they entail. Until real advances have been made in developing methods of assessment, the most fruitful path for research will be to carry out limited inquiries dealing with specific aspects of treatment in limited and homogeneous groups of patients and, to restrict research at first to the simplest forms of treatment.

The work of Frank and his colleagues on placebo responses, on patients' expectations of treatment and on the effects of role induction interviews [16, 21] show how much can be achieved by concentrating attention on a small clearly defined part of psychotherapy. It can always be objected that research which has such limited objectives produces trivial results. But they are not trivial; they are the answers which must be obtained before more ambitious problems can be investigated. Research into psychotherapy has too often tried to move ahead too fast. It can only move slowly; there is no substitute for painstaking and systematic research which must go on for many years before it will be ready to tackle the larger problems.

REFERENCES

1. BLAKEMORE, C. D., THORPE, J. G., BARKER, J. C., CONWAY, C. G., and LAVIN, N. I. (1963) The application of faradic aversion conditioning in a case of transvestism, *Behav. Res. Ther.*, **1**, 29–35.
2. BRENGELMANN, J. C. (1959) The effect of repeated electroshock on learning in depressives, *Monograph aus dem gesamtgebiete der Neurologie und Psychiatrie*, Vol. 84, Berlin.
3. BRENGELMANN, J. C. (1960) Extreme response set, drive level, and abnormality in questionnaire rigidity, *J. ment. Sci.*, **106**, 171–86.
4. CHAPPLE, E. D. (1949) The interaction chronograph. Its evolution and present application, *J. Personality*, **25**, 295–307.
5. COOPER, J. E. (1963) A study of behaviour therapy in thirty psychiatric patients, *Lancet*, i, 411–15.
6. COOPER, J. E., GELDER, M. G., and MARKS, I. M. (1965) Results of behaviour therapy in 77 psychiatric patients, *Brit. med. J.*, i, 1222–5.
7. EDWARDS, G. (1963) Duration of the post-hypnotic effect, *Brit. J. Psychiat.*, **109**, 259–66.

8. Edwards, G. (1964) Hypnosis and lobeline in an anti-smoking clinic, *Med. Offr*, **111**, 239–43.
9. Edwards, G. (1964) Double blind trials of lobeline in an anti-smoking clinic, *Med. Offr*, **112**, 158–60.
10. Edwards, G. (1965) Motivation and post-hypnotic effect, *Brit. J. Psychiat.*, **111**, 983–92.
11. Edwards, G. (1965) Signal specificity and post-hypnotic effect, *Brit. J. Psychiat.*, **111**, 326–33.
12. Edwards, G. (1965) Post-hypnotic amnesia and post-hypnotic effect, *Brit. J. Psychiat.*, **111**, 316–25.
13. Edwards, G. (1966) Hypnosis in treatment of alcohol addiction, *Quart. J. Stud. Alcohol*, **27**, 221–41.
14. Foulkes, S. M. (1964) *Therapeutic Group Analysis*, London.
15. Frank, J. D. (1961) *Persuasion and Healing: A Comparative Study of Psychotherapy*, Baltimore.
16. Frank, J. D., Gliedman, L. H., Imber, S. D., Stone, A. R., and Mash, E. H. (1959) Patient's expectancies and relearning as factors determining improvement in psychotherapy, *Amer. J. Psychiat.*, **115**, 961–8.
17. Gelder, M. G. (1965) Verbal conditioning in psychiatric patients, Unpublished thesis for D.M., University of Oxford.
18. Gelder, M. G., and Marks, I. M. (1966) Severe agoraphobia: a controlled prospective therapeutic trial, *Brit. J. Psychiat.*, **112**, 309–19.
19. Gelder, M. G., Marks, I. M., and Wolff, H. H. (1967) Desensitization and psychotherapy in phobic states. A controlled inquiry, *Brit. J. Psychiat.*, **113**, 53–73.
20. Goldman-Eisler, F. (1951) The measurement of time sequence in conversational behaviour, *Brit. J. Psychol.*, **42**, 355–62.
21. Hoehn-Saric, R., Frank, J. D., Imber, S. E., Nash, E. H., Stone, A. R., and Battle, C. C. (1965) Systematic preparation of patients for psychotherapy. I. Effects on therapy behaviour and outcome, *J. psychiat. Res.*, **2**, 267–81.
22. Krasner, L. (1963) Reinforcement, verbal behavior and psychotherapy, *Amer. J. Orthopsychiat.*, **33**, 601–13.
23. Lader, M. H. (1968) Predictive value of autonomic measures in patients with phobic states, *J. Psychosom. Res.* [in press]
24. Lader, M. H., and Wing, L. (1966) *Physiological Measures, Sedative Drugs, and Morbid Anxiety*, Maudsley Monographs, No. 14, London.
25. Marks, I. M. (1965) *Patterns of Meaning in Psychiatric Patients*, Maudsley Monographs, No. 13, London.
26. Marks, I. M. (1966) Semantic differential uses in psychiatric patients, *Brit. J. Psychiat.*, **112**, 945–51.
27. Marks, I. M., and Gelder, M. G. (1965) A controlled retrospective trial of behaviour therapy in phobic patients, *Brit. J. Psychiat.*, **111**, 561–73.
28. Marks, I. M., and Gelder, M. G. (1966) Common ground between behaviour therapy and psychodynamic techniques, *Brit. J. med. Psychol.*, **39**, 11–23.

29. Marks, I. M., and Gelder, M. G. (1967) Transvestism and fetishism. Clinical and psychological changes during faradic aversion, *Brit. J. Psychiat.*, **113**, 711–29.
30. Marks, I. M., Birley, J. L. T., and Gelder, M. G. (1966) Modified leucotomy in severe agoraphobia: a controlled serial inquiry, *Bri. J. Psychiat.*, **112**, 757–69.
31. McGuire, R. H., and Vallance, M. (1964) Aversion therapy by electric shock: a simple technique, *Brit. med. J.*, i, 151–2.
32. Pearce, J. D. (1963) The application of behaviour therapy to transvestism. Dissertation for the Academic Diploma in Psychological Medicine, The University of London.
33. Sainsbury, P. (1954) A method of measuring spontaneous movements by time sampling motion pictures, *J. ment. Sci.*, **100**, 732–8.
34. Sainsbury, P. (1954) The measurement and description of spontaneous movements before and after leucotomy, *J. ment. Sci.*, **100**, 732–41.
35. Sainsbury, P. (1955) Gestural movement during psychiatric interviews, *Psychosom. Med.*, **17**, 458–69.
36. Sakinofsky, I. (1964) Effects 9f discordant feedback during experimental psychiatric interviews. Dissertation for the Academic Diploma in Psychological Medicine, The University of London.
37. Sergeant, H. G. S. (1965) Systematic desensitization. Dissertation for the Academic Diploma in Psychological Medicine, The University of London.

7

Forensic Psychiatry

T. C. N. GIBBENS

FOR many years before 1950 the late Sir Norwood East was Lecturer in Forensic Psychiatry at The Maudsley Hospital. He brought to this task an experience and authority unequalled before or since, for he was not only a senior administrator—a Commissioner of the Prisons—but had also published more studies in forensic psychiatry than any other person in England before him, and was the most experienced psychiatric expert in the criminal courts. He had been a Prison Medical Officer for the astonishing period of 50 years, had witnessed the introduction of the Mental Deficiency Act of 1913, the disappearance of the broad arrow and the shorn head. The evolution of the speciality thenceforward made it certain that these roles could never again be performed by one man.

From the foundation of the Institute of Psychiatry Sir Aubrey Lewis was interested in the development of forensic psychiatry, and in 1948 the author was awarded a Nuffield Fellowship to study the subject in the United States, followed in 1950 by the first whole-time appointment of a Lecturer in Forensic Psychiatry. At about the same time Dr. P. D. Scott was appointed to the staff of The Maudsley Hospital, to devote himself whole-time to providing clinical services for juvenile and adult offenders. His more important papers on this subject are mentioned below.

The delicate problems of public relations which are involved in forensic psychiatry were made immediately apparent, for in 1949 a project was put forward to make a psychological study of those convicted of murder in the previous 3 years. The psychology of murder was again in the public eye, for the Royal Commission on Capital Punishment was about to report. After a preliminary agreement to allow the study had been obtained, and an extension of the Fellowship for a further year had been arranged, further difficulties arose. Comparable studies had to be pursued in the United States.

PSYCHIATRIC ASPECTS OF PARTICULAR CRIMES

Medical training emphasizes the importance of aetiology, and forensic psychiatrists have tended to concentrate on the mental abnormalities of those committing particular crimes or upon the type of crime to which mental illness gives rise. Many of Sir Norwood East's papers were devoted to the extent of mental illness among, for example, exhibitionists or murderers; or to the varieties of crime committed by those suffering from pure paranoia. These can still be valuable as preliminary surveys of some relatively unknown field, but in contemporary conditions they should incorporate two other features. First, the offenders should constitute a definable sample. When Sir Norwood East reported that 15 per cent. of exhibitionists were psychotic when seen in Brixton Prison, this may only have meant that magistrates were adept in picking out mentally abnormal cases when asking for a medical report. The Cambridge Institute of Criminology later made a systematic study of a national sample of sex offenders. It was shown that 80 per cent. of exhibitionists were not re-convicted in 5 years, which does not suggest that a high proportion was psychotic.

Secondly, it is nowadays desirable to put abnormal cases in some relationship with the less seriously disturbed, either to indicate some resemblance in psychopathology and psychology, or suggest recurring syndromes of causation which may have a bearing upon the prevention and treatment of less abnormal cases.

Murder fascinates psychologists as much as the general public. As the principal crime, it is an important touchstone for gauging society's attitude to offenders in general, and has great political significance. Until the abolition of the death penalty it involved psychiatrists in serious issues about criminal responsibility. Yet it has very little importance in the whole field of crime. Many, perhaps most, murderers have no settled intention to kill, but are oblivious to the risks of killing; and it may be pure chance which separates them from many cases of assault. An efficient ambulance and casualty service has perhaps played a greater part in keeping the murder rate steady than anything else. The mystery is that so many cases of grievous bodily harm do not end in death.

For reasons already given, the study of murderers was continued in the United States. The late Sanford Bates, Director of the Department of Institutions and Agencies in New Jersey (which combines in one office the equivalent of the Home Office and Ministry of Health) immediately provided access to the records of all cases of homicide in the State. Homicides were chosen since the definitions of manslaughter and second degree murder constitute an artificial barrier in selection. All 120 homicides convicted in 1947–49 and found to be sane were contrasted with 115 mentally disordered cases of homicide admitted to the State Hospital including a complete sample since 1938, whether dead, discharged or still detained there [5]. The series drew attention to several features which are often overlooked in discussions about 'insane' homicides. Only 53 per cent. were demonstrably psychotic before the crime; and though in another 20 per cent. the abnormality was detected so soon after the crime as to lead to presumption that they were insane at the time, the remainder included many who developed psychoses sometimes many years after the offence, mainly consisting of 'prison psychoses' or 'psychoses with psychopathic personality'. Conversely, although the majority of those insane before the crime committed it in the early stages of their illness, 15 per cent. had been known to be psychotic for 5–10 years. More attention should be paid to these preventable forms of murder, rare as they are.

The diagnostic groups were similar to those found in other studies —40 per cent. schizophrenic, 14 per cent. of typical 'family' murder by the depressed, etc. It was found that the depressed murderers could almost be picked out by the time of day of the crime. Murder at breakfast-time or in the early morning is almost confined to those who are depressed. An interesting 9 per cent. were given the rather indeterminate label of 'paranoid condition'. This last group, a characteristic and difficult group of pathological murderers, has been more recently studied in England by Shepherd [38], and by Mowat [28] who recently surveyed all the morbidly jealous patients in Broadmoor. The declension from excessive jealousy to morbid and frankly delusional jealousy is very gradual and may be spread over many years. The Broadmoor cases were usually quite obviously irrational but they tended to keep their delusions to themselves and to look constantly for further proof of infidelity, so that the danger is overlooked unless there is a proper psychiatric examination.

Most people assume that the insane act from unintelligible motives, yet in only a third of cases was the motive obscure or delusional. In most, the motive, whether of jealousy, hate, or revenge, was as apparent as in the sane but the effect of the psychosis was to remove normal inhibitions, especially, of course, in cases of organic psychosis. A number of the insane, for example, had committed armed robbery which had led to murder. An intelligible motive does not in any way prove that the murderer is sane. The study also showed, as East's had done, that excessive violence in committing murder does not indicate insanity; it is rather more commonly seen in the 'normal'. Multiple methods of killing, and especially multiple victims, are much more closely associated with insanity.

One of the advantages of an academic appointment is that it provides the opportunity to study complete samples instead of the selected groups seen by a single clinic. In 1953, as a result of the initiative of Miss Margery Fry, the author examined all those sent to prison in England and Wales in a year for violent cruelty to children—32 men and 7 women [22, 23]. This showed the usual range of mental abnormality from psychosis to something approaching mental normality, about a third being grossly pathological cases. The time is passing, however, when it is any longer of much value to demonstrate that any particular crime is associated with a high or low proportion with particular diagnoses. If psychological or psychopathological syndromes of behaviour can be established, however, there is hope that methods of prevention and treatment can be suggested. Total samples may also show the prevalence of certain social pressures which may be preventable. In the case of cruel parents, something approaching a typical syndrome emerges. It consists of an aggressive youth who, after a disturbed adolescence, enters the Army and responds well to its protection and discipline. On leaving the Army, however, such a man, who has often had little social experience of the opposite sex, tends to marry a promiscuous or inadequate woman who gives him none of the expected support. Drinking, unemployment, and debt lead to increasing exasperation which is apt to flare up in injury to the child when it is enuretic or dirty. Unexpectedly, cruelty often *followed* rehousing or other improvement in material conditions, partly because this emphasized the persistence of psychological problems, and sometimes because the family came under the observation of critical neighbours in a new housing estate who maintained much higher standards.

In most instances the clinician is forced to throw light upon behavioural syndromes by reporting a series of cases as they pass through a clinic, ignoring the many selecting processes which have brought them there. Two types of disorder have had a topical interest during recent years. The control of prostitution was considered by the Wolfenden Committee in 1958. Few studies of the psychopathology of prostitutes were available, but these aspects could be considered at least in relation to juvenile prostitutes seen in the London Remand Home for Girls [3]. Among 400 juvenile girls in need of care and protection, and later followed up, 16, or 4 per cent. were prostitutes at the time of their arrest. The largest group provided striking confirmation of Glover's [24] view that the prostitution was frequently accompanied by unconscious homosexuality. Four of the main group, intelligent but very unstable girls, were in fact overtly lesbian. Others showed a well-marked hostility to and contempt for men, and inability to form any satisfying relationship with boys, which corresponded to Glover's concept of unconscious homosexuality—in marked contrast to the vast majority of wayward girls who are strongly heterosexual, even if indiscreet or uncontrolled. This 'gold-digger' attitude of being unmoved by affection for males enables them to seize the opportunities for material advantage, again in marked contrast to the majority of teenage girls who think remarkably little about money and poverty when their emotions are involved. Although this may be the most important aspect of the psychopathology of prostitution, there are several variants—deprived girls who are so mistrustful that they cannot become involved in lasting heterosexual relations, those who take to prostitution in a depressed, self-destructive mood to show 'how low they can go', the feeble-minded and uncritical, and the excessively passive.

When 200 of these girls placed on probation or under supervision [8] were followed up it seemed clear that prostitution was usually quite temporary. Many have done very well; several became successful nurses—a profession which, it was suggested, allows similar attitudes to masculine weakness to be expressed in a well sublimated form. A further 8 per cent. of the 200 took to prostitution temporarily.

Fourteen years later, a follow-up is now being completed of the adult convictions of 300 of these girls psychiatrically examined for the Courts in 1952 as well as of all the juvenile girls of all ages—nearly 500—who were before the Courts in London in the course of 6 months from September 1951 to March 1952. Among those remanded for investigation 10 per cent. were convicted of prostitution as adults and 2 per cent. of the total sample came before the Courts.

The theft of motor cars (or taking and driving away) is another type of offence which has greatly increased in the last 10 years. Those convicted are concentrated, perhaps more than any other type of offender, in the age group 16–18. Among 200 boys sentenced to Borstal training in 1952 it could be shown statistically that boys who had stolen cars came from better homes, and were more clearly neurotic, than others [6]. It is a typical 'proving' offence [p. 128] in which a boy, usually with a dominant or over-possessive but affectionate mother, commits an offence for prestige, excitement, or to bolster self-confidence in trying to fulfil a masculine role. This offence, however, provides an interesting example of how psychopathology is modified by social change. Now that driving a car is accepted by almost all strata of society as a normal part of living, it has lost much of its significance as excitement, though joy-riding is still frequently a 'proving' type of offence.

Lastly, *shoplifting* has again attracted attention, partly because it is greatly on the increase with the introduction of self-service stores. Psychiatrists have long recognized and written about the 'neurotic', 'kleptomaniac', or quasi-compulsive shoplifter who impulsively steals for motives other than material gain. The valet of the King of

Sardinia used to go through his master's pockets and return the silver spoons he regularly stole from his hosts; and Henry of Navarre, among his other eccentricities, was apparently unable to resist pilfering in a similar way. The problem is, how important a part do such cases play in general in shoplifting? With a grant from the Prinz Hopkins Fund of California, made to the Institute for the Study and Treatment of Delinquency, Mrs. Joyce Prince and I [18] tried to make a systematic study by collecting information about 500 women shoplifters—all those convicted in a year in a West End, a suburban, and an outer suburban Court. Probation Officers, especially Mrs. Gray, kindly interviewed the majority of cases. We compared the results with brief Court details of all the male and juvenile shoplifters convicted in the same areas; and with the subsequent criminal records of 100 women shoplifters and 100 other thieves convicted in those Courts 10 years before.

The results showed a surprisingly large group (29 per cent.) of young women who were foreign visitors or au pair girls—healthy, untroubled, even if hard-up and exploited, who regarded shoplifting as 'fair game', though quite honest in other respects. The peak age for British women was in the 50's and about a quarter were neurotic or depressed women of good character for whom a conviction for shoplifting was quite unexpected. For many, it seemed to be a 'call for help', like a miniature suicidal attempt, which successfully drew attention to their needs. As with many middle-aged neurotic women attending their doctors, their condition was frequently psychosomatic in character, insomnia, fears and depression being blended with symptoms attributable to such disorders as gynaecological conditions, recent hysterectomies, and miscarriages. Post-menopausal women were commoner than menopausal; and there was no evidence of a close connexion with any particular phase of the menstrual cycle. The remaining women, though they might occasionally be under various forms of social stress, seemed relatively undisturbed psychologically, except that their standards of honesty had sagged, especially in relation to stealing small amounts from self-service stores while paying for the major part of their order. The chances of reconviction after a single fine were, however, low. A small proportion of professional shoplifters (4 per cent.) tended to gravitate to the more lucrative practice of stealing women shoppers' handbags or purses. With such a good prognosis, whether neurotic and depressed or not, it is hardly worth while to attempt to examine all cases thoroughly though a brief interview with an experienced Probation Officer often quickly reveals the exceptional cases. Psychiatric examination was considered desirable, however, in all cases on their second conviction. The detailed psychopathology only emerged clearly in a group of cases given psychotherapy at the Portman Clinic for some months.

PSYCHOLOGICAL TYPES OF OFFENDER

Studies of the varieties of offender committing some particular crime run the risk, as we have suggested, of merely revealing that some particular proportion is psychotic, subnormal, psychopathic or neurotic. It is quite certain that all will be represented in any sizable group. Any particular crime is only a symptom of many different conditions. The understanding of these types may offer better hopes of prevention and treatment.

Rich [30] made a notable contribution to the definition of syndromes of stealing. 'Marauding' theft was typical of boys acting in groups of two or three, setting out to explore without intention to steal but liable to exploit any opportunity for it. 'Proving' theft is usually committed alone, the stolen objects being shown to friends as a mark of prestige, and valued for this rather than for any other purpose. 'Comforting' theft is typical of the deprived or rejected boy who tries to obtain substitutes for lost love, often committed very impulsively and alone. A residual group of 'secondary' thieves stole for gain, with purposeful planning, often in company with similar boys. There was an element of criminal sophistication and such boys had often started as one of the other types. Rich showed differences in the family background of the three types and the author applied this classification also to Borstal boys [10]. Although 'proving' offences have the best prognosis and 'comforting' offences the worst in the immediate future, this has not been confirmed for the long term results. Much depends upon the 'secondary' development, on the acceptance of crime by the individual as compatible with his self-image so that it becomes organized and goal-directed. We shall return later to this important question of the evolution of the criminal career from both the social and psychological points of view.

Scott [35] suggested a classification of sexual offenders, especially detailing the psychological varieties of homosexual offenders, and their treatment needs. He has also [34] evolved a classification of the greatest interest for the main group of property offenders. He discussed the origin and treatment needs of four types of offender—those who are well-trained but to antisocial standards; those ill-trained who have had little consistent education; the 'reparative' whose delinquency represents an attempt to resolve conflicts; and the 'maladaptive' who commit stereotyped repetitive offences.

Psychiatrists are constantly reminded, since a great part of the treatment of offenders must be carried out in Approved Schools or in the penal system, usually without psychiatric treatment, that they could help a great deal if they could establish an accurate prognosis. If they could diagnose those conditions which involve a high risk of further crime, any available treatment, or at least preventive control, could be concentrated upon them. Those with psychopathic personality have always been regarded as having a very poor prognosis—their lack of conscience, impulsiveness, inability to postpone immediate satisfaction, to plan for the future or to learn from experience, make further crime almost inevitable. In 1948 Stafford-Clark, Pond, and Lovett Doust [39] compared 80 severely psychopathic prisoners with controls, with regard to clinical features and EEG examinations. Their criminal careers have been followed for 15 years by the author [16, 17]. Although, as expected, most of these have become serious recidivists, the most interesting finding is that a quarter were never reconvicted after their current offence, and a check was made that this was not because they had died or been admitted to mental hospitals. In the last (unpublished) follow-up period of 5 years the controls, though not reconvicted at first, have shown sporadic reconvictions which are not very much less frequent than those of such psychopaths who have been at liberty. In the earlier studies it was shown that an abnormal EEG, though far more often found in psychopaths, was not strongly related to reconvictions; in fact, in patients over 25 years old it was a slightly favourable sign, perhaps because it provided some hope that a maturation process could occur. Aggressive and inadequate psychopaths were broadly distinguished. A criminal career of many aggressive offences, at any rate of a serious type, is not, however, characteristic of aggressive psychopaths, probably because their hostility cuts them off from normal social contacts and they can only live by committing major property offences. Conversely, a man with a record only of aggressive offences is often a good worker who is, perhaps, violent only when drunk and not so completely disabled as the true aggressive psychopath. Most of the psychopaths who were not reconvicted were young men with few previous convictions; the number of previous convictions, as many criminologists have maintained, is still a surer guide to reconviction than psychiatric diagnosis.

The variety of meanings attached to 'psychopathic personality' has been such a stumbling block to research that the term is almost obsolete. The psychopath in prison, where nearly all are psychopathic to some degree (especially nowadays when the Courts are reluctant to use imprisonment unless there are several previous convictions) is only given this label in extreme cases, approximating to the type of case called by East 'non-sane non-insane'. In the mental hospital population the criteria are less severe. Briscoe, Dell, and the author

[13] have recently examined the criminal behaviour of mental hospital in-patients admitted with a diagnosis of 'pathological' and 'immature' personality (with 13 sub-types in the International Classification) or neurosis (with 7 sub-types). In the course of nearly a decade 111 psychopaths and 75 neurotics were admitted who had mentioned a previous criminal conviction. The criminal convictions of these cases, before or after admission, as well as of twice the number of allegedly unoffending psychopaths and neurotic admissions were then checked so that offenders and non-offenders with mixed diagnoses could be carefully matched for age and subsidiary diagnosis. Those who subsequently received the diagnosis of psychosis were excluded and in the final matching 89 offending and 107 non-offending psychopaths were contrasted and 72 offending with 91 non-offending neurotics.

Psychopaths, especially, would not be admitted to hospital, where they are usually unpopular, unless they presented a serious disturbance; attempted suicide, however, was not a common reason.

The offenders as a whole were sharply distinguished from the non-offenders, as many studies of the normal population have emphasized, by the early history—early lack of maternal and paternal care, poor family relations, unsatisfactory mothering, poor physical environment, etc. These factors did not, however, significantly distinguish the offending from non-offending psychopaths, most of whom had a very unsatisfactory early environment; the main difference was in respect of neurotics. The psychopathic as well as the neurotic offenders were distinguished from controls by poor education, falling work position, frequent unemployment.

With regard to symptoms, the psychopaths of all kinds were distinguished from the neurotics in the expected ways; being more cold-hearted, selfish, aggressive, explosive, carefree and lacking in morals. Their disturbance was more often considered to be constitutional and lifelong and they appeared uninfluenced by treatment. Sibling rivalry and sleep disturbances were much commoner as well as anxiety, apathy, and depression among the neurotics.

The criminal records of these patients were nevertheless far less serious than among those in prison. Nearly half had committed quite minor offences; about 40 per cent., however, had over four convictions, sometimes of a serious kind. But when followed, in most cases for about 5 years after discharge, 70 per cent. of neurotics and 40 per cent. of the psychopaths had no subsequent convictions, and usually there was no more than one reconviction. These were not the grossly abnormal persistent offenders seen in prison; in fact, psychopaths seen in mental hospitals tend to be middle-class, intelligent and well educated, beginning their official criminal career for the first time in their twenties rather than in childhood. The surprise is that such obviously unstable and explosive individuals should be able to avoid breaking the law as much as they do. The neurotic offenders were somewhat older, with more offences in their past record but now settling down at the cost of considerable anxiety and depression. Clearly, the relations of crime to mental abnormality, as the psychiatrist is accustomed to see it, is very uncertain.

Much the same conclusion must be drawn from the follow-up of 200 Borstal boys seen originally in 1952 [20]. At the time they presented a range of mental abnormalities which were clearly not related very closely to the chances of further crime. Some highly neurotic boys might show very little likelihood of further conviction, while about 5 per cent. were severely psychopathic and almost certain to be involved in further crime. In an attempt to study this relationship, they were therefore classified along two dimensions—mental abnormality (including 27 per cent.) and criminal prognosis, making use of the prediction scores devised by Mannheim and Wilkins [26] as well as clinical estimates.

The follow-up of 15 years with regard to subsequent convictions and employment has brought many surprises and demonstrated the complexity of the problem. Some 20 per cent. of the boys have become persistent and serious recidivists, but although half of these were certainly considered to be severely psychopathic, the other half were not considered to be seriously disordered but to present a socially or sub-culturally induced type of delinquency in a relatively well integrated personality. Conversely, some very unstable, conflict-ridden boys with a history of suicidal attempts and the like, have settled down very well and benefited a great deal from Borstal training. Altogether, 65 per cent. of the boys have become free from crime for some time. Apart from the 20 per cent. of seriously persistent offenders and the 45 per cent. who were never reconvicted at all, 15 per cent. were 'late recoveries' abandoning crime after one or two convictions, 10 per cent. were 'late failures', crime-free for some years but relapsing again later. These last two groups may represent dependent or independent types of boy who respectively need or resent supervision. A further 5 per cent. became petty persistent offenders with repeated fines for drunkenness and assault, and probably on their way to becoming chronic alcoholics; 5 per cent. have offended sporadically.

The boys were given extensive psychological tests of personality but these were not found to have much prognostic significance. It was demonstrated that, as compared with controls, the Borstal boys obtained significantly higher scores on the qualitative scores of the Porteus Maze Test [7]; but when tested a year later in their institutions a reduction in the score was not related to whether they had done well, nor was it related to subsequent convictions. They also scored abnormally higher than the controls on the Minnesota Multiphasic Personality Inventory. Later factor analysis showed that the higher scores on the different sub-scales were strongly related to one another and that those with abnormally high scores on the whole were rather less often reconvicted.

More valuable have been the subjective estimates of personality traits. When these were factor analysed it was revealed that a factor consisting of such qualities as 'inadequate response to life, helpless, unrealistic, lacking in energy, solitary, submissive, with weak sex interest, marked conflict and rated as mentally abnormal' were fairly strongly related to failure, while such qualities as 'aggressiveness, over-assertiveness, realistic, extrovert, dynamic' were combined in a factor which had a slightly favourable prognosis. The onset of criminal behaviour varied very much with age and also with personality. The dynamic, defiant type of boy, faced with an unsatisfactory home life to which he is anchored until he becomes an adult, has little opportunity to avoid a delinquent response. Sheldon and Eleanor Glueck have shown that it is these qualities which predict that a child will come before the Courts. Between 17 and 21, however, at Borstal age, these qualities may enable a boy to make his own way, marry and settle down. There are, however, a number of inadequate youths who in late adolescence and early adult life take to crime for the first time when they lose the support of their family. These boys are less able to adjust to adult life and may settle into persistent crime and prison life more frequently. In order to carry out preventive treatment, the Child Care Services would need to detect these children who are maladjusted in a passive and negative way.

In another context, Mitcheson [27] has recently examined the relation of intelligence to recidivism. The subsequent criminal records of 200 juvenile delinquents treated at the Portman Clinic 20 years ago have been studied and related to many details of their personal and family situation when they visited the Clinic. Those of superior intelligence were significantly less often reconvicted; but this relationship became insignificant if a group of boys was excluded who had been referred by their parents or doctors and not through Courts and Probation Officers. A group of factors were associated together with dullness and with reconviction as an adult, namely a mother in poor physical health, with a large family, living in poor circumstances, and attending a non-selective school.

FAMILY AND SOCIAL RELATIONSHIPS

The family background of delinquents in both its effect upon personality development and in current conflicts and dissatisfactions, has long been a principal concern of psychiatrists. The main interest has been to unravel the causes of different types of delinquency or, more recently, to establish whether these family situations predict delinquency or carry a particularly unfavourable prognosis. Almost all the studies mentioned throw some light on these significant relationships; whether it is that car thieves are typical 'proving' offenders who have over-possessive or dominating mothers, against whom they are rebelling, or that juvenile prostitutes frequently have had unsatisfactory relations with their fathers, and so on. Although aetiological interpretation, largely based upon psychoanalytic views of personality development, has proved extremely valuable, the most recent trend is to apply more objective methods of research. The absence of control groups in most of these studies has been a great handicap.

A study by West [40] of the parents of 50 homosexuals and 50 controls is a good example of this more systematic approach. From a verbal description, the mothers were rated by an independent observer (who did not know whether the description applied to a patient or a control) for undue, abnormal, or extreme intensity of relationship with their sons; and the father for 'unsatisfactoriness' of relationship. A significantly higher degree of unsatisfactory relationships of one or the other kind was found in the homosexuals.

The family background and other factors in boy and girl delinquents in Remand Homes were contrasted by Cockburn and Maclay [2]. Girls are more often charged with sexual promiscuous behaviour and boys with property offences, but there are great difficulties about regarding these as 'equivalent' forms of delinquency for, as Barbara Wootton has observed, the girls need boys to be promiscuous with, and the boys' behaviour does not lead to arrest! However, they found that the girls more often came from broken homes, their families when together were less cohesive, their fathers poorer in discipline and more indifferent or lacking in affection. Supervision and affection of the mother towards the girl was also poorer.

Although sexual attitudes and behaviour are regarded by psychiatrists as extremely important in relation to mental health, criminologists have largely ignored them except in relation to sex offenders. In practice, however, a high proportion of chronic property offenders show various forms of sexual maladjustment. The more objective aspects of sexual behaviour of 200 Borstal boys were studied [4].

Although the rate of overt homosexuality was no higher than in the general population (4 per cent.), about a quarter showed evidence of problems in relation to sexual identification with fairly high homosexual potential. Since crime is very largely the activity of males, many of these were involved in anxious attempts to assert or prove their masculinity in crime. A number of others had a strong sexual drive, sometimes of a casual, promiscuous type, which was combined with other defects of personality; others with developed socialized relationships of a more normal type. Strong sexual interest of the latter kind is related to a good prognosis when they leave Borstal; those who married became quite rapidly free from crime. The study threw light on the vexed question of the effect of homosexual seduction. One-third of all the boys had been subjected to attempts at seduction by homosexuals; the proportion was no higher in those who were suspected of homosexual problems; the only difference was in the response to them.

The relation of various disturbances of family life upon the long-term recidivism of Borstal boys has been examined at both 5 and 10 year periods after leaving Borstal [20]. Separation from mother for varying periods in the first 5 years was not related to recidivism; in fact, the 6 boys separated for almost the whole time from birth to the age of 15 were rather more successful than those never separated. Much appears clinically to depend upon the type of separation; but even those with the two most traumatic types of experience—'mother dead; no effective substitute'; and 'mother out of touch for long periods (or permanently); no effective substitute'—were not more frequently reconvicted.

Parental discord appeared to have a more marked effect. There were 22 cases in which the relationship between the parents was rated as poor, with either present or previous separation from one another; in 16 of these cases the boy was also rejected by them. Nine of these boys (56 per cent.) were not merely reconvicted but were in the seriously persistent offender group after 10 years. The range is wide, however; 4 of these extremely deprived boys, 25 per cent. of this small group, were never reconvicted after leaving Borstal. Conversely, 24 per cent. of the seriously persistent offenders had been rated as fully accepted by their parents, whose relationship with one another was also good.

Parental affection, considered alone, did not have any predictive significance. Those rejected or abandoned by both parents were reconvicted no more often than those 'accepted' or 'warmly accepted' by both parents.

Discipline by either parent was rated as in previous studies, as either lax, over-strict, erratic, or normal. Although erratic discipline was, as elsewhere, related to failure, a close analysis showed that estimates of discipline by parents tended to be strongly influenced by the relationship *between* parents. If parents get on well together, discipline tends to be 'lax', which has a quite favourable prognosis, or normal. If the parents quarrel, then one or other parent inevitably transfers his or her exasperation to the child and becomes punitive or erratic. We found, however, that 11 of the 12 boys whose mothers were 'over-strict' were reconvicted and all the 4 boys who had two over-strict parents.

Apart from the lack of controls in many studies, a difficulty has always been that similar family situations are found in the background of many different forms of deviation, whether alcoholism, drug addiction, mental illness or crime, though not to the same extent. The effects are far from specific. A study was made, with Martin Silberman, of nearly 300 patients attending a venereal disease clinic [11, 21]. Like criminals, many owed their condition to transitory situations and were quite normal individuals; but there were many 'recidivists' who were repeatedly reinfected in spite of strong fears or recurrent depressions and many others who could be regarded as psychopathic in their casual promiscuity and lack of development of human relationships of all kinds. The population as a whole were more often neurotic than the prison population, with more nervous symptoms in childhood; but their family situations in childhood were not much more satisfactory than those of prisoners. Parental alcoholism and parental discord were, if anything, slightly commoner in the clinic population, but the prisoners had more often suffered an early or complete breakdown of family life, with periods in children's homes, and were of poorer education; and they came from much larger families. The greatest difference was that the clinic patients were nearly all in regular employment and, however unreliable and unstable, appeared to accept the necessity of work and obtained some satisfaction from it.

Sociological studies of delinquency have, in general, made greater advances since the war than purely psychiatric research, but psychiatrists have contributed to the study of these social aspects. In England there are no well-structured criminal gangs as in America, but Scott [32] has contributed a detailed study of such gangs and groups as we have, emphasizing the different relation which each member may have to the rest of the gang. Among Borstal boys it was shown [10] that those with gang or group attachments had much more often been born and brought up in the same area of London, and knew their friends since early schooldays. The better adjusted members of these large groups had usually left the group at 17 or 18 to start courting or to go with girl friends. The delinquent groups were often the small residue of those who were not able to develop socio-sexual relations.

It is usually assumed that delinquency is much commoner in the lower two Social Classes (IV and V of the Registrar General's classification); but the evidence for this is far from satisfactory. Little and Ntsekhe [25] from a study of nearly 400 boys in a Remand Home and before the Juvenile Courts, found a much less marked preponderance of those of lower social class than had been found in earlier studies; and the question was raised whether delinquency was becoming a more 'middle-class' phenomenon. But these and other studies were based upon Probation and Child Welfare Officers' reports, which are not always available for all cases. A recent unpublished study by Palmai was carried out with much greater care than ever before. Every 25th case appearing before the London Juvenile Courts for a year was considered. In the 40 per cent. of cases in which incomplete information was available, letters were sent to employers or parents or home visits were made until only 14 cases were left undecided so far as occupation of parent was concerned. Palmai found that young offenders in London are derived fairly evenly from all social classes and the type of offence does not vary very much from class to class. Girls committed very different offences and included a higher proportion from the lower social classes.

The wider social aspects of delinquency can often be seen most clearly by international comparison. In 1959 the author was commissioned by the World Health Organization to visit many European countries and to report upon new fashions and forms of delinquency. The report [9] commented on the great variations in delinquent behaviour as well as in its definition and treatment. These cultural variations were considered in detail at an international conference in 1964 sponsored by the World Federation of Mental Health and the outcome of this conference was fully reported [14].

LEGAL AND ADMINISTRATIVE RELATIONSHIPS

How the forensic psychiatrist can improve his effectiveness and collaborate more closely in relation to Courts of Law or the administration of Local Authorities' Children's Departments is a matter of continuing interest. The last 15 years have seen the introduction of the Mental Health Act, with its revolutionary proposals for treating psychopaths, whether offenders or otherwise. International policies in treating or detaining psychopaths have been reviewed [12, 37]. West, Bearcroft and Smith [41] studied the use which the Courts made of remands on bail or to prison to obtain a psychiatric report on offenders. Comparing those referred to two out-patient clinics with those remanded in Brixton Prison, they found that the decision was strongly influenced by the nature of the crime, offences of violence or the vagrancy type almost invariably leading to remand in custody, and also by the number of previous convictions and whether the offender had a settled address. Those referred to clinics on bail included a high proportion of minor sex offenders, although most psychiatrists believe that property offenders are quite as likely to show neurotic disturbances. For a large proportion, the decision seems arbitrary; one-third of prison remands were first offenders, and among minor sex offenders (indecent exposure and homosexuality between adults) this proportion rose to 43 per cent.; yet only 8·7 per cent. of the latter were reconvicted in the next 4 years, slightly less than similar cases referred to clinics. They concluded that if custody were only used for those with such positive indications as were given above, the number would fall by one-third, and if only dangerous or homeless offenders were remanded in custody, the number would fall by two-thirds.

A study by Scott [33] of the juvenile offender's attitude to the Courts, and recollection of Court procedure, pointed out many sources of misunderstanding. Another most unsatisfactory aspect of Court procedure was studied by the author and J. Prince [19]: this is the practice of examining the child victims of sex offences in higher Courts. In some cases the legal consequences of the offence are more damaging to the child than the offence itself. The police interrogation, physical examination, appearance at a Magistrates' Court and again at a higher Court after an interval of perhaps 2 months, with constant indoctrination by parents and repetition of evidence, and the possibility of being cross-examined by the assailant himself in Court, involves a child in a reorientation of attitude which is most undesirable from a mental health point of view. An attempt to verify some of these conclusions was made by examining the records of 80 child victims reported to the Federation of Moral Welfare Committees and comparing them with 40 similar cases who had been exposed to Court proceedings. The results showed that serious disturbances were often shown by those who had been involved in the Court procedures but, of course, this could not be attributed with any certainty to the legal consequences, since such cases had often been the victims of much more serious offences. The problem is unresolved, although some relief has been given more recently by the provision that evidence in lower Courts can be given in writing if the defendant agrees. An Israeli law provides that all child victims under 14 shall be examined by a 'Youth Examiner' (an experienced social worker) who takes the place of the child in all subsequent proceedings and has the right to decide whether or not the child shall be allowed to give evidence. This satisfactory solution has not been accepted in this country because it conflicts with the fundamental principle that hearsay is not admissible. A great deal of expert evidence, e.g. medical and psychiatric, already involves the assessment of hearsay evidence by persons trained to evaluate it; and this barrier may not be insurmountable.

Problems of criminal responsibility, especially in relation to murder, which were once thought to be the only field of interest for a psychiatrist, have been very much reduced by the Homicide Act of 1957 which provides for a verdict of 'manslaughter' in cases of murder in which the offender suffered from a mental abnormality which substantially reduced his mental responsibility. With the abolition of the death penalty this issue, though still argued at length, has become somewhat academic as a defence since the judge may, if he wishes, award a longer prison sentence to someone convicted of manslaughter than the man would be likely to serve if given a statutory life sentence for murder. An area of the law which is undergoing fairly rapid evolution, however, refers to the defence of so-called 'automatism'. It has long been recognized that persons committing a crime without being consciously aware of it, e.g. because of epileptic automatism or sleep-walking, could not be guilty; but they were acquitted on the grounds of 'legal insanity'; they 'did not know what they were doing', which is one requirement of the McNaughten Rules. On the other hand, not having any criminal intent should, according to the doctrine of *mens rea*, entitle one to be absolutely acquitted without an order to be indefinitely detained as an insane person. There have been cases recently in which persons committing serious offences such as grievous bodily harm, when in a hypoglycaemic state or when sleep-walking, have been so acquitted [15].

Apart from Courts of Law, there are administrative bodies such as Local Authorities, who make diagnostic decisions with the aid of psychiatrists; and the use and consequences of these decisions are of the greatest importance in social organization. Asuni [1] compared 105 delinquents in an Approved School with 107 in a Residential School for 'educationally maladjusted' boys; 74 of the Approved School boys were predominantly delinquent and had minimal disturbance or maladjustment in other respects; similarly, 72 of the maladjusted were non-delinquent, with multiple neurotic symptoms, school difficulties, etc. But 31 delinquent and 35 maladjusted boys were very similar in background and symptomatology, having attended Child Guidance Clinics as well as having been before the Court, etc. Maladjusted boys came from smaller families with less family criminality. Many such decisions, especially in borderline cases, depend upon such factors as the education and social class of parents, and whether or not they know how to obtain medical or social help with their problem children.

Although many studies have thrown light on the types of medical or penal treatment which are indicated, few studies have dealt specifically with treatment. Pearce [29] however, made a valuable study of the use of aversion therapy with transvestists [p. 116].

CRIMINAL CAREERS

The task of forensic psychiatry is to find and improve its most effective application to a very wide range of criminal behaviour by people of different ages; but also to collaborate with a long-established penal system which at least in some respects is quite effective. Large numbers of first offenders—perhaps 70 per cent.—are not reconvicted after being fined or put on probation or discharged. At the other end of the scale there is a large group of apparently helpless or incorrigible recidivists, and in between, and often forgotten, are the majority of recidivists who appear resistant for a time but are not, in fact, reconvicted after three or four varieties of penal treatment have been tried. Apart from the cases of psychosis or subnormality who quite evidently need psychiatric care and treatment, where should psychiatrists concentrate their meagre forces with best hope of success?

At present we have only a crude idea of the natural history of criminal careers. The same may be said about the evolution of mental illness; but in this case the health service has full responsibility for treatment, and deals with the situation presented, as the Courts and penal system do with offenders, on an *ad hoc* basis, according to what seems necessary at the time. But where it is a question of one discipline collaborating with another, it is essential to study the interaction in some detail. In relation to the criminal career, which for the vast majority is a short-lived affair leading to 'recovery' by the age of 25–30, are there significant points at which psychiatric intervention would be especially valuable? Should all offenders, as was suggested for adult women shoplifters, be psychiatrically examined on their second conviction? There is little doubt that psychiatric treatment, like probation, is most effective in a semi-preventive way at the first sign of trouble in young people. Is there another period when the early recidivist hopes to abandon crime but without help lacks the means and ability to do so?

In this review several attempts to study criminal careers have been referred to: the follow-up of psychopaths for 15 years, a group of Borstal boys for 12 years, 800 adolescent girls for 15 years, and delinquent boys for 20 years. The record of convictions is not, of course, a completely satisfactory measure of events when only 40–50 per cent. of reported offences are cleared up by arrest. In recent years it has been possible to add observations of the employment record over many years and the picture which emerged was surprising and interesting. The 200 ex-Borstal boys as a whole have not been in recognized employment for an average of 4 out of 10 years, but the relation of unemployment to crime is a complex one. Some repeated offenders have worked well when not in prison. Some groups such as the persistent petty offenders, although never sentenced to anything more serious than fines for drunken assaults and the like, have rarely done anything but casual and occasional work. The Borstal Governors' opinions about whether boys would be reconvicted tended, as other studies have shown, to be rather inaccurate; but their reports about a boy's industry, interest, and application in work during training have tended to remain fairly accurate. These qualities affecting employment are perhaps more basic and permanent personality features than whether or not a crime is committed and detected; this may remain largely unpredictable, like the exact location of the origin of a forest fire.

Criminal behaviour is naturally very varied in gravity, which can often be judged only by the severity of sentence. Scott [36], however, using Sellin and Wolfgang's [31] method of measuring severity, showed that many ex-Approved School boys who were reconvicted had been guilty of only very minor offences.

Adult male offenders in prison were sampled in collaboration with Martin Silverman, who interviewed 300 prisoners in three London prisons, chosen at random to represent the proportional output of these prisons and lengths of sentences served; they were compared with 100 ex-prisoners reporting for after-care at the Royal London Discharged Prisoners' Aid Society offices. Any reconvictions in the 12–18 months after release have been recorded.

The striking feature of these prisoners, who included offenders of every type from men in prison for their first offence or their thirtieth, was the varied ages at which they were first convicted. Only a third had had convictions as juveniles. No less than 18 per cent. had no convictions before the age of 30, yet 29 per cent. of these late beginners had amassed six or more convictions by the time they were interviewed. A relatively high proportion (17 per cent.) of these recidivists of late onset had had previous mental hospital treatment, but their history showed that in other respects they had been most inadequate individuals. Once convicted, they seemed to resign themselves to being cared for in prison.

Nowadays, the Courts use imprisonment with reluctance, so that even those serving their first prison sentence often have several previous convictions. Those serving their first sentence in Brixton

Prison gave hardly less indication of mental disturbance than the recidivists in Pentonville—10 per cent. for example, had had mental treatment compared with 15 per cent. amongst recidivists. E.S.N. education, obvious subnormality, homosexuality and psychosis (3 per cent.) were about the same, as well as adverse childhood experiences. The symptom which steadily increases with recidivism is alcoholism. In the main, however, the difference lies in the social isolation of recidivists such as loss of contact with wife, relatives or home or being of 'no fixed abode'.

Comparison with the careers of Borstal boys suggests that personality, prognosis and treatment needs vary considerably with the age of onset of crime. The younger, defiant and aggressive adolescent is likely to come before the Juvenile Courts, but when old enough to leave home these active qualities, if not excessive, may help him to find a better life for himself. In the early adult period a group of much more inadequate and passive individuals fall into criminal ways when their home supports are removed, and they may settle to recurrent imprisonment all too readily. Large numbers are unable to draw any benefit from imprisonment and the urgent problem of today is how to provide community support in the form of after-care or probation before imprisonment by personal contact, hostel accommodation, protective employment, etc. For this group of offenders the problems are not very different from those posed by mental illness. It is hoped that current studies of voluntary after-care and hostel schemes will provide some solutions.

REFERENCES

1. Asuni, T. (1960) Examination of the administrative categories of maladjusted and delinquent children receiving residential treatment, M.D. Thesis, Dublin.
2. Cockburn, J. J., and Maclay, I. (1965) Sex differentials in juvenile delinquency, *Brit. J. Crim.*, **4**, 289–308.
3. Gibbens, T. C. N. (1957) Juvenile prostitution, *Brit. J. Delinq.*, **8**, 3–12.
4. Gibbens, T. C. N. (1957) Sexual behaviour of young criminals, *J. ment. Sci.*, **103**, 527–39.
5. Gibbens, T. C. N. (1958) Sane and insane homicide, *J. crim. Law, Criminol. & Police Sci.*, **58**, 110–15.
6. Gibbens, T. C. N. (1958) Car thieves, *Brit. J. Delinq.*, **8**, 257–65.
7. Gibbens, T. C. N. (1958) The Porteus Maze Test and delinquency, *Brit. J. educ. Psychol.*, **28**, 209–16.
8. Gibbens, T. C. N. (1959) Supervision and probation of adolescent girls, *Brit. J. Delinq.*, **10**, 84–103.
9. Gibbens, T. C. N. (1961) Trends in juvenile delinquency, *Wld Hlth Org. Publ. Hlth Pap.*, **5**, 53.

10. GIBBENS, T. C. N. (1963) *Psychiatric Studies of Borstal Lads*, Maudsley Monographs, No. 11., London.
11. GIBBENS, T. C. N. (1963) Clients of prostitutes, Alison Neilan's Memorial Lecture, Josephine Butler Society.
12. GIBBENS, T. C. N. (1966) Treatment of psychopaths in England, in *Psychopathic Personality*, ed. Craft, M., Oxford.
13. GIBBENS, T. C. N. (1966) Psychiatric research in delinquency behaviour, *Brit. med. J.*, ii, 695–8.
14. GIBBENS, T. C. N., and AHRENFELDT, R. H. (1966) *Cultural Factors in Delinquency*, London.
15. GIBBENS, T. C. N., and HALL-WILLIAMS, J. E. (1966) Medico-legal aspects of amnesia, in *Amnesia*, ed. Zangwell, O. L., and Whitty, C. W. M., London.
16. GIBBENS, T. C. N., POND, D., and STAFFORD-CLARK, D. (1955) A follow-up of criminal psychopaths, *Brit. J. Delinq.*, **6**, 126–36.
17. GIBBENS, T. C. N., POND, D. and STAFFORD-CLARK, D. (1959) A follow-up study of criminal psychopaths, *J. ment. Sci.*, **104**, 108–15.
18. GIBBENS, T. C. N., and PRINCE, J. (1962) Shoplifting, Institute for the Study and Treatment of Delinquency Pamphlet.
19. GIBBENS, T. C. N., and PRINCE, J. (1963) Child victims of sex offences, Institute for the Study and Treatment of Delinquency Pamphlet.
20. GIBBENS, T. C. N., and PRINCE, J. (1965) The results of Borstal training, *Sociol Rev.* Monograph No. 9, 227–36, Keele University.
21. GIBBENS, T. C. N., and SILBERMAN, M. (1960) The clients of prostitutes, *Brit. J. vener. Dis.*, **36**, 113–17.
22. GIBBENS, T. C. N., and WALKER, A. (1956) Violent cruelty to children, *Brit. J. Delinq.*, **6**, 260–77.
23. GIBBENS, T. C. N., and WALKER, A. (1956) Cruel parents, Institute for the Study and Treatment of Delinquency Pamphlet.
24. GLOVER, E. (March 1957) The Psychopathology of prostitution, Institute for the Study and Treatment of Delinquency Pamphlet.
25. LITTLE, W. R., and NTSEKHE, V. R. (1959) Social class background of young offenders from London, *Brit. J. Delinq.*, **10**, 130–5.
26. MANNHEIM, H., and WILKINS, L. T. (1955) *Prediction Methods in Relation to Borstal Training*, London, H.M.S.O.
27. MITCHESON, M. (1966) Intelligence and recidivism, Dissertation for the Academic Diploma in Psychological Medicine, The University of London.
28. MOWAT, R. R. (1966) *Morbid Jealousy and Murder*, London.
29. PEARCE, J. F. (1963) The application of behaviour therapy to transvestism, Dissertation for the Academic Diploma in Psychological Medicine, The University of London.
30. RICH, J. (1956) Types of stealing, *Lancet*, i, 496–8.
31. SELLIN, T., and WOLFGANG, M. E. (1964) *Measurement of Delinquency*, New York.
32. SCOTT, P. D. (1956) Gangs and delinquent groups in London, *Brit. J. Delinq.*, **7**, 4–26.

33. Scott, P. D. (1959) Juvenile courts: the juvenile's point of view, *Brit. J. Delinq.*, **9**, 200–11.
34. Scott, P. D. (1960) Assessing the offenders for the courts, *Brit. J. Crim.*, **1**, 116–29.
35. Scott, P. D. (1964) Sexual perversions, in *The Pathology and Treatment of Sexual Deviation*, ed. Rosen, I., London.
36. Scott, P. D. (1964) Approved school success rates, *Brit. J. Crim.*, **5**, 525–56.
37. Scott, P. D. (1965) Provisions for the treatment of psychopaths, in *Psychiatric Hospital Care*, ed. Freeman, H., London.
38. Shepherd, M. (1961) Morbid jealousy, *J. ment. Sci.*, **107**, 687–753.
39. Stafford-Clark, D., Pond, D., and Lovett Doust, J. W. (1951) The psychopath in prison, *Brit. J. Delinq.*, **2**, 117–30.
40. West, D. J. (1959) Parental figures in the genesis of male homosexuality, *Int. J. soc. Psychiat.*, **3**, 2.
41. West, D. J., Bearcroft, J. S., and Smith, A. (1960) The choice of bail or custody for offenders remanded for a psychiatric report, *Int. J. soc. Psychiat.*, **6**, Nos. 1 and 2.

PART II

CHILD PSYCHIATRY, GENETICS AND EDUCATION

8

Child Psychiatry

MICHAEL RUTTER

THE studies in child psychiatry described in this chapter started in 1952 with the appointment of Dr. (now Professor) James Anthony as Senior Lecturer in Child Psychiatry. When Sir Aubrey Lewis extended the interests of the Department of Psychiatry in this way to include the psychiatry of childhood, it was the first senior academic appointment in child psychiatry to be made in this country and, indeed, the appointment today remains the only one of its kind in Great Britain.

The history of research in child psychiatry is a short one. Before this century, any kind of interest in childhood was rare [10] and until some 40 or 50 years ago most references to the psychiatry of childhood were in terms of adult conditions [21]. Even Freud's epoch-making theory of infantile sexuality was based on the reminiscences of neurotic adults and was published before Freud saw his first child patient [21]. Many of the early studies of abnormal child development were carried out by psychologists and in this country Sir Cyril Burt was one of the pioneers. At first, investigations were limited by the inadequacies of child psychiatry itself, in particular by the absence of well defined diagnostic categories so that much research was necessarily concerned with the unsatisfactory global concept of the 'maladjusted' child. That this is no longer the case today is due in part to careful clinical studies in the 1930s and 1940s by some of the foremost child psychiatrists of that time; for example by Kanner [20] in his delineation of 'infantile autism' and by Levy [22] in his study of 'maternal overprotection'.

CLINICAL-EXPERIMENTAL STUDIES

Nevertheless a need for clinical studies remained. Lewis [26] has emphasized the value of integrating the findings of psychological research with the study of child pyschiatry, and it was appropriate that Anthony's first clinical studies should reflect this. Thus, in a series of clinical-experimental studies of psychiatric disorders in children, he sought to relate children's abnormalities in behaviour and emotions to factors important in normal maturation. In this endeavour recourse was often made to Piaget's theories on the process of development. Anthony [1, 2] argued that Piaget's emphasis on the close links between intelligence and affect and his finding that there were different styles of thinking at different stages of development might have important implications for psychopathological studies. Differences in cognitive styles at different ages might offer clues as to the nature and development of the various emotional and behavioural disorders which are characteristic of different periods of childhood. This might be particularly so in relation to those disorders which were essentially delays or distortions in the course of normal behavioural development.

Encopresis was selected by Anthony as the first syndrome to be studied in this way, using a combination of clinical and experimental methods [3]. Thirty children with 'continuous' encopresis who had never shown normal control of defaecation were compared with 30 children with 'discontinuous' encopresis, that is, where soiling had developed after a period in which there was normal bowel control. It was found that whereas the 'continuous' encopretic had usually been trained in a neglectful way, the 'discontinuous' encopretic had been subjected to a coercive approach. Co-operative training was infrequent in both groups. Animistic attitudes towards faeces were elicited using Piaget's methods of free interrogation; children who had experienced coercive training usually expressed fearful or hateful feelings towards their faeces, whereas most of those trained neglectfully spoke of erotic, affectionate or solicitous feelings. Children's disgust reactions to stimuli associated with faeces or toileting were tested by means of a battery of perceptual tests. Smell reactions were tested by the use of a smell prism and touch reactions were assessed by asking the children to determine the warmest and coolest of a series of open vessels containing fluids which ranged from water to a disgusting squelchy black mess. The 'discontinuous' encopretics showed increased disgust reactions in keeping with their negative attitude towards faeces, whereas the 'continuous' encopretics showed little disgust, in line with their positive attitudes towards faeces. It was concluded that the 'continuous' encopretic (who more often came from a socially deprived home, frequently exhibited antisocial behaviour and was usually enuretic as well as encopretic) required habit training under a more consistent regime than available at home. In contrast, the 'discontinuous' encopretic (who was usually *not* enuretic and who tended to be inhibited and obsessional in personality) was generally a deeply disturbed child who needed prolonged psychotherapy and some measure of protection from his mother.

The much rarer phenomenon of micropsia was examined in a

study of 17 cases by Anthony [7]. In general, the microptic children emerged as introspective, sensitive and emotionally unstable, with a tendency towards experiencing unusual subjective sensations and reacting excessively to them. In comparison with control children they showed a low constancy in size judgement, a poor appreciation of size-distance relationships that blinded them to gross artificial discrepancies, and a 'realism' that caused them to interpret as actual the apparent shrinking of the object with distance. Microptic illusional attacks could arise through factors affecting either the retina or the central visual organization. Central effects could be organic (7 of the 17 children were epileptic), developmental (the children were often predominantly visual and eidetic in their perceptual capacities) or emotional (in a few cases the micropsia seemed to have developed on the basis of anxiety).

Sleep disturbances also follow a characteristic developmental course. Hypnagogic hallucinations form a prominent aspect of some disorders of sleep, and as animism and imagery also show developmental transformations it was postulated that different types of sleep disturbance might be related to differences in capacity for imagery [6]. Thirty children with night terrors, 16 with nightmares and 30 who walked in their sleep, were compared in relation to their eidetic, visualizing, substantializing, and dreaming capacity. The groups differed in age; night terrors were most common under the age of 8 years, nightmares between 8 and 10 years, and sleep-walking over 10 years. With regard to perception, the major differences lay between the night terror/nightmare group and the sleep-walking group. Visualizing capacity was greater and eidetic imagery more marked in the first group, the differences being most obvious in the young children. It seemed that the developmental patterning of sleep disturbances was related to the developmental patterning of imaginal processes; night terrors appeared at the highest point of the imaginal curve and sleep-walking at the lowest. It was concluded that the 'choice of symptom' was largely governed by factors within the children rather than in the environment.

TEMPERAMENTAL DEVELOPMENT IN CHILDHOOD

Temperamental factors within the child which influence his emotional and behavioural development were also later investigated by Rutter when collaborating with Birch, Chess, Thomas and their colleagues in the New York longitudinal study. It had been found that children differed sharply in their temperamental characteristics even in infancy [50]. These patterns of temperamental functioning showed a certain consistency and continuity over time [40, 50] but also there was sufficient flux and change for the correlation on any variable between age periods separated by more than a year or so (in the pre-school period) to be quite low [46]. A pilot study of twins and sibs included in the study showed that non-genetic as well as genetic influences were important in the development of temperament, and also that those characteristics with the strongest genetic loading were not necessarily the most stable over time [46].

Although temperament became modified in various ways during the course of development, it was found that the temperamental characteristics shown in infancy were related to the child's later behavioural development [40]. Quantitative measures of temperamental style obtained between the ages of 12 and 24 months significantly differentiated those children later referred to a psychiatrist. Children with irregular patterns of function in infancy as shown, for example, in the sleep cycle, who were slow to adapt to novel circumstances, whose emotional responses were usually of high intensity and whose preponderant mood was negative were those most likely to be referred to a psychiatrist because of behaviour problems when older. These temperamental characteristics differentiated the psychiatric cases from their sibs as well as from the general population of children in the study.

Although temperamental attributes were important in relation to development, they were not of themselves determining factors. Behavioural disturbance was thought to result from an interaction between certain kinds of temperamental patterns and certain features in the environment—both intrafamilial and extrafamilial. Highly irregular, non-adaptable children with intense negative reactions are particularly likely to induce negative feelings in their parents. Parental attitudes are shaped by the child's characteristics as well as by the parents' personality and background. The intense, active, independent child, by getting into situations never experienced by less adventurous children, will also have differing life experiences and learning opportunities. Of course, too, the child's experiences may in turn influence temperamental development. If children who are slow to adapt to new situations are given a wide variety of experiences, then later they will adjust more quickly to situations which to other children of similar initial temperament but who have had a more sheltered existence will be new and stressful [40].

So far, the findings refer only to early childhood and only to relatively mild disorders of behaviour. However, the interaction between temperamental attributes and stressful circumstances in later childhood is now being examined by Graham in relation to an older group of more deviant children in families containing a mentally ill parent.

LINKS BETWEEN DISORDERS IN CHILDHOOD AND IN ADULT LIFE

In a cross-sectional study of clinic children, Grant [17] found age and sex trends in the psychiatric disorders present at each age-period which were similar to those reported by Macfarlane *et al.* [28] in their longitudinal study of normal children. Developmental disorders such as hyperkinesis, enuresis, speech disorders and sleep disturbances were most characteristic of early childhood. Tearfulness and jealousy were also common in young children, while shyness and fears reached their peak in middle childhood. In contrast, delinquency, sexual abnormalities and overt neurotic disorders were much more typical of later childhood and adolescence. Similar age and sex trends were apparent in a follow-up study of pre-school children with psychiatric disorder [53].

Warren [51] followed up 157 children for 6 or more years after they had been in-patients in the adolescent unit at Bethlem Royal Hospital. Children who were psychotic in adolescence had the worst outcome, and the neurotics (especially the neurotic girls) had the best prognosis. However, one in six neurotics still required in-patient treatment at follow-up. Two fifths of the children with conduct disorders continued to exhibit serious antisocial behaviour in adult life. On the whole the disorders shown during the follow-up period were similar to those at the time of admission, but a few children diagnosed as neurotic later became psychotic.

The relationship between psychosis in adult life and psychiatric disorder in childhood was also considered by Anthony and Scott [9] in relation to a case study of manic-depressive psychosis with an onset at age 12 years. A review of the literature showed the rarity of manic-depressive psychosis before puberty and it was concluded that although depression and anxiety were common in childhood, depressive psychosis was rare and mania even rarer. Nevertheless, the question of what behavioural and emotional characteristics in childhood are shown by persons later to develop manic-depressive psychosis remained unresolved.

This question of associations between disorders in childhood and in adult life was considered by Pritchard and Graham [29] in their investigation of 75 patients who attended both the child and adult departments of The Maudsley Hospital. Most of the childhood neurotics exhibited depression, anxiety or some other neurotic disorder in adult life. However, in some the main problem, when adult, was an immature or inadequate personality and a few became schizophrenic. The delinquent children who returned to The Maudsley Hospital when adult usually showed continuing antisocial characteristics. Children with conduct disorders who were not taken to Court in childhood also usually had deviant personalities when adult but the disorder of personality was as likely to show itself in general inadequacy as in antisocial behaviour. Very few of the group studied had either a schizophrenic or a manic-depressive psychosis and the childhood problems of these groups are now being examined by Graham and Pritchard in relation to a larger number of patients.

INFANTILE PSYCHOSIS

The question of the link between child and adult psychiatric disorders also arose in relation to infantile psychosis, which has sometimes been considered to be the first manifestation of schizophrenia. Anthony [4] stressed the need to relate the onset of psychosis in infancy to the process of development rather than to view the disorder in terms of adult disease. He divided psychotic disorders into those beginning in early infancy, those in which massive regression occurred between 3 and 5 years of age, and those beginning in middle and later childhood which were associated with minimal regression.

Study of some 100 cases of child psychosis led Anthony [4] to reject the somatic-psychological dichotomy in relation to aetiology, as multiple causation appeared to be so common. Attitudes and behaviour of the parents of the psychotic children were examined by means of a Shoben type questionnaire, the Rorschach test [11] and the Fels scales [13]. Some differences were found between the parents of children thought to have an organically determined psychosis and parents of children with psychosis apparently due to environmental factors, but the differences were very slight and the findings did *not* support the view that the parents were 'psychotogenic' [5].

Noting that many of the children had been investigated for deafness, and that there was visual avoidance and auditory imperception, Anthony [5] postulated the existence of a psychotic 'sensory barrier'. He found that psychotics showed no startle response to a single loud sound and in marked contrast to a group of neurotic controls they showed no preparatory set after the first experience. Whether the 'barrier' was psychological or physiological in nature remained uncertain.

These issues were considered further by Rutter [31, 34, 35, 36, 37, 45, 47] in relation to a 5–15-year follow-up study of the psychotic children in Anthony's group who had had an early onset of psychosis. Each of the 63 psychotic children in the study was individually matched with another child of the same sex, attending the same psychiatric department at about the same time and with the same age and measured intelligence.

By comparison of the behaviours shown by the psychotic and control children, both initially and when older, it was shown that the following items were those most characteristic of psychosis:

1. Autism (as shown by aloofness, apparent lack of interest in people, avoidance of eye to eye gaze, little variation in facial expression, and a relative absence of warmth, sympathy or empathy).
2. A marked lack of response to sounds in early childhood (so that often the child appeared deaf).
3. Retardation of speech development (half never acquired speech).
4. Echolalia (present in three-quarters of those who spoke).
5. Pronominal reversal (usually as part of an echolalia).
6. Severe ritualistic and compulsive phenomena (including abnormal attachments to objects, morbid preoccupations, a resistance to change, and other obsessive phenomena).
7. Non-distractibility.
8. A tendency to self-injury (especially wrist-biting and head-banging, and
9. Stereotyped repetitive movements consisting of either complicated whole body movements (not including rocking) or hand and finger mannerisms.

It was notable that all of these items occurred in at least a few control children so that no single symptom could be said to be pathognomonic of psychosis.

The psychotics' pattern of scores on the Wechsler scales showed that they were defective in language as well as in speech production [34]. Their scores were very low on performance tests (such as picture arrangement) which did not require the use of speech but which did require some use of verbal concepts, such as symbolization or sequential logic. Their scores on performance sub-tests which required neither speech nor verbal concepts (e.g. block design) were much higher. Furthermore, this pattern of scores significantly differentiated those children *within* the psychotic group who had continuing speech handicaps. These differences were large; for example, in the speech-retarded group the mean weighted score on picture arrangement was 1·69 whereas on block design it was 8·15. Other features suggested that this defect in inner language was often (at least in early childhood) accompanied by an inability to comprehend sounds—of a type similar to that found in developmental speech disorders involving receptive difficulties. That the language disorder was a primary handicap rather than a secondary consequence was also suggested by the importance of language development in relation to prognosis [35, 45], and by the finding that some children ceased to be autistic during the follow-up period but none the less remained without speech [31].

Although none of the children had shown abnormalities on neurological examination when they first attended The Maudsley Hospital, evidence became available during the follow-up period (especially by the development of fits at adolescence which occurred in 16 per cent. of the psychotic children) to suggest the likelihood of 'brain damage' in 18 of the 63 children [45].

Although sometimes it has been thought that infantile psychosis is an early manifestation of schizophrenia the follow-up findings suggested that this is a mistaken view [8, 37]. The two conditions differ in the rate of schizophrenia in relatives (low in infantile psychosis), in the occupational level of the parents (high in infantile psychosis), in pattern of cognitive functioning, and in the course of the condition (hallucinations and delusions rarely develop in the child with infantile psychosis).

Although most of the psychotic children reached only a very limited level of social adjustment by the time they reached late adolescence (14 per cent. had a good adjustment, 25 per cent.—fair, and 60 per cent.—poor or very poor), a sizeable proportion had made considerable educational progress [36]. A quarter were reading at the 8-year level or better; this was as many as in the control group, although neither group was reading as well as expected on the basis of its age and intelligence.

Four factors were shown to be of prognostic value in terms of later social adjustment: I.Q., speech, severity of disorder, and schooling [45]. The I.Q. (even in the mute or in those under 5 years of age) proved to be highly stable and also a very good predictor of intellectual functioning and social adjustment in late adolescence [35]. The disorder in children untestable on any I.Q. test or with an I.Q. below 60 had an almost uniformly poor outcome, however it was measured. Children with a profound lack of response to sounds or without useful speech at 5 years often achieved a fair level of adjustment but never a good one. Those who did well usually had a less severe disorder from the outset. They were also differentiated in terms of the amount of schooling they had received. This last issue is now being considered further in a prospective study of the effects of different forms of special educational treatment for children with infantile psychosis.

OTHER CLINICAL STUDIES

The value of these clinical studies often lay in the way findings suggested better ways of classifying the disorders which had been investigated; for example, the different mechanisms involved in 'continuous' and 'discontinuous' encopresis, the differentiation of nightmares and night-terrors from somnambulism in terms of perceptual variables, and the distinction between infantile psychosis and schizophrenia. Diagnostic issues were also important in Hersov's study of persistent non-attendance at school [18]. He demonstrated clear differences between the syndromes of 'school refusal' and of 'truancy'. School refusal, in which the child stayed away from school with the parents' knowledge, was usually part of a psychoneurotic condition in which fear of separation from the parents was often a prominent factor in aetiology. In contrast, truancy, in which the child concealed his frequent absences from school, was usually part of a delinquent pattern.

A study of peptic ulcer in adults [30] showed the importance of psychiatric factors in relation to short-term prognosis, but it was also concluded that the influence of these factors on somatic disease may be seen in most illnesses, not just in a restricted group of so-called 'psychosomatic' disorders. This issue has recently been taken further by Graham in relation to asthma in childhood [16]. He found that psychiatric factors were important in this condition but they were as important in cases where there was a heavy allergic or genetic loading as in those where there was not. It was suggested that a dichotomy between asthma of 'psychogenic' origin and asthma of 'organic' origin was misleading.

CLASSIFICATION

Lewis' comment that the standing of psychiatry has been 'darkly overcast by those psychiatrists who belittle diagnosis as futile labelling' [27] applies with particular force to the history of child psychiatry. However, in recent years psychiatrists have increasingly recognized the need for a classification, 'not (as) the discovery of a fixed pattern of ordained forms, but (as) a convenient, arbitrarily determined grouping according to common attibutes, for purposes of identification and as a basis for induction' [23]. Much of the dispute over classification has been concerned with theoretical or philosophical differences but there are research findings which are relevant; some of these have been mentioned in connexion with the account of clinical studies, others were reviewed by Rutter [32]. He argued that classification in no way implied the existence of disease entities; the child is a developing organism and it was also essential that classification take this into account. Maturation sometimes caused the same abnormality to manifest itself in different ways at different ages. For example, it was shown that children severely *over*active in early childhood often became *under*active in adolescence [45]. Rutter suggested that three principles were important: (1) the classification should be based on facts rather than concepts and it should be defined in operational terms; (2) it should convey information relevant to the clinical situation and should have predictive value; and (3) it should classify disorders, *not* children. Children might have one sort of psychiatric disorder at one age and another sort at another age.

Research findings were reviewed in relation to symptom clusters and factor analysis, response to treatment, long-term prognosis, aetiology, epidemiology, age and sex trends, and the severity and duration of disorders. More recently findings in relation to educational retardation [49] and child psychosis [37] have also been considered. An outline which might form the basis of an acceptable classification was suggested.

FAMILY STUDIES

Lewis [24] has urged the '. . . need to study the family, not only from the psychoanalytical and psychological standpoint but also to discover how mental illness impinges upon it, and what effects this sort of incapacity has on the family structure'. It was in response to his stimulus that a series of investigations into these questions were initiated.

First, there was a study [33] of illnesses and death among the parents of the 922 children who first attended The Maudsley Hospital during the course of a 2 year period. Children attending dental and paediatric clinics comprised the two main control groups which were closely matched with the Maudsley group for age and for social class.

One in five of the Maudsley children had a parent who had been or still was under psychiatric care or who had attempted or committed suicide—a rate three times that in the matched control groups. Referral biases were unlikely to be relevant as a similar difference in the rate of parental mental disorder was found *within* the Maudsley group, i.e. between those children with neurotic or behavioural disorders and those with some condition (such as mental subnormality or epilepsy) which was *un*associated with any disorder of behaviour.

It was found that parental psychopathy or personality disorder was especially likely to be associated with psychiatric disorder in the children, but in keeping with other studies, schizophrenia was not. Nevertheless, the diagnosis of the parental mental disorder was not necessarily the relevant feature in relation to the effects on the children. The various types of parental illness differed in three other variables which may have been more important with respect to the development of disorder in the children: (1) the frequency with which mental illness occurred in *both* parents; (2) breakdown of the marriage; and (3) admission to hospital.

In nearly a third of the Maudsley children, *both* parents had been mentally ill, whereas in a control group of adult psychiatric patients who were also parents, this occurred in only 1 in 30 cases. Thus, the risk to the child appeared to be particularly great when both parents had psychiatric disorder. However, in this study as in others, most of the spouses of the schizophrenics were mentally healthy. In contrast, when the diagnosis was neurosis or personality disorder, psychiatric disability was often present in both parents. There was also an association between disruption of the parental marriage and psychiatric disorder in the children, and again marital breakdown was much commoner when the diagnosis was psychopathy or neurosis than when it was schizophrenia. The important factor might not be the type of parental illness but rather the presence or absence of a spouse who is healthy and able to cope with the children. The third factor, admission to hospital, also differentiated the groups. At the time of the study (early and mid 1950s) schizophrenics were still being admitted to hospitals where they often remained for many years. As more schizophrenics are being treated in the community, sometimes with a considerable strain on family relationships [52], the risk to their children may now be greater.

Perhaps the most striking feature of illnesses in the parents of children attending The Maudsley Hospital was the high frequency with which symptoms of the parental illness directly involved the child, often with hostile feelings, either overt or covert. Formal diagnosis or symptomatology was less important in relation to the risk of psychiatric disorder in the children.

The incidence of parental *physical* illnesses was also examined [33] and it was found that chronic or recurrent illnesses—that is to say, illnesses which had produced substantial disability and which had lasted intermittently or continuously for at least 1 year—were twice as common among the Maudsley parents as in any of the control groups. There was no increase in the rate of acute physical illnesses among the parents.

There was a higher rate of parental deaths in the Maudsley group than in the control groups but the numbers were rather small and a more reliable comparison was made directly with the expected rate calculated from the Registrar General's figures, making a separate calculation for each year during the child's lifetime according to the parents' age, sex, and marital status in that year [33]. The observed number of deaths of fathers and mothers was more than double the expected figure; paternal and maternal deaths were equally associated with psychiatric disorder in the child. The death could not be considered in isolation for it preceded and succeeded many changes; over a third took place after a chronic and incapacitating illness and several were due to suicide or took place in the context of a mental illness. Furthermore, in some cases the spouse's bereavement reaction was so severe or so prolonged that psychiatric treatment was necessitated. It might be that the parental distress before dying and the grief of the surviving parent were sometimes as important to the child as the death itself.

The temporal aspects of the association between bereavement and the onset of psychiatric disorder in the child were also important. Children bereaved between 2 and 5 years of age were most likely to develop psychiatric disorder. Nevertheless in most cases the onset of symptoms was considerably delayed—often until early adolescence. Factors consequent upon the death (grief of the spouse, family poverty and loneliness, parental remarriage, etc.) might have been more important than the stress of the event of death itself.

Neither parental death nor parental illness was associated with a specific behavioural syndrome in the children, but like other children attending psychiatric clinics about two-thirds exhibited socially disapproved behaviour (although only a minority had been before the Courts). The lack of specificity in the type of disorder associated with parental death or parental illness was particularly striking in view of the marked differences between neurotic and antisocial disorders in relation to other factors—such as family background, sex of child, and educational retardation [32, 42, 49]. It may be that illness or death of a parent acts as a non-specific stress, increasing the likelihood that the child will show deviant behaviour, but that the characteristics of the child himself determine what form the disorder takes. Alternatively, the changes in family life and relationships associated with the parental illness, but not specific to any one diagnostic type, may be the relevant factors in relation to the form of disorder shown by the child.

Although psychiatric disorder in the child was equally associated with illness or death in the mother or in the father, the sex of the dead or ill parent was important in another connexion. When mental illness occurred in the *mother* or when the mother died, there was a particular association with psychiatric disorders in the *daughter*, rather than the son. It was thought that parental illness and death might be influential through those aspects of affectional and disciplinary relationships which are to some extent determined by the sex of the parent or it might be that behaviour culturally appropriate to the child's sex relies heavily upon an adequate parental model.

The possible mechanism of the relationship between illness in the parent and psychiatric disorder in the child was considered in terms of possible genetic and environmental factors [33]. A number of children had both a natural parent and a step-parent and when comparable situations were examined, mental illness was found to occur in the step-parent nearly as often as in the natural parent. This suggested that those genetic influences important in the parental disorder were not the major factor in relation to the child's disorder. In addition, there was considerable cirumstantial evidence suggesting the importance of non-genetic influences in the association between illnesses in parents and their children. Genetic factors could scarcely be invoked to account for the relationship between parental physical illness and disorder in the child, and the effects of physical and mental illnesses were similar in many respects. The lack of relationship between the type of parental disorder and the type of disorder in the child argued against a genetic link, as did the very heterogeneity of child disorders. The sex link between the ill parent and the deviant child also suggested an environmental effect (a genetic explanation is less likely in the absence of evidence suggesting a recessive gene and in view of the fact that parental illness was associated with an increased risk of disorder for both boys and girls). Environmental influences were also suggested by the finding that direct involvement of the child in the symptoms of the parental illness was more important than the form the parental disorder took. Other studies have suggested that genetic factors play a part in the development of child psychiatric disorder, but although certainly important in other respects, they did not appear to account for the association between parental illness and disorder in the child. It was concluded that the effect of parental illness on the child's behavioural development was probably through the impact of illness on family life and relationships and that prospective studies of families in which one parent was ill were required to determine this. Before such studies could be initiated it was necessary to develop adequate measures of family interaction and family pathology.

THE MEASUREMENT OF FAMILY LIFE AND RELATIONSHIPS

A review of the literature showed that many of the published measures of the family lacked satisfactory reliability and validity. Between 1962 and 1965 new measures were developed and given preliminary testing [12, 41]. A basic distinction was made between actual events or activities (e.g. the number of quarrels within a specified period, how much the husband assisted the wife with household tasks or child care, etc.) and feelings or attitudes about these events (e.g. warmth or hostility to the spouse, dissatisfaction with various aspects of the marital relationship, etc.). An interview designed to measure both types of variables was developed. By the use of a particular kind of flexible and detailed questioning about recent events an attempt was made to free the measurement of events and activities from attitudinal bases. The method used had much in common with the technique described by Hoffman [19] and also that used in the study of temperament [40, 50]. On the other hand, a different approach was used for the measurement of emotions. By the use of tape recordings and group discussions [41], interviewers were trained to recognize differences in tone of voice as shown in the speed, pitch and intensity of speech.

A methodological study was carried out in 1965 with 30 families in all of which there were children of school age or younger and in which one parent had newly attended a psychiatric facility [12, 41]. For each family there was an interview with the spouse, with the patient, and with the patient and spouse together. The emotional scales were shown to be highly reliable and by the comparison of ratings made at different interviews it was shown that similar feelings were expressed about the spouse in different situations, suggesting that ratings were valid as well as reliable. The measurement of most family events and activities was also found to be reliable and, more important, good agreement was found between the accounts of husbands and wives when interviewed separately. However, it was found that, compared with the other marriage partner, dissatisfied spouses showed some tendency to underestimate the other's participation in the home. There was also a slight trend suggesting that patients sometimes gave a more negative picture of the marriage than did their spouses. These influences were shown to have important implications for methodology in relation to family studies, but it was possible to modify the methods used so that these biases were kept to a minimal level.

RESEARCH INTO THE DIAGNOSTIC PROCESS

Before proceeding with a prospective study of patients and their families it was also necessary to develop adequate measures of psychiatric state in children. Lewis [25] has emphasized the weakness of depending on symptom scores in field studies and a particular effort was made to develop satisfactory measures of diagnosis.

Screening questionnaires for completion by teachers [38] and by parents [48] were devised and shown to be reliable and valid. For more intensive studies, diagnostic interviews with children [42] and with parents [15] were developed. The reliability of the parental interview was tested primarily by interviewing 36 mothers twice, with a different interviewer on each occasion and an interval of 1–4 weeks between interviews. Over-all judgements concerning the presence or absence of psychiatric disorder and concerning the diagnosis were found to be reliable when based on systematic questioning of the mothers in these two independent interviews, but mothers' spontaneous complaints about their children were not reliable. Mothers' complaints differed very considerably between the two interviews. Also, *many* parents who said at the beginning of the interview that their child had no problems, when asked specific questions later, went on to describe manifestly abnormal behaviour. The converse was also true; some parents said their child was a severe problem but on closer questioning it became clear that the child was essentially normal—it was the parents' concept of how children should behave that was deviant. It was concluded that the history-taking procedure had to include detailed questioning on *all* kinds of emotional and behaviour problems, not just those of which the parent complained. However, even after systematic questioning, there were certain areas of the child's behaviour on which most mothers could not give reliable information. They knew very little of their child's activities and relationships with other children and mothers' accounts of their child's interpersonal relationships also proved to be rather unreliable. There were some interesting differences between parents and teachers in the kinds of complaints they made about their children [14]. For example, with 10- and 11-year-old children much the commonest single complaint from mothers concerned temper tantrums—an item scarcely ever present in teachers' complaints.

The reliability of the interview with the child was tested in a similar fashion; one series of children was seen together by two psychiatrists who rated the children independently and without discussion at the end of the interview, and another series seen separately by the same two psychiatrists with an interval of 1–4 weeks between interviews [43]. Validity was tested by comparing the findings at interview with other measures and by comparing the interview findings concerning a general population sample (seen 'blind') with those of a group of psychiatrically abnormal children (as judged from information from parents and school). These, too, were seen 'blind'. Although the over-all ratings based on this diagnostic interview with the child were both reliable and valid, certain more specific items of behaviour were less reliable (e.g. muscular tension) or less useful as indicators of psychopathology, (e.g. habitual mannerisms). It was also possible to examine some inferences involved in the diagnostic process. For example, it was shown that, contrary to most views, fidgetiness was not a valid indicator of anxiety—indeed it was actually commoner among anti-social children than among neurotic children.

THE EFFECTS OF PARENTAL MENTAL ILLNESS ON THE CHILDREN

The earlier study of illnesses among the parents of children attending a psychiatric clinic showed that there was a significant relationship between mental illness and psychiatric disorder in the children, and the findings suggested that the mechanism involved lay in the impact of parental mental illness on family life and relationships. Using the measures developed during the methodological studies described above, a prospective study of families containing a mentally ill parent was started in 1966. Using the Camberwell Psychiatric Register [p. 26] a virtually complete population-based sample has been obtained of newly referred patients who are parents of children aged less than 15 years. Analysis of data on the first 50 families confirmed the original hypothesis that there would be an excess of psychiatric disorder in the children. A high rate of marriage breakdown in relation to psychiatric disorder was also found—26 per cent. of the patients were not living with their marriage partner and in a further 18 per cent. the marital situation was characterized by gross open discord. These families will be studied over the course of several years to determine how and in what circumstances mental illness in a parent adversely influences the behavioural development of the children. Particular attention is being paid to those factors in the child which may modify the impact of the parental disorder. Over the last two years Graham has extended the earlier studies of children's temperamental characteristics [40, 50] to produce improved measures of temperament which have been shown to have satisfactory reliability and which are being used with children aged 3–8 years in the longitudinal study of families of mentally ill parents.

EPIDEMIOLOGICAL STUDIES

In order that the findings from the family studies should be seen in proper perspective it was necessary to examine the distribution of deviant behaviour among children in the general population and also to study child psychiatric disorder in relation to those biological and educational variables which could not be included in the family studies. It was partly in order to fill these gaps that epidemiological studies of school age children were undertaken on the Isle of Wight by Rutter and Graham in collaboration with Professor Tizard, Dr. Pless, and Mr. Yule of the Institute of Education and Dr. Whitmore of the Department of Education and Science. Excluding educational disorders, mental subnormality, and some monosymptomatic disorders such as enuresis, a minimum prevalence rate of 6·3 per cent. was obtained for psychiatric disorder among 10- and 11-year-old children. The rate for severe psychiatric disorder was 2·2 per cent. but only a third of these severely handicapped children were under psychiatric care. Neurotic disorders were about equally common in boys and girls but antisocial disorders were much commoner in boys [42, 48].

Information was obtained from parents and teachers on the behaviour of the *total* population of children aged 10 and 11 years on the Isle of Wight (some 2,300 in all). It was found that even in those without psychiatric disorder there was a high frequency of individual behaviour sometimes thought to indicate psychopathology; for example, 8 per cent. of boys still wet their beds occasionally, 30 per cent. were reported by their mothers as worrying and over 30 per cent. bit their nails [48]. Thus, it was seen that *isolated* difficulties occurred in nearly all children at some time or other and could not be taken as necessarily indicating any significant psychiatric problem. It was also found that some behaviours commonly thought to indicate psychopathology (e.g. nail biting) were quite *un*-related to psychiatric disorder as evidenced in other ways.

A strong association was found between antisocial behaviour and educational difficulties [49]. A third of the children with an antisocial disorder were reading at a level *at least* 28 months below that expected on the basis of their age and intelligence (compared with a rate of about 4 per cent. in the general population). Similarly a third of the total number of severely backward readers in the general population also exhibited psychiatric disorder. Severe reading retardation was found to be associated with a strong family history of reading difficulties (and to a lesser extent speech difficulties). It was also associated with developmental or 'constitutional' factors in the child associated with handicaps in language, motor and perceptual functioning. These developmental handicaps were just as common in the antisocial backward readers as in those without psychiatric disability and it seemed unlikely that the difficulties in reading were often directly emotional in origin.

Neurological disorders were also examined in relation to psychiatric conditions in childhood [44]. A distinction was made between syndromes of brain dysfunction involving definite *abnormalities* of function (such as spasticity or paralysis) and those involving only limits or *delays in the development* of normal functions (e.g. delayed speech development or poor co-ordination) [39, 44]. Both groups were found to be associated with a considerably increased rate of psychiatric disorder but apart from an excess of certain rare conditions (such as psychosis and the hyperkinetic syndrome) the types of psychiatric disorder were similar to those found in children without organic brain dysfunction. It seemed probable, therefore, that the behaviour difficulties did not arise directly from damage to the brain but rather through rendering the child more susceptible to stresses at home and at school.

Although the importance of interrelationships between developmental handicaps, neurological disorders, psychiatric disorders and educational retardation has been demonstrated, the mechanisms which are involved remain ill-understood. Some aspects of this problem are being examined in the family studies already described, other aspects are being considered as part of prospective and epidemiological studies of both younger and older children. The implications for services for handicapped children are also being studied [see Chapter 3].

REFERENCES

1. ANTHONY, E. J. (1956) The significance of Jean Piaget for child psychiatry, *Brit. J. med. Psychol.*, **29**, 20–34.
2. ANTHONY, E. J. (1957) Symposium on the contribution of current theories to an understanding of child development, IV. The system markers: Piaget and Freud, *Brit. J. med. Psychol.*, **30**, 255–69.
3. ANTHONY, E. J. (1957) An experimental approach to the psychopathology of childhood: encopresis, *Brit. J. med. Psychol.*, **30**, 146–75.
4. ANTHONY, E. J. (1958) An aetiological approach to the diagnosis of psychosis in childhood, *Rev. Psychiat. Infant.*, **25**, 89–96.
5. ANTHONY, E. J. (1958) An experimental approach to the psychopathology of childhood: autism, *Brit. J. med. Psychol.*, **31**, 211–25.
6. ANTHONY, E. J. (1959) An experimental approach to the psychopathology of childhood: sleep disturbances, *Brit. J. med. Psychol.*, **32**, 19–37.
7. ANTHONY, E. J. (1960) An experimental approach to the psychopathology of childhood: micropsia. *Psychiat. Res. Rep. Amer. psychiat. Ass.*, **13**, 63–99.
8. ANTHONY, E. J. (1862) Low grade psychosis in childhood, in Proc. London Conf. Scient. Stud. Ment. Def., ed. Richards, B. W., **2**, May and Baker, Ltd.
9. ANTHONY, J., and SCOTT, P. (1960) Manic-depressive psychosis in childhood, *J. Child Psychol.*, **1**, 53–72.
10. ARIÈS, P. (1962) *Centuries of Childhood*, trans. Baldick, R., London.
11. BENE, E. M. (1958) A Rorschach investigation into the mothers of autistic children, *Brit. J. med. Psychol.*, **31**, 226–7.
12. BROWN, G. W., and RUTTER, M. (1966) The measurement of family activities and relationships: a methodological study, *Hum. Rel.*, **19**, 241–63.

13. DONNELLY, E. M. (1960) The quantitative analysis of parent behaviour toward psychotic children and their siblings, *Genet. Psychol. Monogr.*, **62**, 331–76.
14. GRAHAM, P. (1967) Perceiving disturbed children, *Spec. Educ.*, **56**, 29–33.
15. GRAHAM, P. J., and RUTTER, M. (1968) The reliability and validity of the psychiatric assessmentof the child, II–Interview with the parent, *Brit. J. Psychiat.* [in press].
16. GRAHAM, P. J., RUTTER, M. L., YULE, W., and PLESS, I. B. (1967) Childhood asthma: A psychosomatic disorder? Some epidemiological considerations, *Brit. J. prev. soc. Med.*, **21**, 78–85.
17. GRANT, Q. A. F. R. (1958) Age and sex trends in the symptomatology of disturbed children, Dissertation for the Academic Diploma in Psychological Medicine, The University of London.
18. HERSOV, L. A. (1960) Persistent non-attendance at school, *J. Child Psychol.*, **1**, 130–6.
19. HOFFMAN, M. L. (1960) Power assertion by the parent and its impact on the child, *Child Develop.*, **31**, 129–43.
20. KANNER, L. (1943) Autistic disturbances of affective contact, *Nerv. Child*, **2**, 217–50.
21. KANNER, L. (1959) Trends in child psychiatry, *J. ment. Sci.*, **105**, 581–93.
22. LEVY, D. (1943) *Maternal Overprotection*, New York.
23. LEWIS, A. (1952) *Congrès Mondial de Psychiatrie, 1950,* Comptes Rendus, II. Psychiatrie Clinique, Paris.
24. LEWIS, A. (1956) Social psychiatry, in *Lectures on the Scientific Basis of Medicine*, VI, 1956–57, London.
25. LEWIS, A. (1961) Current field studies in mental disorders in Britain, in *Comparative Epidemiology of the Mental Disorders*, ed. Hoch, P. H., and Zubin, J., New York.
26. LEWIS, A. (1963) Symposium: training for child psychiatry, *J. Child Psychol.*, **4**, 75–84.
27. LEWIS, A. (1963) Medicine and affections of the mind, *Brit. med. J.*, ii, 1549–57.
28. MACFARLANE, J. W., ALLEN, L., and HONZIK, M. P. (1954) *A Developmental Study of the Behaviour Problems of Normal Children Between 2½ and 14 Years*, Berkeley, Calif.
29. PRITCHARD, M., and GRAHAM, P. (1966) An investigation of a group of patients who have attended both the child and adult departments of the same psychiatric hospital, *Brit. J. Psychiat.*, **112**, 603–12.
30. RUTTER, M. (1963) Psychosocial factors in the short-term prognosis of physical disease: I. Peptic ulcer, *J. psychosom. Res.*, **7**, 45–60.
31. RUTTER, M. (1965) The influence of organic and emotional factors on the origins, nature and outcome of childhood psychosis, *Develop. med. Child Neurol.*, **7**, 71–83.
32. RUTTER, M. (1965) Classification and categorization in child psychiatry, *J. Child Psychol.*, **6**, 71–83.
33. RUTTER, M. (1966) *Children of Sick Parents: an Environmental and Psychiatric Study*, Maudsley Monographs, No. 16, London.

34. RUTTER, M. (1966) Behavioural and cognitive characteristics of a series of psychotic children, in *Childhood Autism: Clinical, Educational and Social Aspects*, ed. Wing, J. K., London.
35. RUTTER, M. (1966) Prognosis: psychotic children in adolescence and early adult life, in *Childhood Autism: Clinical, Educational, and Social Aspects*, ed. Wing, J. K., London.
36. RUTTER, M. (1967) Schooling and the 'autistic' child, *Spec. Educ.*, **56**, 19–24.
37. RUTTER, M. (1967) Psychotic disorders in early childhood, in *Recent Developments in Schizophrenia: A Symposium*, ed. Coppen, A. J., and Walk, A., London.
38. RUTTER, M. (1967) A children's behaviour questionnaire for completion by teachers: preliminary findings, *J. Child Psychol.*, **8**, 1–11.
39. RUTTER, M. (1967) 'Brain damage' in childhood, *New Educ.*, **3**, 10–13.
40. RUTTER, M., BIRCH, H. G., THOMAS, A., and CHESS, S. (1964) Temperamental characteristics in infancy and the later development of behavioural disorders, *Brit. J. Psychiat.*, **110**, 651–61.
41. RUTTER, M., and BROWN, G. W. (1966) The reliability and validity of measures of family life and relationships in families containing a psychiatric patient, *Soc. Psychiat.*, **1**, 38–53.
42. RUTTER, M., and GRAHAM, P. (1966) Psychiatric disorder in 10- and 11-year-old children, *Proc. roy. Soc. Med.*, **49**, 30–35.
43. RUTTER, M., and GRAHAM, P. J. (1968) *The Reliability and Validity of the Psychiatric Assessment of the Child, I. Interview with the Child, Brit. J. Psychiat.* [in press].
44. RUTTER, M., GRAHAM, P., and YULE, W. (1968) *Neuropsychiatric Disorders in Childhood: A Study in a Small Community*, London [in press].
45. RUTTER, M., GREENFELD, D., and LOCKYER, L. (1967) A five- to fifteen-year follow-up of infantile psychosis, II. Social and behavioural outcome, *Brit. J. Psychiat.*, **113**, 1183–99.
46. RUTTER, M., KORN, S., and BIRCH, H. G. (1963) Genetic and environmental factors in the development of 'primary reaction patterns', *Brit. J. soc. clin. Psychol.*, **2**, 161–73.
47. RUTTER, M., and LOCKYER, L. (1967) A five- to fifteen-year follow-up of infantile psychosis, I. Description of sample, *Brit. J. Psychiat.*, **113**, 1169–82.
48. RUTTER, M., TIZARD, J., and WHITMORE, K., (eds) (1968) *Education, Health, and Behaviour*, London [in press].
49. RUTTER, M., YULE, W., TIZARD, J., and GRAHAM, P. (1967) Severe reading retardation: its relationship to maladjustment, epilepsy, and neurological disorders, Proc. Assoc. Spec. Educ. Int. Conf. London, 1966.
50. THOMAS, A., CHESS, S., BIRCH, H. G., HERTZIG, M., and KORN, S. (1963) *Behavioral Individuality in Early Childhood*, New York.
51. WARREN, W. (1965) A study of adolescent psychiatric in-patients and the outcome six or more years later, II. The follow-up study, *J. Child Psychol.*, **6**, 141–60.

52. WING, J. K., MONCK, E., BROWN, G. W., and CARSTAIRS, G. M. (1964) Morbidity in the community of schizophrenic patients discharged from London mental hospitals in 1959, *Brit. J. Psychiat.*, **110**, 10–21.

53. WOLFF, S. (1961) Symptomatology and outcome of pre-school children with behaviour disorders attending a child guidance clinic, *J. Child Psychol.*, **2**, 269–76.

9

Psychiatric Genetics

JAMES SHIELDS

MOST of the work done in the Department of Psychiatry on the subject of genetics has come, understandably enough, from the Unit which Dr. Eliot Slater directs. Its association with the Institute began in November 1949. On the expiry of a grant from the Medical Research Council to complete his large twin study, interrupted by the war, Dr. Slater and the writer were taken on to the academic staff of the Department to continue work along genetic lines; they were joined in 1957 by Dr. Valerie Cowie. In October 1959 we became a Medical Research Council Unit, but still remained attached alongside the Institute to the Teaching Hospital.

Psychiatrists in the Department other than those working in the Genetics Unit have, of course, also made contributions to psychiatric genetics; and conversely the work of the Unit may at times have strayed from a narrowly defined genetic field. This chapter will first mention briefly some of the publications from outside the Unit, of which those of Sir Aubrey Lewis are notable examples.

STUDIES MADE OUTSIDE THE GENETICS UNIT

In 1956 Lewis [52] read a paper at the First International Congress of Human Genetics in Copenhagen on the offspring of parents both mentally ill. His subject was one which it is as difficult as it is important to investigate. As long ago as 1932–3 he had succeeded in collecting information about the children of forty such couples where both parents had a non-organic psychosis. He was characteristically diffident about presenting his results: the war had made a follow-up impossible; information may have been less than complete; diagnosis, much of it from nineteenth century records, could not always be certain; and there were the difficulties of analysing a numerically small material. Nevertheless, his series 'was of a respectable size, on the whole', when set alongside those of others. Twenty-three of their 153 children, or about 1 in 5 of the total at risk, were known to have been psychotic. Thirty-nine had other psychiatric abnormalities. With some qualification, the illnesses of parents and child tended to fall into the same broad category. Some of the other affections could have been related to the psychosis in the parents. In the nine families where the illnesses of both parents were typical the risk for similar illness in the children was higher.

In his 1958 Galton Lecture, Lewis [53] again chose a genetic topic, the fertility of the mentally ill. He covered his subject from an historical aspect and discussed what was known of fertility in the commonest psychiatric conditions. He believed the occurrence of fresh mutations to be the most likely explanation of why schizophrenia remained as prevalent as ever, despite the lowered fertility of those who suffer from it. In the following year he discussed in more detail the problem as it related to the families of manic-depressives, concluding that up to the present 'there is still room for doubt as to whether we here have any striking quantitative departures to account for' [54].

The scope and variety of the numerous studies relevant to genetics made by other workers in the Department illustrate many of the methods used in clinical genetics. Pedigrees of rare or interesting combinations of disorders were made by Johnson [40], Shepherd [69], and Wheelan [108]. Single cases of twins were investigated by Wheelan [107] with a view to exploring the reasons for discordance and by Benaim [1] who studied their response to drugs. Normal twins or siblings were compared in studies of normal reaction patterns by Rutter *et al.* [68] and of anxiety by Lader and Wing [48]. Leigh and Marley [50] made a family study of asthma. The maternal age of psychiatric patients was examined by Goodman [30] and Granville-Grossman [34, 35]. As new laboratory techniques became available biochemical studies were made in Huntington's chorea by Kenyon and Hardy [45] and in phenylketonuria by Pare *et al.* [59]; and the nuclear or chromosomal sex of male homosexuals was studied, with negative results, by Pare [58] and Pritchard [63]. In the course of epidemiological studies Hare [37] gathered data on resemblances between relatives.

THE GENETICS UNIT

For convenience the work of the Unit may be divided into: (1) studies of normal twins; (2) studies based on the Maudsley Twin Register; (3) genetic investigations in adult psychiatry, other than twin studies; (4) genetic investigations in mental subnormality along organic lines; and (5) other miscellaneous studies.

If the following account is devoted in greater part to the first two or three of these topics, the reason is not simply the writer's greater familiarity with them but also the fact that they represent the part of the work of the Unit with which the Institute has, since 1959, been most directly concerned; for throughout this period the writer has remained a lecturer in the Department of Psychiatry, seconded to work in the Medical Research Council Psychiatric Genetics Research Unit.

Presentation according to method rather than diagnosis or chronology has been preferred as, on the whole, being less disjointed. A central topic has, of course, been the problem of schizophrenia. This is dealt with first in the section on twins. Having answered in the positive the question of whether genetics is relevant in schizophrenia at all, the thread is immediately taken up again in the following section, which deals with homogeneity and the mode of inheritance of schizophrenia.

Essentially there are two kinds of information which one hopes to obtain through investigating twins. The classical twin method compares resemblance within genetically identical pairs with resemblance within fraternal pairs for evidence of the effects of hereditary differences. The historical method compares the life histories of identical twins in the hope of discovering something about the effects of environment. Two studies made on groups of normal twins serve as an illustration of the method.

Studies of Normal Twins

Schoolchildren. In 1953 an investigation was made by Shields [70], in parallel with one done in the Psychology Department, of the personalities and behaviour of 62 same-sexed 12–15-year-old twin pairs from the ordinary London County Council secondary schools. The results are not unlike those of other twin studies. There was not much difficulty in showing that identical pairs tended to be more alike than fraternals. This was not so much because the genetically identical pairs were strikingly similar in behaviour; many differed in important ways. It was rather the relatively marked differences not infrequently observed in fraternal pairs, despite the similar family environment, that led to the contrast between the groups. Genetic factors seemed to have a closer bearing on basic temperamental traits, and on the type of reaction in the case of behaviour disturbances, than they did on the presence or severity of disturbance. The latter was more dependent on the common family environment. As for differences between identical twins, these could often be related, directly or indirectly, to factors such as an initial difference in birth weight or to differences in the social relationships within the pair.

Ten years later these twins were followed up (Harrison and Shields, unpublished). It did not appear that the fact of being a twin had handicapped them in any way. For instance, from the number and distribution of married twins there was no suggestion that the fact of being one of identical twins had held them back from marriage. Nor had any social or psychological problems arising from twinship led to either kind of twins having, as a group, a raised neuroticism or lowered extraversion score. Within pairs, identicals of both sexes were more alike than fraternals in respect of extraversion, a tendency which has been found in most twin studies. As for neuroticism, it was only in female pairs that identicals could be shown to be more alike than fraternals in this sample.

Twins Brought up Apart. Conclusions as to the importance of heredity derived from twin studies become open to question if there are grounds for suspecting that the external environments of identical twins are more alike than those of fraternals in features relevant to the character in question. For instance, a tendency for mothers to treat identical twins more alike than fraternals might be considered, at least in part, to account for any greater personality resemblance that might be observed. Likewise, the tendency for identical twins to go about together or to identify with one another might contribute largely to their resemblance. From the retrospective accounts obtained in the 1953 study it seemed unlikely that these factors were of primary importance. Many parents and twins looked for special differentiating features in identical twins. There was no apparent tendency for those who were most closely attached to be the ones who were the most alike in personality. However, the best test would be provided by pairs of identical twins brought up by different mothers and with little or no opportunity to identify. If subtle parent-child and inter-twin relationships are all-important, identical twins brought up apart, but in otherwise similar environments, should be no more alike than fraternal twins brought up together. Twins brought up apart, especially those in whom there has been a considerable difference in background, can, of course, also provide a unique opportunity of observing the effects of environment. It was therefore a stroke of luck when, thanks largely to an appeal on a B.B.C. Television programme, Shields [71] was able to investigate 44 pairs of identical twins brought up apart, more than twice the size of the largest series to have been studied hitherto. These twins were compared with a matched group of 44 pairs of identical twins brought up together, obtained from the same source, and with 32 same-sexed fraternal pairs. The subjects were mostly normal adults. Life histories, interviews with the twins, intelligence tests and personality questionnaires were used. The extent of environmental differences found in the twins brought up apart varied from pair to pair. One twin was brought up by a doctor in South America, her sister by a psychopathic ship's carpenter in a Scandinavian country. More typical were pairs in which one twin was brought up by a grandmother as an only child, the other by the mother along with other sibs but under poorer circumstances.

On the intelligence and personality tests there was no clear difference in resemblance between identical twins brought up apart and those brought up together. Resemblance was significantly greater than zero in both groups in all tests, and fraternal pairs were consistently less alike. Thus the tests were sufficient to reveal the influence of heredity but failed to show the effects of early environment. Similarities between identical twins, including those reared apart, were also noted in a variety of personal characteristics, ranging from voice and mannerisms to smoking habits. Twins separated in the first few months could not be shown to be less alike than those separated later on in childhood. Some pairs remained alike despite quite considerable differences in environment. Among those most alike in personality was a pair, separated at 16 months and adopted into different families, who had not met until the day they were investigated at the age of 36. In another pair, obtained through The Maudsley Hospital, one twin was brought up in a half-Chinese home in Limehouse, the other being adopted by a self-employed builder in a middle-class suburb. They displayed similar problems of intelligence and behaviour and both eventually became schizophrenic. The study thus showed that family environments could vary quite a lot without obscuring the basic similarity in a pair of genetically identical twins.

Environmental effects were, of course, not lacking. A global rating of personality resemblance by the investigator suggested that the twins brought up apart were less alike than the control group, as one would expect; and there was an association between poorness of psychological environment and later mental health record. Associations were also found between extraversion and the age of the mother who brought up the twin, between neuroticism and social class, and between intelligence and age at menarche. Differences between twins brought up together were sometimes attributable to one twin taking the lead in childhood.

It may be surprising that identical twins brought up together differ as much as they do. Various reasons suggest themselves as to why a clearer difference was not found between pairs brought up apart and brought up together. One reason is the tendency, already alluded to, for the social proximity of identical twins to act as a differentiating factor, leading to a division of role. Another possibility is that in some pairs the effects of early family environment were obscured by physical factors and the influence of the later environment. It can also be pointed out that not many extreme differences in background were observed; nevertheless, differences in regard to family structure and the ages and personalities of the parents who took the twins were generally considerable. A further possibility is that there may well be considerable interaction between environment and genotype, the effect of a given environment differing according to the genetic constitution. It was hoped that any bias that may have arisen through having to rely on volunteers was controlled by studying twins brought up together from the same source. A later study of Danish identical twins brought up apart [41], obtained mostly from a register of all twins born, confirms the observation of considerable resemblance in personality in many such pairs, a resemblance sometimes extending to surprising details.

Perhaps the main lesson to be drawn from studies of separated twins is that personality resemblance between identical twins is not merely due to their having been treated alike by the same mother or to their having influenced one another.

The Maudsley Twin Register and Studies Based on it

The first two years' work under the Institute was devoted in part to analysing and preparing for publication the findings of Slater's [82] recently completed study of twins based on 295 index cases from the pre-war London County Council mental hospitals and their families. Notable features of the report were the presentation of case histories and the detailed analysis of clinical features and the previous histories of the twins. Rather than elaborate further on this widely cited investigation, it will be more appropriate here to describe in greater detail some of the more recent twin research.

Meanwhile, work started in 1950 on the register of Maudsley Hospital twins. It has long been realized that twin studies, if they are to avoid biased selection, should be based on a total sample of twins within a defined population. In 1948 the practice instituted by Slater before the war was reintroduced, whereby every patient admitted to any department of the Joint Hospital was routinely asked whether he was born one of twins. The Unit is fortunate in being able to compile a register of all such cases. At present (August 1967) the register consists of 590 cases with same-sexed twin partners surviving at least till the age of 15 (or 5 for Children's Department patients), including 21 cases of twins systematically ascertained at Belmont Hospital, 1950–53. Many pairs are studied at the time of admission. From time to time particular clinical groups are selected for follow-up and special investigation. These are described below. A point worth noting is that the proportion of patients who are twins, and the relative proportion of identical and fraternal twins among them, are close to what one would expect from the general population in the United Kingdom. There is thus no evidence that twins as such, or identical twins in particular, are especially liable to suffer from psychiatric disorders of the kind treated in the Maudsley.

The accuracy of twin studies depends in large part on the correctness with which pairs are classified as identical or fraternal. The result of blood grouping only rarely contradicts the opinion previously reached as to zygosity on the basis of outward appearances. Special studies have been made from time to time of the best application of fingerprinting to zygosity determination [56, 82, 87, 100]. Of these it would appear that Slater's method of 1963 gives the best combination of simplicity and accuracy.

Affective Illnesses in Twins. The first group of twins to be reported in any detail was that of 60 cases on the register by the end of 1956 who were considered by da Fonseca [28, 29] to have suffered from an endogenous affective disorder. Without any correction for age, 75 per cent. of the 21 identical co-twins and 37·5 per cent. of the 39 fraternal co-twins were likewise considered to have had an affective disorder. Restricting concordance to cover only hospitalized cases, the rates were 60 per cent. and 31 per cent. respectively. Da Fonseca thought the findings supported previous theories of a dominant gene with reduced manifestation. In his 1963 paper he developed the idea that in some relatives the same hereditary predisposition which resulted in a recurrent affective disorder in the index case could manifest itself in relatives in the form of recurrent attacks of rheumatism, asthma, peptic ulceration or certain dermatoses.

Hysteria in Twins. Negative findings as regards concordance can be as revealing as positive ones. In the 1960 Maudsley Lecture, Slater [85] described his investigation of all twins on the register who, up to the end of 1958, had received a formal diagnosis of hysteria at The Maudsley Hospital. Field work on these twins had been done by Miss M. Malherbe and the present writer. There were 12 identical and 12 fraternal pairs. The most striking finding was that no single co-twin of the index cases had ever received a psychiatric diagnosis of hysteria, though 5 identical and 4 fraternal co-twins were abnormal in other ways. The suggestion arose that the aetiology of hysteria, unlike that of schizophrenia, does not depend to any great extent on specific genetic factors. One of the 'hysterics' turned out to have a schizophrenic illness (and a schizophrenic twin), 5 were regarded as suffering from affective illnesses and 1 died of a temporal lobe abscess, while others were probable or possible epileptics suffering from atypical fits. A number were considered as having had anxiety states. While the diagnosis of a symptom as hysterical was usually reliable, the identification of an illness as hysterical was much more dubious. These conclusions were confirmed [91] in a study of cases diagnosed 'hysteria' in a neurological hospital.

Neurosis and Personality Disorder in Twins. The twins diagnosed as 'Hysteria, 311' form part of the larger series of all those admitted by the end of 1958 who at some time had received an official hospital diagnosis other than psychosis or organic disorder. There were 192 such cases, 80 from identical and 112 from fraternal pairs. Since diagnoses were made by many different consultants and follow-up information was obtained, in some cases up to 14 years later, it will come as no surprise that the final diagnosis sometimes turned out to be other than one of neurosis or personality disorder. In order to ensure some measure of diagnostic consistency and at the same time to avoid a contamination of diagnosis by knowledge of the clinical state of the other twin and the zygosity of the pair, summaries were prepared by one author (J.S.) [78], for each twin separately, and diagnosed by the other author (E.S.) according to the *International Classification of Diseases*. Seventy-eight index cases were finally diagnosed as neurosis, 68 as personality disorder and 46 as endogenous depression (25), schizophrenia (13) or organic disorder (8).

Identical pairs in which the index case was regarded as having had an anxiety state or a personality disorder were more often concordant than those in which the index case had another neurosis (mostly cases of reactive depression). As in many other twin studies, such as that of the twin schoolchildren mentioned above, the qualitative similarities in identical twins show themselves to be genetically influenced to a greater extent than the presence of disturbance. Taking as the criterion of concordance the simple presence of a psychiatric diagnosis in the co-twin, 50 per cent. of identical and 29 per cent. of fraternal pairs proved to be concordant. Evidence of the importance of genetic factors is not very striking, since half the identical co-twins are within normal limits; and identical pairs are only 1·7 times as often concordant as fraternal pairs. The contrast between the two kinds of twin, and hence the presumptive operation of biological causes, was much greater when account was taken of the nature of the psychiatric disorder in the co-twin and not just its presence. It can be seen from TABLE 3 (previously unpublished) that the identical: fraternal concordance ratio increased as an attempt was made to make diagnosis more precise. There was no clear sex difference in concordance rate. This part of the twin study may perhaps be regarded as an application of the nosological twin method, in which resemblance in twins is used as an aid in the most meaningful classification of disorders. It appears to show that, even in the field of the neuroses and personality disorders, psychiatric diagnosis still has some biological meaning in a wide sense.

Parker [60, 61, 62] examined 21 neurotic and personality-disordered twins who came to the Maudsley between 1959 and 1961. He considered that formal psychiatric diagnosis was too unreliable and superficial for it to be of much value in assessing similarities and differences in his material. He was impressed by the fact that, as in previous series from the Unit, there was no tendency for the twins who appeared to have identified most closely to be alike in morbidity. There was no tendency for females to be more alike than males. His neurotic series did, however, show a tendency for female identical twins to be unmarried. In one of his papers Parker [60] reports on three pairs, discordant in respect of sexual deviation. One of these was an identical male pair in which only one twin was homosexual. A difference from an early age in the attitude taken to the twins by their

TABLE 3

DIAGNOSTIC SIMILARITY AMONG TWINS ACCORDING TO SPECIFICITY (MAUDSLEY NEUROTIC SERIES, INDEPENDENT DIAGNOSIS)

	IDENTICAL TWINS	SAME-SEXED FRATERNAL TWINS	I:F RATIO
NO. OF PAIRS OF TWINS	80 (100%)	112 (100%)	
Diagnostic resemblance:			
Any coded psychiatric abnormality in co-twin	40 (50·0%)	33 (29·5%)	1·7
Both twins Neurosis or Personality disorder (310–326); *or* both psychiatric disorder outside 310–326	30 (37·5%)	16 (14·3%)	2·6
Both twins Psychosis (30 . . .), both Neurosis (31 . . .) or both Personality disorder (32 . . .)	25 (31·3%)	10 (8·9%)	3·5
Both twins same diagnostic code (whole number)	23 (28·8%)	4 (3·6%)	8·1
Both twins same diagnostic code (smallest subdivision used)	20 (25·0%)	3 (2·7%)	9·3

mother, who had wanted one of them to be a girl, may have contributed to their very different behaviour. Since the publication of Parker's paper, 3 more cases of male homosexuality in identical twins have entered the series [39]. One pair is discordant, like Parker's case, the other two concordant. One of the latter comes from a large sibship in which there were three sets of male identical twins; in two sets both twins were homosexual, in the third both heterosexual.

Slater [89] has reviewed the genetic basis of neurosis, preferring a pluridimensional theory, with polygenic inheritance, to the simpler bi-dimensional view of personality adopted by Eysenck. The findings in twin research support the view of a genetic contribution to the neuroses, and family studies have shown an increased incidence in relatives of similar affections, especially anxiety states and obsessional disorders (e.g. Lewis, [51]). However, the psychometric study of Coppen, Cowie, and Slater [3] failed to produce findings capable of interpretation along genetic lines. The M.P.I. was given to 266 neurotic patients from Belmont Hospital and 735 of their relatives. Pairs of spouses were significantly alike in neuroticism. There were no significant correlations between female patients and their first degree relatives. The largest correlations were between the mothers of male patients and their children.

Twins from the Children's Department of The Maudsley Hospital. Over the period 1948–58, 53 twins from 40 pairs attended the Maudsley Children's Department. They were followed for an average of 7 years (Shields, unpublished). Many different criteria were used to assess concordance in respect of behaviour disorder, and according to most of them the identical pairs were about twice as often both affected as the same-sexed fraternal pairs. The contrast between resemblance in identical and fraternal pairs was greatest where dull intelligence was part of the presenting problem. It was least when it was a question of aggressive or delinquent behaviour in boys, indicating that genetic factors play relatively little part in predisposing towards juvenile delinquency.

Schizophrenia in Twins. We now come to the problem of the genetics of schizophrenia. Most of the index cases in Slater's twin study of 1953 were schizophrenics. In that investigation the best estimates of the risk of schizophrenia for the identical and fraternal co-twins of a schizophrenic were considered to be 76 per cent. and 14 per cent. respectively; and from this it was concluded that 'genetical causes provide a potentiality for schizophrenia, perhaps an essential one, though environmental factors play a substantial role which may be decisive in the individual case.'

In 1963 the time was ripe to look again at schizophrenia in twins. The concordance rates reported in the earlier studies, such as those of Slater [82] and Kallmann [44], had recently been suspected of being misleadingly high. According to Rosenthal [65, 66], this was largely because these studies had mostly been based on chronic hospital cases who might tend to be the more genetically determined ones and on samples with an over-representation of females who were thought to have a higher concordance rate than males. Methods of ascertaining twinship might have led to discordant pairs being missed, and bias, due for example to a knowledge of zygosity, might have entered into the diagnosis of schizophrenia. Further, two recent studies from Scandinavian countries [46, 102] reported low or zero concordance in male identical twins. Some of the problems raised by the older and more recent series of schizophrenic twins have been discussed by members of the Unit [32, 73, 75].

After 16 years of ascertaining twins from a psychiatric population of about 45,000, the Maudsley Twin Register had accumulated enough cases of schizophrenia to provide a series which meets most of the criticisms of earlier work. It was based on consecutive admissions to a short-stay hospital and out-patient department where twinship had been inquired about systematically on admission. Gottesman and Shields [31] investigated 57 pairs on the register where one or both twins had received a psychiatrist's diagnosis of schizophrenia at the Maudsley or since discharge. The sexes were equally represented. In 10 out of 24 (42 per cent.) identical pairs and in 3 out of 33 (9 per cent.) fraternal pairs both twins had been diagnosed as schizophrenic by a psychiatrist. There was no marked sex difference in this respect. These uncorrected concordance rates are comparable with those obtained by Kringlen [47] in his second Norwegian study and in a population-based Danish investigation [27]. The expectation of schizophrenia in a member of the general population is about 1 per cent. It was concluded that 'genetic factors are largely responsible for the specific nature of most of the schizophrenias'.

An interesting association was noted in the Maudsley study between severity of schizophrenia in the index case and frequency of schizophrenia in the identical co-twin, as predicted by Rosenthal. Assessing severity by total length of hospitalization or by outcome on follow-up, the concordance rate for 'severe' cases was comparable to the uncorrected rates reported by Kallmann and Slater, while only about 20 per cent. of the twins of 'mild' schizophrenics were affected. Similar differences were obtained using independent 'blind' diagnoses made on the twins by Slater. Illnesses in concordant pairs tended to be hebephrenic or catatonic, those in discordant pairs to be atypical or doubtful schizophrenias.

One possible explanation of the findings relating to severity and concordance is along genetic lines. If we assume that several genes contribute to the schizophrenic diathesis it might be thought that the more such genes a person carried the more severe would be his illness and at the same time the more likely it would be that his identical twin would break down. An attempt to estimate how much the liability to schizophrenia is determined polygenically has been made by Gottesman and Shields [33], applying the method of Falconer; the resulting estimate was around 86 per cent.

By comparing the histories of the twins it is hoped to learn something of the predisposing and precipitating environmental causes of schizophrenic breakdown. However, it does not appear that such factors as being underweight at birth or a submissive twin or brought up by an overprotective or even irrational mother are sufficient to produce a schizophrenic psychosis in a person who does not possess a specifically predisposing genetic constitution. The index cases, their twins and their parents have, when possible, been tested psychologically in an attempt to identify schizotypic signs.

Genetic Investigations in Adult Psychiatry, other than Twin Studies

The Mode of Inheritance and Possible Heterogeneity of Schizophrenia. From the combined evidence of twin and family investigations, there seems to be little doubt of the importance of genetic factors in the aetiology of schizophrenia. One of the main tasks of psychiatric genetics is to shed further light on the so far unsolved problems of the mode of inheritance, the possibility of genetic heterogeneity and the genetic relation of schizophrenia to other disorders. These problems have received attention over the years.

Investigations of special classes of person have suggested aetiological heterogeneity: 'there might well be a large number of different genotypes in schizophrenia ... Some forms might not be genetical at all' [81]. Thus, pairs of mentally ill relatives, consisting of maternal uncle and nephew, revealed an excess of pairs of paranoid illnesses associated with mental deficiency; the suggestion was that sex-linked recessive genes might play a part in some illnesses called schizophrenic, though the evidence was admittedly slender [80]. Patients whose parents were cousins [57, 76], were more often schizophrenics than patients in a series of controls; a tentative conclusion was that one-sixth of the totality of schizophrenia might be accounted for by an autosomal recessive gene. In families of patients in whom schizophrenia was associated with epilepsy there was no raised incidence of schizophrenia, suggesting that a proportion of cases of schizophrenia might have an organic, non-genetic aetiology [95]. Schizophrenics of a sexually-deviant body-build revealed no anomalies of nuclear sex [16], which suggests that cases such as the one described by Slater and Zilkha [99] are rare.

A view of schizophrenia as a heterogeneous collection of disorders is an unsatisfactory one, however, if most of the evidence can be accounted for more economically. Schizophreniform psychoses, unrelated to 'true' schizophrenia, are probably rare [90], and it could yet be that most schizophrenias are genetically similar. In his monogenic theory of schizophrenia of 1958 Slater [83] showed that the then most widely accepted figures for the incidence of schizophrenia in the sibs of schizophrenics, in the children of one and of two schizophrenics, in the children of cousins and in the general population were consistent with the view that nearly all schizophrenias could be accounted for by a gene which manifests itself in all homozygotes (or double gene carriers) and in a proportion of heterozygotes (or single gene carriers).

Other models besides the monogenic one can also be put forward to explain most schizophrenias as biologically related. One such theory, mentioned earlier, is polygenic inheritance with a threshold effect, though this theory is often difficult to distinguish from the monogenic model, a point which Slater [93] has discussed. On the other hand, the so-called monogenic theory could be regarded as a special class of polygenic theory. The hypothetical gene, though necessary for the development of schizophrenia, is far from sufficient if, as required by the monogenic theory, most schizophrenics are heterozygotes and manifestation occurs in only 26 per cent. of heterozygotes. The big difference in incidence in identical and fraternal twins of schizophrenics suggests that many other genes, in addition to the major gene and environmental factors, affect the manifestation, perhaps with varying degrees of specificity. The genetics of schizophrenia has recently been reviewed by members of the Unit [74, 79].

Resemblances between affected relatives may cut across diagnostic boundaries. With a view to discovering what was inherited in mental illnesses, Tsuang [104] compared pairs of sibs both treated in a psychiatric hospital. A significant resemblance in diagnosis, though not a striking one, was found. From the information available from medical notes, schizophrenic and affective illnesses occurred together in sibs more often than could be accounted for by independent monogenic inheritance of each disorder. The possibility arose from Tsuang's observations that schizophrenia and affective disorders may each be largely polygenic on separate dimensions but with some overlap. There was not sufficient resemblance within families to suggest that schizophrenia could be split up into a large number of distinct genetic entities.

The relationship of schizophrenia and other psychoses to neuroses was investigated by Cowie [7] who examined over 300 offspring of Maudsley-diagnosed psychotics by means of the M.P.I., a Teachers' Rating Form and psychiatric history. Though neurotic disturbances when they occurred in the children tended to be associated with the onset of parental psychosis, there was no evidence in this study of an over-all increase in neuroticism among the children, compared with that found in the children in a control series. These findings supported the hypothesis that psychoses and neuroses were genetically distinct.

Heston [38], on the other hand, found more psychiatric disturbance of all kinds in the children of schizophrenics than in the children of non-psychotic mothers. The principal interest of Heston's study, however, was the fact that his experimental subjects were 47 children born to schizophrenic mothers but brought up apart from them. They were compared with a matched group of children with similar foster-home experiences but whose mothers were not psychotic. Five of the children of schizophrenics themselves had schizophrenia (age-corrected morbidity risk 16·6 per cent.), a rate as high as is generally found in the children of schizophrenics brought up in their parental home. There were no schizophrenics among the children of the control group.

Identification of Carriers in Huntington's Chorea. In 1952 Leese, Pond, and Shields [49] investigated the family of a Maudsley patient with Huntington's chorea in which a number of other abnormalities also occurred. Linkage data were collected. Electroencephalograms of 21 family members were recorded. Three or possibly four so far unaffected sibs had a low-voltage fast rhythm, such as is frequently found in the disease. The suggestion arose that this EEG abnormality might represent preclinical signs of the condition. Four years later one of these sibs had developed the disease and one of her daughters, whose EEG was previously normal, now had a low-voltage fast record.

The next Huntington's chorea family to be reported [21] by the Unit came to notice in an unexpected way. In the course of a screening test for phenylketonuria among inmates of Remand Homes, the Phenystix test gave an apparently false positive. The boy in question was found not to be phenylketonuric, but both he and a brother had a raised serum alanine level and their mother had Huntington's chorea. It was thought there might be a connexion between the serum alanine level and the gene for Huntington's chorea. Following on this suggestion, investigation of serum proteins was made [17] in 14 cases of Huntington's chorea in the hope that biochemical changes might be found that antedated the disease and so could be useful in the identification of carriers. A significant increase of gamma globulin was observed in the Huntington patients compared with matched controls.

Effect of Birth-order in Psychiatric Illness. Deviations from expectation in respect of place in sibship or in age of parent at birth suggest profitable fields for further exploration, whether along genetic or environmental lines. For instance, a genetic explanation for an increased parental age might be chromosomal changes (as in mongolism) or fresh mutation (as in achondroplasia). Slater [86] found that 389 male homosexuals from The Maudsley Hospital came significantly late in the birth order, and mean maternal age at birth lay between that of the general population and that of mongols. If chromosomal abnormalities play an aetiological role in at least some cases of homosexuality, which is one possible explanation, their nature has yet to be identified. In this paper Slater introduced a useful and simple method for expressing in the form of a ratio a person's ordinal position in a sibship.

Tsuang [103] has made a detailed study of maternal age and birth order for 1,435 Maudsley patients of all diagnoses, using more than one method. The only significant birth order effects were in male alcoholics (who tended to come late in the sibship) and female immature personalities (who tended to come early).

Genetic Investigations in Mental Subnormality along Organic Lines

Advances in techniques in the past decade have encouraged developments on these lines. Work done in the Medical Research Council Genetics Unit in this field has been expanding increasingly since Dr. Cowie's appointment, the establishment of a cytological laboratory for chromosome analysis and the many fruitful contacts that have been made with paediatricians, biologists, and hospitals for the subnormal. Since the results of these developments are less directly concerned with the Department of Psychiatry than the work described in this chapter so far, they will be referred to in less detail.

Papers describing work on phenylketonuria carried out by Cowie at the Fountain Hospital or Galton Laboratory were published while she was working in the Institute or Unit [5, 14, 20, 64]. More recently a wide variety of work has been done on different aspects of mental subnormality and genetics [6, 9, 19, 24, 26, 42, 43]. The main effort has, however, been concentrated on mongolism.

A number of studies have been made of the health and reproductive histories of the mothers of mongols. Positive findings might throw light on the origins of the chromosomal abnormality. While abnormalities of thyroid function [15] or of an increased output of male steroid [101] were not confirmed, the mothers of mongols did, however, have a high abortion rate [2]; and mothers with previous abortions, and those who had borne a mongol at a relatively early age, were found to have a body-build deviating in a masculine direction. One possible explanation of the finding was a raised incidence among the younger mothers of a balanced chromosomal translocation [67]. Investigation of the family of a case of translocation mongolism and analysis of others known at the time [36] showed a tendency for an inherited chromosomal translocation to be associated with mongolism only when transmitted by the female.

The problem of the excess of abortions produced by mothers of mongols was looked at again when Cowie and Slater [23] analysed a large material of case reports provided by Hanhart. It was thought that some of the excess might be accounted for by monosomic gametes produced by women who also produced trisomic mongols.

Papers have also appeared on the age at which a diagnosis of mongolism is made [111], a topic relevant to the calculation of the incidence of the disorder, and on the cerebellar and brain-stem weight and its possible relationship to muscular hypotonia in mongolism [25]. Mention may be made of studies published from the Unit [105, 106], which showed that mongolism in Formosa has many clinical, familial and chromosomal characteristics in common with mongolism in the West.

The major project on mongolism has been a longitudinal, population-based survey of all mongols born in a defined area of Surrey and South London between December 1963 and January 1965. Studies based on institutional cases may not be representative of the variety of the condition by reason of increased early mortality. Special investigation has been made of the chromosomes and dermatoglyphics of the mongols and their parents, of morbidity and mortality, and of neurological findings and the results of tests of childhood development at successive ages.

Some results relating to mortality and cytological findings have been reported [11]. Twelve out of 65 cytologically-examined cases in the survey died within the first 10 months. Sixty-two were apparently trisomic, while 3 were translocation mongols. Of the latter, two died. The third, who survived, was unusual, having a B/C or B/X translocation, also carried by the mother, together with trisomy-G. This case was closer to the normal neurologically than any other in the series. The question of whether the balanced translocation conferred a biological advantage therefore arose. Alternatively, as only blood cultures could be done, the possibility of mosaicism could not be ruled out.

One of the three translocation cases could be interpreted as having extra F rather than extra G chromosomal material and a small deletion in a G chromosome [18]: the father carried a reciprocal F/G translocation. This finding of Cowie and Kahn suggested that the chromosomal variations in mongolism might be more complex than at first appeared. Points of similarity between mongolism and other congenital abnormalities have been discussed [10]. Further evidence of possible aetiological complexity comes from the provisional results from the Unit's laboratory in 85 families where a mongol child and a parent have been investigated cytologically. Chromosome breakages and rearrangements have been shown in about a third of both fathers and mothers. Clearly the hypothesis requires confirmation.

In work with mental subnormality and congenital malformations, the problem frequently arises of the best way to advise parents who are concerned about the risk for any subsequent children [8]. There is sometimes a difference of opinion as to when to tell parents that their child is abnormal. In the course of the mongolism survey, it appeared that most parents prefer to be told early [12].

Other Miscellaneous Studies

Over the course of the years various general accounts of psychiatric genetics have been published by members of the Unit [e.g. 10, 22, 55, 77].

Some of Slater's contributions to areas bordering on psychiatric genetics may be mentioned—his study with Moya Woodside [98] of working-class marriages and the evidence it provided of possible assortative mating for neurotic personality; his personality study of Galton [84] the pioneer of modern human genetics; and his pathographic studies [94, 96, 97] of men of genius. A study of the German composers gave support to the hypothesis that cyclothymic traits of personality are unusually abundant in such persons, but the majority are psychiatrically normal. In a contribution to Manfred Bleuler's *Festschrift* [88] he demonstrated a distinctive colour imagery in individual English poets, conceivably resting on a genetic basis.

It was indicated early on that the work of the Unit has not always been confined strictly to psychiatric genetics. When Cowie planned her study of neurosis in the children of pychotics, it was intended to make a parallel study of psychosis and other psychiatric abnormality in the families of delinquents. Though a genetic study of a delinquent population proved to be impracticable, valuable information could be obtained about the backgrounds and later histories of 318 consecutive admissions to the Magdalen Classifying School for delinquent girls. Some of the factors regarded as of aetiological significance in male juvenile delinquency showed their effects in even more striking degree in these girls [4].

FUTURE RESEARCH

It is surprising that so few studies have been made comparing patients with their first degree relatives, and especially with their healthy same-sexed sibs. One such study is at present being carried out in the Unit by Price on patients in Bethlem and their relatives with a view to investigating constitutional factors associated with a predisposition to mental illnesses of different kinds. Measurements are made of physique (with special attention to ectomorphy and androgyny), and information gathered on biographical data and premorbid personality. Personality inventories are given so that the scores of the relatives of patients of different diagnoses can be compared.

In the short-term future, those attached to the Institute who are interested in the wide field of psychiatric genetics are finding no shortage of suitable material, whether from the Joint Hospitals for twin and sibship studies or from the subnormality and paediatric hospitals which have been providing the most promising cases for cytological work. But wherever one looks, one can see hopeful lines of expansion, both extensive and intensive. On the twin side, the time may have come for a new look at affective illnesses, incorporating an investigation of the electrolyte balance. On the chromosomal side, much basic scientific investigation calls out to be done, while on the practical level, facilities in the Unit for growing skin cultures would be welcome.

More generally, collaborative studies would seem to be called for with those interested in sociology, psychopathology, psychometry and biochemistry. A healthy development would be the setting of genetic work in a sound epidemiological context. The population-based mongolism survey was a step in this direction; and there is always scope for the systematic study of morbidity in the close families of a representative or clearly defined sample of the psychiatric population.

Even in large, densely populated areas the number of certain special classes of case that can be investigated at a given time remains small. With a growing interest in genetics itself and in twin studies as a means of testing environmental hypotheses, there is an increasing desire for international co-operation and exchange of information [109, 110]; and the Unit has been collaborating with the World Health Organization in this regard [72, 92]. Some workers are interested in comparing data on twins discordant for schizophrenia. Others have suggested carrying out parallel studies of congenital malformations in different countries.

To say whether or not, or how soon, there will be a major breakthrough in our knowledge of the genetic aspects of the commoner psychiatric disorders, and in what area it is most likely to occur, would be to make a prediction which may well be based more upon the innate temperament and the professional environment of the individual who is rash enough to make it, than on the available evidence. Whether by reason of his training in the Department of Psychiatry or not, the writer would sooner not hazard a guess. But he does express the hope and belief that some of the careful work in genetics carried out at the Institute of Psychiatry over the past 17 years and more will prove a source of scientific progress.

REFERENCES

1. Benaim, S. (1960) The specificity of reserpine in the treatment of schizophrenia in identical twins, *J. Neurol. Neurosurg. Psychiat.*, **23**, 170–5.
2. Coppen, A. J., and Cowie, V. A. (1960) Maternal health and mongolism, *Brit. med. J.*, i, 1843–7.
3. Coppen, A. J., Cowie, V. A., and Slater, E. (1965) Familial aspects of 'neuroticism' and 'extraversion', *Brit. J. Psychiat.*, **111**, 70–83.
4. Cowie, J., Cowie, V. A., and Slater, E. *Delinquency in Girls*, London [in press].
5. Cowie, V. A. (1951) An atypical case of phenylketonuria, *Lancet*, i, 272.
6. Cowie, V. A. (1960) The genetics and sub-classification of microcephaly, *J. ment. Defic. Res.*, **4**, 42–47.
7. Cowie, V. A. (1961) The incidence of neurosis in the children of psychotics, *Acta psychiat.* (*Kbh.*), **37**, 37–87.
8. Cowie, V. A. (1963) Genetic counselling and the changing background of medical genetics, pp. 371–6, Proc. 2nd internat. Cong. congen. Malformns., at New York, 15–19 July 1963, Internat. Med. Cong., New York.
9. Cowie, V. A. (1964) Survey of a mentally subnormal sample taking congenital cardiac defects as an index lesion, pp. 754–7, Proc. internat. Copenhagen Congr. on the Scientific Study of Mental Retardation, Denmark, 7–14 Aug. 1964.
10. Cowie, V. A. (1965) Genetical aspects of child psychiatry, in *Modern Perspectives in Child Psychiatry*, ed. Howells, J., Edinburgh.
11. Cowie, V. A., (1966) Chromosomal findings in a population-based sample of mongols, Proc. internat. Seminar on Medical Genetics, University of Alabama Medical Center, September 1966, *Ala. J. Med. Sci.*, **3**, 493–5.
12. Cowie, V. A. (1966) Genetic counselling, *Proc. roy. Soc. Med.*, **59**, 149–50.
13. Cowie, V. A. (1966) Chromosomal aspects of mental subnormality, in *Genetic and Environmental Factors in Human Ability*, ed. Meade, J. E., and Parkes, A. S., pp. 163–72, Edinburgh.
14. Cowie, V. A., and Brandon, M. W. G. (1958) Follow-up note on an atypical case of phenylketonuria, *J. ment. Defic. Res.*, **2**, 55–58.
15. Cowie, V. A., and Coppen, A. J. (1959) Protein-bound iodine in phenylketonuria, *J. ment. Defic. Res.*, **3**, 94–95.
16. Cowie, V. A., Coppen, A. J., and Norman, P. (1960) Nuclear sex and body-build in schizophrenia, *Brit. med. J.*, ii, 431–3.
17. Cowie, V. A., and Gammack, D. B. (1966) Serum proteins in Huntington's chorea, *Brit. J. Psychiat.*, **112**, 723–6.
18. Cowie, V. A., and Kahn, J. (1965) A mongol child without trisomy G, *Lancet*, ii, 58–59.
19. Cowie, V. A., Kahn, J., and O'Reilly, J. N. (1965) Congenital abnormalities in a child with an apparently balanced karyotype carrying a reciprocal D/F translocation, *Lancet*, i, 1043–4.

20. COWIE, V. A., and PENROSE, L. S. (1951) Dilution of hair colour in phenylketonuria, *Ann. Eugen.* (*Lond.*), **15**, 297–301.
21. COWIE, V. A., and SEAKINS, J. W. T. (1962) Urinary alanine excretor in a Huntington's chorea family, *J. ment. Sci.*, **108**, 427–31.
22. COWIE, V. A., and SLATER, E. (1959) Psychiatric genetics, in *Recent Progress in Psychiatry*, Vol. III, ed. Fleming, G. W. T. H., pp. 1–53, London.
23. COWIE, V. A., and SLATER, E. (1963) Maternal age and miscarriage in the mothers of mongols, *Acta genet.* (*Basel*), **13**, 77–83.
24. CREAK, M., COWIE, V. A., *et. al.* (1961) Schizophrenic syndrome in childhood. Progress report of working party, April 1961, *Cerebr. Palsy Bull.*, **3**, 501–4.
25. CROME, L., COWIE, V. A., and SLATER, E. (1966) A statistical note on cerebellar and brain-stem weight in mongolism, *J. ment. Defic. Res.*, **10**, 69–72.
26. ERDOHAZI, M., COWIE, V. A., and LO, S. S. (1964) A case of haemophilia with Marfan's syndrome, *Brit. med. J.*, i, 102–3.
27. FISCHER, M. Schizophrenia in twins, Proc. 4th World Congr. Psychiat., Madrid, 1966 [in press].
28. FONSECA, A. F. da (1959) *Análise Heredo-clínica das Perturbaçoes Afectivas Atraves de 60 Pares de Gémeos*, Faculdade de Medicina, Oporto.
29. FONSECA, A. F. da (1963) Affective equivalents, *Brit. J. Psychiat.*, **109**, 464–9.
30. GOODMAN, N. (1957) Relation between maternal age at parturition and incidence of mental disorder in the offspring, *Brit. J. prev. soc. Med.*, **11**, 203–13.
31. GOTTESMAN, I. I., and SHIELDS, J. (1966) Schizophrenia in twins: 16 years' consecutive admissions to a psychiatric clinic, *Brit. J. Psychiat.*, **112**, 809–18.
32. GOTTESMAN, I. I., and SHIELDS, J. (1966) Contributions of twin studies to perspectives on schizophrenia, in *Progress in Experimental Personality Research*, Vol. 3, ed. Maher, B. A., pp. 1–84, New York.
33. GOTTESMAN, I. I., and SHIELDS, J. (1967) A polygenic theory of schizophrenia, *Proc. nat. Acad. Sci.*, **58**, 199–205.
34. GRANVILLE-GROSSMAN, K. L. (1966) Parental age and schizophrenia, *Brit. J. Psychiat.*, **112**, 899–905.
35. GRANVILLE-GROSSMAN, K. L. (1966) Birth order in schizophrenia, *Brit. J. Psychiat.*, **112**, 1119–26.
36. HAMERTON, J. L., COWIE, V. A., GIANNELLI, F., BRIGGS, S., and POLANI, P. E. (1961) Differential transmission of Down's syndrome (Mongolism) through male and female translocation carriers, *Lancet*, ii, 956–8.
37. HARE, E. H. (1965) A comparison of the health of fathers, mothers and children, *Brit. J. Psychiat.*, **111**, 467–71.
38. HESTON, L. L. (1966) Psychiatric disorders in foster home reared children of schizophrenic mothers, *Brit. J. Pyschiat.*, **112**, 819–25.

39. Heston, L. L., and Shields, J. Homosexuality in twins: a family study and a registry study, *Arch. gen. Psychiat.* [in press].

40. Johnson, J. (1961) Juvenile amaurotic idiocy, *J. ment. Sci.*, **107**, 931–5.

41. Juel-Nielsen, N. (1965) Individual and environment, *Acta psychiat.* (*Kbh.*), Suppl. 183.

42. Kahn, J., Ashwood-Smith, M. J., and Robinson, D. M. (1966) A cautionary note on the use of pronase in tissue culture, *Exp. Cell Res.*, **50**, 445–6.

43. Kahn, J., and Dernley, N. (1966) Chromatid behaviour during mitosis of human leucocytes, abstracts of contributed papers, p. 53, 3rd Internat. Congr. hum. Genet., Chicago, Sept. 1966.

44. Kallmann, F. J. (1946) The genetic theory of schizophrenia: an analysis of 691 schizophrenic twin index families, *Amer. J. Psychiat.*, **103**, 309–22.

45. Kenyon, F. E., and Hardy, S. M. (1963) A biochemical study of Huntington's chorea, *J. Neurol. Neurosurg. Psychiat.*, **26**, 123–6.

46. Kringlen, E. (1964) Schizophrenia in male monozygotic twins, *Acta psychiat.* (*Kbh.*), Suppl. 178.

47. Kringlen, E. (1966) Schizophrenia in twins, an epidemiological-clinical study, *Psychiatry*, **29**, 172–84.

48. Lader, M. H., and Wing, L. (1966) *Physiological Measures, Sedative Drugs, and Morbid Anxiety*, Maudsley Monographs, No. 14, London.

49. Leese, S. M., Pond, D. A. and Shields, J. (1952) A pedigree of Huntington's chorea, *Ann. Eugen.* (*Lond.*), **17**, 92–112.

50. Leigh, D., and Marley, E. (1967) *Bronchial Asthma, a Genetic, Population, and Psychiatric Study*, Oxford.

51. Lewis, A. J. (1935) Problems of obsessional illness, *Proc. roy. Soc. Med.*, **29**, 325–6.

52. Lewis, A. J. (1957) The offspring of parents both mentally ill, *Acta genet.* (*Basel*), **7**, 349–65.

53. Lewis, A. J. (1958) Fertility and mental illness, *Eugen. Rev.*, **50**, 91–106.

54. Lewis, A. J. (1959) Families with manic-depressive psychosis, *Eugen. Quart.*, **6**, 130–7.

55. Mayer-Gross, W., Slater, E., and Roth, M. *Clinical Psychiatry*, 3rd ed., London [in press].

56. Nixon, W. L. B. (1956) On the diagnosis of twin-pair ovularity and the use of dermatoglyphic data, in *Novant' Anni delle Leggi Mendeliane*, ed. Gedda, L., pp. 235–45, Rome.

57. Nixon, W. L. B., and Slater, E. (1958) A second investigation into the children of cousins, *Acta genet.* (*Basel*), **7**, 513–32.

58. Pare, C. M. B. (1956) Homosexuality and chromosomal sex, *J. psychosom. Res.*, **1**, 247–51.

59. Pare, C. M. B., Sandler, M., and Stacey, R. S. (1958) Decreased 5-hydroxytryptamine decarboxylase activity in phenylketonuria, *Lancet*, ii, 1099–101.

60. Parker, N. (1964) Homosexuality in twins: a report on three discordant pairs, *Brit. J. Psychiat.*, **110**, 489–95.
61. Parker, N. (1964) Close identification in twins discordant for obsessional neurosis, *Brit. J. Psychiat.*, **110**, 496–504.
62. Parker, N. (1964) Twins: a psychiatric study of a neurotic group, *Med. J. Aus.*, ii, 735–42.
63. Pritchard, M. (1962) Homosexuality and genetic sex, *J. ment. Sci.*, **108**, 616–23.
64. Renwick, J. H., Lawler, S. D., and Cowie, V. A. (1960) Phenylketonuria: a linkage study using phenylalanine tolerance tests, *Amer. J. hum. Genet.*, **12**, 287–322.
65. Rosenthal, D. (1961) Sex distribution and the severity of illness among samples of schizophrenic twins, *J. psychiat. Res.*, **1**, 26–36.
66. Rosenthal, D. (1962) Problems of sampling and diagnosis in the major twin studies of schizophrenia, *J. psychiat. Res.*, **1**, 116–34.
67. Rundle, A., Coppen, A. J., and Cowie, V. A. (1961) Steroid excretion in mothers of mongols, *Lancet*, ii, 846–8.
68. Rutter, M., Korn, S., and Birch, H. G. (1963) Genetic and environmental factors in the development of 'primary reaction patterns', *Brit. J. soc. clin. Psychol.*, **2**, 161–73.
69. Shepherd, M. (1955) Report of a family suffering from Friedreich's disease, peroneal muscular atrophy and schizophrenia, *J. Neurol. Neurosurg. Psychiat.*, **18**, 297–304.
70. Shields, J. (1954) Personality differences and neurotic traits in normal twin school children, *Eugen. Rev.*, **45**, 213–45.
71. Shields, J. (1962) *Monozygotic Twins, Brought up Apart and Brought up Together*, London.
72. Shields, J. (1965) Findings and applications of the twin method in psychology and psychiatry. Working paper, World Health Organization Meeting of Investigators on Methodology of Twin Studies, Geneva.
73. Shields, J. (1965) Review of 'Psychiatric Illnesses in Identical Twins' by Pekka Tienari, *Brit. J. Psychiat.*, **111**, 777–81.
74. Shields, J. (1967) The genetics of schizophrenia in historical context, in *Recent Developments in Schizophrenia*, ed. Coppen, A. J., and Walk, A., *Brit. J. Psychiat*, Spec.Publ. No. 1, pp. 25–41, Ashford, Kent.
75. Shields, J., Gottesman, I. I., and Slater, E. (1967) Kallmann's 1946 schizophrenic twin study in the light of fresh data, *Acta psychiat.* (*Kbh.*) [in press].
76. Shields, J., and Slater, E. (1956) An investigation into the children of cousins, *Acta genet.* (*Basel*), **6**, 60–79.
77. Shields, J., and Slater, E. (1960) Heredity and psychological abnormality in *Handbook of Abnormal Psychology*, ed. Eysenck, H. J., pp. 298–343, London.
78. Shields, J., and Slater, E. (1966) La similarité du diagnostic chez les jumeaux et le problème de la spécificité biologique dans les névroses et les troubles de la personnalité, *Évolut. psychiat.*, **31**, 441–51.

79. SHIELDS, J., and SLATER, E. (1967) Genetic aspects of schizophrenia, *Hosp. Med.*, **1**, 579–84.
80. SLATER, E. (1953) Sex-linked recessives in mental illness?, *Acta genet.* (*Basel*), **4**, 273–80.
81. SLATER, E. (1953) Psychiatry, in *Clinical Genetics*, ed. Sorsby, A., pp. 323–49, London.
82. SLATER, E. (with the assistance of Shields, J.) (1953) Psychotic and neurotic illnesses in twins, *Spec. Rep. Ser. med. Res. Coun.* (*Lond.*), 278, London, H.M.S.O.
83. SLATER, E. (1958) The monogenic theory of schizophrenia, *Acta genet.* (*Basel*), **8**, 50–56.
84. SLATER, E. (1960) Galton's heritage, *Eugen. Rev.*, **52**, 91–103.
85. SLATER, E. (1961) The thirty-fifth Maudsley lecture: 'Hysteria 311', *J. ment. Sci.*, **107**, 359–81.
86. SLATER, E. (1962) Birth order and maternal age of homosexuals, *Lancet*, i, 69–71.
87. SLATER, E. (1963) Diagnosis of zygosity by fingerprints, *Acta psychiat.* (*Kbh.*), **39**, 78–84.
88. SLATER, E. (1963) The colour imagery of poets, *Schweiz. Arch. Neurol. Neurochir. Psychiat.*, **9**, 303–8.
89. SLATER, E. (1964) Genetical factors in neurosis, *Brit. J. Psychol.*, **55**, 265–9.
90. SLATER, E. (1964) Review of Faergeman's *Psychogenic Psychoses* and Labhardt's *Die schizophrenieähnlichen Emotionspsychosen*, *Brit. J. Psychiat.*, **110**, 114–18.
91. SLATER, E. (1965) Diagnosis of 'hysteria', *Brit. med. J.*, i, 1395–9.
92. SLATER, E. (1965) Interdisciplinary investigations (Working paper No. 1), World Health Organisation Scientific Group on Research on Genetics in Psychiatry, November 1965, Geneva.
93. SLATER, E. (1966) Expectation of abnormality on paternal and maternal sides: a computational model, *J. med. Genet.*, **3**, 159–61.
94. SLATER, E. The problems of pathography, *Acta. psychiat.* (*Kbh.*), Suppl. in honour of Prof. E. Essen-Möller [in press].
95. SLATER, E., BEARD, A. W., and GLITHERO, E. (1963) The schizophrenia-like psychoses of epilepsy, *Brit. J. Psychiat.*, **109**, 95–150.
96. SLATER, E., and MEYER, A. (1959) Contributions to a pathography of the musicians: 1. Robert Schumann, *Confin. psychiat.*, **2**, 65–94.
97. SLATER, E., and MEYER, A. (1960) Contributions to a pathography of the musicians: II. Organic and psychotic disorders, *Confin. psychiat.*, **3**, 129–45.
98. SLATER, E., and WOODSIDE, M. (1951) *Patterns of Marriage*, London.
99. SLATER, E., and ZILKHA, K. (1961) A case of Turner mosaic with myopathy and schizophrenia, *Proc. roy. Soc. Med.*, **54**, 674–5.
100. SLATER, P., SHIELDS, J., and SLATER, E. (1964) A quadratic discriminant of zygosity from fingerprints, *J. med. Genet.*, **1**, 42–46.
101. STERN, M. I., COWIE, V. A., and COPPEN, A. J. (1966) Dehydroepiandrosterone excretion in the mothers of mongols, *Acta endocr.* (*Kbh.*), **53**, 79–83.

102. TIENARI, P. (1963) Psychiatric illnesses in identical twins, *Acta psychiat.* (*Kbh.*), Suppl. 171.
103. TSUANG, M.-T. (1966) Birth order and maternal age of psychiatric inpatients, *Brit. J. Psychiat.*, **112**, 1131–41.
104. TSUANG, M.-T. (1967) A study of pairs of sibs both hospitalized for mental disorder, *Brit. J. Psychiat.*, **113**, 283–300.
105. TSUANG, M.-T., and LIN, T.-Y., (1964) A clinical and family study of Chinese mongol children, *J. ment. Defic. Res.*, **8**, 84–91.
106. TSUANG, M.-T., and LIN, T.-Y., (1965) A chromosome study of Chinese children with Down's syndrome, *J. ment. Defic. Res.*, **9**, 1–3.
107. WHEELAN, L. (1951) Aggressive psychopathy in one of a pair of uniovular twins, *Brit. J. Delinq.*, **2**, 130–43.
108. WHEELAN, L. (1959) Familial Alzheimer's disease, *Ann. Eugen.* (*Lond.*), **23**, 300–10.
109. WORLD HEALTH ORGANIZATION (1966) The use of twins in epidemiological studies: report of the W.H.O. Meeting of Investigators on Methodology of Twin Studies, *Acta genet.* (*Roma*), **15**, 109–28.
110. WORLD HEALTH ORGANIZATION (1966) Research on genetics in psychiatry: report of a W.H.O. sientific group., *Wld Hlth Org. techn. Rep. Ser.*, 346, Geneva.
111. ZAPPELLA, M., and COWIE, V. A. (1962) A note on time of diagnosis in mongolism, *J. ment. Defic. Res.*, **6**, 82–86.

10

Psychiatric Education and Training

D. L. DAVIES

WHEN Dr. Edward Mapother [6] wrote his report of the first year of The Maudsley Hospital's activities in 1924, he devoted rather less than one of the seventeen pages to the arrangements for teaching. He reported recognition of the clinical practice of the hospital for postgraduate diplomas in psychological medicine, as well as for undergraduate instruction by certain examining bodies; and he referred to recognition for himself, through his recent appointment to King's College Hospital and its medical school, for instruction he was giving to undergraduates at the Maudsley and at King's College Hospital. Reference to postgraduate instruction included the lectures and demonstrations of the diploma course, which was to be strengthened in the middle month 'at the suggestion of the Fellowship of Medicine and Postgraduates' Association which are jointly undertaking the re-organization of postgraduate teaching in London'. The only specific teaching occasions additionally mentioned were a monthly conference of all medical officers of the London County Council's Hospital Service, a weekly ward conference, and some out-patient demonstrations twice weekly.

It would seem praiseworthy that so much clinical teaching was encompassed, when the in-patients amounted to 157, the out-patient department was demanding, and the staff amounted to only one medical superintendent, one deputy medical superintendent, one senior medical officer and two assistant medical officers.

Of course this was not the whole story. The Claybury Laboratory, which had been transferred to the newly founded Maudsley Hospital, was already very well known for its researches in the field of mental illness under its distinguished director, Sir Frederick Mott, F.R.S. Very soon both the clinical and laboratory facilities were made available for the training of medical officers from the L.C.C. mental hospitals, under an arrangement which Golla [3] described in the following words:

'With a view to training medical officers in scientific methods of investigation and at the same time affording them the opportunity for study of early and "borderland" cases, four medical officers chosen from the mental hospitals' staffs are seconded for a period of three months to the Maudsley Hospital. Part of their training is clinical in the wards of the hospital and the remainder of their time is spent in the Laboratory.'

A course of instruction was started, geared to the Diploma in Psychological Medicine of the Conjoint Board, and attended by medical officers from L.C.C. service and 'various provincial and colonial mental hospitals'. The course was in two parts: (1) anatomy and physiology of the nervous system and normal psychology; and (2) lectures and demonstrations in psychiatry. Initially it extended over six months.

In the succeeding 2 years Mapother reported that 29 medical officers from L.C.C. hospitals had been seconded to the Maudsley for periods of 3 months, while 28 others had acted as voluntary clinical assistants, whole-time for 6 months or part-time for a year, to meet D.P.M. requirements, usually in conjunction with the lecture course.

In the next report, covering the 5 years to 31 December 1931, Mapother [7] was able to announce a significant increase in staff from five to nine whole-time medical officers (including the medical superintendent), with a temporary assistant medical officer and two part-time assistant medical officers. Dr. Aubrey Lewis, who had held a Maudsley Research Grant in 1928–29, was mentioned as having been appointed assistant medical officer on 15 April 1929, and promoted to first assistant medical officer on 15 December 1931. In this post he ranked third in the hierarchy, after the medical superintendent (Dr. Mapother) and the deputy (Dr. Thomas Tennent).

In addition to temporary medical officers who served for varying periods, there were clinical assistants in three groups. First, those who came from the L.C.C. mental hospitals for three months' secondment prior to sitting for the D.P.M.; secondly, others from the same source who came for a short period similarly after gaining the D.P.M.; and thirdly, psychiatrists from other sources who attended voluntarily whilst pursuing the lecture demonstration course, again with the D.P.M. in mind. The total number of these was 28 in 1927, declining to 17 in 1931, mainly because 'those long in the service have nearly all been to the Maudsley, and only new entrants to the service are now available'. Though there is a reference to 'overseas visitors' the context suggests that these were not postgraduate students as the term is now understood.

This is not the place to deal with the early research activities of The Maudsley Hospital, but one can hardly give an account of teaching developments fully without some reference of this kind, since it clearly has a bearing on the quality of the teachers. The list of publications in the 5 years to 1931 which Mapother gives, includes well known papers by Lewis on melancholia, genetic problems in psychiatry, paranoid disorders, psychopathology of suicide, and the experience of time in mental disorder.

The report [8] of the 5 years to December 1935 refers to the building plans of a garden villa about to be fully implemented, and the provision of an out-patients' block, as well as a children's block, so releasing some existing accommodation to provide a large lecture theatre, a library and increased laboratory space. The report mentions that Lewis had 'of late years' acted as tutor to the three groups of the postgraduate students mentioned earlier, and that he was one of the four staff members recognized as teachers of the University of London, which body had confirmed its recognition of The Maudsley Hospital and the Central Pathological Laboratory as a school of the University following a visit of inspection in 1933.

The number of clinical assistants was fairly constant between 1932 and 1935 in annual totals of between 22 and 34, with the majority as voluntary attenders from outside the L.C.C. service. Little extension of the case conference programme seems to have occurred over the previous years but already outside clinics, and especially the Unit at what is now called St. Francis' Hospital, were mentioned among the available teaching facilities. Considerable strengthening of the academic staff occurred in this period with grants from the Rockefeller Foundation, amounting to £3,000 a year for 3 years from August 1935, to support five research workers. Dr. Mayer-Gross and Dr. Eric Guttmann worked in the hospital, with this support, and Dr. Adolf Beck, Dr. Alfred Meyer, and Dr. Grey Walter were appointed to the Laboratory.

This development of clinical research, as well as the tendency to increasing specialization in the field of psychiatry (as witnessed by the growth of the children's department) raised serious problems. As Mapother [8] wrote:

> 'Even up to the date of my last report, the medical staffing had the relatively simple pattern traditional at a mental hospital. As a mental hospital the two senior colleagues of the medical superintendent have to take charge of the male and female side of the institution respectively, and to deputise for him administratively... No one conversant with modern psychiatry could suppose that the Maudsley would ever attain full efficiency if its senior staff, in climbing by promotion, must pass from work with adults in wards and out-patient departments (both diagnostic and psychothera-

peutic) to similar duties with children, thence again to the training of post-graduates and organisation of clinical research (which needs close acquaintance with the frontier of current knowledge) and finally to the administrative routine of the medical superintendent or his deputy. No single person is capable of being by turns for a year or two so expert in each function as to equal those who permanently devote themselves to one. Moreover the sort of gifts and personality required in each case are entirely different.'

As part of the solution to this problem Lewis was appointed clinical director with the rank equivalent to deputy medical superintendent, and given charge of about half the beds, because of his responsibilities for clinical training of the postgraduates. This was virtually the forerunner of the professorial unit as we know it today. Mapother's report [8] was clear:

> 'It is intended that while clinical research and teaching shall not be confined to this Unit it shall be the chief and co-ordinating centre of these. Such purposes are among the most important at this hospital.'

The rest of the hospital was divided into 'Firms', under an assistant medical officer, two of whom came under the deputy medical superintendent, Dr. Thomas Tennent, and one under Lewis.

This foreshadowed the subsequent development of multiple firms under independent heads. This system exists today when some, if not all, the firms are highly specialized. Though the system was set out as an operative scheme in the Report of 1935, it is clear from a later document [9] that it was still only under consideration as late as December 1938. Nevertheless, to whatever extent it was or was not implemented, Mapother's views and intentions at the time are beyond doubt.

War-clouds were beginning to form in 1938. In 1939 The Maudsley Hospital split into two groups, one going to Mill Hill and one to Sutton, on the outskirts of London. When these reassembled at Denmark Hill after the war, the wards were empty, the staff just beginning to return from national service, and the demand for further education and training in psychiatry, the public image of which had been transformed in the war years, was greater than ever. The whole problem of postgraduate education in London had been the subject of a Report [10] published by the Goodenough Committee: this recommended, in general, the arrangement of Institutes under the British Postgraduate Medical Federation as we know it today, and in particular that teaching and research in psychiatry should be developed further at The Maudsley Hospital. In saying this, reference was made particularly to the high reputation of the hospital, and the urgent need for more well-trained teachers of psychiatry in Great Britain.

Plans for the National Health Service were also being made, and before the inception of that service in 1948 The Maudsley Hospital merged with Bethlem Royal Hospital, to form one institution under a single Board of Governors. The newly formed body consisted now of two previously distinct hospitals, separated by about 8 miles, each contributing about half the joint total of about 500 beds. At the same time as the new hospital unit took shape, the Institute of Psychiatry became part of the University of London, with formal responsibilities for teaching and research.

The full development of a teaching and training programme in psychiatry now became possible. The shape which the postgraduate teaching institution was to take is best understood by recalling the presidential address entitled 'Education of Psychiatrists' which Lewis [4] gave to the section of Psychiatry of the Royal Society of Medicine on 26 September 1946. In his address he pointed out the deficiencies of the then existing system, and especially the limitations of what he called 'the D.P.M. outlook', and' the D.P.M. course'. He outlined the aim of training, the foundations of teaching, and referred also to the content of teaching, a subject to which he made reference again in his Harveian Oration [5]. This address is of great historical interest, not only for its lucid exposition of the problems involved, and the key it holds to the development of teaching at the Maudsley, but also because it foreshadows the role of regional hospitals in postgraduate medical education, which has culminated in the post-graduate medical centre.

As Lewis saw it:

'. . . we must get away from the D.P.M. outlook, as I may call it, in psychiatric education. At its worst this outlook has created bare empirics, and teachers of psychiatry who are like the sophists that Aristotle denounced—they used to suppose that they trained people by imparting to them not the art but its products.

What are its outstanding faults? Too many examining bodies have made a uniform standard impossible, and a high standard quite impossible. The psychiatrist has been encouraged to nibble at many branches of knowledge instead of studying them, and has often come to regard the experts in these—for example the psychologists—as rivals or subordinates, as technicians, or as academic playboys, as masters of strange and efficacious arts, as anything but scientists and collaborators on whom he intelligently depends. His training has not saved him, in psychopathology, from a weak syncretism. Therapeutic effort has prospered at the expense of therapeutic discrimination.'

Behind the D.P.M. outlook lay the D.P.M. course, comprising lectures, demonstrations, and classroom instruction given to students assembled to receive such.

In Lewis' view:

'. . . the training of psychiatrists—even the least ambitious of them—clearly cannot continue to rest on so flimsy and outworn a basis, which, clinically, did little more than supply the deficiencies of undergraduate education in psychiatry, and on the theoretical side practised the vices of spoon-feeding and fact-cramming, which are inescapable in such compressed mass teaching.

There is no need to doubt that the last state of those who were thus prepared for the ordeal by examination was nevertheless often better than the first, and that much positive good has been done by "D.P.M. courses"; but they do not answer the needs of psychiatry at its present stage of development. Although lectures and demonstrations will, of course, be a valuable part of psychiatric teaching in the future, they are educationally of less account than supervised work in clinic and laboratory, seminars or discussion, factual reading, and tutorial sessions—all of which take up so much more of teachers' time.'

As Lewis saw it, clinical teaching must be the core of the psychiatrist's education:

' "taking cases", studying and testing individual patients, arranging and digesting the findings, formulating the problem, relating it to what may be learnt elsewhere than in the company of the patient—this is the body of psychiatric opportunity.'

Indeed, 17 years later in Lewis' Harveian Oration we hear the echo of this view, not only for postgraduates but for undergraduates, when he says:

'close study of the phenomena of mental disorder, appraisal of evident causes, information about pathology, balanced considerations of prognosis—these are the preliminaries and the stable elements in the teaching of psychiatry to medical students.'

Returning to his views on postgraduate education, it is clear from the earlier address that clinical opportunities need to be supplemented by laboratory experience in various disciplines. Further, these disciplines should include not only those dealing with the sick, but also those, such as psychology and anthropology, which deal with normal people as well.

Training and education so based would have the aim of producing the 'all purposes psychiatrist':

> 'When he is asked to treat a child, to report on a criminal, to explain the origins of a strange symptom, to supervise a course of insulin, to diagnose a high-grade defective, or to avail himself of the results of psychological tests, he should not have to choose whether he will excuse or hide his deficiencies; he ought not to be nonplussed and as much off his own ground as if he had been called to deliver a baby. His all-round training is not designed to make him a sciolist who thinks he can answer every question, but to put him in the way of getting the experience that will give him scientific grounding, standards, and a sure frame of reference, and will fit him for the general practice of psychological medicine as our times require it.
>
> The psychiatrist, like other specialists, must acquire knowledge, a technical skill, and an attitude fit for what he has to do: he cannot, for example, dislike human beings with a Swiftian rancour, he cannot view his patients' conduct censoriously or be indifferent to their motives and feelings, any more than he can afford to be clumsy in carrying out therapeutic measures or in getting patients to talk to him freely. He may, it is true, become an administrator, or a psychoanalyst, or a forensic expert, or even a professor—very diverse activities, but all requiring the broad training.'

Some of the facilities, but by no means all, nor in enough quantity, for training such psychiatrists were to hand when the hospital reassembled in Denmark Hill, at about the time when these views were being expressed. There was also a very grave lack of teachers who might provide the clinical instruction, and the extensive academic curriculum referred to. Nevertheless, over the succeeding years Lewis was able to build up a teaching programme adequately staffed in its various parts which fully incorporated the ideals he had set out in the address quoted, so that at his retirement there was a complex of clinical teaching facilities and academic instruction operating for a registrar establishment of about 70 psychiatrists on the staff of the Joint Hospital, as well as for other categories of students who will be described later.

The clinical basis, in the main, rests on the Joint Hospital. The Unit is a firm, a collection of facilities (in-patient beds, out-patient clinics or both) under a consultant or a small group of consultants, expert in a particular field. Adult psychiatry is an example of one such specialty, child psychiatry another. Over the years there has been further differentiation, to include the psychiatry of adolescence, geriatric psychiatry, forensic psychiatry, social psychiatry, psychotherapy, to mention only some.

With the growth of interest in psychosurgery a Neurosurgical Unit was set up in 1952, located on our site, but as a joint venture with Guy's Hospital. This arrangement had the advantage of preventing the field of interest becoming too narrow for good practice, whilst allowing access to the neurological material provided by Guy's Hospital for teaching purposes.

It has never been supposed that the comprehensive resources needed to provide a broad training in psychiatry, and the wide opportunities for clinical investigation, could be satisfactorily provided solely in a psychiatric hospital. To cover the field of forensic psychiatry, for example, it is necessary to have access to prisons which come under the Home Office, and to Remand Homes and Classifying Centres, which come under Local Authorities. Arrangements were therefore made of mutual advantage to the authorities concerned, for our specialists and their attached postgraduate students to have access to prisons; in the case of Remand Homes the Joint Hospital undertook to give the necessary clinical service gratuitously for the sake of the clinical opportunities.

In similar fashion the Unit, formerly the Observation Ward, at the nearby St. Francis' Hospital has been staffed night and day from the Joint Hospital for corresponding teaching advantages. Other examples could be quoted of this policy, especially the consulting service given to a nearby general hospital in East Dulwich which had previously lacked such facilities. In this way access to a variety of patients with 'psychosomatic' complaints, who might not otherwise appear at a psychiatric hospital, was ensured.

Another reason for undertaking a clinical responsibility from the Joint Hospital was that the existing firms were inadequate in size to form part of a planned programme for the number of postgraduate students involved. In a rotating system of allocated experience a balance must be preserved. In one instance, child psychiatry, our own department was too small in extent for our needs: in this case the problem was solved by undertaking the clinical service to the Brixton Child Guidance Clinic, which is administratively the responsibility of the Local Authority.

Where all else failed, the bold step was taken of seconding our students to another special hospital for the necessary experience. Neurological experience for 6 months, whole-time, has been made available to our registrars by arrangement with the Institute of Neurology at Queen Square.

In rather similar fashion, but without going so far afield, certain of our registrars are enabled to spend 6 months to a year on secondment to one of the departments of the Institute of Psychiatry to learn research method while pursuing a research task.

The value of supplementary experience for the registrar outside the clinical and laboratory complex described has not been decried. It has been possible nearly always to have one or more registrars on special leave at centres of psychiatry in other countries, e.g. in the United States, in Switzerland, France or other European countries, for periods of 3 months to 2 years. Such registrars have derived enormous benefits from the attachments.

Nearer home, it has proved possible also, by informal and *ad hoc* arrangements, to have selected registrars spend periods of attachment to the growing undergraduate departments of psychiatry in London, where they have been able to see something at first hand of the particular problems—clinical and educational—to be met in these situations.

Joint senior registrarships have enabled others, similarly, to spend some time in a regional psychiatric hospital, or at the Hammersmith Hospital.

No administrative difficulties have been encountered to including periods of almost pure student status in a comprehensive scheme of in-service training. The registrars, as the past junior staff members are known collectively, are appointed to the hospital and not to serve individual consultants, or firms. Their programme involves rotation between firms, and as the Dean has been also the consultant charged with the allocation of registrars' assignments, no insuperable problems have been encountered in meeting the hospital's staffing needs whilst preserving a balanced programme for the individual registrars, designed to meet the clinical requirements of the Academic Diploma in Psychological Medicine of the University of London.

In general these requirements amount to 3 years of clinical instruction at a School of the University under recognized teachers, as well as instruction by lectures, seminars and laboratory work, and also a dissertation on an approved topic. Six months of neurological work and 6 months of child psychiatry are specifically demanded in this programme.

The Academic Diploma in Psychological Medicine of the University of London grew out of the system of training which developed at the Maudsley. It did no more than recognize the system and formally embody the elements of it as necessary requirements for admission to the examination. The first diploma was granted in 1953, and since that time the numbers have grown so that an average of 16 are awarded annually.

From the University standpoint, this diploma has been something of an anomaly, in that the length of study and the requirements generally are beyond what is usual for the grant of a mere diploma and approximate far more to the requirements for a higher degree. It is logical therefore that following a current review by the University of London of its higher degrees in general, this course is to lead to a Master's degree.

The more formal teaching programme has developed from the original case conferences and lectures for the diploma in psychological medicine to which Mapother made reference in his earlier reports quoted above.

The case conference programme has been elaborated considerably. In the background are the rounds which each consultant does in the wards, usually in the morning, and the teaching given in the outpatients' department where registrars clerk by arrangement. Every day at noon, however, one or more conferences are held: a main weekly conference is presided over by the Professor of Psychiatry, whilst on the other days conferences earmarked for childrens' problems, social problems, psychotherapy problems and so on, are held.

From time to time individual consultants are invited to hold a series of, say, six weekly seminars on some special topic, to replace or supplement parts of the main programme.

On alternate Saturday mornings it has been customary for the Professor of Psychiatry to preside at a Journal Club at which two papers of interest were reviewed by designated registrars. On the alternate Saturday mornings either clinicopathological conferences were held, or the Institute departments would take turns to describe research in progress in various fields.

Apart from the Saturday morning meetings the case conferences were not always easily accessible to all registrars: some would be at Bethlem, or at other hospitals and be prevented from attending by reason of distance, whilst some would be so recently joined as to be unable to derive much profit from some of the topics. To overcome this difficulty Professor Michael Shepherd [11] introduced a tutorial system under which in their first year all incoming doctors, including clinical assistants, enter tutorial groups of six to eight people for a three-term course devoted to clinical psychiatry. These meet regularly with a clinical tutor throughout each term; basic texts are used by each member on which are initiated discussions lasting 1–1½ hours; the subjects covered are the central themes of clinical psychiatry, i.e. the organic reactions, functional psychoses, neurotic reactions and personality disorders. In the second 2 years attention is paid to various branches of knowledge, e.g. genetics, biochemistry, which are related to the subject matter of psychiatry. Initially outside experts in these fields were invited to provide the texts and conduct the discussions, but this function is now continued by the growing corpus of lecturers and senior registrars in the Institute and Hospital most of whom have grown up in this system.

The so-called lecture demonstration has continued, side by side with this tutorial system. The formal lectures have been divided up, perhaps too much so in the past, between experts in various fields. Since registrars meet these teachers elsewhere, this formal information by lectures is of most value to those clinical assistants who are not attached so closely, and by junior staffs from psychiatric hospitals in the London area who come in on, say, two afternoons weekly during term for this purpose. Neuroanatomy, neurophysiology and neuropathology lend themselves best to this method of teaching which also involves practical laboratory instruction: these are the most heavily patronized sections of this two-year course.

Lewis fostered several ventures in the educational field, in addition to those already described, which have become well established in the curriculum. One of these is a weekly admission and discharge conference for the staff of the professorial unit. At these each newly admitted patient is briefly described, with provisional diagnosis and aetiology; a formulated plan is presented of the goals and means of treatment, together with a forecast of investigations to be done and the length of stay. At discharge, each patient's stay is reviewed, and particular notice is taken of any changes in assessment or deviation from the proposed plan at admission. Arrangements for further treatment and follow-up are also formulated. In this way the registrar acquires the habit of thinking clearly about his patient, and learning the scope and limitations of the means available to help. Psychologists, psychiatric social workers and occupational therapists participate in these conferences, the documented records of which are preserved along with the other information relating to the patient.

This information includes an item sheet, which is an account of the conventional hospital record of the patient's stay in question and answer form.

It also includes the results of follow-up which, on the professorial unit, was entrusted to a special office. As long as the patient continues to attend after discharge, the out-patient record provides the necessary information. Otherwise, at intervals of 6 months at first, and later of 1 year, detailed inquiry letters go out (usually to the nearest relative) about the patient's state, his complaint, his demand on doctors or other hospitals, his working ability, and so on. Change of address is noted, so that a high proportion of patients have been successfully followed-up for the intended period of 10 years.

These two records, the item sheet and the follow-up, have provided the raw material for many inquiries which the registrars are encouraged to make and have fostered an interest in what may be called the natural history of mental illness. Several of the dissertations which registrars are required to produce at the time of their final examination for the Academic Diploma have derived from these sources.

These dissertations reflect in some measure the influence of a comprehensive training on the candidates for the Academic Diploma to which reference has already been made, as is borne out by the findings of Dr. G. F. M. Russell (personal communication) quoted here with his permission. The majority (68 per cent.) of these involve examination of patients, and 22 per cent. the consultation of case notes as an alternative. The methods used derive mainly from psychology (30 per cent.), physiology (15 per cent.) and biochemistry (12 per cent.); it is noteworthy that an aspect of social psychiatry has been involved in 25 per cent., whilst no less than 72 per cent. have used statistical techniques. Over half the dissertations are subsequently communicated in various ways. Those doctors writing the dissertations have no doubts about the value of the exercise: 82 per cent. believe that it provided a helpful training towards further investigations, and almost as many believe that they have gained in awareness of the literature and the confines of knowledge.

It may be appropriate to give some information about the registrars in more detail than has been included up to this point.

They are whole-time junior staff members of the Bethlem Royal and Maudsley Hospital, up to and including the grade of senior registrar. A good deal of information about them, on arrival, during their stay, and their subsequent careers, has been published by Davies and Stein [2] and Davies [1], in an attempt to evaluate the success of Lewis in meeting the challenge of the Goodenough Committee [10]. More recently a further 118 leavers in these grades have been followed up, making a total of 417 who left between 1946 and 1964.

By grouping leavers into four periods, some trends are seen to emerge from the statistics [see TABLE 4].

Noteworthy among these is the change in composition of the doctors by countries of origin, a sharp drop in the number of those coming from overseas being evident in the latest group followed-up. Among the factors bearing on this phenomenon is the increasing number of young doctors from the United Kingdom who have been turning to psychiatry as a career in the course of time and the exclusion by the American Boards, for domestic reasons, of all overseas hospitals in all specialties (which of course included the Maudsley) from the list of institutions approved by them for their training.

Equally noteworthy is the tendency towards increasing length of training from 11·8 months in the early group to 35·3 months in the latest group. As might be imagined, longer duration of stay is associated with a wider range of experience, as shown by the increasing number of training assignments with time.

It is doubtful if much can be concluded from the change in the percentages originally domiciled in the United Kingdom who are abroad at the time of follow-up. This is always a mixed group, made up of those who have gone for a limited period with a clear objective, those who have gone with the definite object of permanent emigration, and a less clearly defined group in between.

The whole-time postgraduate students are men and women, usually fairly senior and from overseas, who come on fellowships and

TABLE 4

SOME CHANGES AFFECTING REGISTRARS LEAVING THE STAFF OF THE MAUDSLEY HOSPITAL AT VARIOUS PERIODS OF TIME

		PERIOD OF LEAVING			
		EARLY 1946–49	MIDDLE 1950–53	RECENT 1954–58	LATEST 1959–64
DOCTORS LEAVING		(n= 64)	(n = 110)	(n = 125)	(n = 118)
Women	(%)	11	12	14	14
Originally domiciled abroad	(%)	25	30	34	15
Originally domiciled in U.K. now abroad	(%)	15	18	17	12
Average time spent in training	(months)	11·8	21	27·3	35·3
Average no. of training assignments		1·6	2·3	2·8	3·7

scholarships from their governments or from bodies such as the World Health Organization or the British Council, for further study in psychiatry. They stay for at least 6 months, most usually now 2 years before returning, with or without an extra higher qualification, to serve in their own countries. They number 50–60 at any one time. The more senior fit easily into the pattern of registrar training outlined as clinical assistants attached to firms. Most are not so senior, and come for longer periods, 2–3 years, aiming at a diploma. Some of these become clinical assistants at a later stage in their training, but most are accommodated in small groups of up to six in some eight regional hospitals, either psychiatric or general with a psychiatric department, where the clinical instruction is usually in the hands of former registrars now holding senior appointments in those hospitals. These students attend the lecture course and the tutorial groups described above.

The regional registrars are the junior staffs of regional hospitals, who come usually just for the lecture course. They are given time off from clinical duties at their parent hospitals for this purpose, and because of the good travel arrangements can come in from a radius of 60 miles or more around London.

Thus three groups of doctors, who number around 180 at any one time, look to the Institute of Psychiatry and the Joint Hospital for some or all of their postgraduate education in psychiatry. This highly organized system has grown from the early arrangements which Mapother described, under the active guidance and purposeful planning of Lewis, who has aimed at a balance between clinical training and academic instruction. It has only become fully developed in perhaps the last 5 years, since before then the number of younger teachers and research workers was hardly adequate to man the system.

The system has produced offshoots in all parts of Britain and abroad, in the form of newly founded departments and chairs of psychiatry, which have begun by drawing their teachers and methods from the Maudsley, and have gone on to sending their young trainees back to London to swell the student lists of the Institute.

The task of training the 'all purposes psychiatrist' was made more difficult by the paucity of undergraduate departments of psychiatry, and the inadequate instruction of the newly graduated doctor in his period as a medical student. This aspect of medical education in British and Commonwealth universities has begun to be transformed over the last decade, but though the Institute may well change to adapt to these new circumstances, the debt it owes to Sir Aubrey Lewis for the developments he has fostered between 1948 and 1966 will remain incalculable.

REFERENCES

1. Davies, D. L. (1964) in *Psychiatric Education*, ed. Davies, D. L., and Shepherd, M., London.
2. Davies, D. L., and Stein, L. (1963) What becomes of Maudsley registrars, *Proc. roy. Soc. Med.*, **56**, 115–19.
3. Golla, F. L. (1927) The functions of the Central Pathological Laboratory of the London County Mental Hospitals, *Arch. Neurol. Psychiat.*, L.C.C. *IX*.
4. Lewis, A. J. (1947) The education of psychiatrists, *Lancet*, ii, 79–83.
5. Lewis, A. J. (1963) Medicine and the affections of the mind. *Brit. med. J.*, ii, 1549–57.

6. Mapother, E. (1924) Medical Superintendent's Annual Report, Year ended 31st January 1924, Maudsley Hospital, London County Council.
7. Mapother, E. (1927) Medical Superintendent's Annual Report, 1st February 1925 to 31st December 1926, Maudsley Hospital, London County Council.
8. Mapother, E. (1932) Medical Superintendent's Annual Report, 1st January 1927 to 31st December 1931, The Maudsley Hospital, London County Council.
9. Mapother, E. (1936) Medical Superintendent's Annual Report, 1st January 1932 to 31st December 1935, The Maudsley Hospital, London County Council.
10. Report of the Interdepartmental Committee on Medical Schools (1944), H.M.S.O., London.
11. Shepherd, M. (1964) in *Psychiatric Education* (vide supra).

PART III
BIOLOGICAL STUDIES

11

Sensorimotor Physiology

CYRIL RASHBASS

THE sensory and motor systems are the frontier posts of the central nervous system. Not only do they represent the gateways through which almost all information passes on its way to and from the brain, but they also impose restrictions on the flow of information. Only those events in the outside world that are acceptable to the sense organs can penetrate into central nervous territory, and all incoming traffic is stamped with the characteristic patterns imposed by these organs. The motor system regulates the way in which processes going on within the brain can manifest themselves to the environment. Just as the social state suffers if severe restrictions are imposed on the passage of persons and commerce across its frontiers, so is the normality of the central nervous system threatened by impairment of its interaction with the outside world. Examination of the information entering and leaving the nervous system can reveal much about the matters which concern it, its inherent resources, and its ability to transform the raw materials of sensation into the end product of action.

In 1954 Dr. Peter Sainsbury [10, 11, 12] published the first results he had obtained from experiments in which he measured motor activity in patients with mental illness. He was concerned with two aspects of motor behaviour: the general level of activity in the motor system and the measurement of abnormal movements.

The first of these investigations [10] dealt with the physiological changes in the muscular system which accompanied symptoms of anxiety and tension. These symptoms were scored by means of an inventory designed by Professor J. G. Gibson. The inventory was completed in the course of an interview with the patient and assessed both his affective state in terms of anxiety and tension, and the frequency of bodily symptoms of muscular origin.

The electromyogram was recorded from several sites: the extensors of the forearm, the muscles of the forehead, the posterior muscles of the neck and the extensors of the foot. The magnitude of muscle activity was scored by processing the electromyogram in a way that gave a numerical index that increased with both the frequency and the amplitude of the wave-form. Muscle activity was assessed during periods when the patient was relaxing and various tests for the reliability of this measure were satisfied.

The results that emerged from this investigation showed a relationship between the clinical manifestation of anxiety and tension and muscular over-activity. Separating the patients into two groups, those whose symptom scores lay above and below the median, divided the muscle tension scores into two significantly different groups. Patients with symptoms located in the head, neck or arm showed significantly higher muscle activity in the relevant muscle. Onset of headache during recordings was accompanied by increases in the activity of the frontalis muscle. Bodily symptoms attributable to a generalized alteration in muscular innervation, such as tremor and startle, were accompanied by significant increases in muscle activity in well-separated areas.

Sainsbury [10] also used the electromyogram to measure the spontaneous movements made by patients before and after leucotomy. The electromyogram, integrated as described above to give an over-all measure of muscular activity, was recorded from the extensors of the fingers and wrist. The apparatus had an inbuilt threshold which could be so adjusted as to record only the muscle activity in excess of the resting tone. Records were obtained during interview and during periods of isolation. Movements occurring during isolation were considered to be mainly autistic or self-directed, whereas movements occurring during interview were considered to be mainly communicative. In general these measurements were made on two occasions before operation and at 3, 6 and 12 months after operation.

These observations showed first that before leucotomy the patients made significantly more autistic movements than did healthy controls. The patients made significantly fewer autistic and communicative movements after leucotomy than they did before it. Three features in the pre-operative mental state were significantly associated with the decrease in movement following leucotomy. They were anxiety and tension, depression, and restlessness.

The patients investigated had operations differing in extent. It was found that the more extensive operation was consistently followed by a decrease in movements, but the operation localized to areas 9 and 10 was not.

Communicative movements decreased relatively less than the autistic in 8 out of 10 patients. The autistic mannerisms peculiar to each patient were unaltered by the operation, but occurred less emphatically when there was diminished muscular tension after leucotomy.

In addition to this method of recording spontaneous movements by means of the electromyogram, Sainsbury [11] developed a technique for doing the same thing with time-sampling motion pictures. The pictures were taken with a concealed ciné camera. Filming was carried out for 45 seconds in every period of 120 seconds. Each 45 seconds' run of film was subdivided into nine periods of 5 seconds and the occurrence or otherwise of the movement being studied was recorded. Thus a strip of film recording 45 seconds of activity would yield a score ranging between 0 and 9. A final score was obtained by repeating this analysis on five such strips of film and expressing the result in terms of score per minute.

The usefulness of this technique was assessed by various methods. The split-half reliability of the movement scores obtained from the films was 0·93. Autistic movements scores obtained from time-sampling 100 ft. of film correlated highly with the scores obtained from counting them with an electromyogram during 20 minutes. Tics were scored from short films and compared with the scores found during 12–30 minutes of direct observation. The results corresponded closely. Sainsbury concluded that although the numbers investigated were small, the results suggested that the method could be a reliable and valid one.

Sir Aubrey Lewis considered that these researches might be profitably assisted by adopting a more fundamental physiological approach to the problem of muscular activity. As a result a different set of problems were tackled in an attempt to relate the motor output of the central nervous system to its sensory input. In order to do this with a reasonable hope of success it was decided to investigate a neurological system in which the motor response is fairly simply related to the sensory input. The investigation would be directed to analyse the way in which the central nervous system transforms the information it receives into the instructions that it issues.

The neurological system that controls the way in which the eye can follow the movements of a moving target is an ideal subject for an analysis of this sort for many reasons. The most important of these is that it has a suitable degree of complexity. It is not as simple as the spinal reflexes, which throw little light on the functions of the higher parts of the central nervous system. Nor is it as complex as the many behavioural functions of the brain which must deter all but the most intrepid investigators. The movements of the eyes are voluntary in the sense that they can usually be prevented by an effort of will. Nevertheless there is no way in which the form that eye movements take can be shaped by the will of the subject. The physical nature of the structures in the orbit is such that they can largely be ignored in the interpretation of the way in which the eyes move. The friction, inertia and elasticity of these structures have no effect on the time course of eye movements other than to modify the finer details of the very fastest movements. The movements that we see are therefore a direct representation of the demands of the central nervous system.

Further, the dimensions of both the sensory input and the motor output are the same: the angular direction of a line to the mid-sagittal plane. This allows direct comparison of the two, and a description of the central transformations in a dimensionless form. Finally, the control of eye position is directly analogous to the control of man-made direction-finding systems. This allows the type of analysis that has been developed with great sophistication for the description of man-made control systems to be applied to the problem of understanding this neurological system.

In order to investigate this control system it is necessary to have a way of recording the direction in which the eyes are looking. It is also necessary to have a method of presenting tracking tasks to the subject and to produce tasks selected to bring out the special characteristics of the system.

The method of recording eye movements [4] that was devised for this purpose was itself a position-finding control system. The spot of light on the face of a cathode-ray tube is a light source that can be moved with great speed and precision by a suitable electrical signal. An optical image of a cathode-ray tube spot is projected on the surface of the eye somewhere near the most lateral part of the intersection of sclera and cornea. Because the optical properties of the cornea and sclera differ this projected image appears bright when it falls on the sclera but dull when it falls on the cornea. A photo-electric cell placed near the eye can detect this difference in brightness and transform this information into electrical form. Now, suppose that we arrange suitable electrical connexions such that when the projected image is lying on the sclera and appears bright the cathode-ray tube spot is moved to bring the projected image on to the cornea, and when the image is on the cornea and appears dull the cathode-ray tube spot is moved to bring the projected image on to the sclera. If this arrangement is made then the projected image will find a position of rest in equilibrium at the junction of the cornea and sclera. This junction moves as the eye moves and the spot of light moves with it. In this way it is possible to detect movements of the eye without encumbering it mechanically. The method is also inherently linear; it gives an output directly proportional to the eye movement. The speed of response of the recording system is measurable in milliseconds.

Analogy with man-made control systems would suggest that

certain tracking tasks would be expected to yield the most easily interpreted responses from the eyes. For simplicity the eyes should fixate a small spot of light in an otherwise dark visual field. This spot of light should be made to move in a variety of ways, among which the most important are: a stationary spot moving at an instant to another position where it remains stationary; a spot that is initially stationary being made to move at constant speed; and a spot being made to oscillate from side to side with a variety of amplitudes and frequencies.

It has long been known [2] that when tracking a moving target the movements of the eyes can be of two different types, rapid jerky movements and slow smooth movements. The eye movements recorded in response to the tracking tasks described above clearly show these two types of movement [5]. Responses to the sudden change of position of a stationary target are always rapid jerky movements, whereas the responses to target movements of constant speed or oscillations consist of a mixture of smooth movements and jerks. The jerks or jumps that the eyes make are recognized by being isolated events lasting under 50 milliseconds. It is unusual for two such movements to occur with an interval between them of less than 150 milliseconds so there is no difficulty in recognizing each one individually. The precise time-course of these jerky movements has recently been interpreted in terms of the mechanical properties of the orbital structures [9], but this was not the concern of this investigation. These movements, which can be looked upon as the way in which the brain demands a change in position of the eyes, are called saccadic movements.

When presented with the task of fixating a stationary spot of light that suddenly changes its position, the eyes reach the new position of fixation by means of a saccadic movement. This occurs after a reaction time of 200–250 milliseconds. It sometimes happens that this saccadic movement does not completely succeed in directing the eyes to the new position of the target so that there is a residual error in fixation when the movement is finished. When this happens, there is a second saccadic movement made to correct this residual error. The second saccadic movement never follows the first by an interval of less than 150 milliseconds.

When fixating a stationary target the eyes perform small saccadic movements around the direction of fixation irregularly at a frequency of one every second or so. These movements have been called physiological nystagmus and have been the subject of intensive study. It sometimes happens when tracking a target that a saccadic movement leaves a residual error which is rather small—less than a quarter of a degree. This is comparable in size to the size of the movements occurring spontaneously during physiological nystagmus. When a residual error as small as this is left it is unusual for it to evoke a corrective saccadic movement after a reaction time of 200 milliseconds but it is left for the next spontaneous movement to care for it. A similar threshold in the size of corrective saccadic movements can be demonstrated by making the jump in the position of the target spot very small.

When presented with the task of maintaining fixation on a target that moves from an initially stationary position with constant speed, the movements that the eyes make are very different from those just described. From the moment that the target starts to move the eyes do nothing for about 150 milliseconds. After this reaction time has elapsed the eyes begin to move in the direction of the target gathering speed during the next 150 milliseconds. By that time the speed at which the eyes are slewing round just about matches the speed at which the target is moving. Were nothing else to happen the eyes would, at that time, be directed at a point moving along some distance behind the moving target. However, at about that time, but sometimes a little sooner, a saccadic movement occurs in which the direction in which the eyes are looking leaps forward to be directed at the target. Thereafter the eyes continue to fixate the moving target with a precision that is not worse than it would have been had the target been still.

From this observation, and from similar observations about the way in which the eyes follow oscillating targets, it is clear that saccadic movements are supplemented by smooth movements when the target itself moves smoothly. What is not clear from these observations is the way in which the smooth movements of the target bring this about.

An experiment which sheds considerable light on this problem was performed. Imagine fixating a stationary target spot which is suddenly displaced to a new position to the left of its original position and at the same time is made to start travelling smoothly towards the right. We would expect the eyes to have a smooth movement component in addition to one or more saccadic movements, but in which direction will it be? If it is towards the left then we would see that smooth eye movements are concerned with making the eye look in the direction of the target. If the smooth eye movement is towards the right, then we would infer that it is concerned with making the eye travel round at the same speed as the target.

The result of this experiment is that the smooth movement that the eyes make is towards the right even though at the time that the eyes start moving to the right the fixation spot is well to the left of the direction in which they are looking. This error in the direction in which the eyes are looking, which is being aggravated by the smooth eye movement, is not allowed to exist for long, and is soon corrected by a saccadic movement to the left. This experiment shows that smooth eye movements are invoked in order to get the eye moving at the same speed as the target, irrespective of whether or not this helps to centralize the target in the visual field. A close analogy exists in the way in which photographs are taken of objects moving rapidly across the front of the photographer. As it approaches he prepares to swing the camera round at the same speed of traverse as the object he is photographing. At a time when it is approximately in front of him he presses the shutter release. The developed picture may well show the object at some distance from the centre of the frame, an error which can be independently corrected, but the picture will at least not be blurred by the motion of the object. We have seen that tracking eye movements are the result of compounding the demands of two systems each with its own aim; saccadic movements being produced with the aim of directing the line of sight at the target, smooth movements being produced to prevent the target moving about in the visual field. These two systems can be dissociated from each other by their markedly different pharmacological sensitivities [3]. A quite small dose of a barbiturate drug is sufficient completely to abolish any smooth tracking eye movements. FIGURE 3 shows the effect of the intravenous injection of 100 mg. of sodium thiopentone on the ability of the eyes to track a spot moving at constant speed. The upper record shows the movements that the eyes make before the drug is taken. The reaction time, the smooth movement and the saccadic movements can be seen. After the drug is taken (lower record) the smooth movement is completely absent and the eyes attempt to follow the retreating target by a succession of saccadic movements.

A study [7], similar to the one described above of the eye movements occurring in the tracking of a target moving from side to side, was carried out on the way in which the eyes follow targets moving to and from the subject. When a fixation target that is directly in front of the subject moves directly towards him, both eyes are required to turn towards his nose if they are to remain directed at the target. In order to record this eye movement it is not sufficient to record the movement of one eye and assume that the other eye does likewise in the opposite direction, for it is known that the eyes perform spontaneous small side-to-side movements which would be represented in the record. In order to examine only the way in which the eyes turn towards or away from each other without corrupting the record with movements in which both eyes are moving in the same direction, it is necessary to record from both eyes simultaneously. A method somewhat like that described above was used, duplicated for the other eye. The technical problems involved in operating two sensitive devices simultaneously were much greater than twice the difficulties experienced with only one, but they were successfully

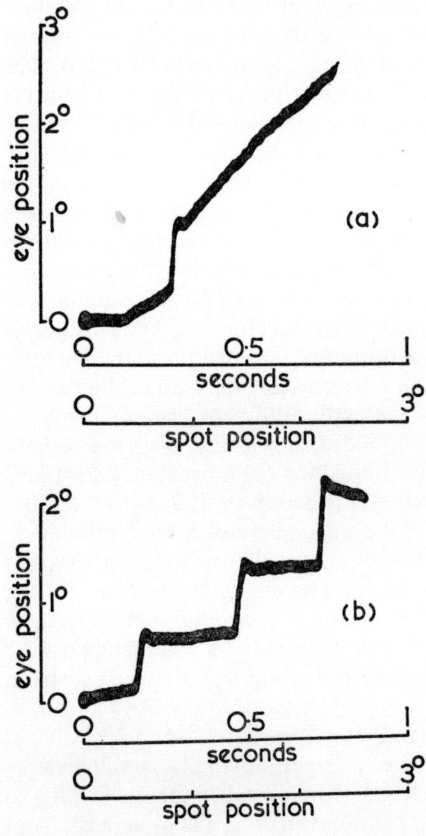

FIG. 3. Records of the eye movements caused by watching a fixation spot moving with constant velocity (a) before and (b) after the administration of 100 mg. of sodium thiopentone (*Pentothal*) intravenously.

overcome. Instead of just displaying and recording the positions of the two eyes on separate channels it was possible to manipulate the electrical signals in such a way that one channel could be used to display the extent to which the eyes moved in the same direction, and another channel to display the movements of the eyes towards and away from each other without contamination from side-to-side movements.

The characteristics of the eye movements involved in tracking fore-and-aft movements of the target are very different from those of side-to-side movements. There is no equivalent of the saccadic movement; all movements are carried out smoothly and slowly. When the target moves suddenly from a far position to a near one, the reaction time of about 200 milliseconds is followed by a movement that lasts about 800 milliseconds before the final position of the eyes is reached. In some subjects the final position is only reached after a period of decaying oscillation of the eyes about the final position at a frequency of some 2 cycles per second. The system is easily fatigued. Attempts to track a target moving towards and away from the subject at a frequency of 1 cycle per second are abandoned after the first few cycles, whereas side-to-side tracking at this frequency could be sustained indefinitely.

Quantitative analysis of the responses showed that basically the eyes converge or diverge at a rate that is directly proportional to the magnitude of the convergence or divergence required of them, the movement being delayed some 200 milliseconds. Because there is this substantial delay between the time that a movement becomes necessary and the time that it occurs the system would be expected to be unstable, with large oscillations occurring in the attempt to find the correct position of convergence. It was possible to show that the system was stabilized by being able to utilize information about the rate at which the target was moving. This information, coming from the eyes, permits the central nervous system to predict where the target is about to be and so reduce the effect of the delay which conduction and processing in the central nervous system inevitably introduce.

It was also possible to show that the convergence system and the side-to-side tracking system carry out their functions and bring about their eye movements completely independently of each other. A special case of this had already been demonstrated elegantly by Yarbus in the U.S.S.R. We were able to generalize this observation [8] and show that each system can accept and respond normally to stimuli irrespective of whether the other system is being stimulated, is within a reaction time, is responding or is suffering overload or fatigue.

Like smooth tracking movements, movements of convergence and divergence of the eyes are sensitive to small doses of the barbiturate drugs [13]. The limits of convergence and divergence are narrowed by these drugs and the speed at which movements are performed within these limits is reduced. It was of interest to show that accommodation of the lens, a reflex closely linked in many ways to convergence movements of the eyes, remained totally unimpaired by a dose of barbiturate that severely restricted the range of convergence.

It was tempting at this stage to imagine eye movements to be of two sorts: the fast saccadic movements and the slow movements of smooth tracking and convergence. The action of barbiturates would be seen in this light as blocking some process essential to the performance of slow movements. We [6] were able to demonstrate that this is not so by investigating the effect of barbiturate drugs on the slow component of the eye movements induced by vestibular stimulation. We induced vestibular eye movements by caloric stimulation and took some trouble to overcome the irregularity in the magnitude of the response. The speed of the slow component of the eye movement was measured at various times during and after a period of caloric irrigation of the ear. Before any drug was administered the speed of the slow component depended on whether or not the subject had anything on which he could fixate. With the light switched on it was possible, by fixating stationary objects in the room, for him to hold his eyes almost steady. In the dark a nystagmus of considerable magnitude was evoked. The effect of barbiturate drugs was to make the nystagmus with the light on as large as the nystagmus in the dark. We interpret this finding as indicating that the action of the drug is to incapacitate the smooth tracking mechanism. The smooth movements evoked by the vestibular reflex are not prevented by the drug. They are normally reduced in the light by being counteracted by smooth tracking of stationary objects and are released to their full extent when smooth tracking is blocked pharmacologically.

Another investigation carried on at that time concerned the relationship between eye movements and the ability to localize objects in space. Whether or not we have conscious knowledge of the position of our eyes was a matter of dispute among classical physiologists. Helmholtz held the view that there is no position sense in the eye; Sherrington argued that there is. Recent experiments [1] have shown beyond argument that Helmholtz was right. However, it is clear that, in order to explain certain observations about the way in which we interpret what we see, the brain has access to certain information about what the eyes are doing. Thus, if the eyes are kept stationary and a spot of light moved from one place to another, the appearance of this movement is very different from the appearance of a stationary spot of light viewed before and after a voluntary saccadic movement. In the first case the spot is seen to move in space; in the second case it is seen to be in the same place. In both cases the information from the retina is the same. The difference in the appearance of the two cases lies in the way the brain interprets the change in the retinal position of the image, in the light of whether the eyes moved or not.

Since the evidence is incontrovertible that the brain receives no information from the eye or the structures around it about its position or movements, it follows that the information that the brain uses in order to allow for movements of the eyes is information concerning the outflow of instructions to the eye muscles. This view is supported by many observations. For instance, if movement of the eye is mechanically impeded and an attempt is made to turn the eye voluntarily, the outside world appears to swing in the direction of the attempted movement. The brain interprets a stationary image on the retina of an eye that was instructed to move as being due to a movement of the observed object, even though the eye did not in fact move. So we see that the brain monitors information that it is sending out to the eyes in order correctly to interpret the movement of images on the retina. Is all such outflowing information monitored? The answer is certain that it is not. When the eyes move reflexly from stimulation of the vestibular system the information that they are moving is not taken into account by the brain in interpreting what is seen. This is why, during a nystagmus of vestibular origin, whether it be post-rotational or calorically induced, the world appears to swing round. Had the eyes made the same movements voluntarily or by tracking a moving object, the world would not appear to move.

The question that we set out to answer was whether movements that the eyes make involuntarily in the dark are monitored or not. The experiments, which were carried out by Mr. Hugh Norris, involved making two sets of measurements under comparable conditions. The first was to measure the extent to which the eyes move during various periods of darkness; the second, to determine the magnitude of errors in the judgement of position after the same periods of darkness. To measure the first, the subject sat fixating a small light which was suddenly extinguished leaving him in total darkness. After a period of time of 1, 3 or 10 seconds a bright brief flash was released from a point in the position of the fixation spot. This flash produced an easily identifiable after-image. If the eye did not drift during the time in the dark, this after-image would be seen straight ahead; if the eye had moved it would be seen at a point some distance away from the centre of fixation. By fixating the zero of a suitable scale the subject could read off the position of the after-image and thereby determine the position of his eye at the moment the flash was released.

To determine the magnitude of the errors in the judgement of position after a period of darkness the subject again fixated a small light. This was extinguished, and after a period of total darkness of 1, 3 or 10 seconds another indistinguishable light was lit. This second light was one of an array of ten lights, five at various small distances to the right and five to the left of the original fixation spot. The subject was required to say whether the second light was to the left or right of the original light.

The findings that emerged from these experiments were that the mean position of the eyes after various periods in the dark barely deviated from straight ahead. However, the standard deviation of the position of the eye increased as the time in the dark increased. Over the period of time investigated the standard deviation of eye position increased rather precisely in proportion to the square root of the time in the dark, a property that would be expected were the eyes to perform a 'random walk' type of movement. The number and magnitude of errors in the judgement of position also increased as the period of darkness increased and it was possible to show that the errors could be accounted for if the eye moved in the way it did and the information about its movement was not monitored by the central nervous system.

A precisely analogous experiment was performed to measure movements of convergence and divergence in the dark, and errors in the assessment of distance arising therefrom. It was shown that in the dark the eyes move rather rapidly to be directed at a point some 2 metres from the subject, thus converging if they start by looking at a far object, diverging if they start looking at a near object. Superimposed on this trend towards a neutral position of convergence is a variation in the position of convergence that increases with the length of time spent in darkness. Errors in the judgement of distance were made of a magnitude and direction that could be attributed to this increasing variance in the state of convergence. No errors were attributable to the trend of the eyes to the neutral position. From this it was concluded that the movement that brought the point of convergence to 2 metres away from the subject was allowed for by the brain but a degree of variation occurred of which the brain was ignorant.

The problems that have concerned us most recently have been devoted to the eye as an organ of vision. The general problem has been to discover the way in which the brain analyses fluctuations in brightness. It will only be possible here to outline the problems, indicate the approach to their solution, and summarize some of the findings.

Changes in brightness are sometimes seen and sometimes not seen, depending on their magnitude. This is to say that there is a threshold in vision. Measurements of visual thresholds may be made from an initial state of total darkness, or from an initial state of constant illumination; these are known as absolute thresholds and incremental thresholds and differ in many important respects. The present study concerns only incremental thresholds.

A classical observation is that if an incremental flash is presented and its intensity measured at threshold, there is a simple relationship between this intensity and the duration of the flash. For durations less than a certain duration of about 100 milliseconds the intensity is inversely proportional to the duration. Thus, within this range of durations the total amount of light energy entering the eye determines whether or not it is seen. This ability of the visual system to add up the amount of energy arriving over an extended period is known as temporal summation. For very long durations, about 500 milliseconds and more, the threshold intensity is constant independent of the duration. This shows that the visual system cannot go on adding energy for an unlimited period. For intermediate durations (100–500 milliseconds) the threshold intensity decreases with the duration of the flash, but does not decrease as much as would be expected if the energy of the flash were added together. So we see that there is a period of total summation, followed by a period of partial summation, followed by a period in which no further summation takes place.

It is not difficult to do an experiment that shows that this model of the visual system is inadequate to account for the observations. One such experiment is to measure the threshold intensity of two equal brief (1 millisecond, say) flashes, separated by varying intervals of time. Another, and more dramatic, experiment is to relate the threshold intensity to the interval separating two flashes that are equal in duration and magnitude but opposite in direction, i.e. a momentary brightening of the visual field followed by a momentary dimming. When separated by an interval of about 40 milliseconds two such flashes, one of brightness and one of dimness, have a threshold intensity that is only about 0·6 times the threshold of either one of them presented by itself. This observation is quite inexplicable in terms of a system that does nothing more complex than summate energy extended in time.

In attempting to resolve the way in which the visual system analyses temporal changes in intensity, it is necessary to allow for an effect, essentially irrelevant to the problem, that arises from the statistical nature of the visual threshold. If a subject is asked to report whether or not he sees single brief flashes that are presented at different intensities it is found that he probably never sees the very dim ones and probably always sees the very bright ones. However, the dividing line between the intensities that he sees and those that he does not see is not clear-cut. There is an extended range of intensities of flashes that are sometimes reported as seen and sometimes reported as not seen. If a sufficient number of flashes are presented it is found that, within this range, the proportion of seen to unseen flashes increases as the intensity increases. The probability of seeing a flash increases with its intensity. To measure a visual threshold an arbitrary probability of being seen is selected—0·5 say—and the intensity of the flash seen with that probability is defined as threshold.

Now suppose that we wish to measure the threshold intensity of two equal flashes separated by various intervals. At short intervals we would expect to find interactions of various sorts including summation, but at large intervals we would expect the flashes to be independent of each other and to have thresholds equal to the threshold of a single flash. In the course of the experiment we would present the subject with two flashes separated by an interval of perhaps 1 second and he would report whether or not he has seen anything. If the intensity of the flashes is such that the probability of seeing either one of them is 0·5, a level that we have defined as threshold, he will report having seen something, either the first or the second or both, on more than half the presentations. If the two flashes vary in visibility independently, he will report having seen something on three out of every four presentations. We would then say that this intensity was above threshold, and reduce it until he reports seeing as many as he does not see. Because of the statistical nature of the visual threshold we would be led to believe that two flashes separated by a large interval nevertheless interact with each other. Experiments have to be designed in a way that takes this effect into account.

One can enunciate a general rule of experimentation, that in investigating a complex system simplification can be achieved by investigating the effect of very small disturbances to the system. Many of the experiments in this series are based on this principle and involve measuring the changes in the threshold of a single flash when certain very small changes are imposed on the continuous level of illumination. These very small changes are themselves well below the threshold of visibility. This sort of experiment poses some special problems of methodology. It is required to detect and measure with some precision very small changes in the threshold of a flash. Owing to the statistical nature of thresholds a determination can only be reached by recording the responses to a number of flashes. The greater the precision that is required the larger is the number of flashes that needs to be presented. At best, the standard error in the estimate of the threshold decreases by a factor inversely proportional to the square root of the number of flashes. In fact, fatigue and tedium tend to increase the variability of the responses if the number of judgements required of the subject is very large, so that increasing the number of flashes presented is, to a certain extent, self-defeating.

It is necessary to design an experiment with maximum efficiency. Inefficiency arises when many of the flashes presented are either far above or far below threshold. Techniques that are available for increasing the efficiency of measures like the determination of drug doses producing 50 per cent. mortality are open to objection when applied to psychophysical measurements. A method in which the intensity of the present flashes is dependent on the subject's previous judgements, but dependent in a complex way, has been devised. It is efficient and at the same time not subject to the criticisms usually levelled against this type of technique.

The conclusions drawn from these experiments are only tentative, and further work is required, either to support or demolish them. At the time of writing it appears that the visual system analyses temporal changes in the following way. The wave-form of the changes in brightness is first subjected to a filtration process that attenuates the high frequencies present in it, and, to a lesser extent, the low frequencies. After filtration the wave-form is subjected to a process that, in effect, computes a running estimate of its variance. If this estimate of variance should reach a certain level then the subject will report seeing the brightness changes.

Should this suggestion stand up to critical experimentation, the analysis will be extended in two directions. First, it is of interest to see how the parameters of the system, the frequencies of filtration, the epoch over which variance is estimated and the level at which the criterion for seeing is set, vary with certain changes in the initial conditions. The initial conditions can be varied in brightness, hue, size of the field and its position on the retina. Secondly, it is of interest to see whether this type of analysis is unique to the visual system or is a more general property of the organization of the central nervous system.

REFERENCES

1. Brindley, G. S., and Merton, P. A. (1960) The absence of position sense in the human eye, *J. Physiol.* (*Lond.*), **143**, 127–30.
2. Dodge, R. (1903) Five types of eye movements in the horizontal meridian plane of the field of regard, *Amer. J. Physiol.*, **8**, 307–29.
3. Rashbass, C. (1959) Barbiturate nystagmus and the mechanisms of visual fixation, *Nature* (*Lond.*), **183**, 897–8.
4. Rashbass, C. (1960) New method of recording eye movements, *J. opt. Soc. Amer.*, **40**, 642–4.
5. Rashbass, C. (1961) The relationship between saccadic and smooth tracking eye movements, *J. Phsyiol.* (*Lond.*), **159**, 326–38.
6. Rashbass, C., and Russell, G. F. M. (1961) Action of a barbiturate drug on the vestibulo-ocular reflex, *Brain*, **85**, 329–35.

7. RASHBASS, C., and WESTHEIMER, G. (1961) Disjunctive eye movements, *J. Physiol.* (*Lond.*), **149**, 339–60.
8. RASHBASS, C., and WESTHEIMER, G. (1961) Independence of conjugate and disjunctive eye movements, *J. Physiol.* (*Lond.*), **159**, 361–4.
9. ROBINSON, D. A. (1964) The mechanics of human saccadic eye movement, *J. Physiol.* (*Lond.*), **175**, 245–64.
10. SAINSBURY, P. (1954) The measurement and description of spontaneous movements before and after leucotomy, *J. ment. Sci.*, **100**, 732–41.
11. SAINSBURY, P. (1954) A method of measuring spontaneous movements by time-sampling motion pictures, *J. ment. Sci.*, **100**, 742–8.
12. SAINSBURY, P., and GIBSON, J. G. (1954) Symptoms of anxiety and tension and the accompanying physiological changes in the muscular system, *J. Neurol. Neurosurg. Psychiat.*, **17**, 216–24.
13. WESTHEIMER, G., and RASHBASS, C. (1961) Barbiturates and eye vergence, *Nature* (*Lond.*), **191**, 833–4.

12

Research Conducted in the Metabolic Unit, 1956—66

G. F. M. RUSSELL

INTRODUCTION

In 1955, at the prompting of Sir Aubrey Lewis, a metabolic unit was set up at The Maudsley Hospital to investigate the physiological and chemical aspects of mental illness. It was the first unit of its kind in Britain, but has since been followed by others. Until the time of his retirement in 1966 Lewis directed the clinical research in the Metabolic Unit, and conducted weekly ward rounds. He was influenced by the pioneer work of Rolv Gjessing who in 1924 built a metabolic ward and a biochemical research laboratory at Dikemark Hospital, Asker, Norway, primarily for the study of the periodic psychoses. Lewis' immense admiration of Gjessing's precise clinical observations and his painstaking laboratory studies made it natural that the first investigations at the Maudsley should be run along similar lines and attempts were made to find patients with periodic catatonia corresponding to the descriptions of Gjessing. But the patients were difficult to come by, and the phases of their periodic illnesses were seldom easy to predict. While limited investigations were carried out in periodic catatonia [48], interest soon shifted to less frustrating areas of research. These have proved more rewarding and have yielded information about the metabolic and endocrine aspects of anorexia nervosa, depressive illness and premenstrual tension. Before describing the outcome of this work, however, Lewis' approach to the subject of metabolic research in psychiatry should be mentioned.

Lewis never favoured the term 'psychosomatic'. He considered that in the mere use of the terms 'psyche' and 'soma' there lay implied acceptance of two distinct entities—the mind and the body; a semantic marriage could not succeed in bringing them together once they had been torn asunder. In a masterly review of psychosomatic medicine [37], he has discussed the philosophical issues which have guided or bedevilled research in this field:

> 'The strictly dualist point of view has lost so much ground in this century however that the "double aspect" theory may be regarded as the prevalent one; it fits well with the operational point of view and the old controversies about monism and dualism can be discussed as pseudo-problems.'

His view of the complexity of the problems probably came close to that of Jaspers [33] who spoke of a gulf that separated our understanding of mental and physical phenomena and of man's puny efforts to bridge this gulf. To quote again:

> 'The unbridgeable transition between physically and mentally viewed phenomena may well be recognized in some instances, just as it remains most obscure and practically irrelevant in others. The pragmatic strength—and the metaphysical weakness—of the "double aspect" manner of describing and relating phenomena lies in its ready acceptance of the interplay and sequence of the physically viewed and the mentally viewed processes in the individual, the physical or mental view being allowed to predominate according to the adequacy of our physical or mental theoretical formulations and concept language.'

Characteristically, Lewis eschewed the glittering prizes of research if he thought the risk of nugatory results was too great. Though the history of biological research in psychiatry is relatively short, it is littered with examples of high but unfulfilled expectations. Ambitious studies aimed at the solution of the fundamental problems of schizophrenia have foundered. Among the more respectable examples of such disappointments may be listed the sagas of adrenochrome, the toxic phenols and amines, and the story of the 'pink spot'. Such endeavours are not to be discouraged, but when they fail they may be fruitless or add very little to knowledge that is fundamental. It is regrettable that their contribution to normal physiological, biochemical and psychological processes has been so small. Research aimed at understanding the disturbances of these processes is unlikely to bring forth brilliant results immediately, but the rewards though modest will probably be more enduring. Step by step progression in laying these foundations of psychiatry will eventually lead to advances in the treatment and prevention of mental illness.

It is essential to formulate as clearly as possible the psychiatric problems themselves. The imperfections of psychiatric classifications are so well recognized that there is no need to labour the fact that the researcher is in danger of studying a heterogeneous collection of disorders. The best policy is to study the 'typical case' and reject patients who show unusual clinical features. Unfortunately, so-called typical cases may be rather rare specimens. Initial studies conducted in the Metabolic Unit concentrated on patients with typical and severe depressive illnesses, thus increasing the chances of homogeneity of the group and of detecting the physical changes in question. Subsequent studies were even more circumscribed, when it was thought that alterations in body physiology or chemistry might be linked with individual symptoms rather than with the so-called psychiatric illnesses. Depression was studied rather than depressive illness; the complex feeding disturbances that pass under the name of anorexia nervosa were dissected into their different components.

But no solution is perfect when knowledge of psychiatry is still in a rudimentary stage. By his example Lewis taught his students to steer a course between Scylla and Charybdis—to avoid the temptations of easy answers and yet not to become spellbound by the philosophical issues. Clarity in thinking about psychiatric concepts should never get in the way of research, but if the researcher is put off by this need for intellectual lucidity, either his ideas or his persistence are at fault. Once the problem has been defined there comes a time for action. In a way which might be thought to be out of character, Lewis was once heard to quote John Hunter's dictum 'why think? why not try the experiment?'. A final quotation from his article on psychosomatic research should serve as a clarion call:

> 'Any method that is reliable, any set of concepts that fits the phenomena, any theory that provides fruitful hypotheses, any function, any disease, might properly be employed or studied in so wide and difficult an undertaking: any critical procedure that can detect premature or misleading inferences needs also to be used to the full'.

TRAINING IN PSYCHIATRIC RESEARCH

The primary requirement of the clinical investigator is the ability to carry out research, while ensuring that the patient receives the best available treatment. Such ability has to be acquired together with other clinical and scientific skills. At the Institute of Psychiatry, Lewis recognized that training in research was the highest form of postgraduate education. In the field of metabolic research he urged his students first to become sound psychiatrists, and then to acquire special knowledge in one of the scientific disciplines relevant to psychiatry. The research worker thus equipped can use the specialized techniques he has acquired in the study of his patients. A sophisticated knowledge of psychiatry is necessary to ensure an enlightened direction to the research and to avoid over-simplification of the clinical problems. Only by possessing a thorough understanding of at least some aspects of physiology or biochemistry, or both, is the investigator able to interpret the results of his research. He must guard against ascribing unwarranted significance to findings which are the consequences of the psychiatric disorder and not its cause. For instance, as a result of his illness the patient may change his diet or his physical activity, he may become constipated or he may be treated with drugs. Any of these factors may produce alterations in body physiology or chemistry which may delude the investigator into thinking that he has made a fundamental discovery. Hence he must study these complicating factors in their own right, so as to understand how they affect the manifestations of mental illness. He must in fact be willing to wander from time to time into physiological or biochemical researches in normal subjects, and apply what he has thus learned to his clinical studies.

To induce clinicians to undertake metabolic research in psychiatric patients is no easy task. Professional selection and self-selection operates in such a way as to lead into psychiatry doctors who are more interested in pursuing inquiries into applied psychology or sociology. Nevertheless, under Lewis' stimulus twelve Maudsley registrars have so far been encouraged to pursue researches in the Metabolic Unit which led to dissertations for the Academic Post-graduate Diploma in Psychological Medicine of the University of London [6, 7, 8, 10, 17, 26, 32, 39, 44, 60, 62, 65]. Their studies ranged from purely clinical observations on the course of thyroid disorders to laboratory inquiries into the survival of red blood cells in schizophrenia; they inquired into the metabolic aspects of alcoholism, premenstrual tension, old age, anorexia nervosa and depressive illness. These doctors were given the opportunity to acquire particular skills in laboratory work extending to chemical, electro-physiological and isotope-detection techniques. The results have constituted modest but valuable contributions to psychiatric knowledge. More important still was the inculcation of the scientific method and the realization by the registrars that they were capable of conducting original research.

THE FUNCTIONS OF A PSYCHIATRIC METABOLIC UNIT

A metabolic unit provides an excellent opportunity for the detailed investigation and treatment of patients. Their environment—both external and internal—is controlled to a maximum degree; they are scrutinized from day to day, and they are treated in the proximity of laboratories. If an investigation merely requires specimens of blood or urine from patients to be sent to a laboratory, it matters little if this is 10 yards or 10 miles distant. To obtain the samples is relatively easy and the investigator's efforts are virtually confined to the laboratory work. In clinical research the situation is more complex. For instance, the test may require the active participation of the patient, e.g. in the use of recording apparatus, the infusion of a drug, or the injection of an isotope. In these circumstances it is best to set up the clinical laboratory within the ward so that the investigator retains the assistance of the nursing staff and the patient remains in surroundings which are familiar to him.

Even greater participation of the patient is required when a metabolic balance is determined. This is a dynamic study at a particular period in time chosen with regard to the phase of the patient's illness, or his physiological or emotional state. The total body intake and output of the substance in question is determined; the difference constitutes the 'balance' and indicates whether the patient is at the time retaining or eliminating this substance. Only in a metabolic unit do the conditions prevail which ensure that the patient accepts the prescribed regimen and yields the required specimens. The investigation of psychiatric patients in a metabolic ward presents special difficulties. A co-operative patient is often said to be the most essential requirement of a successful metabolic study [30], but the psychiatrist cannot afford the luxury of excluding difficult and disturbed patients from his researches. The mentally ill patient may decline his diet because of loss of appetite or through fear that he is being poisoned. He may withhold specimens of urine or faeces because of negativism or inability to grasp the reasons for the investigation. For these reasons, it is essential to set up a research team whose members collaborate in their endeavours to understand their patients' anxieties and the nature of their illnesses, as well as in the research. The team consists of the clinical psychiatrist, the nurse, the dietitian and the laboratory technician. Because of her close contact with the patients, the nurse's role is all-important. Her training in the management of psychiatric patients equips her for the task of obtaining their confidence and their co-operation. The nursing staff of the Metabolic Unit of the Maudsley Hospital were led by Sister C. Gillies who has described the nursing principles involved in the investigation and care of patients in a psychiatric metabolic ward [57]. All members of the team must learn to readjust their orientation, which must now comprise a quest for knowledge as well as a zeal for treatment.

When a patient purposely seeks to evade the prescribed diet or goes out of his way to deceive the staff, special supervision and restrictions will be required. For this reason 'dry toilets' are essential in the psychiatric metabolic ward; collections of urine and faeces are made more reliable and the patient can less easily vomit or dispose of his food without escaping detection. The unco-operative patient usually learns that evasion of the rules is so difficult that he might as well comply with them. Nevertheless, on rare occasions the patient may be so wily as to elude surveillance, and to guard against such a contingency over-all checks of the reliability of the metabolic balances are advisable.

The best check is the measurement of the patient's insensible weight loss (I.W.L.) [45]. In a subject living and working under uniform conditions the I.W.L. remains relatively constant from day to day and indicates the expenditure of energy. It represents mainly the evaporative losses of water from the lungs and skin, and is calculated in the course of 24 hours from the known exchanges by the body, as shown in the formula:

$$\text{I.W.L.} = \text{Weight of ingested materials} - (\text{Weight of excreted materials} + \text{Gain in body weight})$$

If the body weight decreases, the gain in weight is counted as a negative quantity in the above formula. Although the I.W.L. is seldom used to measure energy expenditure, it is very useful as a check. For any individual patient the I.W.L. should remain fairly constant between 600 and 1,200 g. per day. Any significant deviation means that the patient's recorded intake of food or fluids is unreliable, that he is vomiting, or that the collections of urine or faeces are incomplete. Further inquiry will disclose which of these explanations is correct.

Another approximate check is provided by measuring the daily urinary excretion of creatinine which remains roughly constant and reflects the subject's lean body mass. The constancy of the urinary creatinine output is used as an index of the accuracy of the 24-hour collections of urine. This check is not foolproof, however, and in any case fails to detect other errors that may arise in the determination of the metabolic balance.

MORAL ASPECTS OF RESEARCH IN PSYCHIATRIC PATIENTS

At first glance the environment of the metabolic unit with its emphasis on physical investigations might seem inimical to the patient's recovery. It might, for example, encourage hypochondriacal tendencies, or reinforce the patient's wish to maintain the passive role of the sick person instead of grappling with his psychological problems. In short, it might be said that the research is likely to interfere with the patient's recovery. This was seldom, if ever, found to be the case. The patients soon accepted the idea of co-operating in the research and, far from retarding their recovery, the ward environment had a positive therapeutic effect, probably because of the intensive nursing and medical care provided.

The commonest moral problem encountered when carrying out

research on psychiatric patients is that of withholding treatment which would interfere with the investigations. For instance, chlorpromazine is said to be the treatment of choice in patients with anorexia nervosa [16]. Its administration to the patients studied would, however, almost certainly have altered their metabolic and endocrine status, and made it impossible to interpret the findings obtained. It was decided, therefore, to try to increase the weight of these patients without resorting to the drug. A comparable therapeutic benefit was obtained by concentrating on nursing and by administering a liquid high-calorie diet [57, 59]. Withholding treatment is always a burning question and much of the skill of clinical research lies in the investigator's ability to plan the treatment and the experiments so that they do not interfere with each other.

In general, the moral issues that face the investigator of mentally ill patients do not differ from those encountered in patients with physical illnesses. They have been fully described elsewhere [2, 38]. It is accepted that the research procedure should not endanger the health or life of the patient, or cause him distress unless the risk is heavily offset by the likelihood that he will benefit personally by the experiment. If the patient is unlikely to benefit from the research, his consent must be sought if he is to be considered a true volunteer. He must understand fully the nature of the investigation and the risks involved, and give his consent freely. Here lies the crux of the question of conducting research in psychiatric patients. From the experimental point of view the mentally ill are often grouped with condemned prisoners, conscientious objectors and children in whom there is serious doubt about the nature of the consent given or the understanding of the research procedure. The objections to experiments in these groups of subjects are obviously very strong, but these restrictions do not necessarily apply to mentally ill patients. The Medical Research Council in a statement on the responsibility of clinical investigators has given the following advice [41]:

> 'In the case of those who are mentally sub-normal or mentally disordered the reality of the consent given will fall to be judged by similar criteria to those which apply to the making of a will, contracting a marriage or otherwise taking decisions which have legal force as well as moral and social implications.'

The patient's capacity to understand the implications and risks of an experiment is likely to cut across diagnostic categories and may be fully preserved in spite of serious psychological aberrations. A patient detained under the Mental Health Act for the compulsory treatment of his mental illness may be capable of expressing consent, but it is difficult to accept that such a consent could ever be freely given.

Under such circumstances experiments involving risk or significant distress should in general not be undertaken. The investigator should also guard against conducting research in patients who give their consent too readily as a result of abnormal attitudes stemming from their illness. For example, a hypochondriacal patient may too eagerly accept repeated investigations because he is convinced that a physical disorder will thus be unearthed; or a masochistic patient may obtain positive gratification from being subjected to physical procedures which other persons would regard as painful or distressing.

Another consideration that applies particularly to psychiatric patients is whether it is always desirable to explain fully the nature of the investigation. When the experiment involves no risk and only minimal discomfort, it may be unnecessary to go through this procedure for the reason that an apprehensive patient may become unduly alarmed or an irritable patient may respond with anger or suspicion. Such situations arise with minor procedures as when blood is withdrawn by venepuncture, or when a drug known to be safe is administered. On these occasions it seems officious to labour the experimental nature of the investigation, and the formal request for consent may be omitted. Occasionally a patient responds adversely to the knowledge that he has been asked to participate in research. One such patient in the Metabolic Unit consented to having his eye movements recorded by a modified EEG apparatus. The test involved the intravenous administration of a small dose of amylobarbitone to measure his sedation threshold. Several years later he returned to hospital with a paranoid illness and accused the investigator of implanting microphones in his head and thus transmitting his thoughts to the outside world. Had he not been told that the test was a research procedure he would probably not have developed this particular delusion. Although he would undoubtedly have shown other delusions, and the experiment almost certainly played no part in the causation of his paranoid illness, nevertheless it was a mistake to give this patient information which he later distorted, with a resulting resentment towards the doctor on whom he depended for treatment. It might be argued, of course, that it would have been better not to have undertaken the investigation. Yet it is the clinician's duty to carry out research in man if experiments in animals cannot contribute to advances in the understanding and treatment of disease. This consideration certainly applies to psychiatric disorders.

Thus psychiatric research often raises serious moral issues. The Medical Research Council has proffered advice on how to resolve difficulties in the case of research in physically ill patients. They recommend that the research worker should allow himself to be influenced by professional discipline and accept the advice of his colleagues who have the requisite medical expertise which enables them to understand the complications and risks of the experiments. This procedure can also be applied to research in psychiatric patients with the proviso that it becomes highly desirable for the medical arbiter to know the clinical details of the patient's illness, and thus judge his reaction as a mentally ill person to the investigation in question. In his personal contact with the patients and researchers in the Metabolic Unit Lewis frequently undertook this role. At times he may have been unaware that his advice was being actively sought, but he combined so harmoniously a concern for the welfare of his patients with a curiosity for knowledge that his guidance was always carefully heeded.

The research undertaken in the Metabolic Unit until the time of Lewis' retirement will now be reviewed. Reference has already been made to the work on recurrent mental illness [48] which was initiated by Drs. J. H. Rey and D. R. C. Willcox, and which preceded the main stream of this research. Unfortunately, shortage of space makes it necessary to omit some of the papers which have emanated from the Metabolic Unit [21, 22, 42].

ANOREXIA NERVOSA

Lewis frequently questioned whether anorexia nervosa deserves a privileged place in a classification of psychiatric disorders. Is it not more likely that anorexia nervosa is merely a symptom which might arise as a result of a psychiatric illness such as depression, or as a manifestation of various disturbances of the personality, namely, hysteria, hypochondriasis or obsessional neurosis? To this question affirmative answers have often been given [4, 34]. On the other hand, experience with 50 patients admitted to the Metabolic Unit over the course of 7 years has shown that a syndrome of anorexia nervosa can be identified with relative ease. It is true that the fundamental causes of this syndrome remain unknown, but its place in psychiatric nosology seems no less assured than that of schizophrenia or manic-depressive psychosis. The criteria for the recognition of the syndrome are as follows:

1. The patient is resolved to lose weight. This end is achieved usually by eating less, but it may be attained with even greater speed by the addition of self-induced vomiting or purgation, or by excessive exercise.

2. The patient displays a more or less specific psychopathology characterized by a morbid fear of becoming fat. There is a disturbed awareness of the body image, so that the patient believes that her ideal weight is at a level which is ridiculously low by normal standards. She is liable to over-estimate her weight: her belief that she is

adequately nourished, or even fat, in the presence of gross emaciation may acquire the intensity of a delusion.

3. In female patients who develop the illness during the reproductive span of their lives, cessation of menstruation is an early and protracted manifestation.

4. There is no primary psychiatric disorder to account for the psychopathology, e.g. depression, or any physical disease responsible for the malnutrition, e.g. a malabsorption syndrome.

Anorexia nervosa is much commoner in females than in males by a ratio exceeding 10–1; it may occur for the first time in childhood or in middle age, but is commonest in adolescent girls soon after the onset of puberty. Since the clear delineation of Sheehan's syndrome (panhypopituitarism) there is no longer any excuse for diagnostic confusion between this condition and anorexia nervosa.

Studies of the Development and Nature of the Malnutrition in Anorexia Nervosa

The malnutrition of anorexia nervosa has suffered from academic neglect at the hands of nutritionists. Yet this form of malnutrition is interesting because it is an extreme example of caloric deprivation with a relative sufficiency of protein intake. This particular choice of diet by the patient is presumably due to her belief—probably justified—that she will lose weight most rapidly by depriving herself of starchy foods which are usually the main source of calories in a normal diet. TABLE 5 shows the composition of an average diet in normal subjects with respect to carbohydrate, fat and protein [54]. Also shown is the mean intake of these chief dietary constituents in a series of 9 patients with anorexia nervosa who were permitted a free choice of food during the first few days of their admission to the Metabolic Unit. It is evident that they selectively cut out carbohydrate-containing foods while they consumed relatively adequate amounts of fat and protein.

TABLE 5

CHOICE OF DIET IN ANOREXIA NERVOSA (MEAN OF 9 PATIENTS).

		SOURCE OF CALORIES (%)		
	CALORIES	PROTEIN	FAT	CARBOHYDRATE
Anorexia nervosa	1030	18·2	48·5	33·3
Normal	1500+	10–12	33–39	50–53

It is not surprising therefore that in spite of severe weight loss and emaciation, there may be little evidence of impaired protein metabolism until the malnutrition becomes extreme. For example, the levels of plasma free aminoacids remain normal in anorexia nervosa [54], in contrast with the findings in kwashiorkor, an illness caused primarily by an insufficiency of protein [31]. An analysis of the body tissue laid down after refeeding was made in 4 female patients treated in the Metabolic Unit [59]. The methods consisted of nitrogen balances to deduce the rate of protein synthesis, and indirect calorimetry to determine the caloric balance and the assimilation of fatty tissue. From these measurements and a knowledge of the weight gain, it was possible to calculate the retention of water and hence complete the tissue analysis. The average proportions were as follows: protein 7 per cent., fat 77 per cent., and water 16 per cent. It was also found that, on the average, for each kg. gain in weight the patient had to ingest a surplus of 7,500 calories over and above the calorie expenditure required for basal metabolism, the maintenance of body temperature and any physical work that was carried out. Instead of expressing the results in chemical terms they may also be given as proportions of the reconstituted body tissues: 1 kg. gain in weight would consist of 230 g. cellular tissue and 770 g. fatty tissue. The high proportion of fat deposited was confirmed by estimations of the respiratory quotients which exceeded unity when the patients were rapidly gaining weight. Direct measurements of skinfold thickness also showed rapid increases at different body sites. The low rate of protein synthesis suggests that the patients were not markedly depleted of protein at the start of the investigation. Some protection against protein depletion may be due to the reserves of fatty tissue in female subjects as opposed to males. Support for this view came from nitrogen balance studies in 3 male subjects with anorexia nervosa in whom protein depletion was more evident than in the female patients [54]. Nevertheless, even if the malnutrition of anorexia nervosa does not affect protein metabolism primarily, it leads to considerable ill health and may endanger life.

Complications of the Malnutrition in Anorexia Nervosa

The view is sometimes expressed that all the disturbances of body physiology and chemistry in anorexia nervosa are secondary to the malnutrition. It is certain that many of them are but the amenorrhoea at least is probably an exception, as will be shown later.

In severely emaciated patients oedema of the lower extremities may develop—the so-called famine oedema. Of greater significance, however, is the depletion of potassium which, when severe, may lead to hypokalaemia. Muscular paralysis may follow, though this complication must be very rare, and vacuolar degeneration of the renal tubules has also been ascribed to potassium deficiency [66]. Patients who vomit repeatedly are most likely to develop hypokalaemia but a depletion of body potassium may also occur in the absence of vomiting, and is probably present before there is any fall in the serum level. This has been demonstrated by metabolic balances of nitrogen and potassium carried out while the patients were being refed and gaining weight [52]. Potassium and nitrogen were both retained but the ratio of potassium (expressed in mEq.) to nitrogen (expressed in g.) varied from 3·2 to 6·9, whereas this ratio is normally lower (2·4–3·5) [18]. The relatively high retention of potassium on refeeding indicates that this electrolyte is selectively depleted in the malnourished patient.

Another consequence of long-standing malnutrition in anorexia nervosa is the impaired diuretic response to drinking a water load [56]. FIGURE 4A shows that in a normal subject urinary dilution begins within one hour and the water load is completely excreted within 4 hours. In contrast, FIGURE 4B shows the delay in dilution of the urine in a patient with anorexia nervosa: many hours may be needed before the urinary osmolality falls below the plasma osmolality. As a result the excretion of the water load is long delayed. This phenomenon is neither due to adrenal insufficiency nor to excessive or inappropriate secretion of antidiuretic hormone. The exact mechanism is uncertain but diminution in the glomerular filtration rate may play a part in the delayed diuresis. The patients usually suffer no ill effects from this complication unless they drink large quantities of water when water intoxication may occur. They report frequency of micturition at night because of increased excretion of urine from lying down. The normal diuretic response can be restored by correcting the malnutrition, but recovery sometimes takes several months.

The Possible Hypothalamic Basis of Anorexia Nervosa

Following the demonstration that bilateral destruction of the lateral hypothalamic areas may cause animals to starve themselves to death [1], the possibility has been considered that a disturbance of hypothalamic function may be the cause of anorexia nervosa. In addition to the anorexia, some of the other clinical features have their counterparts in the results of experimental lesions—the failure of reproductive function and disturbances in the regulation of water balance. So far, however, the only support for this hypothesis arises from the observation that the cessation of menstruation in anorexia nervosa is not solely due to the malnutrition [53]. Clinicians have been aware that amenorrhoea frequently precedes weight loss [34]. Hormone studies in 7 female patients receiving treatment were conducted in the Metabolic Unit [3, 58]. FIGURE 5 shows the results in a patient in whom, when she was malnourished, there was a

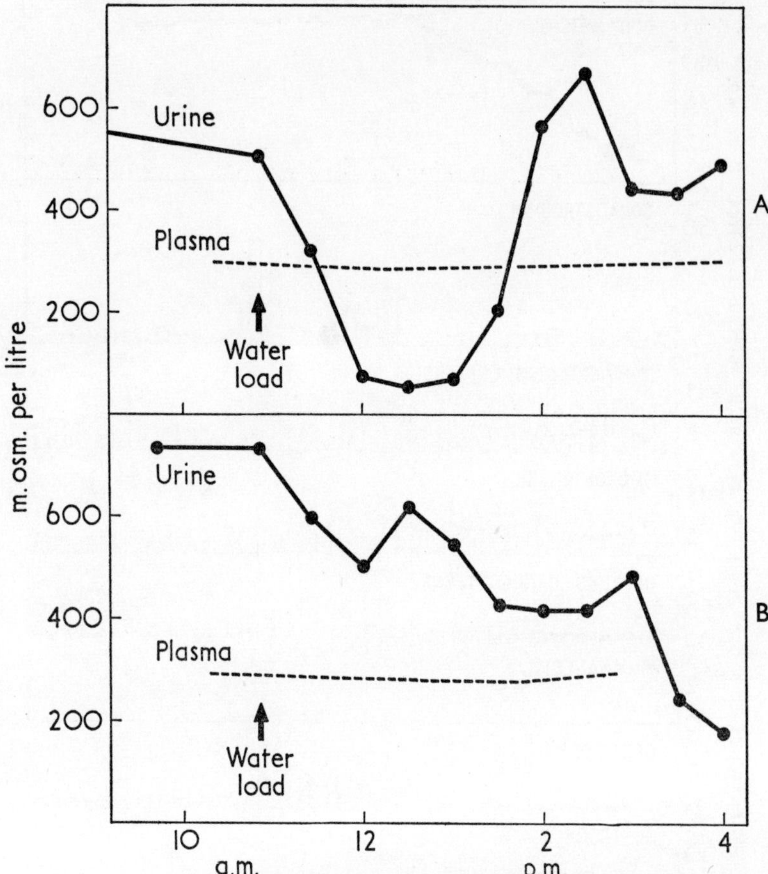

FIG. 4. A. Normal response to drinking 1,200 ml. water. Within 1 hour the osmolality of the urine fell below that of the plasma. B. Abnormal response in a patient with anorexia nervosa to the water load. The urine osmolality fell below the plasma osmolality only after 4 hours.

considerable diminution in the urinary output of human pituitary gonadotrophins (HPG) and in the 3 oestrogen fractions measured—oestriol, oestrone and oestradiol. The reduction of oestriol was even greater than that of the other two oestrogen fractions. Refeeding resulted in a gradual rise in the output of HPG and of the oestrogen fractions, with a return to the more normal proportions of oestriol, oestrone and oestradiol. On the other hand, the HPG did not always reach normal levels, and in no patient was there a return to a cyclical pattern of excretion of oestrogens and HPG such as would

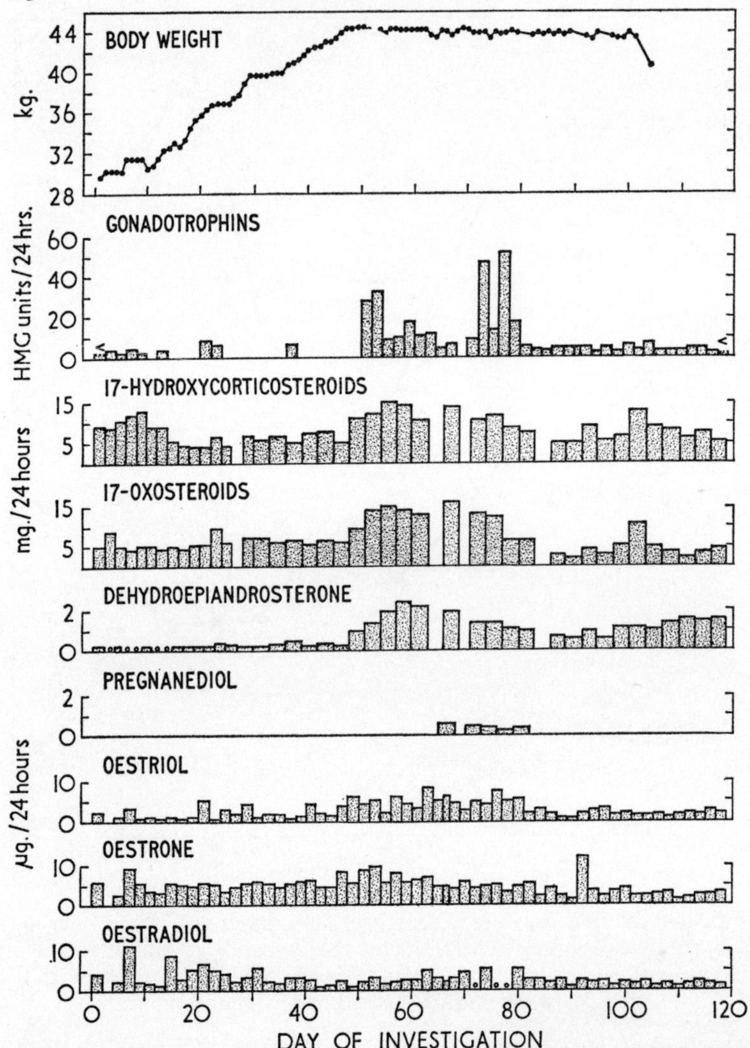

FIG. 5. Weight chart, and urinary output of hormones in a patient with anorexia nervosa while she was being refed.

HMG. Human Menopausal Gonadotrophin, First International Reference Preparation.

portend the resumption of menstruation and ovulation. This was true in spite of continuing the hormone studies for several weeks during the course of which vigorous treatment had led to a considerable weight gain. The patients were followed up for 3–27 months and in only one was there a return of normal menstruation after 11 months. Thus there is some evidence supporting the hypothesis of a primary hypothalamic disturbance to account for the amenorrhoea of anorexia nervosa. The other clinical features, however, and the psychopathology in particular, still defy explanation in these terms.

The Persistence of Morbid Attitudes to Feeding in Anorexia Nervosa

After receiving treatment in the Metabolic Unit most patients returned to a normal weight or fell just short of it. Although the psychotherapy they received was not intensive the majority of patients showed a considerable psychological improvement, losing their general symptoms of depression, agitation and irritability. On discharge from hospital they were usually confident that they had lost their unhealthy desire to become thin. Experience has taught, however, that this confidence is often misplaced. The illness tends to run a chronic course, or is punctuated by frequent relapses. A study of the variations in the patients' food intake immediately before discharge demonstrated the persistence of feeding problems [54]. Negative correlations were found between their calorie intake and their mental state from day to day: when the patients forced themselves to eat, they often reacted by becoming somewhat tense or depressed. It is not surprising that such patients gradually reduce the amounts they eat in order to obtain relief from their worst psychological symptoms.

Physiological Studies of the Disorder of Appetite

It has become increasingly recognized that the description 'anorexia nervosa' is at times a misnomer, as some patients have no true loss of appetite but wilfully deprive themselves of food. Other patients, however, may say that they have lost all desire for food. In them a derangement of the mechanisms regulating hunger may be postulated. Two studies were carried out to test this hypothesis. In the first [61] gastric motility was recorded and compared in a series of patients and in matched normal subjects. No significant changes were found. A patient with anorexia nervosa may protest that she can no longer experience hunger, but her gastric contractions are likely to remain normally active. In the second study [55], capillary and venous glucose levels were increased in patients after a glucose tolerance test. The difference between these two levels is said to indicate the rate of glucose utilization which in turn may be detected by glucoreceptors in the hypothalamus [40]. This theory received no support from the reported study. Although significant differences were found between patients with anorexia nervosa, normals, and obese subjects, they vanished within a few days of feeding the patients with corrective diets. The failure to detect any disturbance of the mechanisms controlling hunger may reflect the limitations of our understanding of the factors which normally regulate the intake of food.

DEPRESSIVE ILLNESS

Three sets of studies were undertaken, the first dealing with endocrine aspects of depression, the second with changes in body weight, water and electrolytes, and the last with sleep disturbances.

Endocrine Aspects of Depression

An early study conducted in the Metabolic Unit and initiated by Dr. (now Professor) J. G. Gibson indicated that during the course of a depressive illness thyroid function was normal and remained stable, whereas adrenocortical function showed some fluctuations usually in the direction of enhanced activity [24]. The increases in adrenocortical activity appeared to occur mainly in patients with anxiety or agitation or with preoccupations of a sexual nature. These observations needed confirmation, however, for they were based on urinary steroid assays which have been superseded by more satisfactory methods. This study provided a lead which was followed by Drs J. L. Gibbons and P. R. McHugh who carried out further investigations of adrenocortical function in depressed patients.

The plasma cortisol level was measured [25] in 17 patients with severe (so-called endogenous) depression. The method used was that of Peterson *et al.* [46] which depends on the production of a chromogen (the Porter-Silber reaction); normally cortisol accounts for 90–95 per cent. of the chromogen thus measured. Care was taken to carry out the test on blood removed from the patients at a set time of the morning so as to allow for the diurnal variation in the cortisol level which falls during the day. The mean level was 22 μg. per 100 ml. when the patients were first tested 1 week after admission to hospital. Serial measurements at approximately weekly intervals over periods of 8–12 weeks showed a fluctuating decline in the plasma cortisol commensurate with clinical improvement of the depression. The mean level of the last samples taken from each patient was 11 μg. per 100 ml. which was now close to that reported for normal subjects in other studies [5]. This elevation of plasma cortisol in general reflected the severity of the illness. This finding was not considered to be specific for the depressive illness itself, but was thought to indicate the degree of emotional turmoil and distress experienced by the patients. It was interesting that the markedly retarded patients showed at least as great an elevation in plasma cortisol as did severely agitated patients. This finding lends force to Lewis' early observations on the turbulence of distressing thoughts in retarded patients: their slowness of reaction and their poverty of speech conceal the 'ceaseless roundabout of painful thought' from which they suffer [36].

Although the finding of elevated plasma cortisol levels in depression was highly significant, it was considered desirable to leave no room for doubt. After all, the increased Porter-Silber chromogen might conceivably have represented a steroid other than cortisol: or again, it might have been due to an increase in protein-bound steroid whereas it is probably only the free steroid which is biologically active. Accordingly, in a further series of depressed patients, the secretion rate of cortisol was measured at the height of their illness, and after they had recovered [23]. The method was based on that of Cope and Black [11] and depended on measuring the degree of dilution in the body cortisol pool of a known quantity of isotopically-labelled cortisol (4-C^{14}) administered orally. The mean secretion rate of cortisol before treatment was 26 μg. per 24 hours, and after recovery or improvement, it had decreased to 14 μg. per 24 hours, irrespective of the kind of treatment the patient had received or whether improvement had been spontaneous. There was a high positive correlation between the measurements of plasma cortisol and those of cortisol secretion rates, thus confirming the conclusion already drawn that depressed patients show increased adrenocortical activity. The biological importance of this phenomenon is uncertain: it may have represented an adaptive function in primitive man but its benefits are no longer obvious. On the other hand, the raised levels of cortisol in depression are unlikely to be harmful. In contrast with the persistent elevations of plasma cortisol in Cushing's syndrome, the levels in depressed patients decline during the day as they still show a normal diurnal variation; hence there is less sustained exposure of the tissues to the possibly harmful effects of cortisol. In a full review, Michael and Gibbons [43] have discussed further the interrelationship between adrenocortical function and psychiatric disorders.

Changes in Body Weight, Water and Electrolytes in Depression

Loss of weight is sometimes a conspicuous feature of depressive illness and the clinical progress of patients can be gauged by observing whether they are regaining their lost weight. Such changes in body weight are most likely to be due to alterations in appetite and food intake, but the possibility remained that they might represent shifts in the balance of water and sodium. These shifts have been described in mental illness [15, 27, 35, 49, 63].

The first study designed to investigate this question relied on metabolic balances in fifteen depressed patients who were all treated with electro-convulsive therapy [50]. They were fed on diets of constant composition containing sufficient quantities of sodium and potassium to allow the detection of shifts of these electrolytes should they occur; the water intake was also kept fixed. The intake and output of water, sodium and potassium were measured each day and the average daily balance (intake minus output) was calculated over the period when the patients were depressed and again after they had improved or recovered; the balance studies lasted from 14 to 35 days. No significant changes in the balance of water, sodium or potassium followed recovery. The patient's body weight was also recorded daily on a sensitive beam balance. Recovery from the depression did not bring about any change in the trend in body weight so long as the patients' food intake remained constant. This finding confirms that the clinical recovery from the depression is not accompanied by any significant changes in body water. The gain in weight that accompanies recovery is chiefly due to a return of appetite and an increase in the intake of food. An incidental observation was that the ECT administered was followed by a small but significant retention of sodium and water during the ensuing 24 hours. To extend this study the real ECT was interspersed with 'mock' ECT when the electrical shock was omitted from the therapeutic procedure. Again there resulted a retention of sodium and water so that it was concluded that this effect was caused by the patient's anxiety while awaiting his treatment rather than by the electrical shock itself.

In a second study on body electrolytes in depression, the method used depended on the principle of isotope dilution [20]. After administering small known amounts of radioactive isotopes of sodium (Na^{24}) and potassium (K^{42}), a period of 24 hours was allowed for equilibration throughout the body. The specific activity of a 'spot' sample of urine was then measured for Na^{24} and K^{42}, sometimes supplemented by counting the activity of a serum sample take around the same time. By comparing these specific activities with those of the original amounts of the administered isotopes, suitably diluted, it was possible to calculate the total body exchangeable sodium and potassium. A total of twenty-four depressed patients were tested before and after treatment which consisted usually of ECT. Sixteen patients recovered from their depression and in them there was a mean decrease of 9 per cent. in the total exchangeable sodium; 8 patients failed to recover and showed no significant change in their total exchangeable sodium. There was no significant alteration in the exchangeable potassium after recovery. The findings suggested that depression is accompanied by a retention of sodium which is excreted after recovery.

This conclusion appears at first to be at variance with the results of the balance studies. The explanation may be that the isotope technique did not measure strictly the total body sodium, but rather that proportion which is exchanged within the course of 24 hours. The dynamics of the exchange of sodium in the body is therefore an important factor to consider, as is the distribution of sodium within the different body compartments. The greatest proportion of body sodium is in the extracellular space, but there is also a considerable component in bone, some of which does not exchange or does so only slowly. These factors therefore complicate the interpretation of the results of the isotope technique. At present the best evidence is that depressive illness is not accompanied by an alteration in total body sodium. Nevertheless there is scope for further examination of the transfer and distribution of sodium, as is shown by the findings of Dr. A. J. Coppen who has reported an abnormal distribution of sodium between the different compartments where exchange takes place [14].

Coppen has also reported a study on the transfer of sodium from the blood into the cerebrospinal fluid of depressed patients [12]. This work will be summarized here as it was conducted while he was a member of the Metabolic Unit. The subjects were given a small dose of radioactive sodium (Na^{24}) intravenously. The specific activities of a sample of plasma and a sample of cerebrospinal fluid both taken 1 hour later were compared, and the rate of entry of sodium into the cerebrospinal fluid expressed as a ratio of these two values. The one-hour ratio was measured in three groups of patients who were not suffering from a depression at the time, namely schizophrenics, patients who had recovered from a depressive illness, and psychiatrically normal subjects who were given a spinal anaesthetic for an abdominal operation. The mean values obtained were very similar in the three groups and averaged 3·9 per cent. In contrast, the one-hour ratio was significantly diministed in a group of depressed patients before treatment (2·7 per cent.), and in another group of patients who remained depressed even after receiving a course of 5 ECT's (2·4 per cent.). It would seem therefore that the rate of entry of sodium from the plasma into the cerebrospinal fluid of depressed patients is significantly low and that its return to normal depends on an improvement in the clinical state rather than on any effect of electro-convulsive therapy. This finding has been partly confirmed [19]. It remains uncertain, however, whether the reduced sodium entry is a fundamental metabolic change responsible for the depression, or whether it is merely secondary to the abnormal mental state, and the reduced physical activity of the patients.

Sleep Disturbances in Depression

In the final study to be reported on depressive illness [29], Dr. (now Professor) J. M. Hinton investigated sleep patterns by means of an activity bed which recorded electrically the motility of the patients [28]. These observations were supplemented with the patients' self-ratings of their sleep and records kept by the night nurses. In addition to finding that depressed patients slept poorly and were restless at night, there emerged two patterns of insomnia—delayed sleep and early waking. The early waking pattern usually occurred in the more agitated patients whose insomnia was the more severe and who showed greater restlessness at night. The pattern of insomnia bore no relation to the groupings of patients according to the subdivisions of endogenous and reactive depressions.

PREMENSTRUAL TENSION

If Lewis had some doubts about the clinical identity of anorexia nervosa he was even more sceptical that premenstrual tension represented anything more than an accentuation of pre-existent neurotic symptoms at a time of stress. Nevertheless he encouraged a study which aimed at testing the prevailing view on the cause of the premenstrual syndrome [9]. This was that a hormonal imbalance during the second half of the menstrual cycle leads to an abnormal retention of sodium and water which in turn causes the symptoms of tension, depression and irritability comprising the premenstrual syndrome. In support of this theory it is often said that premenstrual symptoms are accompanied by a gain in body weight and that the patient may complain of swollen ankles, hands or breasts. Psychiatric patients who reported these symptoms were therefore investigated.

In the first study, 24 patients who were not subjected to any major restrictions or disturbance of their living routine were weighed daily throughout their monthly cycles. There was no constant weight gain in the group as a whole during the premenstrual phase.

In the second study, metabolic balances of water, sodium and potassium were determined during at least one menstrual cycle while the patients were kept on a constant food intake in the manner already described in the section on depressive illness. The patients were weighed daily on a sensitive beam balance. Positive and significant correlations were found between the daily changes in body weight and the balances of water and sodium, thus testifying to the reliability of the balances. The gain in weight during the premenstrual phase of the cycle seldom exceeded 500 g. with a corresponding retention of water and sodium. These minimal physiological changes were overshadowed by more abrupt and, therefore, more convincing, weight gains during the middle of the menstrual cycle at the time of ovulation. The results in a typical patient are illustrated in FIGURE 6. FIGURE 7 shows the weight charts of the 10

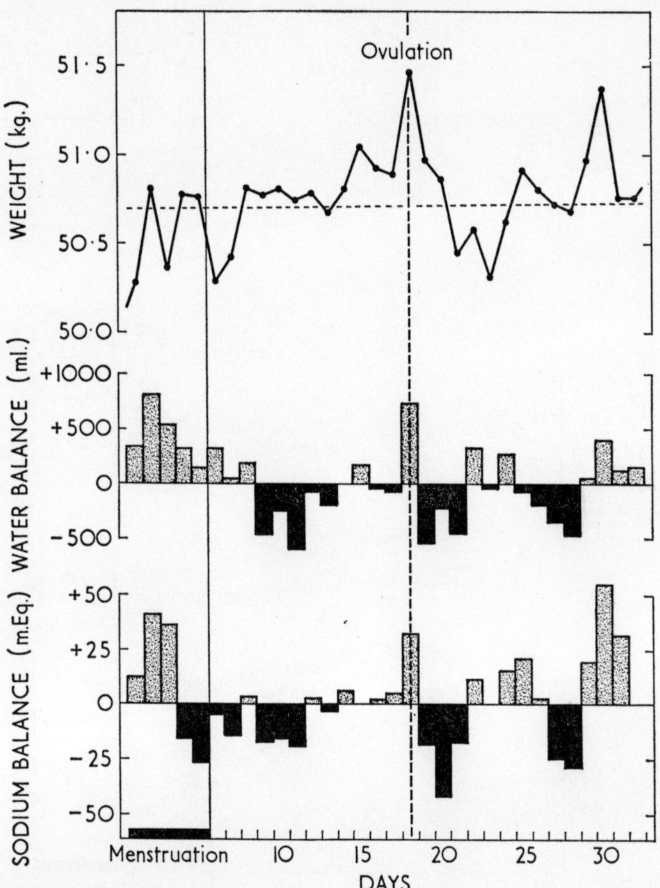

FIG. 6. Weight chart, water and sodium balance in a patient who had reported premenstrual tension. The gain in weight and the retention of water and sodium are more marked at the time of ovulation than premenstrually.

patients studied. The premenstrual physiological changes were not regularly accompanied by an accentuation of the psychiatric symptoms; the mid-cycle retention of water and sodium never caused any psychological disturbance to the patients. It was concluded that

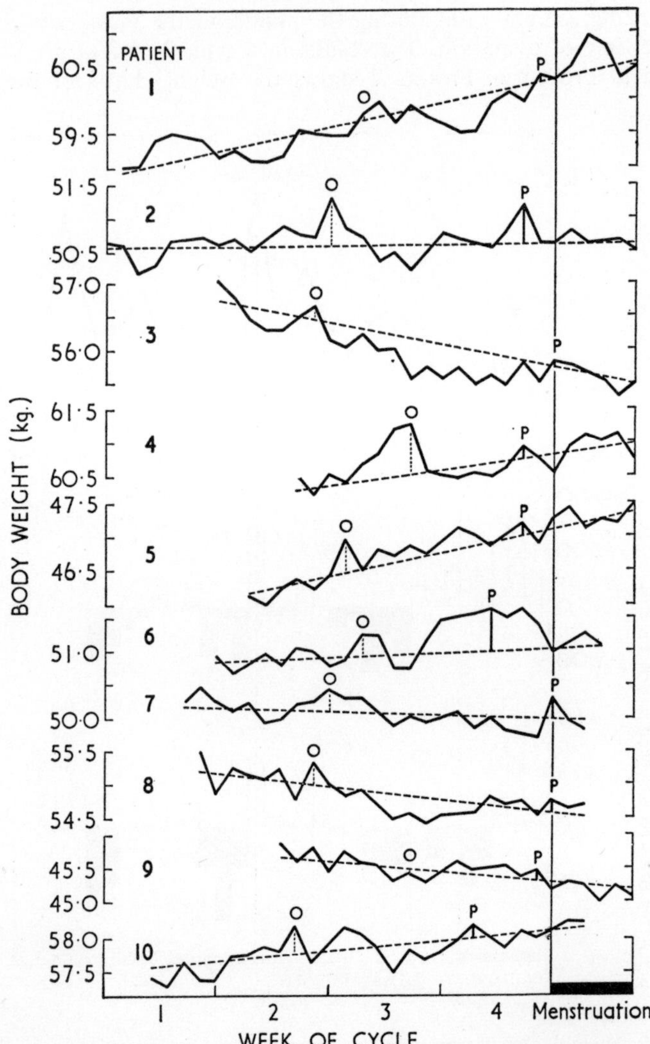

FIG. 7. Weight charts of ten patients with reported premenstrual symptoms. The vertical line (P) shows the greatest premenstrual weight gain. The vertical interrupted line (O) shows the weight change at ovulation.

premenstrual symptoms are not necessarily accompanied by any significant retention of water and gain of body weight. Neither do such metabolic changes, whether at ovulation or premenstrually, inevitably give rise to symptoms.

FUNDAMENTAL RESEARCH

A number of basic studies were carried out to increase the understanding of the physiological mechanisms relevant to the clinical research which was in progress.

The Action of a Barbiturate Drug on the Vestibulo-ocular Reflex

As it was intended to measure the sedation threshold to amylobarbitone sodium in psychiatric patients, a preliminary investigation was carried out on the effects of this drug on eye movements in normal subjects [47]. It is known that visual fixation tends to inhibit the nystagmus induced by caloric stimulation of the semicircular canals of the inner ear. The barbiturate drug was given to two normal subjects and it was found that this inhibitory effect of visual fixation was abolished. The reason is that the barbiturate interferes with the mechanism for smooth eye movements which maintains the stationary image on the retina, whereas the drug has no effect on the smooth movements resulting from the vestibular stimulation. This selective action on the smooth pursuit movements of the eyes is a conspicuous effect of barbiturates, and amylobarbitone was subsequently used to measure the sedation threshold in depressed patients [26].

The Effects of Varying the Composition of Diets on Body Weight, Water and Sodium Balance

While depressed patients were being investigated for the effects of their illness on body weight and the balance of water and sodium, it was noted that variations in diet had more profound consequences than the illness itself. It was already known that variations in the calorie, salt or water content of the diet produced these changes, but it was also suspected that the relative proportions of carbohydrate, fat and protein might be important. This was shown to be the case by varying the proportions of carbohydrate in diets given to obese patients while keeping the intake of calories, sodium, and water constant [51]. A high carbohydrate diet was found to cause retention of sodium and water with a corresponding change in body weight. On a diet relatively rich in protein and fat, the reverse was true. It is evident that the only way to avoid these dietary artifacts while conducting metabolic balances is to ensure that the patients receive a constant diet throughout the investigation.

Saliva-serum Ratios of Tritium after the Administration of Tritiated Water

Total body water can conveniently be estimated by the method of isotope dilution using tritiated water. The method depends on the principle that when the isotopic label becomes uniformly distributed throughout the body water, the total water content of the body can be deduced from measuring the specific activity of water obtained from a sample of a body fluid. But doubt has been cast on this method by workers [64] who had suggested that human salivary glands could distinguish between hydrogen and its isotopes: they used deuterium for the purpose. It was therefore decided to test this finding by comparing the specific activities of saliva and serum water after giving a small dose of tritiated water to normal subjects [13]. The specific activities were found to be equal. There is, therefore, no reason to doubt the validity of the isotope dilution method using tritiated water for the measurement of total body water.

This brief review shows that during the first years of its existence the Metabolic Unit has already made good progress under Sir Aubrey Lewis' guidance. The future should witness the continued development of metabolic research in psychiatry.

REFERENCES

1. Anand, B. K., and Brobeck, J. R. (1951) Localization of a 'feeding centre' in the hypothalamus of the rat, *Proc. Soc. exp. Biol.* (*N.Y.*), **77**, 323.
2. Beecher, H. K. (1960) *Experimentation in Man*, American Lectures in Medicine, Monograph No. 352, Springfield, Ill.
3. Bell, E. T., Harkness, R. A., Loraine, J. A., and Russell, G. F.M. (1966) Hormone assay studies in patients with anorexia nervosa, *Acta Endocr.* (*Kbh.*), **51**, 140.
4. Bliss, E. L., and Branch, C. H. H. (1960) *Anorexia Nervosa. Its History, Psychology, and Biology,* Psychosomatic Medicine Monograph, New York.
5. Bliss, E. L., Migeon, C. J., Branch, C. H. H., and Samuels, L. T. (1956) Reaction of the adrenal cortex to emotional stress, *Psychosom. Med.*, **18**, 56.
6. Briscoe, O. V. (1962) The red cell life in schizophrenia, Dissertation for the Academic Postgraduate Diploma in Psychological Medicine, The University of London.
7. Brothwood, J. (1964) The plasma proteins in anorexia nervosa, Dissertation for the Academic Postgraduate Diploma in Psychological Medicine, The University of London.
8. Bruce, J. T. (1960) Weight changes and metabolic studies in patients with premenstrual symptoms, Dissertation for the Academic Postgraduate Diploma in Psychological Medicine, The University of London.
9. Bruce, J. T., and Russell, G. F. M. (1962) Premenstrual tension—a study of weight changes and balances of water, sodium and potassium, *Lancet*, ii, 267.

10. CHISHOLM, I. D. (1966) Psychiatric in-patients with hyperthyroidism, Dissertation for the Academic Postgraduate Diploma in Psychological Medicine, The University of London.

11. COPE, C. L., and BLACK, E. (1958) The production rate of cortisol in man, *Brit. med. J.*, i, 1020.

12. COPPEN, A. J. (1960) Abnormality of the blood-cerebrospinal fluid barrier of patients suffering from a depressive illness, *J. Neurol. Neurosurg. Psychiat.*, **23**, 156.

13. COPPEN, A. J., and GIBBONS, J. L. (1960) Saliva-serum ratios of tritium after administration of tritiated water, *Nature* (*Lond.*), **186**, 724.

14. COPPEN, A. J., and SHAW, D. M. (1963) Mineral metabolism in melancholia, *Brit. med. J.*, ii, 1439.

15. CRAMMER, J. L. (1959) Water and sodium in two psychotics, *Lancet*, i, 1122.

16. DALLY, P., and SARGANT, W. (1966) Treatment and outcome of anorexia nervosa. *Brit. med. J.*, ii, 793.

17. DEWHURST, W. G. (1961) Amine metabolism in depressive illness with deductions on function drawn from other clinical data, Dissertation for the Academic Postgraduate Diploma in Psychological Medicine, The University of London.

18. ELKINGTON, J. R., and DANOWSKI, T. S. (1955) *The Body Fluids—Basic Physiology and Practical Therapeutics*, Baltimore, Md.

19. FOTHERBY, K., ASHCROFT, G. W., AFFLECK, J. W., and FORREST, A. D. (1962) Studies on sodium transfer and 5-hydroxyindoles in depressive illness, *J. Neurol. Neurosurg. Psychiat.*, **26**, 71.

20. GIBBONS, J. L. (1960) Total body sodium and potassium in depressive illness, *Clin. Sci.*, **19**, 133.

21. GIBBONS, J. L. (1961) Psychological factors in ovarian and uterine dysfunction, in *Modern Trends in Endocrinology*, p. 201, 2nd series, London.

22. GIBBONS, J. L. (1963) Electrolytes and depressive illness, *Postgrad. med. J.*, **39**, 19.

23. GIBBONS, J. L. (1964) Cortisol secretion rate in depressive illness, *Arch. gen. Psychiat.*, **10**, 572.

24. GIBBONS, J. L., GIBSON, J. G., MAXWELL, A. E., and WILLCOX, D. R. C. (1960) An endocrine study of depressive illness, *J. psychosom. Res.*, **5**, 32.

25. GIBBONS, J. L., and MCHUGH, P. R. (1962) Plasma cortisol in depressive illness, *J. Psychiat. Res.*, **1**, 162.

26. GILLAN, R. U. (1962) Barbiturate sensitivity, A study of the changes associated with recovery in depressed patients, Dissertation for the Academic Postgraduate Diploma in Psychological Medicine, University of London.

27. GJESSING, R. (1953) Beiträge zur Somatologie der periodischen Katatonie, VII. *Arch. Psychiat. Nervenkr.*, **191**, 247.

28. HINTON, J. M. (1961) The actions of amylobarbitone sodium, butobarbitone and quinalbarbitone sodium upon insomnia and

nocturnal restlessness compared in psychiatric patients, *Brit. J. Pharmacol.*, **16**, 82.

29. HINTON, J. M. (1962) Sleep and motility in depressive illness, *Proc. roy. Soc. Med.*, **55**, 907.
30. HODGES, R. E., and BEAN, W. B. (1960) The operation of a metabolic ward, *Nutr. Rev.*, **18**, 65.
31. HOLT, L. E., SNYDERMAN, S. E., NORTON, P. M., ROITMAN, E., and FINCH, J. (1963) The plasma aminogram in kwashiorkor, *Lancet*, ii, 1343.
32. ISAACS, A. D. (1962) Comparison of the effect of an anabolic steroid (methandienone) and dietary modification on body weight and nitrogen balance in elderly patients, Dissertation for the Academic Postgraduate Diploma in Psychological Medicine, The University of London.
33. JASPERS, K. (1962) *General Psychopathology*, German 7th ed. trans. Hoenig, J., and Hamilton, M. W., Manchester.
34. KAY, D. W. N., and LEIGH, A. D. (1954) The natural history, treatment and prognosis of anorexia nervosa, based on a study of 38 patients, *J. ment. Sci.*, **100**, 411.
35. KLEIN, R. (1950) Clinical and biochemical investigations in a manic-depressive with short cycles, *J. ment. Sci.*, **96**, 293.
36. LEWIS, A. J. (1960) Psychological medicine, in *Price's Textbook of the Practice of Medicine*, p. 1180, ed. Bodley Scott, R., London.
37. LEWIS, A. J. (1967) Aspects of psychosomatic medicine, in *Inquiries in Psychiatry*, London.
38. MCCANCE, R. A. (1951) The practice of experimental medicine, *Proc. roy. Soc. Med.*, **44**, 189.
39. MCNAMEE, H. B. (1966) Radio-isotope study of tryptophan metabolism, Dissertation for the Academic Postgraduate Diploma in Psychological Medicine, The University of London.
40. MAYER, J. (1955) Regulation of energy intake and the body weight: the glucostatic theory and the lipostatic hypothesis, *Ann. N.Y. Acad. Sci.*, **63**, 15.
41. MEDICAL RESEARCH COUNCIL REPORT FOR THE YEAR 1962–63–(1964) Responsibility in investigations on human subjects, p. 21., London, H.M.S.O.
42. MEZEY, A. G., and COPPEN, A. J. (1961) Respiratory adaptation to exercise in anxious patients, *Clin. Sci.*, **20**, 171.
43. MICHAEL, R., and GIBBONS, J. L. (1963) Interrelations between the endocrine system and neuropsychiatry, *Int. Rev. Neurobiol.*, **5**, 243.
44. MORGAN, H. G. (1966) Acute neuro-psychiatric complications of chronic alcoholism, Dissertation for the Academic Postgraduate Diploma in Psychological Medicine, The University of London.
45. PETERS, J. P., KYDD, D. M., and LAVIETES, P. H. (1933) A note on the calculation of water exchange, *J. clin. Invest.*, **12**, 689.
46. PETERSON, R. E., KARRER, A., and GUERRA, S. L. (1957) Evaluation of Silber-Porter procedure for determination of plasma hydrocortisone, *Analyt. Chem.*, **29**, 144.

47. Rashbass, C., and Russell, G. F. M. (1961) Action of a barbiturate drug (amylobarbitone sodium) on the vestibulo-ocular reflex, *Brain*, **84**, 329.

48. Rey, J. H., Willcox, D. R. C., Gibbons, J. L., Tait, H., and Lewis, D. J. (1961) Serial biochemical and endocrine investigations in recurrent mental illness, *J. psychosom. Res.*, **5**, 155.

49. Rowntree, D. W., and Kay, W. W. (1952) Clinical, biochemical and physiological studies in cases of recurrent schizophrenia, *J. ment. Sci.*, **98**, 100.

50. Russell, G. F. M. (1960) Body weight and balance of water, sodium and potassium in depressed patients given electro-convulsive therapy, *Clin. Sci.*, **19**, 327.

51. Russell, G. F. M. (1962) The effects of diets of different composition on weight loss, water, and sodium balance in obese patients, *Clin. Sci.*, **22**, 269.

52. Russell, G. F. M. (1964) Psychological factors in the control of food intake, in *Diet and Bodily Constitution*, p. 69, Ciba Foundation Study Group No. 17, London.

53. Russell, G. F. M. (1965) Metabolic aspects of anorexia nervosa, *Proc. roy. Soc. Med.*, **58**, 811.

54. Russell, G. F. M. (1967) The nutritional disorder in anorexia nervosa, *J. psychosom. Res.*, **11**, 141.

55. Russell, G. F. M., and Bruce, J. T. (1964) Capillary-venous glucose differences in patients with disorders of appetite, *Clin. Sci.*, **26**, 157.

56. Russell, G. F. M., and Bruce, J. T. (1966) Impaired diuresis in patients with anorexia nervosa, *Amer. J. Med.*, **40**, 38.

57. Russell, G. F. M., and Gillies, C. (1964) Anorexia nervosa—investigation and care of patients in a psychiatric metabolic ward, *Nursing Times*, **60**, 852.

58. Russell, G. F. M., Loraine, J. A., Bell, E. T., and Harkness, R. A. (1965) Gonadotrophin and oestrogen excretion in patients with anorexia nervosa, *J. psychosom. Res.*, **9**, 79.

59. Russell, G. F. M., and Mezey, A. G. (1962) An analysis of weight gain in patients with anorexia nervosa treated with high calorie diets, *Clin. Sci.*, **23**, 450.

60. Silverstone, J. T. (1964) Gastric motility in anorexia nervosa, Dissertation for the Academic Postgraduate Diploma in Psychological Medicine, The University of London.

61. Silverstone, J. T., and Russell, G. F. M. (1967) Gastric 'hunger' contractions in anorexia nervosa, *Brit. J. Psychiat.*, **113**, 257.

62. Smith, E. B. O. (1962) The study of erythrocyte potassium levels in depressive illnesses, Dissertation for the Academic Postgraduate Diploma in Psychological Medicine, The University of London.

63. Ström-Olsen, R., and Weil-Malherbe, H. (1958) Humoral changes in manic-depressive psychosis with particular reference to the excretion of catechol amines in urine, *J. ment. Sci.*, **105**, 696.

64. TAGGART, N., and HYTTEN, F. E. (1959) Saliva-serum ratios of deuterium oxide after administration of heavy water, *Nature* (*Lond.*), **184**, 457.

65. TONKS, D. C. M. (1962) Hypothyroidism and mental illness, Dissertation for the Academic Postgraduate Diploma in Psychological Medicine, The University of London.

66. WIGLEY, R. D. (1960) Potassium deficiency in anorexia nervosa, with reference to renal tubular vacuolation, *Brit. med. J.*, ii, 110.

13

Pharmacological Studies

E. MARLEY

It was no paradox that Sir Aubrey Lewis [49] advocated caution in interpreting the benefits wrought by psychotropic drugs yet freely encouraged research in the applications of pharmacology to psychiatry. Under his guidance, there was no restriction of interest to areas of immediate applicability to psychiatry; rather he welcomed and encouraged investigation on a wide basis. Consequently, although the pharmacological research has centred around amines of biological importance particularly with regard to the central and autonomic nervous systems, it extended also to the physiology and pharmacology of the adrenal medulla [64] and to interactions between monoamine oxidase inhibitors and foodstuffs such as cheese or yeast extracts which contain amines [8, 9]. This chapter confines itself to the action of sympathomimetic and allied amines on the nervous system.

A preliminary word of explanation is necessary. A variety of species are used in pharmacological tests. In most cases, they are selected according to their value in determining a particular aspect of drug action. Consequently, the species tested may be quite remote from man but nevertheless the one most suitable for investigating the effect of a group of drugs or for determining their mode of action.

ACTION OF SYMPATHOMIMETIC AMINES

On the grounds of biological expediency it would be reasonable to suppose that the mechanisms of the peripheral and the central actions of the sympathomimetic amines have much in common. Since their peripheral actions, i.e. on the autonomic nervous system and the smooth muscle it innervates, have been the more extensively investigated it is helpful to begin with these.

PERIPHERAL ACTIONS OF SYMPATHOMIMETIC AMINES

The sympathomimetic amines tend to have similar peripheral effects; thus they raise the blood pressure, contract the nictitating membrane, and dilate the iris. These effects are abolished by phenoxybenzamine, a pharmacological antagonist at α-receptors for catecholamines, suggesting that they have a common mode of action. This supposition can be shown to be incorrect by examining the effect of sympathomimetic amines on chronically denervated tissues. Suitable test objects are the cat's nictitating membrane or iris, both innervated by the cervical sympathetic trunk. Following excision of the superior cervical ganglion and degeneration of the cervical sympathetic postganglionic nerve the effects of the catecholamines on the nictitating membrane are still obtained and are in fact enhanced, a phenomenon known as supersensitivity. In contrast, response of the membrane or iris to amines such as phenylethylamine, which lacks hydroxyls on the phenyl-ring, are substantially reduced or abolished [36, 54, 55]. This implies that the effects of the catecholamines are independent of, whereas those of phenylethylamine and allied amines are dependent on, sympathetic innervation. By the same token their mode of action must differ. A similar division of the amines can be made after treating cats with guanethidine or with reserpine [15, 55, 66, 67, 82]. The effects of phenylethylamine-like amines are reduced or abolished; those of catecholamines remain, but in contrast to denervated tissues, their effects are often not enhanced.

The terminals of sympathetic postganglionic nerves contain noradrenaline which disappears as the nerve degenerates [32] or after treatment with reserpine [40]. These findings together with those from denervated tissues led Burn and Rand [15] to suggest that catecholamines act directly on smooth muscle, whereas phenylethylamine-like amines act indirectly by releasing noradrenaline from granules within the nerve terminals which then diffuses to receptors in smooth muscle. The disappearance of noradrenaline from the nerves due to degeneration or to reserpine accounts for the reduced or absent response to β-phenylethylamine.

Another type of action was described by Vane [83] who found that whereas catecholamines relaxed a rat stomach strip, phenylethylamine and amphetamine-like amines contracted it. The effect was independent of noradrenaline release; it was not due to an action on nerves and was considered to be an action on tryptamine receptors. This action of amphetamine-like amines on tryptamine receptors has considerable implications for the effects of excitant amines on the central nervous system.

CENTRAL ACTIONS OF SYMPATHOMIMETIC AMINES

Species in which Catecholamines and Amphetamine-like Amines Evoke Arousal

Just as the sympathomimetic amines have similar peripheral effects, i.e. mydriasis, so they have similar central effects inasmuch as they evoke alertness. Electrocortical and behavioural arousal have been obtained with catecholamines in rats [10], in rabbits [51], guinea-pigs [61], ducklings [60], and cats [19, 71]. Amphetamine-like amines evoke behavioural and electrocortical arousal in cats [11, 39], dogs [73], guinea-pigs [61], ducklings [60], rabbits [52], and monkeys [11].

Representative effects of a catecholamine, α-methyl noradrenaline, and of dexamphetamine in a 17-day duckling are shown in FIGURE 8; integrals of electrocortical activity and cheeping are shown. By the method of electrical integration [25], large voltage changes with respect to time—large amplitude electrocortical activity of sleep, loud cheeping—give large integrals; on the other hand, small voltage changes in respect of time—low amplitude alert electrocortical activity, soft or little cheeping—give small integrals. Integrals are recorded each minute and provide continuous quantification of spontaneous or drug-induced changes in behaviour or other variables under test.

In the duckling, α-methyl noradrenaline (1·0 μmol./100 g., i.v.) produced electrocortical alerting lasting about 5 minutes associated with a 50 per cent. reduction of electrocortical (ECoG) integrals; a larger dose of α-methyl noradrenaline (2·0 μmol./100 g., i.v.) had a correspondingly longer effect. Although the duckling was alert, cheeping was not increased. The amphetamine-like amines also produced behavioural and electrocortical arousal although the effects were much longer lasting. Electrocortical alerting in the same duckling elicited by dexamphetamine (1·0 μmol./100 g., i.v.) is shown in FIGURE 8D associated with a 70 per cent. reduction of ECoG integrals [FIG. 8E] and increase in cheeping [FIG. 8F].

In all these species, the similarity in effect of the amines allows no differentiation of their mode of action. A further difficulty in adult animals is that the catecholamines probably only penetrate the blood-brain barrier in small quantities [87], so their apparently central effects may be secondary to their peripheral action. In addition, the approaches used so successfully in analysing the effects of the amines on the peripheral adrenergic nervous system are of less value in analysing the central actions of the sympathomimetic amines. Denervation sensitivity has been achieved in the central nervous system but is impracticable when effects on behaviour are to be studied. Noradrenaline is present in the brain [85], where it is found, together with the appropriate inactivating enzymes, in the varicose terminals of adrenergic axones [21]. Consequently it might have been supposed that reserpine or guanethidine would abolish the central effects of indirectly-acting amines. However, the central effects of amphetamine-amines were unaffected and even enhanced

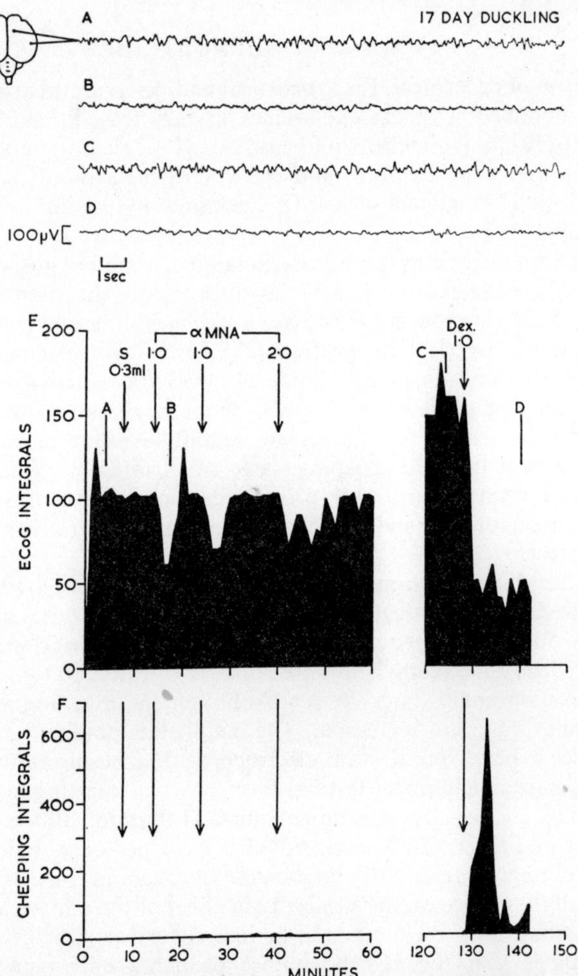

FIG. 8. Effect of α-methyl noradrenaline (αMNA) and of dexamphetamine (DEX) on electrocortical activity and integrals of electrocortical activity (ECoG integrals) and on cheeping. Records from an unanaesthetized unrestrained 17-day duckling. Upper four traces are of electrocorticograms. A, is of drowsy electrocortical activity and corresponds in E with ECoG integral of 100/min. B shows the electrocortical alerting after the injection of α-methyl noradrenaline (1·0 μmol./100g., i.v.) with reduction of ECoG integrals to about 60/min. Further doses of α-methyl noradrenaline (1·0 and 2·0 μmol./100g., i.v.) produced electrocortical alerting with brief reduction of ECoG integrals (E) but did not produce cheeping (F). Testing was stopped for 60 min. after which the duckling was more drowsy (C) with ECoG integrals of about 170/min.(E). Dexamphetamine (1·0 μmol./100g., i.v.) produced electrocortical alerting (D) with reduction of ECoG integrals to 40/min.(E) and evoked cheeping (F). S = Saline control. (Reproduced from Marley, 1967.)

[76, 77] in animals in which the peripheral effects had been prevented by prior treatment with reserpine, suggesting that the central effects were independent of noradrenaline release.

USE OF IMMATURE ANIMALS

A different approach to studying the central action of these drugs was required. One such approach was to test the effects of sympathomimetic amines in immature animals [44, 45, 79].

At first sight the disadvantages of studying immature animals considerably outweigh any advantages. In general, they have poor temperature control, are often unable to feed themselves, have a limited behavioural repertoire, a restricted capacity for learning and poorly developed cerebral electrical activity. The possible advantages are twofold. The enzymes which inactivate sympathomimetic amines are present in low concentrations in immature animals [7, 31] so that central effects might be obtained with amines that are inactivated rapidly in adult animals. Secondly, in the immature brain the blood-brain barrier is absent or not fully effective [4, 46, 86] and this should allow penetration to the brain of substances such as the catecholamines which are excluded in adult animals. The reduced entry of many biologically important substances into the brain as the animal matures may be a reflection of cerebral metabolic requirements rather than a measure of blood-brain barrier function [46]. There may be better transport mechanisms capable of restoring physiological levels faster or to a greater degree in the adult than in the new-born brain [47].

Regardless of other considerations, behaviour and cerebral electrical activity must be sufficiently established in order to record clear-cut changes with drugs. For this reason, not all immature animals proved suitable for testing.

CEREBRAL ELECTRICAL ACTIVITY IN IMMATURE ANIMALS

The development of cerebral electrical activity was studied in five species. Sections of electrocorticograms (ECoGs) at various ages from some of these are shown in FIGURE 9. Even on the first day of life, the alert and sleeping electrocortical pattern of chickens, ducklings [FIG. 9A–D] and guinea-pigs were like those of the adult; phasic and tonic electrocortical arousal were elicited and there was high correlation between wakefulness and sleep and the type of cerebral electrical activity. The ECoG of an alert freely-moving one-day-old chick consisted of 15–20 c/sec. activity of 20–40 μV amplitude; slower components of 3–6 c/sec. and 30–70 μV amplitude were also present. As the chick matured, there was a shift in the frequency spectrum with the emergence of faster electrocortical frequencies up to 30 c/sec., the amplitude now reaching 50–100 μV. In young and adult birds, electrocortical signs of sleep consisted of irregular, high amplitude (100–400 μV) slow activity predominantly in the 2–3 c/sec. frequency range [FIG. 9B]. Occasionally, bursts of a faster rhythm of 4–6 c/sec. appeared but this was more pronounced in the older than the newly hatched chicks. Similar developmental changes were observed in ducklings and guinea-pigs with the addition that 6–12 c/sec. 'spindle' bursts were present in the ECoGs of sleeping guinea-pigs.

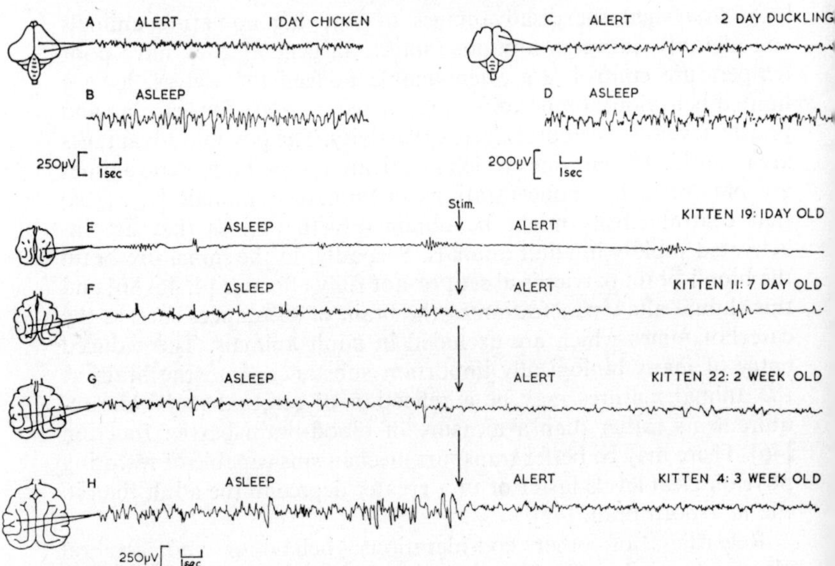

FIG. 9. ECoGs, A, from an alert and B from a sleeping 1-day-old chicken; C from an alert and D from a sleeping 2-day-old duckling; E, F, G, H from kittens at various stages of development showing maturation of electrocortical activity and the changes accompanying transition from the sleeping to the alert state. A tactile stimulus was given at Stim. (A, B reproduced from Key and Marley, 1962; E-H from Marley and Key, 1963.)

Electrocorticograms from kittens showing maturation of electrocortical activity [61], and the effect of a tactile stimulus (Stim) are exemplified in FIGURE 9. At 7 days, tactile stimuli elicited vocalization and movement but without altering electrocortical activity [FIG. 9F]. By 9–15 days auditory stimuli evoked tonic as well as phasic electrocortical arousal. By the third to fourth week, the electrocorticogram exhibited adult characteristics [FIG. 9H]. A similar delay in development of cerebral electrical activity in spite of more advanced behaviour was found in the squab (young pigeon). The contrast between the state of cerebral electrical activity of newly hatched chickens and ducklings compared to that of squabs suggests that precocial birds (young hatched with down) have well-developed cerebral electrical activity whereas altricial birds (those hatched relatively naked) have poorly developed cerebral electrical activity

BEHAVIOUR IN IMMATURE ANIMALS

The behaviour of kittens was insufficiently advanced to merit testing drugs during the crucial first 4 weeks of life. That of squabs was more advanced but like kittens the poor correlation between behaviour and cerebral electrical activity made it unattractive for drug investigations. Behaviour of guinea-pigs, chickens or ducklings was sufficiently developed to allow drugs to be tested on the first day of life. Such behaviour is innate, but it is important to test the effects of drugs on learned as well as innate behaviour. Experiments were therefore made to ascertain what degree of learned behaviour could be established in young animals. Operant conditioning methods were employed although these had been previously restricted to mature animals.

For reasons presently to be considered, young chicks proved eminently suitable for studying the effects of sympathomimetic amines. The newly hatched chicken might not seem a favourable species to study with regard to operant behaviour maintained by food-reinforcement since swallowing of food or water is not present on hatching but has to be learnt [20]. However, key-pecking for food can be developed in chicks within a few days of hatching [62], and this is shown for a 3-day-old chicken in FIGURE 10. The schedule evolved was a multiple alternating Fixed Interval, Fixed Ratio. A Fixed Interval (FI) is a schedule of intermittent reinforcement in which the first response occurring after a given interval of time, measured from some event, is reinforced. A Fixed Ratio (FR) is a schedule of intermittent reinforcement in which a response is reinforced upon completion of a fixed number of responses counted from some event.

FIGURE 10 consists of cumulative-response records showing development of performance on multiple FR30, FI 2 min. In FIGURE 10A (3rd day post-hatching) the first pecks occurred and each was reinforced (FR 1). Invariably chickens trained to respond in the presence of either a white or a red key light did not respond initially when the colour was changed, i.e. there was no stimulus generalization. Thus when the white key light was changed to red between b and d, the chicken stopped responding until the white

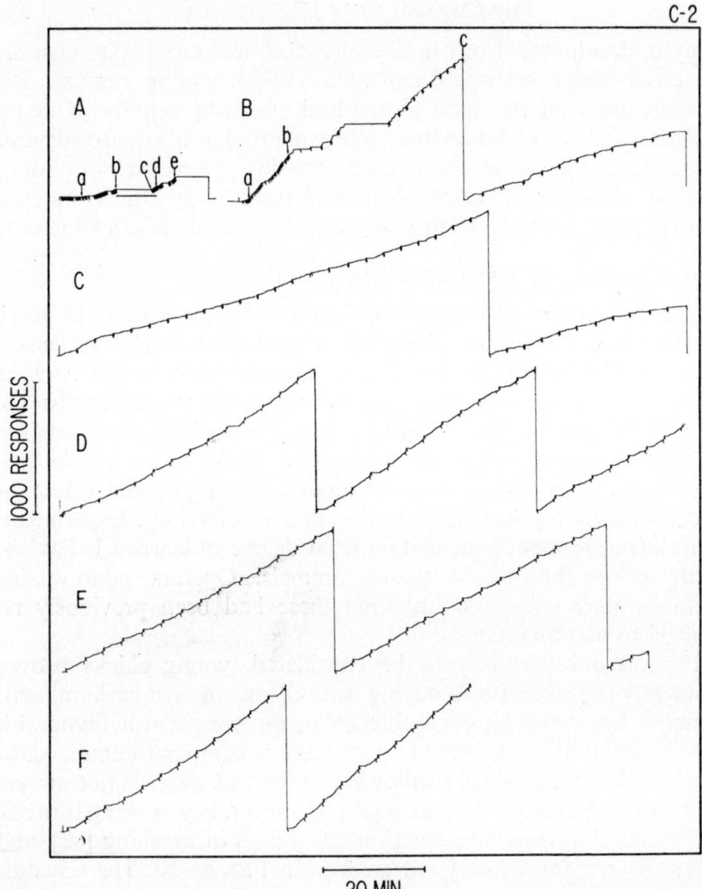

FIG. 10. Cumulative-response records showing development of performance on multiple FR 30, FI 2 min. In this and subsequent figures downward strokes of the recording pen indicate the delivery of food. Record A (from 3-day-old chicken) shows the end of the first session of shaping in the presence of a white key light. At a the first peck occurred, shaping was stopped and the schedule was FR 1. The key light was red between b and d (bar under record). The chicken did not respond after the key light was red until the white light flashed on momentarily at c. At e the schedule was made FR 10 and pecking stopped. Record B (second daily session; fourth day post-hatching) started with FR 1 (white light), and changed to FR 10 at a, multiple FR 10 (white light), FI 1 min. (red light) at b, and multiple FR 10, FI 3 min. at c. The performance was maintained and showed characteristics of initial fixed-interval performance. Records C–F show the daily sessions for the seventh to tenth days after hatching. The schedule was changed to multiple FR 30, FI 3 min. during Record D. (Reproduced from Marley and Morse, 1966.)

light flashed on momentarily at c, when responding recommenced. At e, the schedule was made an FR10 and pecking stopped. Record [10B] (second daily session; 4th day post-hatching) started with FR 1 (white light) and changed to FR 10 at a, and to multiple FR10 (white light) FI 1 min. (red light) at b, and multiple FR 10, FI 3 min. at c. Thus by the 4th day of life, the chicken was responding on a multiple alternating FI, FR schedule. Records [10C–F] show the daily sessions for the 7th to 10th days after hatching. The schedule was changed to multiple FR 30, FI 3 min. during D. The records show the features of initial FI performance. The characteristics of a fully developed FI when plotted on a cumulative recorder include a pause at the beginning of the interval, a region of positive curvature, and a fairly constant terminal rate of responding. The features of a fully developed FI are shown in FIGURE 11C, obtained from a 2-month chicken.

Observations on normal behaviour are highly relevant for interpreting behavioural changes produced by drugs. For example, it is clear from FIGURE 11 that different forms of behaviour compete with each other. When locomotor activity was marked [FIG. 11A] there was corresponding diminution in the same chicken of another type of activity, namely cheeping [11B]. A further example of this reciprocity is given in FIGURE 11C and D. FIGURE 11C is a section taken from a cumulative pecking record of a 2-month chicken. The schedule was a multiple alternating FI, FR of positive reinforcement. The characteristics of such a record are that providing the FR is short (FR 25, in this case) then pecking will be rapid, and provided that the FI is not too short (7 min. in this case) then pecking will be minimal at the beginning and maximal at the end of the interval. In contrast [FIG. 11D] cheeping was maximal at the beginning of the FI when pecking was minimal and waned as pecking increased. Similar kinds of relations were observed after central depressant or excitant drugs; if the drug decreased pecking then cheeping increased [63] although exceptions were found.

SYMPATHOMIMETIC AMINES AND IMMATURE ANIMALS

It was hoped that the young of a species would be found which responded to catecholamines by drowsiness and to the amphetamine-like amines by alerting. This hope was based on observations that catecholamines injected by a route which surmounts the blood-brain barrier, e.g. intracisternally in dogs or into the cerebral ventricles of cats, produce drowsiness [35, 48] whereas amphetamine-like amines produce arousal [48]. Of the immature animals examined, the late development of electrocortical activity or behaviour in kittens or squabs precluded them from consideration. Guinea-pigs [61] and ducklings responded to both groups of amines with behavioural and electrocortical alerting so that their effects could not be pharmacologically differentiated. Young chicks proved suitable, however, since the catecholamines induced sleep and amphetamine-like amines

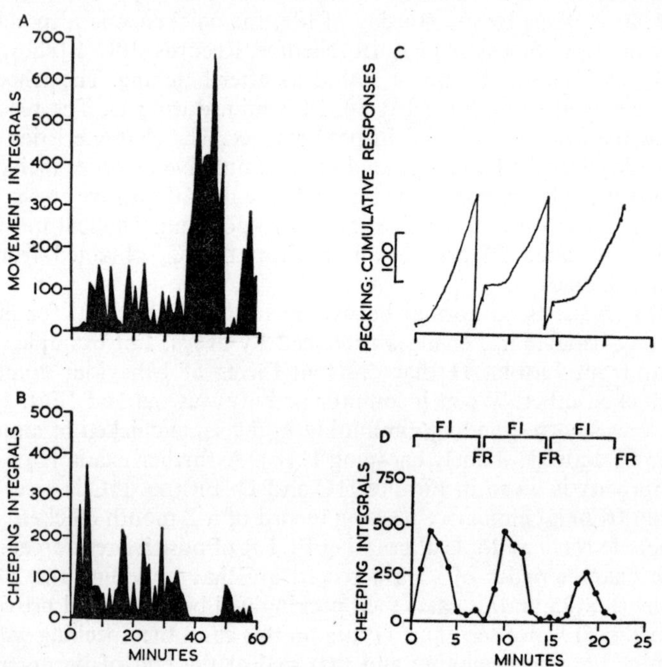

FIG. 11. Reciprocal relation of activity in chickens. A, B. Integrals of movement and cheeping from a 10-day chicken. Marked increase of locomotor activity during the 37th to 48th min. was associated with a corresponding decline in cheeping. C, D. Cumulative pecking record and integrals of cheeping in a 2-month-old chicken on a multiple Fixed Ratio (FR) 25, Fixed Interval (FI) 7 min. schedule. Cheeping was maximal at the beginning of the FI when pecking was minimal and declined as pecking increased towards the end of FI. (A, B, reproduced from Dewhurst and Marley, 1965; C, D, reproduced from Marley and Morse, 1966.)

evoked arousal [23, 26, 27, 44, 45]. Some of the amines tested in young chicks are shown in TABLE 6. They are divided into three groups according to their effects and their chemical structure. These are the central depressant catecholamines, the central excitant amphetamine-like amines and an intermediate group with biphasic or equivocal actions.

TABLE 6 FUNCTIONAL AND CHEMICAL GROUPINGS OF SOME SYMPATHOMIMETIC AMINES TESTED ON BEHAVIOUR AND CEREBRAL ELECTRICAL ACTIVITY IN YOUNG CHICKENS (ADAPTED FROM DEWHURST AND MARLEY [23])

COMPOUND	FUNCTIONAL GROUPING	STRUCTURE: ring 5	ring 4	ring 3	ring 2	CH	CH	NH	CHEMICAL GROUPING OF RING
(−)-ADRENALINE	CENTRAL DEPRESSANTS	H	OH	OH	H	OH	H	CH_3	CATECHOL
(−)-NORADRENALINE		H	OH	OH	H	OH	H	H	
(±)-ISOPRENALINE		H	OH	OH	H	OH	H	$CH(CH_3)_2$	
(±)-α METHYLNORADRENALINE		H	OH	OH	H	OH	CH_3	H	
DOPAMINE		H	OH	OH	H	H	H	H	
(−)-PHENYLEPHRINE		H	H	OH	H	OH	H	CH_3	PHENOL
(±)-HYDROXY METHYL AMPHETAMINE	INTERMEDIATE GROUP	H	OH	H	H	H	CH_3	CH_3	
TYRAMINE		H	OH	H	H	H	H	H	
(±)-HYDROXY AMPHETAMINE		H	OH	H	H	H	CH_3	H	
(−)-EPHEDRINE		H	H	H	H	OH	CH_3	CH_3	BENZENE
(±)-PHENYLPROPANOLAMINE		H	H	H	H	OH	CH_3	H	
(+)-AMPHETAMINE	CENTRAL EXCITANTS	H	H	H	H	H	CH_3	H	
(±)-METHYL PHENIDATE		H	H	H	H	$COOCH_3$	CH_2 (ring: CH_2–CH_2)	CH_2	
(±)-PHENMETRAZINE		H	H	H	H	O (ring: O–CH_2)	CH_3	CH_2–CH_2	
(±)-α-METHYL TRYPTAMINE		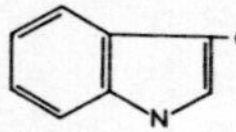 indole–CH_2–$CH{\cdot}CH_3$–NH_2							INDOLE
(±)-CYCLOPENTAMINE		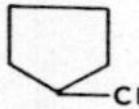 cyclopentyl–CH_2–$CH{\cdot}CH_3$–$NHCH_3$							CYCLOPENTANE
(±)-TUAMINOHEPTANE		CH_3–CH_2–CH_2–$CH_2{\cdot}CH_2$–$CH{\cdot}CH_3$–NH_2							ALIPHATIC

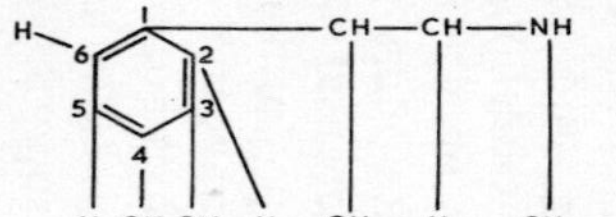

CATECHOLAMINES

Non-operant Situations. The catecholamines, of which adrenaline was the most potent, induced sleep accompanied by large amplitude (150–250 μV) slow frequency (1–4 c/sec.) electrocortical potentials associated with diminution of electromyographic activity and cessation of cheeping. The effects of α-methyl noradrenaline on electrocortical activity and posture are shown in PLATE 1. The sleep was physiological in nature, since the bird was roused by sensory stimuli and arousal was accompanied by electrocortical alerting. 'Paradoxical sleep' electrocortical activity of low amplitude was occasionally observed during deep sleep. The chicken normally sleeps standing or squatting with its head tucked under a wing, and identical postures were assumed during sleep elicited by catecholamines. Similar electrocortical patterns together with loss of electromyographic activity were induced by anaesthetics. Response to the anaesthetics differed inasmuch as electrocortical arousal was not obtained with sensory stimuli; there was loss of postural reflexes and during deep anaesthesia suppression bursts appeared in the electrocorticogram. Sleep produced by catecholamines but not that induced by anaesthetics was reversed by amphetamine-like amines.

As might be expected of compounds with soporific action, adrenaline, noradrenaline and their α-methyl derivatives produced falls in 'core' and 'shell' temperatures with a decline in oxygen consumption [2]. Temperature was measured using implanted thermistors and the chicks were studied in a Richards and Collison [70] oxygen consumption chamber. A dose of α-methyl noradrenaline (10 μmol./kg., i.v.) produced falls of between 1·5° and 5°C. In chickens under 10 days old although there was partial recovery from the fall in temperature, temperature fell again over the ensuing 2 hours and unless the chicken was removed from the chamber and warmed it subsequently died. Apparently these amines interfered with temperature control so that the chicken became poikilothermic. Oxygen consumption was reduced 25–50 per cent. but recovered rapidly. The postures produced by catecholamines, in which the head droops and wings are lowered and applied closely to the trunk [PLATE 1], the head is tucked beneath a wing or the chick squats, all serve to hinder heat loss. In domestic fowls the heat loss while standing is 40–50 per cent. greater than during sitting, and tucking the head beneath a wing reduces heat dissipation by about 12 per cent. [22].

The soporific effects of the catecholamines dwindled from about the 4th or 5th week of life and the adult fowl responded in a similar way to the adult of the other species, i.e. the catecholamines either

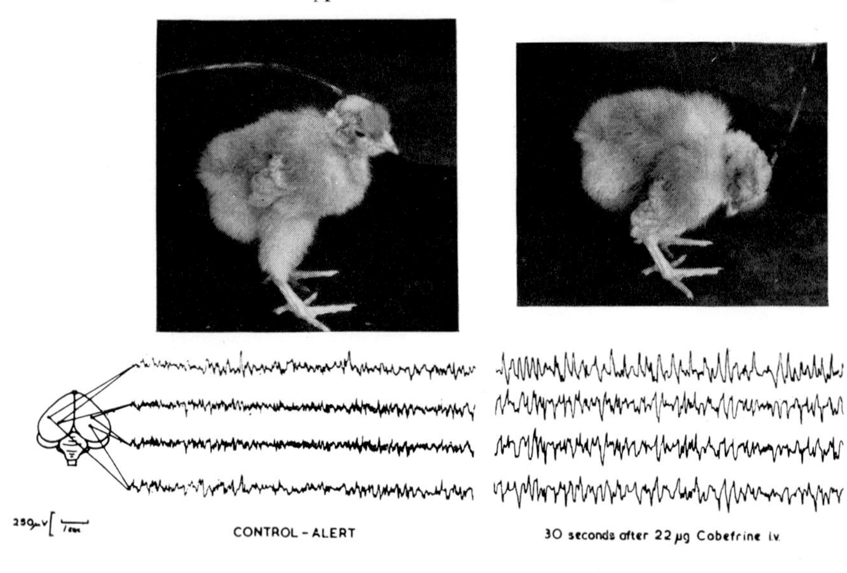

Effect of cobefrine (α-methyl noradrenaline) on behaviour and electrocortical activity. A and C, controls before and after recovery from 22 μg. cobefrine intravenously, which produced (B) behavioural and electrocortical sleep. (Reproduced from Key and Marley, 1962.)

PLATE 2

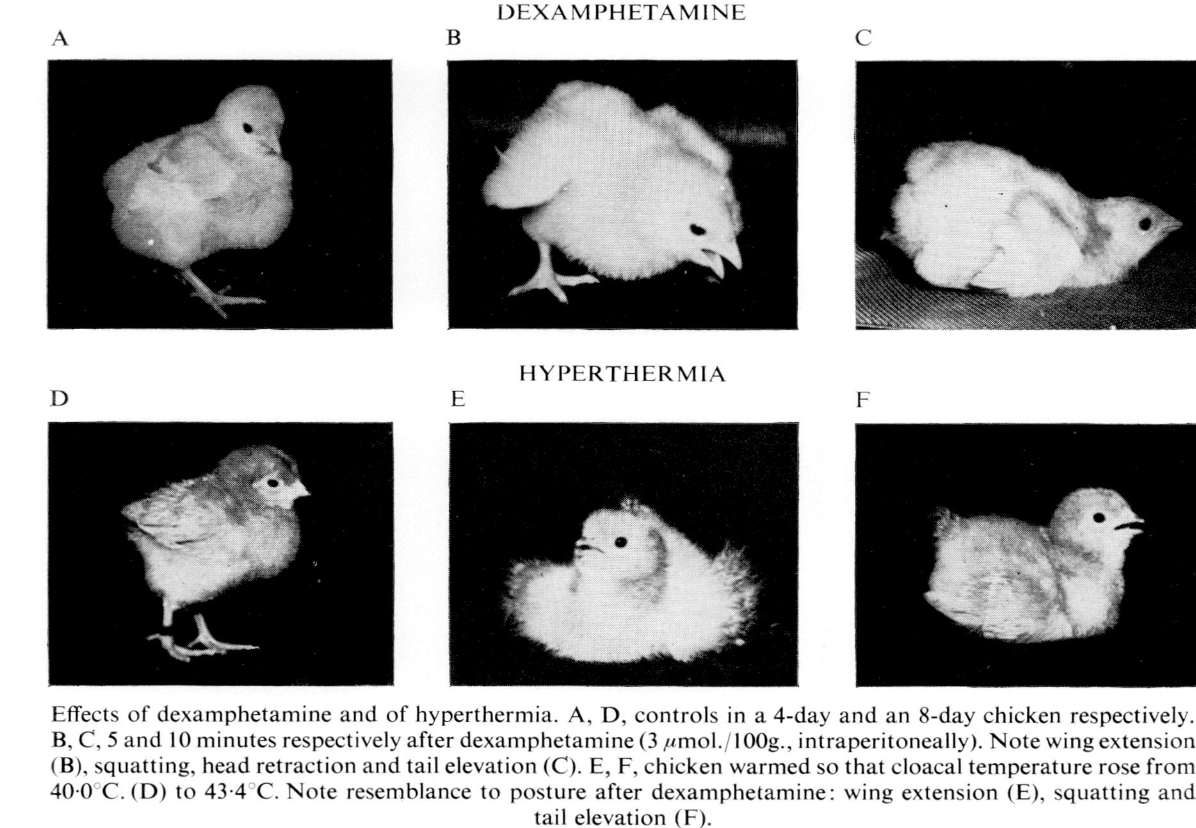

Effects of dexamphetamine and of hyperthermia. A, D, controls in a 4-day and an 8-day chicken respectively. B, C, 5 and 10 minutes respectively after dexamphetamine (3 μmol./100g., intraperitoneally). Note wing extension (B), squatting, head retraction and tail elevation (C). E, F, chicken warmed so that cloacal temperature rose from 40·0°C. (D) to 43·4°C. Note resemblance to posture after dexamphetamine: wing extension (E), squatting and tail elevation (F).

produced brief alerting or had equivocal effects. The effect on temperature from this age was also negligible. Since the adult blood-brain barrier characteristics for the chicken are not present until about the 4th week [86], there is conceivably a significant connexion with the change in response to catecholamines at this age.

Operant Situation. Results in chickens and pigeons were compatible with the catecholamines having central depressant properties. Adrenaline or noradrenaline reduced key-pecking in adult pigeons on a schedule of positive reinforcement [88]. Pecking was also reduced by α-methyl noradrenaline in chickens on a multiple alternating FI, FR schedule for food reinforcement [63]. This is shown in FIGURE 12A and B, portions of cumulative pecking records from two experiments in which there are five alternating FRs and FIs following saline injection and a similar sequence following drug injection. Pecking was reduced in the FI but not the FR [FIG. 12A and B], the more so with the larger dose. Reduction or suppression of pecking was obtained whether the control rate of pecking was fast or slow.

As noted earlier, provided that the FI was not too short there was a reciprocal relation between cheeping and pecking so that when pecking was maximal, as at the end of the FI or during the FR, cheeping was minimal and vice versa. The effects of α-methyl noradrenaline on cheeping appeared to be partly secondary to those on pecking. With doses of up to 5 μmol./kg. α-methyl noradrenaline, pecking was reduced and consequently cheeping was increased. With larger doses of α-methyl noradrenaline which produced sleep, cheeping as well as pecking was suppressed. When pecking recovered, the reciprocal relationship between pecking and cheeping was re-established.

AMPHETAMINE-LIKE AMINES

These amines are central excitants and although the description here applies to chickens their effects in one species are generally similar to those in others. There are minor differences in the pattern evoked, e.g. locomotor activity is particularly increased in rodents, and vocalization particularly increased in aves. Larger doses of the amines elicit species-characteristic stereotyped postures and locomotor activity.

Non-operant Situation. The most potent of these amines in terms of threshold dose was β-phenylethylamine. Their effects were the opposite of those produced by catecholamines. Amphetamine-like amines elicited electrocortical alerting, increased electromyographic activity produced widening of the palpebral fissures and frequent movements of the nictitating membranes. The effects of

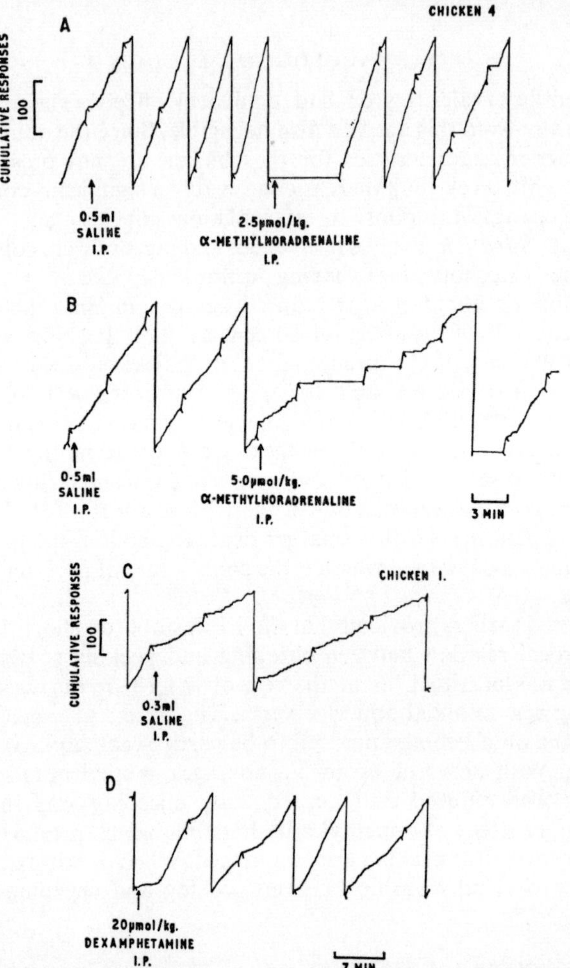

FIG. 12. Cumulative pecking records taken from two chickens; A, B. two experiments in the same chicken on a multiple FR 25, FI 3 min. schedule and C, D from another chicken on a multiple FR 25, FI 7 min. schedule. Ordinate: cumulative pecks. Abscissa: time. The fixed ratio and fixed interval components alternated. The short diagonal lines on the records indicate presentations of the food reinforcer. In each case a series of 5 FIs and 5 FRs are shown following saline injection and a series of at least 5 FIs and 5 FRs following amine injection. In A, pecking is suppressed only in the first FI following injection of α-methyl noradrenaline (2·5 μmol./kg., i.p.). In B, pecking is reduced during the subsequent 5 FIs following injection of α-methyl noradrenaline (5·0 μmol./kg., i.p.) with recovery by the sixth FI. The FRs were unaffected. C, Control response to saline. D. Increased amount of pecking following dexamphetamine (20 μmol./kg., i.p.). (From unpublished experiments in conjunction with Dr. W. H. Morse.)

dexamphetamine on electrocortical and electromyographic activity are shown in FIGURE 13. Compounds with a methyl substituent on the α-carbon atom such as dexamphetamine, phenmetrazine, cyclopentamine and tuaminoheptane produced in addition changes in cheeping and posture which began 2–10 minutes after those in the ECoG and electromyogram. The amount of cheeping was increased, and was succeeded by twittering, a high-pitched low-intensity call repeated at a frequency of 4–5 per second. Dexamphetamine and α-methyl tryptamine have identical effects in chickens and an idea of the delay in onset of cheeping and of the amount it was increased by amphetamines can be obtained from FIGURE 14, taken from an experiment with α-methyl tryptamine. In contrast to the postural changes produced by α-methyl noradrenaline, in which the head droops and the wings were lowered [PLATE 1], the head became erect and the wings were raised and extended away from the trunk after dexamphetamine [PLATE 2]. With larger doses of the amphetamines there was head retraction and elevation of the tail and extreme flexion of the hip and knee so that the legs were tucked under the body [PLATE 2]. At this stage the chicken was incapable of movement and while these postural changes were maximal, cheeping and twittering stopped but returned *pari passu* as postural effects abated.

Twittering and postural changes produced by benzedrine in chicks were first described by Selle [74] and by other amphetamine-like amines by Clymer and Seifter [16]. These effects were thought to be stereotyped and characteristic only of amphetamine-like amines. That the response could be elicited by tryptamines as well and that it was not necessarily stereotyped but due among other causes to a combination of drug with non-drug factors is now recognized [26]. For example, twittering was relatively difficult to elicit with the excitant amines if the chicken was studied in isolation in a sound-proof box. However, if another chicken was present, if the chicken was handled or if it was studied in the open laboratory, then twittering developed. The presence of another chicken underlined the importance of social cues although, surprisingly, vocal interactions were unlikely to be influential. Collias and Joos [17] consider that chicks hear little but the low clucking (*ca* 400 c/sec.) of their mother while the hen reacts preferentially to the high cheeping (*ca* 3,000 c/sec.) of her young. On this basis young chicks are unlikely to hear one another cheeping!

The mechanisms involved in the postural changes remain as yet obscure. The head retraction and tail elevation suggest contracture of the dorsal axial muscles, the positioning of the wings suggests contracture of the supracoracoid muscles; and that of the hind limbs suggests contracture of the iliotibialis and posterior thigh muscles.

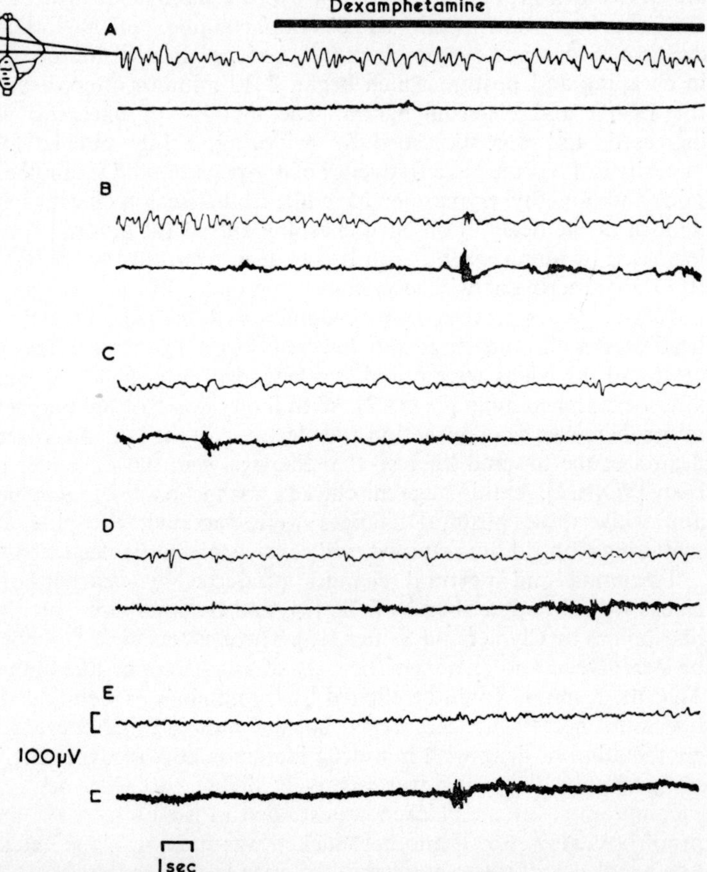

FIG. 13. Effects of dexamphetamine on electrocortical and electromyographic activity. Records from unanaesthetized, unrestrained 5-day-old chicken. From above downwards consecutive records of electrocortical activity (upper trace) and electromyographic potentials (lower trace) over 100 sec. Slow intravenous injection of dexamphetamine, 1 μmol./100g. at bar. Drowsy 150 μV, 4 c/sec. electrocortical potentials and 20 μV electromyographic activity (A) change to 50 μV fast-frequency electrocortical potentials and 60 μV electromyographic activity within 80 sec. (E). Chicken previously drowsy, now alert. (Reproduced from Dewhurst and Marley, 1965.)

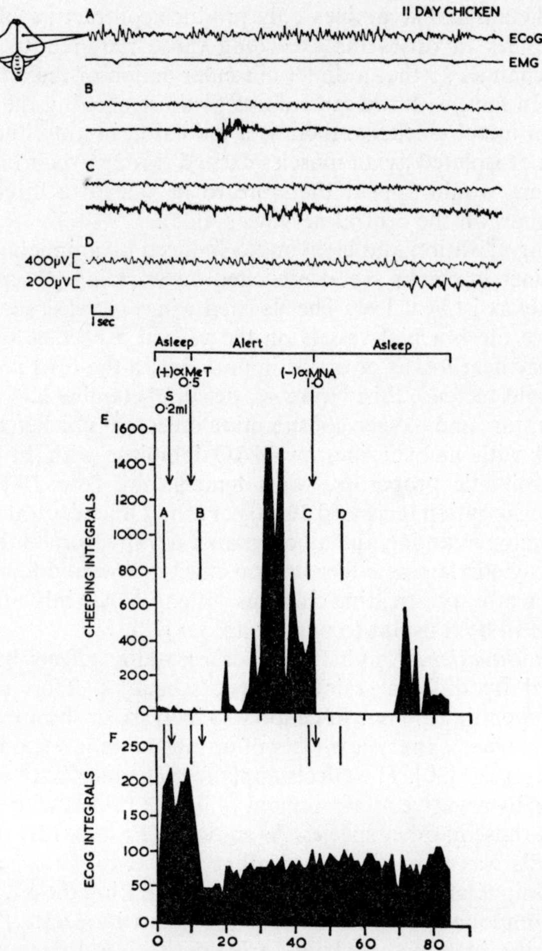

FIG. 14. Effect of (+) α-methyl tryptamine (αMeT) and of (−) α-methyl noradrenaline (αMNA) on electrocortical (ECoG) and electromyographic (EMG) activities and on integrals of electrocortical activity (ECoG integrals) and cheeping in an 11-day chicken. A. Electrocortical and electromyographic activity of a sleeping chicken, with ECoG integrals of about 200/min. (F). B and C. Electrocortical alerting and increased electromyographic potentials produced by (+) α-methyl tryptamine (0·5 µmol./100g., i.v.) was associated with a 75 per cent. reduction of ECoG integrals (F) and an increase in cheeping (E). Sleep was restored (D) by an injection of (−) α-methyl noradrenaline (1·0 µmol./100g., i.v.) and cheeping halted for 22 min. (E). ECoG integrals did not increase (F).

The amphetamine-like amines only produce contracture of isolated avian muscles in doses far exceeding those required to elicit the postural changes so that a direct muscular action of the amines was unlikely. In fact, with the same doses as those eliciting the postural changes in intact chickens, there is a reduction in amplitude of the responses of isolated avian muscles excited through their nerve [41]. The posture would appear therefore to be due to a direct action of the amines on the central nervous system.

The wing-elevation and tachypnoea induced by amphetamine and allied amines in chicks are also elicited on warming [PLATE 2] and presumably assist heat loss. The elevated wings increase surface area and expose the brachial vessels on the ventral aspect of the wings. Respiratory heat loss is of major importance in the fowl and tachypnoea would increase this. However, dexamphetamine had no effect on temperature and oxygen consumption unless the chicken had been pretreated with mebanazine, an MAO inhibitor with little or no sympathomimetic properties, when temperature rose 1°–2°C. and oxygen consumption increased 30–50 per cent. Other central excitants such as cyclopentamine, tuaminoheptane, tetrahydronaphthylamine and β-phenylethylamine either had no effect or lowered temperature briefly even after pre-treating chickens with an MAO inhibitor. Birds are known to be resistant to pyrexic agents [78].

Operant Situation. Amphetamine differentially affects behaviour maintained by different reinforcement schedules. Thus sustained rates of responding are not susceptible to increase or show only small increments, whereas very low rates of or intermittent responding are readily increased [30]. The effects apply for schedules maintained by positive or by negative reinforcement [43]. The results with chickens resembled those in other species. As shown in FIGURE 12D, in which the schedule was a multiple alternating FI, FR for food reinforcement dexamphetamine increased key-pecking during the FI, whereas the FR component was unaffected. As noted by Dews [29] dexamphetamine increases pecking early in the interval so that the usual pause at the beginning of the FI disappears. With larger doses of dexamphetamine and as observed in other species, responding during the FI and finally the FR was reduced or suppressed. In chickens suppression of responding could be related to the development of postural changes. Cheeping was increased by dexamphetamine, irrespective of whether pecking was increased or decreased; it subsided only if marked postural changes developed.

INTERMEDIATE GROUP OF AMINES

This group included compounds such as hydroxyamphetamine, tyramine, ephedrine [TABLE 6] which are intermediate in chemical structure between those of the central depressants and central excitants. They had either no effects, or equivocal or mixed effects. The lack of or brevity of effect was not due to their rapid inactivation since 4 of the 5 compounds tabulated possessed a methyl group on the α-carbon atom.

The division of the amines into three groups [TABLE 6], a central depressant, a central excitant, and an intermediate group of amines, corresponds closely with those into which they were divided according to their mode of action on the mammalian autonomic nervous system [23, 45, 57, 58]. The young chicken proved therefore ideal for integrating findings for the effects of sympathomimetic amines on classical pharmacological smooth muscle preparations and on the central nervous system.

TRYPTAMINES

Tryptamines were tested since Vane [83] suggested that the central effects of the amphetamine-like amines are mediated via an action on tryptamine receptors in the brain. These substances would also be of interest because tryptamine and 5-hydroxytryptamine (5-HT) are present in the brain and other tissues [3, 38, 69] and are presumed to act either as synaptic transmitters or as modulators of synaptic transmission. A role has been proposed for 5-HT in temperature regulation [34].

α-Methyl tryptamine was preferred to tryptamine for testing since its effects were longer-lasting. The drug was investigated in a variety of animals, for a relation between tryptamine and amphetamine-like amines would be strengthened if it could be shown that amphetamine and α-methyl tryptamine had similar effects on behaviour and cerebral electrical activity in a number of species.

Tryptamines, depending on their chemical structure, had effects in chickens similar to those of amphetamines or of catecholamines [27]. The tryptamines have been divided into those like α-methyl tryptamine with predominantly excitant properties (tryptamines lacking substituents on the indolyl ring), and those like 5-HT or 6-HT with mixed excitant or depressant, or solely depressant properties (tryptamines with substituents on the indolyl ring).

Tryptamines Lacking Substituents on the Indolyl Ring

Non-operant Situation. In chickens α-methyl tryptamine and dexamphetamine had identical effects [23, 26]. The effects of (+) α-methyl tryptamine (0·5 μmol./100g. i.v.) on cheeping, electrocortical and electromyographic activity in a sleeping chicken are shown in FIGURE 14. Some 2 minutes after injecting the amine electrocortical alerting developed associated with a 75 per cent. reduction of ECoG integrals [Fig. 14F]. The alert electrocortical patterns together with increased electromyographic potentials are shown in Figure 14B and C, and should be compared with those due to dexamphetamine in Figure 13. Increased cheeping began 6 minutes after the injection [Fig. 14], reaching a peak after 18 minutes. Twittering and postural changes similar to those due to dexamphetamine were also evoked by α-methyl tryptamine. α-methyl noradrenaline antagonized the effects of α-methyl tryptamine [Fig. 14D, E] as it does those of dexamphetamine; although slow wave large amplitude activity returned to the ECoG [Fig. 14D], this alternated with periods of small amplitude 'paradoxical' activity so that ECoG integrals did not increase. Temperature and oxygen consumption were increased by α-methyl tryptamine [2].

Behavioural and electrocortical alerting were also produced by α-methyl tryptamine in ducklings [60]. In mice α-methyl tryptamine and dexamphetamine increased locomotor activity [84]. Identical changes in locomotor activity with the appearance of stereotyped movements were produced by dexamphetamine or α-methyl tryptamine in rats [68]; electrocortical arousal was also elicited by both compounds [28].

In the species so far discussed, the similarities between the excitant effects of dexamphetamine and of α-methyl tryptamine were the most striking. Cats responded differently, for although amphetamine evoked behavioural and electrocortical arousal α-methyl tryptamine had mainly soporific effects [12]. Intact cats given α-methyl tryptamine intraperitoneally, developed recurrent slow alternating flexor and extensor movements after about 30 minutes. The animals seemed bewildered and were reluctant to move. The changes in cerebral electrical activity due to α-methyl tryptamine were quite unlike those observed in chicks or rats. Thus bursts of 6–10 c/sec. large amplitude electrocortical potentials developed. Initially the bursts were separated by low-voltage activity and occurred about 3 times per minute. Later they became more frequent [Fig. 15B] and after 60 minutes were often continuous. At first, electrocortical arousal with suppression of high-voltage activity was readily obtained on sensory stimulation but as burst activity became continuous this was difficult to achieve. This inability to elicit arousal was not due to habituation to the stimulus.

α-Methyl tryptamine given intravenously to feline *encéphale isolé* preparations produced brief electrocortical alerting together with intensification of hippocampal slow wave activity [Fig. 15E, F] and longer-lasting behavioural arousal although bursts of electrocortical potentials [Fig. 15G] of similar character but briefer duration than those observed in intact cats soon developed. Similar potentials were

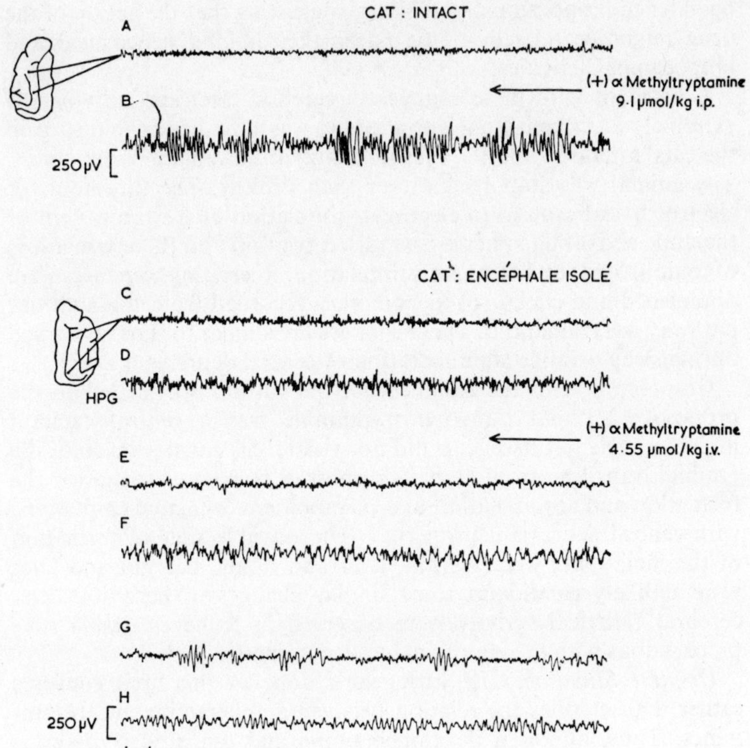

FIG. 15. A, B. The effect of (+) α-methyl tryptamine on cerebral electrical activity in cat with chronically implanted cortical recording electrodes showing the development of large amplitude rhythms (6–10 c/sec.). A. Control record (alert). B. 40 min. after (+) α-methyl tryptamine (9·1 μmol./kg., i.p.). C–H. Neocortical and hippocampal (HPG) electrical activity in a feline *encéphale isolé* preparation. C, D. Control (alert). E, F. 5 min. after (+) α-methyl tryptamine (4·55 μmol./kg., i.v.) showing intensified slow waves in the hippocampus whilst the preparation remained alert. G, H. 145 min. after (+) α-methyl tryptamine showing the time relationship between burst activity in the neocortex and hippocampus. (Adapted from Bradley and Marley, 1965.)

recorded from the thalamus and brain stem. The reciprocal relation between neocortical electrical activity and that of the palaeocortex (hippocampus) which is normally present (compare FIGURE 15C and D) in cats was impaired. Thus the bursts of neocortical slow waves or spindles were associated with either diminished [FIG. 15H] or heightened hippocampal potentials, suggesting that the action of the drug might be related to the pacemaker linking neocortical and hippocampal activities.

Coincident with these changes in cerebral electrical activity, the extremely alert behaviour subsided. It was now impossible to gain the cats' attention and the eyes no longer followed a moving object. The animal was stuporous rather than drowsy. The threshold for electrocortical arousal to electrical stimulation of the brain stem or thalamic activating systems was raised twofold and there was a loss of tonic arousal on brain stem stimulation. Recruiting responses were diminished and click-evoked potentials recorded from the auditory pathway were enhanced. These changes are similar to those observed during sleep or after administration of central depressant drugs.

Consideration of the results from the various species led to the proposal [24] that α-methyl tryptamine was a central excitant molecule. The results in cats did not vitiate this conclusion since the gradual transition from alert to stuporous behaviour suggested the formation and accumulation of a metabolite of α-methyl tryptamine with central depressant properties. The possible sites of formation of the metabolite were the gut, liver and brain. The gut and liver were unlikely candidates since similar changes in behaviour and cerebral electrical activity were observed in feline *encéphale isolé* preparations with the abdominal viscera removed [28].

Operant Situation. The little work done in this area confuses rather than clarifies the relation between amphetamine and tryptamines. Thus, although dexamphetamine and α-methyl tryptamine produced similar behavioural changes in chicks and rats, under the appropriate schedules responding was increased by dexamphetamine but decreased or unaffected by α-methyl tryptamine [63, 80]. In cats responding was reduced by α-alkyl tryptamines [13].

Tryptamines with Substituents on the Indolyl Ring

Non-operant Situation. In mice 5-hydroxytryptamine (5-HT), produced sedation [44, 75]. In chicks pre-treated with mebanazine to prevent rapid inactivation of tryptamines, 5-HT produced brief electrocortical alerting followed by sleep for 30 minutes [26] in contrast to the effects obtained with α-methyl tryptamine. The effect of 6-HT is shown in FIGURE 16. The chicken was initially alert and giving loud distress calls. Following 6-HT cheeping rapidly subsided [FIG. 16E] and sleep developed accompanied by large amplitude 2–4 c/sec. electrocortical potentials [FIG. 16B] and a 100 per cent. increase in ECoG integrals [FIG. 16D]. The soporific action of 6-HT was antagonized by dexamphetamine, following which the animal became alert, cheeping returned [FIG. 16E], the alert electrocortical

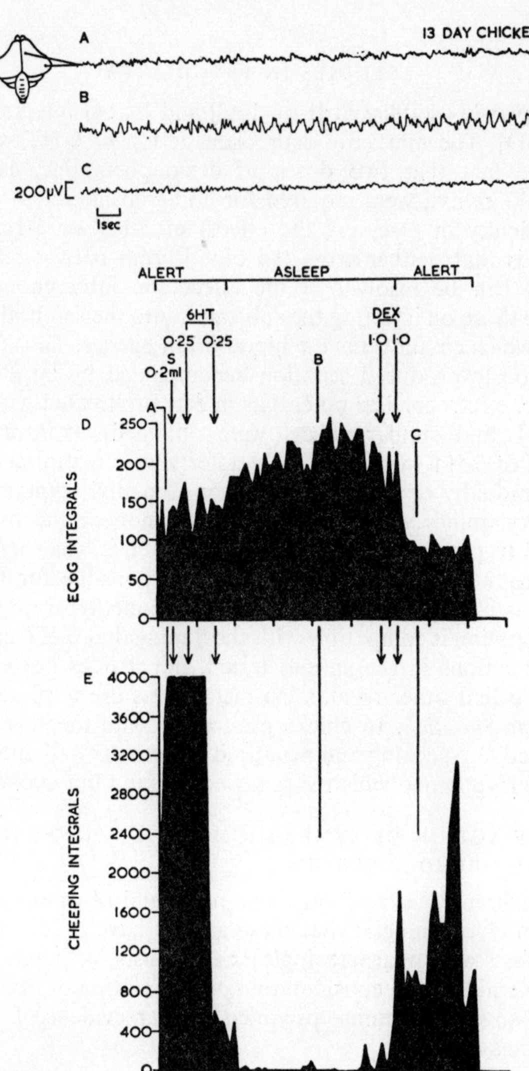

FIG. 16. Effect of 6-hydroxytryptamine (6-HT) and of dexamphetamine (Dex) on electrocortical activity and integrals of electrocortical activity (ECoG integrals) and of cheeping in an unanaesthetized, unrestrained 11-day chicken pretreated with mebanazine (10 μmol./100 g., i.v., 60 min. previously). Upper three traces are electrocorticograms. A, is alert electrocortical activity and corresponds in D with integrals of about 125 min. There was loud distress cheeping (E) and integrals reached 6,000/min. (they are plotted only to a maximum of 4,000/min. in the Figure). B, following the injection of 6-HT (two doses of 0·25 μmol./100 g., i.v.) sleep electrocortical activity developed (B), ECoG integrals rose to 250/min. (D) and cheeping subsided (E). The chicken was re-alerted by dexamphetamine (two doses of 1·0 μmol./100 g., i.v.), the alert electrocortical pattern returning (C), ECoG integrals falling to 80/min. (D) and cheeping recommencing (E). S = Saline control.

pattern was re-established [FIG. 16C] and ECoG integrals declined [FIG. 16D]. The markedly depressant action of 6-HT was evident from the fact that two doses of dexamphetamine, each of 1·0 μmol./100 g., i.v., were required for antagonism.

A difficulty in assessing the effects of 5-HT or 6-HT in adult animals is that neither cross the blood-brain barrier readily. This difficulty can be resolved if the effects on intravenous injection resemble those on injecting the substance into the cerebral ventricles, a route which circumvents the blood-brain barrier. Thus 6-HT given intravenously produced sedation accompanied by large amplitude 4–6 c/sec. electrocortical potentials in cats pre-treated with mebanazine [28], and similar effects were obtained on intraventricular injection of 5-HT in cats [35]. The effects were reminiscent of those which gradually develop in cats given α-methyl tryptamine. Since indolealkylamines which are resistant to monoamine oxidase, e.g. α-methyl tryptamine are 6-hydroxylated [42], it was suggested that a 6-hydroxy derivative may be partly responsible for the central depressant phenomena evoked in cats by α-methyl tryptamine [24]. This suggestion is compatible with the finding that 6-HT had marked soporific actions in the species tested, but it does not exclude the possibility that other tryptamine metabolites are implicated.

Operant Situation. In chicks pre-treated with mebanazine, 6-HT suppressed key-pecking and produced drowsiness [63], in contrast to α-methyl tryptamine which suppressed pecking but evoked arousal.

MODE OF ACTION OF SYMPATHOMIMETIC AMINES IN THE CENTRAL NERVOUS SYSTEM

The different effects of catecholamines and of amphetamine-like amines in chicks suggest that these amines have different modes of action. Tests with pharmacological antagonists, with agents potentiating the amines, and consideration of the relation of potency to the isomeric species of amine provided further evidence for different mechanisms of action.

Pharmacological Antagonists

Central Depressant Amines. Ahlquist [1] defined α- and β-receptors for catecholamines in smooth muscle by the order of potency of certain amines. A decreasing order of central depressant potency in young chicks was from adrenaline via noradrenaline to isoprenaline; this suggests an action on α-receptors similar to those in smooth muscle, but in the brain. Phenoxybenzamine, a pharmacological antagonist, prevents or abolishes the action of catecholamines on α-receptors. Harvey and Nickerson [37] observed that large doses of phenoxybenzamine were required to abolish the pressor actions of adrenaline in fowls. It was clear that large doses of phenoxybenzamine were also needed to antagonize central depressant actions of α-methyl noradrenaline, although antagonism of the more potent adrenaline or noradrenaline was poor. Antagonists at β-receptors did not prevent the central depressant effects of the catecholamines [26, 27]. The hypothermic actions of catecholamines were abolished by phenoxybenzamine [2] as was that of α-methyl noradrenaline on key-pecking in chicks [63]. The results agree with those in another avian species that suppressant action of adrenaline or noradrenaline on key-pecking in pigeons was prevented by phenoxybenzamine [88]. The most crucial evidence would be to antagonize the effects of catecholamines applied iontophoretically to neurones: this has been achieved by Salmoiraghi [72] who found that phenoxybenzamine prevented the action of noradrenaline applied iontophoretically to mitral cells in rabbits' olfactory bulbs.

Studies with antagonists in species in which catecholamines evoke alerting have proved more difficult to interpret and are not discussed here.

Central Excitant Amines. Phenoxybenzamine or reserpine did not reduce the central excitant effect of dexamphetamine in chicks [26]. Its effects, and those of other excitant amines, would appear therefore not to be mediated primarily via α-receptors for catecholamines in the brain, nor by intraneuronal release of noradrenaline. That amphetamine was a central excitant, whereas catecholamines, including noradrenaline, produced sleep and behaved as a physiological antagonist to the amphetamine-like amines in the young chicken, strongly indicated that in this species the central action of amphetamine was unlikely to be primarily mediated via noradrenaline release [45], although it does not entirely exclude this mechanism. Vane [83] suggested that the central effects of amphetamine were due to an action on tryptamine receptors in the brain. The findings in the chicken supported this contention. Thus tryptamine was the most potent of the excitant amines; (+) α-methyl tryptamine was more potent than and had similar effects to dexamphetamine; and the effects of the excitant amines, including dexamphetamine, were prevented or abolished by methysergide, a specific tryptamine antagonist.

The antagonist effect of methysergide is shown in FIGURE 17A and B. In A, electrocortical and behavioural arousal were produced in a sleeping chicken by dexamphetamine (1·0 μmol./100 g., i.v.) associated with a 75 per cent. reduction of ECoG integrals. Methysergide (0·006 and 0·004 μmol./100 g., i.v.) was injected 27 and 40 minutes later respectively. Behavioural and electrocortical sleep returned with gradual restoration of ECoG integrals to pre-injection

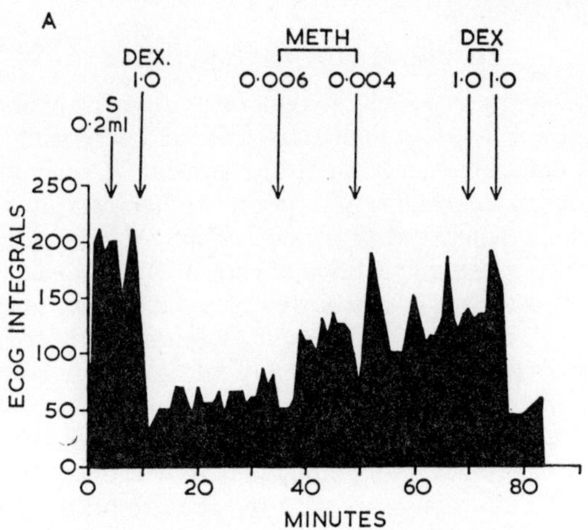

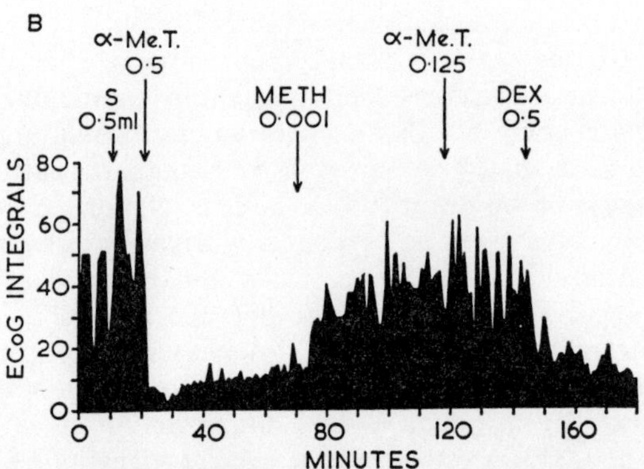

FIG. 17. Histograms of integrals to show antagonism by methysergide of the effects of dexamphetamine or of α-methyl tryptamine. A. 11-day chicken initially asleep with ECoG integrals of 200/min. Electrocortical and behavioural alerting were elicited by dexamphetamine (1·0 μmol./100 g., i.v.) with 75 per cent. reduction of ECoG integrals. These effects were gradually antagonized by methysergide (0·006 and 0·004 μmol./100 g., i.v.). Antagonism was surmounted by dexamphetamine (two doses of 1·0 μmol./100 g., i.v.). B. 12-day chicken initially asleep with ECoG integrals of 70/min. Electrocortical and behavioural alerting were obtained with (+) α-methyl tryptamine (0·5 μmol./100 g., i.v.) accompanied by a 90 per cent. reduction of integrals. These effects were gradually antagonized by methysergide (0·001 μmol./100 g., i.v.). Antagonism was surmounted by dexamphetamine (0·5 μmol./100 g., i.v.) but not by (+) α-methyl tryptamine (0·125 μmol./100 g., i.v.) S = Saline control. (B is reproduced from Dewhurst and Marley, 1965.)

values. Antagonism was surmounted by two successive doses of dexamphetamine (1·0 μmol./100 g., i.v.) which restored the alert state. In FIGURE 17B, electrocortical and behavioural arousal in a drousy chicken were evoked by (+) α-methyl tryptamine (0·5 μmol./100 g., i.v.) with a 90 per cent. reduction of ECoG integrals. Methysergide (0·001 μmol./100 g., i.v.) given 50 minutes later gradually restored the drowsy state with return of ECoG integrals to pre-injection values. Antagonism was surmounted by dexamphetamine (0·5 μmol./100 g., i.v.) but not by a smaller previous dose of (+) α-methyl tryptamine (0·125 μmol./100 g., i.v.).

It would be interesting to know whether methysergide abolishes the effects of dexamphetamine in man. Vane [83] suggested that the hallucinogenic action of large doses of amphetamine may be due to its 'tryptamimetic' properties, and overdoses with amphetamine can precipitate a psychosis with auditory and visual hallucinations of a paranoid [18] or depressive kind [53]. The hallucinogenic properties of a tryptamine analogue, bufotenin, were noted by Fabing [33] and of the N-dimethyl and N-diethyl tryptamine homologues by Szára [81].

Results from operant tests were at variance with those from non-operant situations. Thus the effects of amphetamine on pecking in chicks were antagonized by phenoxybenzamine but not by methysergide [63]. This suggested that part of the central action of amphetamine was mediated via intraneuronal release of noradrenaline.

POTENTIATION

The central depressant effects of adrenaline or noradrenaline were potentiated by cocaine, whereas those of central excitants such as tryptamine or β-phenylethylamine were potentiated by MAO inhibitors.

Potentiation of β-phenylethylamine by mebanazine is shown in FIGURE 18. In the absence of pre-treatment with an MAO inhibitor, behavioural and electrocortical alerting by β-phenylethylamine was brief. Following mebanazine, the sleeping chicken was alerted by β-phenylethylamine (0·5 followed by 1·0 μmol./100 g., i.v.) and electromyographic activity increased [FIG. 18B, E]. The moderate reduction (50 per cent.) of ECoG integrals suggested that MAO inhibition was incomplete. Nevertheless, the chick remained alert for 37 minutes, when sleep was restored by each of consecutive doses of α-methyl noradrenaline (0·5 and 1·0 μmol./100 g., i.v.). Sleep induced by these doses lasted 7 and 8 minutes respectively and then the alert state reappeared [FIG. 18D, E].

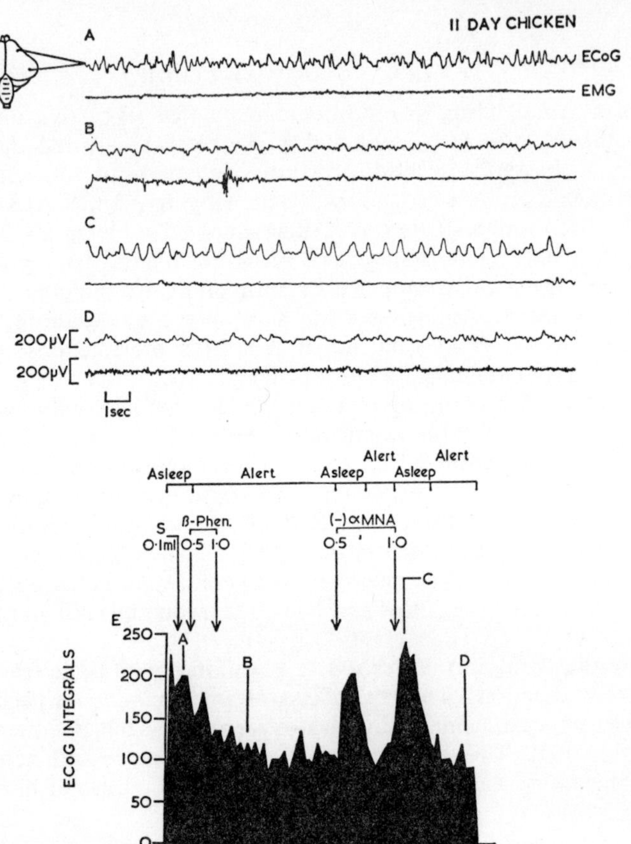

FIG. 18. Effect of β-phenylethylamine (β-Phen) and of (−) α-methyl noradrenaline (αMNA) on electrocortical and electromyographic activity and integrals of electrocortical activity (ECoG integrals) in an unanaesthetized, unrestrained 11-day chicken pretreated with mebanazine (10 μmol./100 g., i.v., 60 min. previously). Upper four traces are electrocorticograms (ECoG) and electromyograms (EMG). A, is electrocortical and electromyographic activity of a sleeping chicken and corresponds in E with ECoG integrals of 200/min. The peak frequencies in the ECoG were at 2–4 and 10–12 c/sec. B, shows the small amplitude fast-frequency electrocortical potentials together with increased amount of electromyographic activity and developed after the injection of β-phenylethylamine (0·5 and 1·0 μmol./100 g., i.v.). The chicken was now alert and ECoG integrals had declined to 110/min. Sleep was restored for 8 and 10 min. respectively by (−) α-methyl noradrenaline (0·5 and 1·0 μmol./100 g. intravenously). Large amplitude activity returned to the electrocorticogram (C) and although there was a peak frequency at 2–4 c/sec., that at 10–12 c/sec. did not develop. ECoG integrals rose to 250/min. (E). EMG activity was reduced (C). The chicken again became alert and alert ECoG and EMG activity returned (D, E) as the effect of α-methyl noradrenaline subsided. S = Saline control.

POTENCY AND ISOMERIC SPECIES OF AMINE

The laevo-isomers were more active than the dextro-isomers of the central depressant amine tested, whereas the dextro-isomers were the more active of the central excitants [26, 27].

The results from these three different types of test suggest that central depressant amines elicit their effects through an action on α-receptors for catecholamines in the brain. The excitant effects of the amphetamine-like amines were likely to be mediated through tryptamine receptors in the brain although a subsidiary action via central noradrenaline release was feasible. The importance of these two modes of action of amphetamine may vary from species to species and amphetamine may have other as yet unknown actions on the nervous system.

Further tests were made with a variety of amines to determine which part of their chemical structure was essential for depressant or excitant activity [27, 45, 57, 59].

STRUCTURE-ACTIVITY STUDIES

For both the central excitant and depressant molecules of the sympathomimetic amines, alkyl substituents larger than a methyl group on the terminal nitrogen atom and any substituents on the α-carbon atom, led to loss of potency. The interaction of sympathomimetic amines with smooth muscle is thought to be due to an ion-pair association between the positively charged nitrogen of the cationic head and a negatively charged site of receptors [6]. The loss of potency in molecules with substituents at the cationic head or at the α-carbon atom would suggest a similar mechanism of action for their effects on the central nervous system, impaired potency being due to steric hindrance or to redistribution of ion charge at the cationic head.

The aliphate side-chain was important for central depressant activity, and molecules without the side-chain but possessing hydroxyls on the ring structure (catechol, pyrogallol) lacked central depressant actions. The central excitant amines also had an aliphatic side-chain attached to one of a number of lipophilic radicals which were aromatic (phenyl, indolyl), alicyclic (cyclopentyl), mixed (tetrahydronaphthyl) or straight chain aliphatic (tuaminoheptane). Excitant activity was also shown by imipramine which has a three ring structure attached to an aliphatic chain with three carbon atoms between the ring and the terminal nitrogen. Potency was maximal when two carbon atoms were interposed between the ring and the terminal nitrogen atom. This accords with the findings of Barger and Dale [5] for the effects of these amines on smooth muscle. Since the aliphatic tuaminoheptane had excitant properties, a ring structure in the molecule was not essential for excitant activity. Potency increased with increase in size of ring structure. One may therefore tentatively conclude that the amine bonds primarily at the cationic head and secondarily at the planar ring structure, presumably through Van der Waal's forces. As a hydroxyl on the β-carbon atom increased central depressant potency, hydrogen bonding may also occur through this substituent.

Leimdorfer [48], on the basis of findings with sympathomimetic amines injected intracisternally in dogs, suggested that with molecules of the phenylethylamine structure the sedative effect was related to the catechol moiety, and the excitant effect to the aliphatic portion. This may be an oversimplification. The results in young chickens showed that both central depressants and excitants contained an aliphatic component. Where a ring structure was present and had electronegative substituents (OH,CH_3O,Cl) so that electrostatic pairing was possible, then the compound was a central depressant; those having none or electropositive substituents (CH_3) had excitant properties. The phenolic groups are little, if at all, ionized in sympathomimetic amines at physiological pH [50]. However the difference between the central depressants α-methyl noradrenaline or α-methyl adrenaline and the central excitants amphetamine or N-methyl amphetamine which were otherwise identical in structure but lacked the phenolic hydroxyls, could be best accounted for by the hydroxyls on the ring structure modifying the electronic properties of the molecule. The central excitants may therefore be thought of as having a positive charge at the aliphatic head of the molecule, and central depressants as having this and a weak negative charge at the other end of the molecule.

CONCLUSIONS

The sympathomimetic amines can be divided into two main groups for their mode of action on the mammalian autonomic nervous system. A third group of amines intermediate in chemical structure and function can also be recognized. This classification has been used as a model and a similar threefold classification of sympathomimetic amines according to their chemical structure and to their effects on behaviour and cerebral electrical activity can be made in young chickens. The catecholamines produced sleep, whereas the amphetamine-like amines evoked arousal. This division had no implication for mode of action, although the catecholamines produced sleep apparently by an action on α-receptors for catecholamines. The effect of amphetamine-like amines appeared to be due primarily to their tryptamine properties, although a subsidiary action via noradrenaline release within cerebral neurones was feasible. The relative importance of these two modes of amphetamine action probably varies from species to species.

Clearly the site of action of the sympathomimetic amines in the avian nervous system has to be ascertained. Experiments have begun using transection techniques [56] and are continuing. The localizations derived from these tests can be made more precise by reproducing the drug effects, when given parenterally, by injection through micropipettes into selected areas of the brain. Similar effects have been obtained in young chickens with catecholamines given intravenously or intracerebrally [65], strongly suggesting they penetrate to the brain from the blood. Localization and mode of action are only two of the many aspects of the central actions of sympathomimetic amines which, although topics of investigation for the last three decades, still await complete solution. One may view with favour or disfavour, according to one's bent, the notion that the eclipse of these problems is but the harbinger of others still to emerge.

ACKNOWLEDGEMENTS

Grants for research by the Bethlem Royal and Maudsley Hospitals Research Fund, the Central Research Fund of London University, the Medical Research Council, the Nuffield Foundation and the Wellcome Foundation are gratefully acknowledged. It is a pleasure also to record indebtedness to colleagues with whom collaborative work was undertaken.

REFERENCES

1. AHLQUIST, R. P. (1948) A study of the adrenotropic receptors, *Amer. J. Physiol.*, **153**, 586–600.
2. ALLEN, D. J., and MARLEY, E. (1966) Actions of amines on temperature in the chicken, *J. Physiol.* (*Lond.*), **183**, 61–62P.
3. AMIN, A. H. T., CRAWFORD, T. B. B., and GADDUM, J. H. (1954) Distribution of substance P and 5-hydroxytryptamine in central nervous system in dog, *J. Physiol.* (*Lond.*), **126**, 596–618.
4. BAKAY, L. (1956) *The Blood-brain Barrier*, p. 86, Springfield, Ill.
5. BARGER, G., and DALE, H. H. (1910) Chemical structure and sympathomimetic actions of amines, *J. Physiol.* (*Lond.*), **41**, 19–59.
6. BELLEAU, B. (1960) Relationships between agonists, antagonists and receptor sites, in *Adrenergic Mechanisms*, ed. Vane, J. R., Wolstenholme, G. E. W., and O'Connor, M., Ciba Foundation Symposium, pp. 223–45, London.
7. BIRKHÄUSER, H. (1940) Fermente im Gehirn geistig normaler Menschen, *Helv. chir. Acta*, **23**, 1071–86.
8. BLACKWELL, B., and MARLEY, E. (1966) Interactions of cheese and of

its constituents with monoamine oxidase inhibitors, *Brit. J. Pharmacol.*, **26**, 120–41.

9. Blackwell, B., and Marley, E. (1966) Interactions of yeast extracts and their constituents with monoamine oxidase inhibitors, *Brit. J. Pharmacol.*, **26**, 142–61.
10. Bradley, P. B., and Burford, R. [Unpublished data.]
11. Bradley, P. B., and Elkes, J. (1957) The effects of some drugs on the electrical activity of the brain, *Brain*, **80**, 77–117.
12. Bradley, P. B., and Marley, E. (1965) Effect of tryptamine and tryptamine homologues on cerebral electrical activity and behaviour in the cat, *Brit. J. Pharmacol.*, **25**, 659–74.
13. Brimblecombe, R. W., Downing, D. F., Green, D. M., and Hunt, R. R. (1964) Some pharmacological effects of a series of tryptamine derivatives, *Brit. J. Pharmacol.*, **23**, 43–54.
14. Brown, B. B. (1957) Lysergic acid diethylamide antagonism of certain drugs, *Ann. N.Y. Acad. Sci.*, **66**, 677–85.
15. Burn, J. H., and Rand, M. J. (1958) The action of sympathomimetic amines in animals treated with reserpine, *J. Physiol.* (*Lond.*), **144**, 314–36.
16. Clymer, N. V., and Seifter, J. (1947) A method of screening sympathomimetic amines for stimulant action on the cerebrum, *J. Pharmacol. exp. Ther.*, **89**, 149–52.
17. Collias, N., and Joos, M. (1953) The spectrographic analysis of sound signals of the domestic fowl, *Behaviour*, **5**, 175–89.
18. Connell, P. H. (1958) *Amphetamine Psychosis*, Maudsley Monographs, No. 5, London.
19. Cordeau, J. P., Moreau, A., Beaulines, A., and Laurin, C. (1953) EEG and behavioural changes following microinjections of acetylcholine and adrenaline in the brain stem of cats, *Arch. ital. Biol.*, **107**, 30–47.
20. Cruze, W. W. (1935) Maturation and learning in chicks, *J. comp. Psychol.*, **19**, 371–408.
21. De Robertis, E. (1966) Adrenergic endings and vesicles isolated from brain, *Pharmacol. Rev.*, **18**, 413–24.
22. Deighton, T., and Hutchinson, J. C. D. (1940) Studies on the metabolism of fowls. II. The effect of activity on metabolism, *J. Agr. Sci.*, **30**, 141–57.
23. Dewhurst, W. G., and Marley, E. (1964) Differential effect of sympathomimetic amines on the central nervous system, in *Animal Behaviour and Drug Action*, ed. Steinberg, H., de Rueck, A. V. S., and Knight, J., Ciba Foundation Symposium, pp. 175–88, London.
24. Dewhurst, W. G., and Marley, E. (1964) Communication to the British Pharmacological Society, January 1964.
25. Dewhurst, W. G., and Marley, E. (1965) Methods for quantifying behaviour and cerebral electrical activity and the effect of drugs under controlled conditions, *Brit. J. Pharmacol.*, **25**, 671–81.
26. Dewhurst, W. G., and Marley, E. (1965) The effects of α-methyl derivatives of noradrenaline, phenylethylamine and tryptamine on

the central nervous system of the chicken, *Brit. J. Pharmacol.*, **25**, 682–704.

27. DEWHURST, W. G., and MARLEY, E. (1965) Action of sympathomimetic and allied amines on the central nervous system of the chicken, *Brit. J. Pharmacol.*, **25**, 705–27.
28. DEWHURST, W. G., and MARLEY, E. [Unpublished data.]
29. DEWS, P. B. (1958) Studies on behaviour, iv, Stimulant actions of methamphetamine, *J. Pharmacol. exp. Ther.*, **122**, 137–47.
30. DEWS, P. B., and MORSE, W. H. (1961) Behavioural pharmacology, *Ann. Rev. Pharmacol.*, **1**, 145–74.
31. EPPS, H. M. R. (1945) The development of amine oxidase activity by human tissues after birth, *Biochem. J.*, **39**, 37–42.
32. EULER, V. S. VON., and PURKHOLD, A. (1951) Effect of sympathetic denervation on the noradrenaline and adrenaline content of the spleen, kidney and salivary glands in the sheep, *Acta physiol. scand.*, **24**, 212–17.
33. FABING, H. D. (1956) On going berserk: a neurochemical inquiry, *Amer. J. Psychiat.*, **113**, 409–15.
34. FELDBERG, W., and MYERS, R. D. (1964) Effects on temperature of amines injected into the cerebral ventricles. A new concept of temperature regulation, *J. Physiol.* (*Lond.*), **173**, 226–37.
35. FELDBERG, W., and SHERWOOD, S. L. (1954) Injections of drugs into the lateral ventricle of the cat, *J. Physiol.* (*Lond.*), **123**, 148–67.
36. FLECKENSTEIN, A., and BURN, J. H. (1953) The effect of denervation on the action of sympathomimetic amines on the nictitating membrane, *Brit. J. Pharmacol.*, **8**, 69–78.
37. HARVEY, S. C., and NICKERSON, M. (1951) Adrenergic mechanisms in the chicken, *Fed. Proc.*, **10**, 307.
38. HESS, S., REDFIELD, B. G., and UDENFRIEND, S. (1959) Tryptamine in animal tissues following the administration of iproniazid, *Fed. Proc.*, **18**, 402.
39. HIEBEL, G., BONVALLET, M., HUVÉ, P., and DELL, P. (1954) Analyse neuro-physiologique de l'action centrale de la d-amphétamine (maxiton), *Sem. Hôp. Paris*, **30**, 1880–7.
40. HOLZBAUER, M., and VOGT, M. (1956) Depression by reserpine of the noradrenaline concentration in the hypothalamus of the cat, *J. Neurochem.*, **1**, 8–11.
41. HOUGHTON, H., and MARLEY, E. [Unpublished data.]
42. JEPSON, J. B., ZALTMAN, P., and UDENFRIEND, S. (1962) Microsomal hydroxylation of tryptamine, indoleacetic acid and related compounds, to 6-hydroxy derivatives, *Biochim. biophys. Acta* (*Amst.*), **62**, 91–102.
43. KELLEHER, R. T., and MORSE, W. H. (1964) Escape behavior and punished behavior, *Fed. Proc.*, **23**, 808–17.
44. KEY, B. J., and MARLEY, E. (1961) The effect of some sympathomimetic amines on electrocortical activity and behaviour of young and adult animals, *J. Physiol.* (*Lond.*), **155**, 39–41P.
45. KEY, B. J., and MARLEY, E. (1962) The effect of the sympathomimetic

amines on behavior and electrocortical activity of the chicken, *Electroenceph. clin. Neurophysiol.*, **14**, 90–105.

46. Lajtha, A. (1957) The development of the blood-brain barrier, *J. Neurochem.*, **1**, 216–27.
47. Lajhta, A. (1962) In *Neurochemistry*, 2nd ed., ed. Elliott, K. A. C., Page, I. H., and Quastel, J. H., p. 399, Springfield, Ill.
48. Leimdorfer, A. (1950) The action of sympathomimetic amines on the central nervous system and the blood sugar. Mechanism of action, *J. Pharmacol.*, **98**, 62–71.
49. Lewis, A. J. (1959) In *Neuro-Psycopharmacology*, Vol. 1, ed. Bradley, P. B., Deniker, P., and Radouco-Thomas, C., pp. 207–12, Amsterdam.
50. Lewis, G. P. (1954) The importance of ionization in the activity of sympathomimetic amines, *Brit. J. Pharmacol.*, **9**, 488–93.
51. Longo, V. G., and Silvestrini, B. (1957) Effect of adrenergic and cholinergic drugs injected by intra-carotid route on electrical activity of brain, *Proc. Soc. exp. Biol.* (*N.Y.*), **95**, 43–47.
52. Longo, V. G., and Silvestrini, B. (1957) Action of eserine and amphetamine on the electrical activity of the brain, *J. Pharmacol. exp. Ther.*, **120**, 160–70.
53. Marley, E. (1960) Response to some stimulant and depressant drugs of the central nervous system, *J. ment. Sci.*, **106**, 76–92.
54. Marley, E. (1961) The significance of mydriasis produced by amphetamine sulphate, *Psychopharmacologia* (*Berl.*), **2**, 243–57.
55. Marley, E. (1962) Action of some sympathomimetic amines in the cat's iris, *in situ* or isolated, *J. Physiol.* (*Lond.*), **162**, 193–211.
56. Marley, E. (1963) Brain-stem receptors for sympathomimetic amines in the chicken, *J. Physiol.* (*Lond.*), **165**, 24–25P.
57. Marley, E. (1964) The adrenergic system and sympathomimetic amines, in *Advances in Pharmacology*, Vol. 3, ed. Garattini, S., and Shore, P. A., pp. 167–266, New York.
58. Marley, E. (1965) Actions of amines on the central and autonomic nervous systems, *J. Psychosom. Res.*, **9**, 137–48.
59. Marley, E. (1966) Behavioral and electrophysiological effects of catecholamines, *Pharmacol. Rev.*, **18**, 753–68.
60. Marley, E. (1967) Action of sympathomimetic and allied amines on the central nervous system, in *Scientific Basis of Medicine: Annual Reviews*. [in press].
61. Marley, E., and Key, B. J. (1963) Maturation of the electrocorticogram and behavior in the kitten and guinea-pig and the effect of some sympathomimetic amines, *Electroenceph. clin. Neurophysiol.*, **15**, 620–36.
62. Marley, E., and Morse, W. H. (1966) Operant conditioning in the newly hatched chicken, *J. Exp. Animal Behav.*, **9**, 95–103.
63. Marley, E., and Morse, W. H. (1967) Effects of α-methyl derivatives of phenethylamine, noradrenaline, and tryptamine on operant conditioning in chickens, *Brit. J. Pharmacol.* [in press].
64. Marley, E., and Prout, G. I., (1965) Physiology and pharmacology of the splanchnic adrenal medullary junction, *J. Physiol.* (*Lond.*), **180**, 483–513.

65. MARLEY, E., and STEPHENSON, J. D. [Unpublished data.]
66. MAXWELL, R. A., POVALSKI, H., and PLUMMER, A. J. (1959) A differential effect of reserpine on pressor amine activity and its relationship to other agents producing this effect, *J. Pharmacol. exp. Ther.*, **125**, 178–83.
67. MAXWELL, R. A., PLUMMER, A. J., SCHNEIDER, F., POVALSKI, H., and DANIEL, A. I., (1960) Pharmacology of [2-(6 octahydro-1-azocinyl) ethyl] guanidine sulfate (SU-5864), *J. Pharmacol. exp. Ther.*, **128**, 22–29.
68. RANDRUP, A., MUNKVAD, I., and UDSEN, P. (1963) Adrenergic mechanisms and amphetamine induced abnormal behaviour, *Acta pharmacol. (Kbh.)*, **20**, 145–57.
69. RAPPORT, M. M., GREEN, A. A., and PAGE, I. H. (1948) Serum vasoconstrictor (serotonin). IV. Isolation and characterization, *J. biol. Chem.*, **176**, 1243–51.
70. RICHARDS, A. N., and COLLISON, L. W. (1928) An apparatus for the continuous recording of the oxygen consumption of small animals, *J. Physiol. (Lond.)*, **66**, 299–306.
71. ROTHBALLER, A. B., (1959) The effects of catecholamines on the central nervous system, *Pharmacol. Rev.*, **11**, 494–547.
72. SALMOIRAGHI, G. C. (1966) Central adrenergic synapses, *Pharmacol. Rev.*, **18**, 717–26.
73. SCHALLEK, W., and WALZ, D. (1953) Effects of d-amphetamine on the electroencephalogram of the dog, *Proc. Soc. exp. Biol. (N.Y.)*, **82**, 715–19.
74. SELLE, R. M. (1940) An effect of benzedrine sulfate on chicks, *Science*, **91**, 95.
75. SHORE, P. A., SILVER, S. L., and BRODIE, B. B. (1955) Interaction of serotonin and lysergic acid diethylamide (LSD) in the central nervous system, *Experientia (Basel)*, **11**, 272–3.
76. SMITH, C. B. (1963) Enhancement by reserpine and α-methyl dopa of the effects of d-amphetamine upon the locomotor activity of mice, *J. Pharmacol. exp. Ther.*, **142**, 343–50.
77. SMITH, C. B. (1964) Effects of d-amphetamine upon operant behavior of pigeons: enhancement by reserpine, *J. Pharmacol. exp. Ther.*, **146**, 167–74.
78. SOLLMANN, T. (1957) *A Manual of Pharmacology*, 8th ed., p. 691, Philadelphia.
79. SPOONER, C. E., and WINTERS, W. D. (1965) Evidence for a direct action of monoamines on the chick central nervous system, *Experientia (Basel)*, **21**, 256–8.
80. STEIN, L. (1964) Self-stimulation of the brain and the central stimulant action of amphetamine, *Fed. Proc.*, **23**, 836–50.
81. SZÁRA, S. (1957) The comparison of the psychotic effect of tryptamine derivatives with the effects of mescaline and LSD-25 in self-experiments, in *Psychotropic Drugs*, ed. Garattini, S., and Ghetti, V., pp. 460–6, Amsterdam.

82. Trendelenburg, U. (1963) Supersensitivity and subsensitivity to sympathomimetic amines, *Pharmacol. Rev.*, **15**, 225–76.

83. Vane, J. R. (1960) The actions of sympathomimetic amines on tryptamine receptors, in *Adrenergic Mechanisms*, ed. Vane, J. R., Wolstenholme, G. E. W., and O'Connor, M., Ciba Foundation Symposium, pp. 356–72, London.

84. Vane, J. R., Collier, H. O. J., Corne, S. J., Marley, E., and Bradley, P. B. (1961) Tryptamine receptors in the central nervous system, *Nature* (*Lond.*), **191**, 1068–9.

85. Vogt, M. (1954) The concentration of sympathin in different parts of the central nervous system under normal conditions and after the administration of drugs, *J. Physiol.* (*Lond.*), **123**, 451–81.

86. Waelsch, H. (1955) Blood-brain barrier and gas exchange, in *Biochemistry of the Developing Nervous System*, ed. Waelsch, H., pp. 187–207, New York.

87. Weil-Malherbe, H. (1960) The passage of catecholamines through the blood-brain barrier, in *Adrenergic Mechanisms*, ed. Vane, J. R., Wolstenholme, G. E. W., and O'Connor, M., Ciba Foundation Symposium, pp. 356–72, London.

88. Wurtman, R. J., Frank, M. M., Morse, W. H., and Dews, P. B., (1959) Studies on behavior. V. Actions of 1-epinephrine and related compounds, *J. Pharmacol. exp. Ther.*, **127**, 281–7.

14

Cerebral Amine Functions in Health and Disease

W. G. DEWHURST

INTRODUCTION

In 1954 two authoritative reports established the presence in mammalian brain of noradrenaline [98] and 5-hydroxytryptamine (5-HT; serotonin) [2]. At this time much was already known about their potency and extracerebral actions (which included neurotransmission) and few doubted their likely importance in cerebral function. Physiologists sought a central synaptic transmitter to complement acetylcholine. Optimistic clinicians looked for a satisfying explanation of pathogenesis in some neuropsychiatric illnesses. In the succeeding decade investigation has been intensive. Other amines such as dopamine [77] and tryptamine [55] were found in brain, and our knowledge of metabolism is richer, but cerebral function, whether physiological or pathological, has proved difficult to specify. Perhaps appearances belie this, for the current view that noradrenaline is an excitant in brain is widely held and often quoted as fact. There are, nonetheless, serious objections to this view. Pathological roles are even more enigmatic and speculations, though ingenious, have yet to find convincing support.

The problem of function is the main theme to be discussed here together with some proposed solutions. Work began in the Department of Psychiatry with studies of hypersecreting tumours and amine oxidase inhibitors, where amine function had clinical impact. Subsequent extension of the biochemical aspects was carried out in collaboration with Dr. R. Rodnight and later F. L. Diggins and W. G. King. The discrepancies from current theory, as well as those in the literature were analysed, and made necessary a re-examination of the physiology by extensive animal experiments with Dr. E. Marley on the basis of which a return to human and clinical investigations in the Metabolic Unit brought the wheel full circle.

The present occasion affords the opportunity to examine the work in a wider setting so that perspective and prospective may be judged. It seems proper, therefore, to present here a full formal statement of a physiological theory to replace the current view. The evidence for and against both standpoints will be examined critically and although references are necessarily selective considerable effort has been made to ensure that all the main types of evidence are dealt with fairly. Thereafter the establishment of a biological basis is considered and specific cerebral receptors identified. Reference to other work is noted which indicates that the same mechanisms subserve mood change in man, thus providing empirical data on the body-mind problem. Finally, the views receive logical extension to clinical problems and are shown to be of help by providing rational explanations and an heuristic basis for further research.

SOURCES OF ERROR

A prefatory word on this seems justified on three counts. First, even a cursory examination of the literature reveals considerable conflict in experimental findings. When the divergencies are analysed the majority can be traced back to differences in method. Second, although some errors seem obvious and some have been publicized [59, 60] the same mistakes recur with depressing regularity as the recent controversy over the 'pink spot' unhappily exemplifies. Third, it may help non-specialist readers to assess the evidence intelligently and reach their own conclusions.

The sources of error can be classified into three groups:

Inadequate Experimental Control. This may be unsuspected, and hence the more dangerous. In *animal* work sufficient time must be allowed for recovery from anaesthesia which takes longer than behaviour suggests: our own observations point to a minimum of 48 hours. The choice of a suitable anaesthetic is important [73] and some types are best avoided altogether, e.g. barbiturates depress spinal cord responses to tryptamine [74]. In *human* studies dietary control is all important and many 'abnormalities' attributed to disease have subsequently been shown to originate in diet. Quantitative studies in addition must allow for more oblique effects associated with urinary volume and pH on amounts of excreted metabolities [28, 31, 76].

Problems Peculiar to Amines. A prominent difficulty in early work was the measurement of the minute amounts present in biological fluids but this has now been largely overcome by advances both in pharmacological and biochemical techniques. A second difficulty, however, is still troublesome and can vitiate the most sophisticated of methods. It is rarely referred to, let alone considered in sufficient detail to enable effects to be assessed. Amine salts, whilst they are relatively stable solids, are destroyed rapidly in solution by increased temperature, high pH and visible or ultra-violet radiation.

The rapidity of such changes is seen clearly when amine solutions are administered to study behavioural and physiological responses. A solution 15 minutes old may have lost all its biological potency. Workers who estimate amines in body fluids have no such signals to warn them but attention to these points is equally vital. Prompt acidification, protection from light, and deep-freezing are required both on the bulk of the sample as well as on a portion to which known amounts of amine are added (the 'recovery') so that destruction may be monitored.

Problems Peculiar to Brain. These are by far the most difficult.

1. The blood-brain barrier. Actions of amines on cerebral sites have been inferred after administering amines in various ways. The commonest route used has been intravenous injection and if the amine is to penetrate brain it must first pass through the blood-brain barrier which in turn depends largely on lipid solubility [75]. Hydroxylated amines such as adrenaline and noradrenaline have low lipid solubility, whereas unhydroxylated amines such as tryptamine and phenylethylamine dissolve readily and are presumed to pass the cell barriers easily. This is one aspect of a more general principle [80]. Its validity is confirmed by the finding that penetration of noradrenaline into brain is slow [102], whereas tryptamine enters easily [52]. No valid conclusions about *cerebral* action, therefore, can be drawn for the hydroxylated group following intravenous (or intra-arterial) administration.

2. Site of action. Even when cerebral entry is reasonably sure, cerebral responses may not be due to *primary* action on brain but arise as secondary consequences from primary action on peripheral tissues. Much care is needed to exclude this error [86] for the classical technique of the isolated organ is denied to neurophysiologists. The whole brain cannot survive without a major part of its vascular supply intact and hence studies *in situ* are unavoidable.

3. Shared metabolism. The difficulties of ensuring cerebral entry have favoured other approaches. One is to give agents such as reserpine which release amines from their cellular sites. This faces the difficulty that a number of different amines with different actions are released at the same time. Other workers have used inhibitors of enzymes but again the results are difficult to disentangle as both indoleamines and catecholamines share a common enzyme (monoamine oxidase) for catabolism and both depend on another for their formation (dopadecarboxylase).

4. The response studied. Physiological parameters have been much used but are insufficient to account for total activity. Behavioural studies in intact conscious animals with concurrent physiological recordings, are essential for valid conclusions. The most scrupulous

environmental control is needed, for merely handling an animal, let alone a needle prick, will have effects far more profound than the contents of the syringe. To demand such control is not unreasonable for it need not be elaborate to be effective [32].

This catalogue of errors leads to two conclusions of value when assessing evidence. First, the weight to be attached to reported findings depends largely on the ways in which these difficulties have been overcome (or ignored). Secondly, no one technique is perfect; evidence from as many valid approaches as possible must be considered to form an accurate picture.

FUNCTIONS IN HEALTH

Although responsible for the discovery of 5-hydroxytryptamine (which he called 'enteramine'), Erspamer has doubted whether that found in brain (where it has a half-life of ten minutes) has any normal function. He has suggested [41] that it may be a vestigial hormone.

It is true that the reasonable expectation that noradrenaline would act as a neurotransmitter has not been realized if acetylcholine be the paradigm. An alternative view is that it modulates synaptic transmission. Whatever the exact cellular action, however, it is still possible to make some general statements on function in the whole animal to unify the large body of data accumulated. Two hypotheses bearing on this will be considered.

BRODIE'S HYPOTHESIS

This may be stated in the following terms:

Noradrenaline is postulated as modulator of the ergotropic division of the diencephalon [14], *activation of which 'elicits arousal, increases central sympathetic output, mobilizes substrates for energy utilization, increases motor activity and results in exaggerated responses to environmental change'. 5-HT is the suggested modulator of the trophotropic system* [13], *activation of which 'elicits drowsiness and sleep, increases central parasympathetic output, decreases motor activity and lowers responsiveness to external stimuli'* [12].

This hypothesis, as fully set out [12], attracts frequent reference which suggests wide support. It adopts concepts of Hess [56] that there are diencephalic ergotropic and trophotropic systems. Though modulators may be inhibitory or facilitatory, activation of the respective systems seems implied.

The evidence adduced by various workers to support the Brodie theory can be categorized by method as follows.

Intravenous Injections. Adrenaline and noradrenaline induce behavioural and electrocortical alerting when given thus in most animals including man. As previously noted, brain penetration is slow and small and the alerting must stem from primary effects on extra-cerebral receptors. Earlier reports found no correlation between alerting and blood pressure changes [6, 84] but our own studies with chicks showed that alterting is entirely dependent on rises in systemic blood pressure, and a similar conclusion was reached by others using different techniques [3, 4].

Intracerebral Injections. To overcome this difficulty noradrenaline has been injected directly into the brain stem. Rothballer [85] produced alerting in this fashion but injections of saline produced the same effect and purely mechanical factors cannot be excluded. Cordeau *et al.* [21] used a similar approach and also produced alerting but, in addition to the mechanical factors mentioned, these workers used large doses (20 μg.) and it is possible that these may also produce local vascular disturbances. More recently in Mexico workers have found that 2–4 μg. of adrenaline in a volume of 10 μl. injected into the olfactory bulb of conscious cats produced behavioural sleep and appropriate EEG changes [83]. These phenomena could be interrupted by external stimuli. Electrical activity from the bulb itself showed increased voltage and frequency.

Microelectrode Studies. The most diverse findings have been reported on neurones from different parts of the spinal cord, brain stem and cortex. Ablation studies suggest that neurones in the brain stem are the most likely sites of action [7, 72]. Curtis and Koizumi [26] found that noradrenaline and 5-HT were inactive on the cells of the cat's *reticular formation* but barbiturate anaesthesia had been used and may have accounted for the results. Curtis [25] claimed that amines such as tryptamine and α-methyl tryptamine were in-effective on *spinal* neurones, but again barbiturate anaesthesia had been used. Experiment has shown that barbiturate profoundly depresses the facilitatory effect of tryptamine on the spinal cord[74]. Other workers have found that substances such as noradrenaline may stimulate some reticular cells and inhibit others [8, 9]. A study of *cortical* neurones [64] showed that most of the amines discussed produced depression, i.e. antagonized L-glutamate-induced firing. The depressants included dopamine, 5-HT, adrenaline, noradrenaline and tryptamine but not amphetamine. Interpretation of these findings at present in terms of total function is impossible. Some reticular cells are stimulated and some inhibited; whereas nearly all cortical neurones are inhibited by all the amines except amphetamine. The difficulty lies in specifying whether effects seen in the whole animal are in fact due to stimulation of inhibitory neurones or inhibition of excitatory ones. Another difficulty reported is that application of drugs by iontophoresis is subject to considerable variation [62]. As far as noradrenaline is concerned, the amounts released were very large or almost none at all. It must be concluded that microelectrode studies provide no clear evidence either for or against the Brodie hypothesis.

Amino Acid Precursors. A number of workers have reported that 3:4-dihydroxyphenylalanine (dopa) the precursor of dopamine and adrenaline [103] causes alerting in reserpinized mice [16]; the effect is more marked in animals pre-treated with amine oxidase inhibitors [17]. 5-Hydroxytryptophan (5-HTP), the precursor of 5-HT, produces drowsiness in animals in small doses and marked locomotor disturbances in large doses [23]. Brodie rejects such evidence on the grounds that the enzyme decarboxylating dopa and 5-HTP is the same; therefore catecholamines will be formed at 5-HT sites and vice versa, with invalid results. It is doubtful whether this objection holds but the matter will be taken up more fully below.

Amine-releasing Agents. Another source of evidence used by Brodie relies on reserpine-like compounds to liberate amines from their cellular stores [12]. If the enzymes catabolizing such amines are also inhibited then large amounts of these substances can accumulate in the brain to produce marked effects. The difficulty with this approach is that it is extremely hard to affect one group of amines, e.g. the indoles, without affecting others, and the total effects produced may be attributable to either group, or, more likely, to both groups. Brodie and Costa claim [12] that by a combination of techniques they were able to release selectively either noradrenaline or 5-HT. With such methods they found that noradrenaline release was accompanied by marked excitement in animals. When they used the technique to liberate 5-HT, on the other hand, the results were unconvincing: 'The animals are not excited; some are even slightly sedated for a short time'. They comment: 'unfortunately it has not been possible thus far to trap only free 5-HT in brain'. Their conclusions on noradrenaline are also open to serious objection. First, it is highly unlikely that noradrenaline, if it is indeed liberated in pure fashion, is released solely in the brain and not at all in extracerebral tissues; as already mentioned, noradrenaline alerting occurs primarily by a peripheral mechanism with secondary actions on the brain. In addition, it is not clear what sort of environmental control, if any, was used.

AN ALTERNATIVE HYPOTHESIS

This may be stated in the following terms:

Cerebral amines fall into two main categories according to their primary cerebral actions. This dichotomy is manifested by: (1)

patterns of response; (2) *physicochemical properties of the amines;* (3) *receptor mechanisms; and* (4) *psychological effects. The groups are called 'excitant' and 'depressant' but wherever confusion is likely the terms 'Type A' and 'Type C' are suggested alternatives. A small biphasic group is termed 'Type B'.*

Type A (*Excitant*) *Amines*

These have the following characteristics:

1. *The response pattern* is typical of the normal alert state. Active exploratory movements, increased vocalization, and sometimes aggresive behaviour, are associated with increased motor activity, tremor, and increased sensory awareness. The EMG shows increased muscle potentials and the EEG desynchronization (fast frequency low amplitude activity).

2. *Physico-chemical properties* comprise: (a) the structure of a β-substituted ethylamine; and (b) a β-substituent which is both planar and *lipophilic.* The most potent is β-indolylethylamine (tryptamine). It is effective in doses of 1 nanomole/100g. body weight, occurs in the brain, and is the main physiological agonist. β-Phenylethylamine is less potent but otherwise similar.

3. *Receptor mechanisms* exist in the brain ('A' receptors), which are specific mediators of excitant amine actions. They are similar to the 'tryptamine receptors' identified in peripheral structures. They are competitively antagonized by methysergide. When excitant amines are so blocked they reveal a potential ability to activate Type C receptors (see below).

4. *Psychological effects* take the form of elevation of mood when A receptors are activated in man, but complex behavioural responses are determined by social as well as chemical stimuli; the excitant amine is a necessary but not a sufficient cause.

Type C (*Depressant*) *Amines*

These have the following characteristics:

1. *The response pattern* is typical of the normal drowsy or sleeping state. Diminished activity and vocalization with adoption of the natural sleeping posture are associated with decreased responsiveness to stimuli (although arousal can be produced normally). The EMG shows diminished muscle potentials and the EEG synchronization.

2. *Physico-chemical properties* comprise: (a) the structure of a β-substituted ethanolethylamine; and (b) a β-substituent which is both planar and *hydrophilic.* Adrenaline is the most potent, being effective in doses of 1 nanomole/100g. body weight. It is the main

physiological agonist. Noradrenaline is less potent but otherwise similar and may act mainly as a precursor of adrenaline.

3. *Receptor mechanisms* exist in the brain ('C receptors') which are distinct from cerebral 'A receptors', peripheral adrenergic α- and β-receptors, histamine and acetylcholine receptors. No certain specific antagonist has been found. Type C amines are not able to activate A receptors. The alerting produced by doses higher than those required for cerebral depressant action depends on blood pressure rises from stimulation of peripheral α-receptors and is antagonized by α-blockers but unaffected by methysergide.

4. *Psychological effects* in terms of associated mood change are at present uncharted.

Type B (Biphasic) Amines

These have the following characteristics:

1. *The response pattern* is truly biphasic, i.e. first excitant (as for Type A) and then depressant (as for Type C).

2. *Physico-chemical properties* are precise. There is either the addition of one hydroxyl group at positions 5 or 6 to the structure of the most potent excitant (tryptamine), or the subtraction of one hydroxyl group from the meta-position of the most potent depressant (adrenaline). 5-HT is the most active of this group which also includes 6-HT and oxedrine (synephrine).

3. *Receptor mechanisms* activated are those of Type A *and* Type C. The former actions are antagonized by methysergide. Type B amines must be distinguished from many inactive intermediates and near relatives representing the end of a continuum in which progressive deviations from optimal Type A or Type C structure entail progressive loss of potency.

4. *Psychological effects* and behavioural responses are those appropriate to the receptor stimulated.

The evidence for items (1) and (2) in each group will now be considered as the ground covered is comparable to that of the Brodie hypothesis and can be dealt with in a similar fashion. Items (3) and (4) pose special and different problems discussed later.

Attention is drawn to two points. First, although the hypothesis proposed at times leads to conclusions which are diametrically opposite to the Brodie view, the theories are not antithetical but different. The one contrasts 5-HT and noradrenaline. The alternative distinguishes between more and less lipophilic ethylamines. Secondly, it is not intended to deal in any detail with the animal and other work on which many of the views are based for this has been covered elsewhere [29–39 inclusive]. The purpose here is to examine all the main types of evidence available so that each falls into perspective and an overall assessment may be obtained. As before, categorization is by method.

Intravenous Injections. Unhydroxylated amines, e.g. amphetamine, produce alerting irrespective of the route of administration and this type of amine readily passes the blood-brain barrier. Peripheral sites of action can be excluded by deafferentation and ablation of the brain stem. With the encéphale isolé and cerveaux isolé preparations of Bremer receptors have been localized in the brain stem [7].

Injections of Cerebrospinal Spaces. The routes used have included lumbar puncture [100], intracisternal injection [65, 66], and intraventricular injection [45]. Leimdorfer found that substances such as amphetamine produced excitement in dogs after intracisternal injection, whereas adrenaline and related compounds produced drowsiness. Feldberg and Sherwood reported a stuporose state in cats after intraventricular injection. A depressant action of catecholamines after intraventricular injections has also been noted in mice [53], sheep [79], and man [94]. Domer and Feldberg [40] also noted that adrenaline given intraventricularly abolished tremor. Feldberg [44] considers that adrenaline may be involved in the control of shivering and tremor.

It may be argued that although the blood-cerebrospinal fluid (CSF) barrier has been passed the catecholamines will still have difficulty in entering cells. According to Mayer *et al.* [75], however, the passage of substances from CSF to brain depends on neuroglial activity rather than lipid solubility.

Two anomalies must be mentioned. First, amphetamine may make the cat lethargic and intensify the depressant action of 5-HT. Our own work shows that tryptamine, after producing alerting for 5 minutes or so, is subsequently followed by a state of stupor with large amplitude slow waves in the EEG. In accordance with the hypothesis proposed it was predicted that these effects indicated that in this species a depressant metabolite is produced, and confirmatory evidence of this has been found. Secondly, at the height of the stuporose phase in cats, the EEG shows desynchronization. The desynchronized pattern after adrenaline may be associated with that stage of sleep called paradoxical [58]. Feldberg [43] ascribed the action of adrenaline to stimulation of midline structures in diencephalon and perhaps mesencephalon. Faure [42] reported that paradoxical sleep may be produced by stimulation of the median and premedian dorsotegmental structures. As indicated, the cat is not always typical of other species.

Injections into Brain. Difficulties attending this method have already been mentioned. It should be noted, however, that in a recent report adrenaline injected in small doses and small volume induced all the phenomena of sleep in cats [83].

Microelectrode Studies. These have been reviewed under the Brodie hypothesis [pp. 292–4] and the conclusion that such studies provide neither proof nor disproof is equally applicable to the hypothesis advanced here. However, the work of Krnjevic *et al.* has supplied valuable information on a paradox which will now be discussed.

Amino Acid Precursors. According to Sjoerdsma *et al.* [95] tryptophan, the precursor of tryptamine as well as 5-HT, has no effect in man, but when given after amine oxidase inhibitors it produces a 'drunken' state with occasional hyper-reflexia. However, the author found that tryptophan does produce clear-cut effects in normal subjects without amine oxidase inhibitors. There is an initial period of alertness and, after about an hour and a half to two hours a feeling of drowsiness which coincides with elevation of hydroxylated indoles in blood. There is also a hypotensive reaction [31]. The effects noted earlier following 5-HTP accord just as well with the present hypothesis as the Brodie position. The effect produced by dopa is, however, an apparent contradiction. Indeed, although these findings apparently support his hypothesis, Brodie rejects such evidence on the grounds that the amine formed will be present at both catecholamine sites and 5-HT sites with invalid results. Brodie's objection does not seem particularly serious and the findings of Carlsson [16], Chrusciel [17] and others must be accepted. In fact, further research has shown an interesting reason for the discrepancy. Chrusciel found that metatyrosine produced effects similar to dopa; as metatyrosine is not metabolized to dopamine it is suggested that the stimulant action is the property of the amino acid itself. Microelectrode studies confirm this and amino acids have been shown to have excitatory or inhibitory actions on cortical neurones [63], as well as on the spinal cord [27]. Krnjevic and Phillis found that dopa applied by micropipette excited cortical neurones, whereas dopamine, adrenaline and noradrenaline depressed them.

Endocrinological Evidence. The examination of patients with hypo- or hypersecretion of different hormones has been a valuable source of physiological data. Such methods were applied to the present problem by the author in 1961 [30]. Deficiency syndromes of catecholamines and indoleamines do not, so far as is known, exist apart from those induced by drugs, notably reserpine. Profound lowering of mood can follow prolonged reserpine treatment, but the difficulty here lies in separating the effects of noradrenaline liberation from those due to 5-HT release. On the other hand, syndromes associated with hypersecretion of both indoleamines and catecholamines are known to occur.

Carcinoid tumours mostly produce excessive amounts of 5-HT but although this produces marked peripheral effects the blood-brain barrier hinders entry to the brain [89] and such cases are unsuitable for study of central actions. However, a small group described by Sandler and Snow [88] secrete large amounts of 5-HTP, the amino acid precursor of 5-HT, which can enter the brain and is then presumably decarboxylated to the amine. Such cases should provide evidence otherwise unobtainable of the effects of 5-HT in man. Experiments along the lines indicated in the earlier part of this paper have been carried out in human subjects [10, 11] but the doses of 5-HTP used were much smaller than those used to produce neurological effects in animals [23]. Patients with 5-HTP-secreting tumours are subjected to large amounts of circulating amino acid over long periods of time and represent more closely the conditions customarily found in clinical disease. Eight such patients were found in the literature up to 1961; and of these, six had no neurological or psychiatric disability whatsoever, despite long-standing high levels of 5-HTP. (When published details were lacking on these points personal inquiry to the authors concerned was made to ensure accuracy on this matter). Of the two patients with abnormalities one had metastases in her liver, lungs, and bones, and had had numerous hospital admissions for investigation and operations: the diagnosis was 'cancerophobia'. The other patient developed a terminal confusional state when in gross heart failure in the last hours of life: there was no neuropsychiatric abnormality during the preceding months during which her tumour was producing large amounts of 5-HTP. 5-HT can hardly be incriminated on the evidence available from these two cases and the absence of effects in the other six is strong evidence against any pathogenic role of 5-HT. Since this study was done other cases of tumours which produce 5-HTP have been reported, but none of the reports seen by the author describe neuropsychiatric sequelae [81, 87].

Phaeochromocytomata provide comparable cases concerning the catecholamines. The majority produce excess noradrenaline and adrenaline which do not easily penetrate the brain, and again one must look for the small number of tumours which produce dopa in excess. Such tumours exist, for example that described by Weil-Malherbe [101]. Unfortunately, no clinical details appear to have been published. Since the survey was done other conditions have been reported in which excess of dopa is produced. Scott [92] found that 22 out of 28 patients with malignant melanomata excreted dopa in the urine. The clinical state was not mentioned except for a note on the melanomata.

Amine Body Levels and Function. 1. Brain levels. According to Vogt [99] a correlation with function cannot easily be made. This is not surprising. The actions of physiological amines last only a few minutes. The functional significance of free amines and those stored in granules is very different. The amines themselves are unstable, and concentration in different parts of the brain vary widely. To allow for all these factors and then relate them to behaviour is difficult indeed.

2. Extracerebral levels. Many studies have been done in health and disease of 5-HT or catecholamines and their metabolites in platelets, blood, and urine [70]. Assuming that dietary control is adequate and that allowance is made for factors like urinary volume [28, 31] such investigations can provide valid and valuable information on general bodily reactions in neuropsychiatric illness, but the tempting extrapolation to cerebral events should not be made unless certain circumstances discussed next prevail.

3. Extracerebral indicators. One instance in which peripheral estimations may properly be extrapolated to indicate cerebral levels occurs in conditions where a known metabolic abnormality affects both brain and extracerebral tissues. Thus the enzyme defect of phenylketonuria is known to be widespread and the detection of such cases by urine analysis depends on this [104].

A legitimate counterpart of these circumstances is the use of agents inhibiting a particular enzyme, provided that there are independent data showing that administration of the substance is followed by significant entry to the brain and, in addition, that it inhibits the cerebral enzymes as effectively as the extracerebral. If these conditions can be established then administration of the substance can be presumed to have similar effects both outside and inside the brain, and extracerebral effects may be used as an indicator of metabolic changes in the brain. In such a study the author made simultaneous measurements of the main substrates of monoamine oxidase, namely metanephrine and normetanephrine, 5-HT, and tryptamine, in human subjects before and after phenelzine. Tryptamine excretion was increased fourfold, 5-HT trebled and the metanephrines doubled. The difference between the differences were statistically significant [30]. Further, the *products* of enzyme action emphasized the greater dependence of indoleamines on catabolism by monoamine oxidase for vanilmandelic acid derived from catecholamines showed only a slight fall after an inhibitor [30], contrasting with another study [39] in which 5-HIAA showed a marked decrease in excretion. Other workers have shown that tyramine, with marked pressor activity, may be affected as much as tryptamine [95]. One would not wish to press such indirect evidence too far but phenelzine has been shown to inhibit the cerebral enzyme just as effectively as the extracerebral, and Levine and Sjoerdsma [67] have demonstrated a close correlation between tryptamine excretion and enzyme inhibition in man. It would therefore seem not unreasonable to assume similar changes in brain.

4. Extracerebral levels affecting brain. Studies such as the last are rightly open to debate, but to concentrate on arguments about the validity of extracerebral changes as indicators of cerebral happenings is to miss completely a more important point. It is this: of the substrates measured, tryptamine shows the greatest increase and can penetrate the blood-brain barrier easily [52]; 5-HT shows a smaller increase and its entry to brain is more restricted [89]; while the catecholamines show least increase and their entry to brain is less still [102]. Hence, irrespective of metabolic changes *within* cerebral tissue the brain is still subject to high concentrations of tryptamine which must overshadow any changes in 5-HT or catecholamines occurring within the brain.

Permeable Blood-brain Barriers. Increased permeability may be the result of disease or immaturity. Many patients presumably have such defects but so far as is known this clinical approach has not been used in the present problem, although Purpura *et al.* [82] employed it for the study of amino acid effects in animals. Similarly, study of the human infant might provide useful data, but again there seem to be no results which are germane. There can be no doubt that some permeability exists, as the phenomena of kernicterus show.

Fortunately animal studies are possible. In 1947 Clymer and Seifter [18], following up an earlier report [93], found that the young chick gave characteristic responses to amphetamine and also noted that adrenaline made the animal drowsy. Key and Marley [61] confirmed and extended this finding and were able to show that the animal's responses, both behavioural and electrocortical, were those of the mature animal. This approach appeared to hold much promise as a means of obtaining information on central mechanisms. Accordingly Dr. Marley and I exploited this as fully as possible. The animal was housed in a carefully controlled physical and social environment. Behavioural and physiological responses were quantified and recorded simultaneously and continuously and amines could be administered, all without handling or disturbing the animal [33, 35, 36, 37]. An extensive series of amines, in fresh solution, was examined so that molecular requirements could be specified in detail. Adrenaline was confirmed as the most potent of some fifteen depressants. Tryptamine was the most potent excitant. Both adrenaline and tryptamine were effective in similar dosage; they had similar durations of action; they were physiological antagonists; and they almost certainly represent true physiological agonists. Deviations from optimal structure were accompanied by progressive loss of potency. An α-methyl group prolonged action. Three molecules had true biphasic actions: these were 5-HT, 6-HT and oxedrine.

An explanation for the excitatory role commonly attributed to adrenaline came from experiments in which blood pressure was recorded concomitantly with the EEG and behavioural variables. The dose required to produce full depressant effects had no effect on arterial blood pressure. If the dose was increased, small rises of blood pressure could be elicited, and the sleeping state was interrupted with episodes of alerting. When the dose was increased still further, hypertensive responses were marked and the behavioural state was entirely alert, with no drowsy component at all. The blood pressure effects could be blocked by an α-antagonist which did not affect the depressant responses but abolished alerting.

CONCLUSION

Many types of evidence have now been cited in connexion with the Brodie hypothesis and the proposed alternative. The experimental work with animals gives the most convincing demonstration of effects but clinical material can also provide important information otherwise unobtainable, which needs no further qualification about species differences.

However, it seems more profitable to consider the data as a whole rather than attempt to assess which is the 'best' approach. Bearing in mind the conclusions reached in 'Sources of error' it is contended that the strength of support for the proposed alternative depends not so much on any one crucial experiment but on the fact that so many radically different approaches point in the same direction. None the less, the evidence so far considered, although giving strong support to the alternative view, does not allow us to claim more than an accurate description. The hope, however, underlying our animal work was that a biological basis could be established for the effects observed and the brain mechanisms elucidated.

BRAIN RECEPTORS AND BIOLOGICAL VALIDITY

To proceed from a descriptive classification of amine actions to the more fundamental cerebral receptor mechanisms involved requires independent and somewhat special evidence. This was obtained in several ways.

Competitive Antagonists. These have been invaluable in elucidating peripheral receptors but application in cerebral studies has hitherto proved difficult. Fortunately methysergide acts as a specific antagonist in brain. It blocks *all* the actions of *all* the excitant amines in minute dosage which given by itself produces no effects [36, 37]. In addition methysergide fulfills most of the criteria laid down by Gaddum for competitive antagonists [48]. Thus it antagonizes all the different actions of excitant amines at receptor sites, it is surmountable, and a chemical link exists between antagonist and excitant module structure.

Antagonism to depressants is not so clearly defined. They are unaffected by methysergide, by β-adrenergic blockers, antihistamines and anticholinergic agents. There is a suggestion that α-blockers given in enormous doses for several days diminish the response to depressant amines but whether this represents a specific antagonistic effect seems at present debatable. It appears fair to say that the C receptor is distinct from the type A receptor as well as the peripheral adrenergic β-receptor and receptors for histamine and acetylcholine; it may also differ from the peripheral α-receptor, or it may turn out that apparent distinctions are merely reflections of the limitations of currently available antagonists. It is also clear that extrapolation from peripheral α-receptors to central excitant receptors is quite erroneous.

Specific antagonists are also powerful tools for unravelling modes of action. They are essential in elucidating the mechanisms of biphasic amine activity, for methysergide specifically abolished the excitatory action only. Similarly the alerting produced by catecholamines could be blocked by antagonists of peripheral α-receptors, which also abolished hypertensive effects.

Cross-tachyphylaxis. Tachyphylaxis induced by an indolethylamine such as α-methyl tryptamine renders the tissues tachyphylactic to other types of excitant amines such as phenylethylamines. Similarly, the specific antagonism of methysergide can be surmounted by one type of an excitant group to allow another member of the group to act.

Order of Potency. Another type of proof suggested by Ahlquist [1] depends on a rank order of potency which is constant for a group of amines acting on a particular type of receptor. This reasoning suggests that type A receptors are similar to peripheral tryptamine receptors and that depressant cerebral receptors are comparable to peripheral α-receptors.

Other Species and Tissues. A final testimony is that the divisions of *cerebral* function observed in the chick studies are entirely similar to divisions of function made in other species and tissues, e.g. the rat's stomach [97], the denervated cat nictitating membrane [47] and the cat denervated iris [71]. The consistency of the patterns observed indicates that the receptor mechanisms probably have a general biological validity in most species including man. Human investigations are still in initial stages but the data so far available support this view. As an example a report by Feldman and Glaser [46] on the treatment of migraine with methysergide while recording the EEG can be noted. The authors reported: 'the most striking observation, however, was that 9 of the 11 subjects receiving methysergide complained of a sudden onset of drowsiness in the immediate period after the injection' and they also found appropriate changes in the EEG. A similar report has also been made by others [90].

MOOD IN MAN

The receptor mechanisms identified gain further importance because there is evidence (both direct and indirect) based on *human* experience that activation of the 'A' receptor produces elevation of mood [31]. The evidence will not be repeated here but one pointer from our animal studies is worthy of emphasis. The peculiar twitterings or 'pleasure calls' [19] require not only an amine but a social stimulus. They occur only when birds are in the flock and rarely when the animal is isolated. The implications for therapeutics are obvious. Although there are a number of reports that type C amines such as adrenaline and noradrenaline given intravenously produce anxiety or apprehension in human subjects there is still doubt if such effects are attributable to the amines or to the psychological circumstances accompanying such administration. However, this may be the *central* actions of type C amines and the function of the type C receptor in relation to mood are quite unknown and more data are needed.

FUNCTIONS IN DISEASE

In this final section it is hoped to show how a logical extension of the views on physiology may have clinical relevance. First, it may provide coherent explanations for apparently diverse clinical phenomena. Secondly, it can furnish an heuristic tool for investigating pathogenesis. Thirdly, it has similar use in further research and treatment. If heuristic value is to be at all genuine it must follow that much of the proof (or the reverse) remains to be determined. The findings assembled to date are cited, therefore, not with any pretence at completeness, but rather to illustrate ways in which applications may be made.

DEPRESSIVE PSYCHOSIS

The clinical features of this illness are comprehensively described in Lewis' classical papers [68, 69]. It has received much less biochemical attention than schizophrenia but a recent increase in interest has been associated with the 'catecholamine hypothesis'. This proposes that '*some, if not all, depressions are associated with an absolute or relative deficiency of catecholamines, particularly norepinephrine, at functionally important receptor sites in the brain. Elation conversely may be associated with an excess of such amines*' [91]. Schildkraut gives a fair-minded assessment of the supporting evidence. This can be placed in three categories. First, substances known to affect mood are linked to changes in noradrenaline. Thus antidepressants all delay noradrenaline destruction, either by enzyme inhibition (monoamine oxidase inhibitors) or by favouring protection of amines by barriers against enzyme attack (imipramine, amphetamine). Reserpine which sometimes is followed by depressive illness has been shown to facilitate noradrenaline destruction by interfering with the granule binding which customarily prevents enzyme attack. Some amino acids such as dopa may have excitant action; and dopa, of course, is a precursor of noradrenaline. A second category of evidence cites studies of patients with affective disorders who might be expected to show associated changes in noradrenaline metabolism. Although it is generally agreed that noradrenaline output is increased in mania, findings in depression are conflicting. Finally, studies of the effects of treatment in depressed patients are noted, such as the increase in normetanephrine excretion after successful imipramine treatment. Such data are, perhaps, more closely allied to the first category linking noradrenaline with drugs rather than affective states, for no studies have yet demonstrated any difference between patients and normal subjects in their biochemical response to antidepressants. It should also be noted that the blood-brain barrier exists for normetanephrine [51] and the provisos noted earlier in the physiological section apply here also, as Schildkraut properly points out. He concludes that it is impossible to confirm or reject the hypothesis definitively.

Aside from minor problems (which may be more apparent than real) one major criticism is necessary. It is that only some of the facts are accounted for and these are the least important both qualitatively and quantitatively. Antidepressants such as monoamine oxidase inhibitors affect other types of amines besides noradrenaline; the same is true for reserpine-like compounds. Amino acid effects perhaps escape such censure but dopa was found to be of only limited benefit in one study and two others were negative, including Schildkraut's own. 5-HTP was also ineffective when trials were controlled, whereas several studies were cited for the euphoriant action of tryptophan. Acceptance of the 'catecholamine hypothesis' leads Schildkraut to the tortuous explanation that the effects of tryptophan are due to noradrenaline release by 5-HTP [22] in spite of the previously noted ineffectiveness of the latter.

An alternative hypothesis consonant with the physiological theory is now proposed. *Lowering of mood and some forms of depressive illness may be due to either deficiency of excitant (type A) amines, or diminished responsiveness of the A receptor. Psychosocial factors are co-determinants of complex behavioural responses. Elevation of mood and some manic states may be caused by an excess of excitant (type A) amines or increased A receptor sensitivity. Psychosocial factors are co-determinants of more complex behavioural features.*

In contrast to the 'catecholamine hypothesis' a number of features should be noted. First, nothing is said here about catecholamines (including noradrenaline) or the type C receptor, for there is no satisfactory evidence linking these with mood; it is, indeed, difficult to specify a particular affective state associated with physiological sleep. Second, involvement of the excitant group of amines is envisaged rather than any particular amine, although tryptamine and phenylethylamine deficiency are presumed to be the most likely. Third, malfunction of receptors is included as well as changes in the amines themselves. Finally, psychosocial determinants are admitted to the scheme.

The hypothesis has an experimental basis as well as clinical supporting evidence. Thus the phenomena of tachyphylaxis in the central nervous system shown by excitant amines [33] are presumably due to diminished receptor responsiveness for there is no evidence that central excitants act indirectly by depleting amine cellular stores. Again, the psychosocial determinants of the animal's vocal responses were clearly demonstrated experimentally as noted previously.

Considering now the type of evidence that Schildkraut cites, studies of monamine oxidase inhibitors discussed earlier show that the preponderant effect is the elevation of tryptamine [30]. This presumably occurs in brain, but, irrespective of this, the ability of tryptamine to pass the blood-brain barrier must have significant cerebral consequences. The effects of amphetamine are due to direct agonistic action on A-receptors and too frequent administration leads to tachyphylaxis. Tranylcypromine has a similar effect in addition to being an amine oxidase inhibitor. Imipramine may have some agonistic action on the receptor as well as its ability to alter permeability. The effects of the reserpine-like compounds do not permit clear distinction between the catechols and indoleamines and are of no use as evidence for either view. The effects of amino acids receive a straightforward explanation in terms of this hypothesis. It may be noted that the effects of tryptophan as an euphoriant are not as clear cut as might be supposed. This is not surprising because tryptophan, as well as forming tryptamine, is also the precursor of 5-HTP and 5-HT. Recently Coppen *et al.* [20], who thoroughly acquainted themselves with the author's views 4 years ago, have reported that tryptamine excretion in affective states changes with recovery, which gives independent confirmation of these views.

Thus even in the initial stages the evidence that one can muster for the alternative hypothesis permits favourable comparison with the catecholamine view. Much, of course, needs to be done. Before leaving depressive illness, however, two other important consequences for treatment and prophylaxis also follow.

First, it is possible to specify a symptomatic treatment with a rational theoretical basis. As the effects of excitant amines include elevation of mood the logical prescription is to foster this, and this may be accomplished in various ways. Excitant amines themselves may be administered, particularly those with long actions such as the α-methylated derivatives. Amine precursors might also be given, namely the amino acids L-tryptophan and L-phenylalanine. Also, destruction of excitant amines might be delayed by inhibiting catabolic enzymes with amine oxidase inhibitors or perhaps by altering permeability with imipramine. Unfortunately, there are difficulties with each of the three procedures. α-Methylated amines cause tachyphylaxis; amino acids are precursors of depressant as well as excitant amines; and, similarly, inhibition of catabolizing enzymes may affect both depressant and excitant groups. Such success as the latter drugs have enjoyed depends partly on the fact that monoamine oxidase has a greater effect on indoleamines than catechols, presumably because the latter have alternative metabolic routes; and also because some are direct agonists on A-receptors, e.g. tranylcypromine. However, the practical limitations besetting currently available treatment must not obscure the fact that such treatment has a logical physiological basis nor need it dim the hope that more effective measures may be developed more quickly than trial and error has permitted in the past.

Secondly, prophylaxis may soon become a practical reality. The amino acid precursors, tryptophan and phenylalanine, are essential amino acids, i.e. they cannot be synthesized by the human, and dietary control which would be an acceptable natural procedure suited to long term use thus becomes feasible. The chief difficulty is that both amino acids lead to excitant and depressant amines. If it is to be fully effective dietary control must be conjoined in the future with some means of regulating the amounts of one or other group formed. Diet, of course, may also need control to avoid unpleasant side-effects, such as those reported by Blackwell [5].

MANIA

The ways in which the hypothesis may be applied to investigate pathogenesis, treatment and prophylaxis follow the lines of depression and should need no further elaboration here. One additional point in connexion with treatment, however, deserves a word. The rational symptomatic treatment is reduction of excitant amine action which may be attempted by withholding amino acid precursors, by inhibiting enzymes forming these amines from amino acids, or by giving agents such as reserpine which deplete cellular stores of formed amines. Unfortunately, as with depression, difficulties occur in practice since all tend to affect both excitant and depressant groups together. Unlike depression of excitant amine action, however, another form of treatment is possible, namely administration of the specific A receptor antagonist, methysergide. I have no knowledge of the results of such a trial in mania but if the theory is correct then benefit should follow, providing that side-effects such as vasospasm permit adequate dosage to be employed.

SCHIZOPHRENIA

This has received the lion's share of biochemical attention over the last few years. One view is that serotonin is at fault; proponents of this view claim that a deficiency of serotonin is the basic defect, although an excess is also considered to produce mental disturbance [105, 106]. In spite of much work and ingenuity, however, this view remains largely unsubstantiated, as Woolley admits, and is likely to remain speculative while much of the physiology of 5-HT remains uncertain. Lack of sequelae in patients with 5-HTP secreting carcinoid tumours discussed earlier provides strong evidence against a pathogenic role for 5-HT [30].

The majority of studies, are based on the postulate of an abnormal amine metabolite. A number of substances produce 'model' psychoses with hallucinations and distortions of time sense. Osmond and Smythies first pointed out the similarity of some hallucinogens to naturally occurring adrenaline metabolites [78]; subsequently indolic hallucinogens have been likened to naturally occurring indoleamine metabolites. High hopes have not been fulfilled mainly for two reasons. The 'model' psychosis is not a model of schizophrenia but a toxic psychosis which most physicians distinguish from schizophrenia without much trouble. One substance, however, namely amphetamine, produces a condition which does cause diagnostic difficulty, but this has received less attention than its more exotic cousins. Furthermore, no abnormal metabolite has been found in spite of intensive search. Many claims for positive findings have been vitiated by demonstrations that the abnormality originates in fact in diet. Such errors are distressingly repetitive in schizophrenic research, as the 'pink spot' shows. A variant of the toxic metabolite theory with eminent sponsors suggests a genetic morphism with adrenochrome as the central biochemical lesion [57]. The genetic aspects have been heavily criticized by geneticists, a matter outside the author's competence, but comment is needed on the alleged biochemical defect. The authors lump together both 'pink' and 'mauve' spots irrespective of the varied location reagents used to produce the colours and cite this as evidence found by many workers which substantiates the adrenochrome theory. They imply that current tests are too insensitive to detect abnormalities and that if only they had better ones they would be able to institute remedial measures. It is a laudable objective, but what measures? Current biochemical and pharmacological techniques have more than adequate sensitivity to measure amines and metabolites, and indeed there is even a Russian claim [15] that they can detect 10^{-16} g. (Such an amount is too small to have a name; after picograms one is officially speechless). It is the author's view that the difficulties are not in the tests but in their application in uncontrolled situations.

By far the most enduring biochemical research in this field has been that of Gjessing whose meticulous studies of a small but homogeneous group demonstrated clear associations between the phases of periodic catatonia and changes in nitrogen balance [50]. Recently Gjessing's son has reported that α-methyldopa lessened the intensity of stupor, but prolonged its duration [49]. These findings can be readily explained in terms of the new physiological views. α-Methyldopa inhibits dopadecarboxylase [96] and also depletes brain of noradrenaline [54]. Hence, accepting noradrenaline as a cerebral depressant, α-methyldopa leads to a fall in depressant actions, as one would predict. Some α-methyldopa is also metabolized along the routes followed by dopa, and α-methyl noradrenaline (cobefrine) and α-methyl adrenaline are formed. The conclusion from the large series of amines studied in the animal work was that substitution of the α-carbon atom with a methyl group diminished the degree of potency but prolonged the duration of action [37].

Stupor, of course, is quite different from the physiological sleep produced by adrenaline. Some responses of the cat, however, may provide a relevant clue. Administration of an *excitant* amine (tryptamine) produces the customary alerting found in all species, but thereafter a curious state develops in which the cat stares ahead with open eyes but gives no response to visual or other stimuli, whilst the ECoG shows bursts of large amplitude, slow frequency 'toxic' waves. The state develops 10–30 minutes after administration of the tryptamine, suggesting a metabolic change. Recently, by giving tryptamine, to cats pre-treated with an amino oxidase inhibitor, evidence of anomalous metabolites has been found in peripherally circulating blood. Similar experiments carried out with the hen (typical of other species in the present connexion) showed no evidence of such a transformation. Thus the physiological approach advocated is *not* antithetical to a toxic theory; it provides, indeed, a rational basis for its understanding.

THE KLEINE-LEVIN SYNDROME

The main features of this rather rare condition are episodic hypersomnia, depression, and overeating [24]. It illustrates how physiological considerations may help to elucidate a syndrome which seems to present very few leads. Bearing in mind that excitant (type A) amines cause diminution of appetite it will be evident that the main symptoms are the reverse of excitant action. It is thus possible to comprehend the major symptoms under a single physiological mechanism, dysfunction of which provides a neat and economical summary of the pathology; the latter, conversely, provides additional and unexpected support for the identity and validity of the physiological mechanisms discussed earlier.

As with depression, dysfunction may be a deficiency of excitant amines or insensitivity of the receptor. This was examined in a patient who presented the classical features during attacks. The EEG, although qualitatively normal, showed quantitatively an increase in slow wave activity when attacks were compared with interval records using continuous integration as a measure. Administration of an excitant amine (N-methylamphetamine, 30 mg. intravenously) produced alerting for a minute or so, but thereafter slow wave activity returned. There was also subjective lack of response with neither elevation of mood nor alleviation of drowsiness. The test was repeated a week later in the same patient in the same attack and on a third occasion in the same patient during another episode with similar findings. The results suggest, therefore, diminished responsiveness of the A-receptor and it is hoped to examine this phenomenon further.

RELEVANCE OUTSIDE PSYCHIATRY

This clinical section has limited its scope to psychiatric conditions. It should be evident, however, that the views are likely to be of use in other clinical and physiological investigations. These comprise the symptom of tremor, the syndrome of Parkinsonism, and normal and pathological sleeping and waking. A more detailed consideration must await another occasion.

It is hoped that enough has been said to show the clinical use of the views expressed in this review. These have already provided explanation for some apparently diverse and puzzling phenomena such as the effects of α-methyldopa in catatonic stupor and the Kleine-Levin syndrome, and have been used heuristically to elucidate physiological changes and the phenomena of affective illness; it will be apparent, however, that there is much more to be done.

To invite others to test the ideas is not a light responsibility, for the burden of suffering in mental illness is enormous. However, the invitation is not a precipitate or hasty one for the ideas expressed here were formulated and written some 4 years ago and subsequently have been discussed with a number of colleagues. The experimental basis is believed to be sound and now that positive results have been obtained further caution seems culpable. It is realized that adoption of the ideas expressed would entail some reorientation in biological research, particularly in psychiatry. On the other hand we must admit that a mountain of dedicated work has brought forth the tiniest of mice. The majority of biochemical studies in mental illness have been founded on an *ad hoc* toxicology which has proved an insecure base from which to mount an attack. This is not to say that toxic metabolites play no part in neuropsychiatric illness but that the insight provided into functions is limited. A framework of physiology seems desirable and may provide better explanations of toxic processes than toxicology itself.

ACKNOWLEDGEMENTS

Thanks are due to the colleagues named in the text and to the Bethlem Royal and Maudsley Hospitals Research Funds whose generous grants have provided support for the bulk of the author's work.

REFERENCES

1. AHLQUIST, R. P. (1948) A study of the adrenotropic receptors, *Amer. J. Physiol.*, **153**, 586–600.
2. AMIN, A. H., CRAWFORD, T. B. B., and GADDUM, J. H. (1954) The distribution of substance P and 5-hydroxytryptamine in the central nervous system of the dog, *J. Physiol.* (*Lond.*), **126**, 596–618.
3. BAUST, W., and NIEMCZYK, H. (1964) Further studies on the action of adrenergic drugs on cortical activity, *Electroenceph. clin. Neurophysiol.* **17**, 261–71.
4. BAUST, W., NIEMCZYK, H., and VIETH, J. (1963) The action of blood pressure on the ascending reticular activating system with special reference to adrenaline-induced EEG arousal, *Electroenceph. clin. Neurophysiol.*, **15**, 63–72.
5. BLACKWELL, B. (1963) Hypertensive crisis due to monoamine-oxidase inhibitors, *Lancet*, ii, 849–51.

6. Bonvallet, M., Dell, P., and Heibel, G. (1954) Tonus sympathique et activité électrique corticale, *Electroenceph. clin. Neurophysiol.*, **6**, 119–44.
7. Bradley, P. B., and Elkes, J. (1957) The effects of some drugs on the electrical activity of the brain, *Brain*, **80**, 77–117.
8. Bradley, P. B., and Mollica, A. (1958) The effect of adrenaline and acetylcholine on single unit activity in the reticular formation of the decerebrate cat, *Arch. ital. Biol.*, **96**, 168–86.
9. Bradley, P. B., and Wolstencroft, J. H. (1962) Excitation and inhibition of brain-stem neurones by noradrenaline and acetylcholine, *Nature* (*Lond.*), **196**, 840 and 873.
10. Brengelmann, J. C., Pare, C. M. B., and Sandler, M. (1958) Alleviation of the psychological effects of LSD in man by 5-hydroxytryptophan, *J. ment. Sci.*, **104**, 1237–44.
11. Brengelmann, J. C., Pare, C. M. B., and Sandler, M. (1959) Effects of 5-hydroxytryptophan on schizophrenia, *J. ment. Sci.*, **105**, 770–6.
12. Brodie, B. B., and Costa, E. (1962) Some current views on monoamines, *Psychopharmacology Service Center Bulletin*, **2**, No. 5, 1–25, reprinted from *Monoamines et Système Nerveux Central*, Geneva.
13. Brodie, B. B., and Shore, P. A. (1957) A concept for the role of serotonin and norepinephrine as chemical mediators in the brain, *Ann. N.Y. Acad. Sci.*, **66**, 631–42.
14. Brodie, B. B., Spector, S., and Shore, P. A. (1959) Interaction of drugs with norepinephrine in the brain, *Pharmacol. Rev.*, **11**, 548–64.
15. Buznikov, G. A., and Manukhin, B. N. (1960) *Zh. Obshch. Biol.*, **21**, 347, quoted by Sandler, M. (1963) in *Clinical Chemistry of Monoamines*, ed. Varley, H., and Gowenlock, A. H., p. 117, Amsterdam.
16. Carlsson, A., Lindquist, M., and Magnusson, T. (1957) 3-, 4-Dihydroxyphenylalanine and 5-hydroxytryptophan as reserpine antagonists, *Nature* (*Lond.*), **180**, 1200.
17. Chrusciel, T. L. (1960) Awakening actions of derivatives of phenylalanine, in *Ciba Foundation Symposium on Adrenergic Mechanisms*, ed. Vane, J. R., Wolstenholme, G. E. W., and O'Connor, M., pp. 440–5, London.
18. Clymer, N. V., and Seifter, J. (1947) A method for screening sympathomimetic amines for stimulant action on the cerebrum, *J. Pharmacol. exp. Ther.*, **89**, 149–52.
19. Collias, N., and Joos, M. (1953) The spectrographic analysis of sound signals of the domestic fowl, *Behaviour*, **5**, 175–88.
20. Coppen, A., Shaw, D. M., Malleson, A., Eccleston, E., and Gundy, G. (1965) Tryptamine metabolism in depression, *Brit. J. Psychiat.*, **111**, 993–8.
21. Cordeau, J. P., Moreau, A., Beulnes, A., and Laurin, C. (1963) EEG and behavioural changes following microinjections of acetylcholine and adrenaline in the brain-stem of cats, *Arch. ital. Biol.*, **101**, 30–47.
22. Costa, E. (1965) Neuropharmacology, presented at the Annual Meeting of the American Psychiatric Association, New York.

23. Costa, E., Himwich, W. A., Goldstein, S. G., Canhan, R. G., and Himwich, H. E. (1959) Behavioural changes following increases of neurohormonal content in selected brain areas, *Fed. Proc.*, **18**, 379.
24. Critchley, M. (1962) Periodic hypersomnia and megaphagia in adolescent males, *Brain*, **85**, 627–56.
25. Curtis, D. R. (1962) Action of 3-hydroxytyramine and some tryptamine derivatives on spinal neurones, *Nature* (*Lond.*), **194**, 292.
26. Curtis, D. R., and Koizumi, K. (1961) Chemical transmitter substance in brain-stem of cat, *J. Neurophysiol.*, **24**, 80–90.
27. Curtis, D. R., and Watkins, J. C. (1960) Amino acids and spinal neurones, *J. Neurochem.*, **6**, 117–41.
28. Dawson, J., and Bone, A. (1963) The relationship between urine volume and urinary adrenaline and noradrenaline excretion in a group of psychotic patients, *Brit. J. Psychiat.*, **109**, 629–30.
29. Dewhurst, W. G. (1960) Opening discussion on monamine oxidase inhibitors in psychiatry, in *Ciba Foundation Symposium on Adrenergic Mechanisms*, ed. Vane, J. R., Wolstenholme, G. E. W., and O'Connor, M., pp. 459–60, London.
30. Dewhurst, W. G. (1961) Amine metabolism in depressive illness: Dissertation, London University.
31. Dewhurst, W. G. (1965) On the chemical basis of mood, *J. Psychosom. Res.*, **9**, 115–27.
32. Dewhurst, W. G., and Marley, E. (1963) Quantification of behaviour and cerebral electrical activity under controlled conditions, *J. Physiol.* (*Lond.*), **168**, 1–3P.
33. Dewhurst, W. G., and Marley, E. (1964) Differential effect of sympathomimetic amines on the central nervous system, in *Ciba Foundation Symposium on Animal Behaviour and Drug Action*, ed. Steinberg, H., de Reuck, A. V. S., and Knight, A., pp. 175–88, London.
34. Dewhurst, W. G., and Marley, E. (1964) Continuous integration of the electrocorticogram and behaviour: the effect of centrally acting amines, *Electroenceph. clin. Neurophysiol.*, **16**, 624.
35. Dewhurst, W. G., and Marley, E. (1965) Methods for quantifying behaviour and cerebral activity and the effect of drugs under controlled conditions, *Brit. J. Pharmacol.*, **24**, 671–81.
36. Dewhurst, W. G., and Marley, E. (1965) The effects of α-methyl derivatives of noradrenaline, phenylethylamine and tryptamine on the central nervous system of the chicken, *Brit. J. Pharmacol.*, **25**, 682–704.
37. Dewhurst, W. G., and Marley, E. (1965) Action of sympathomimetic and allied amines on the central nervous system of the chicken, *Brit. J. Pharmacol.*, **25**, 705–27.
38. Dewhurst, W. G., and Pare, C. M. B. (1961) A clinical and biochemical study of monoamine oxidase inhibition in depressed patients. I. A clinical trial of nialamide, *J. ment. Sci.*, **107**, 239–43.
39. Dewhurst, W. G., and Pare, C. M. B. (1961) A clinical and biochemical study of monoamine oxidase inhibition in depressed

patients. II. 5-Hydroxytryptamine tolerance before and after nialamide, *J. ment. Sci.*, **107**, 244–9.

40. DOMER, F. R., and FELDBERG, W. (1960) Some central actions of adrenaline and noradrenaline when administered into the cerebral ventricles, in *Ciba Foundation Symposium on Adrenergic Mechanisms*, ed. Vane, J. R., Wolstenholme, G. E. W., and O'Connor, M., pp. 386–92, London.
41. ERSPAMER, V. (1956) The enterochromaffin system and 5-hydroxytryptamine (enteramine, serotonin), *Triangle*, **11**, 129–38.
42. FAURE, J. (1962) La phase 'paradoxale' du sommeil chez le lapin (ses relations neuro-hormonales), *Rev. neurol.*, **2**, 190–7.
43. FELDBERG, W. (1960) In *Ciba Foundation Symposium on Adrenergic Mechanisms*, ed. Vane, J. R., Wolstenholme, G. E. W., and O'Connor, M., p. 570, London.
44. FELDBERG, W. (1963) *A Pharmacological Approach to Brain from its Inner and Outer Surfaces*, London.
45. FELDBERG, W., and SHERWOOD, S. L. (1954) Injections of drugs into the lateral ventricle of the cat, *J. Physiol.* (*Lond.*), **123**, 148–67.
46. FELDMAN, R. G., and GLASER, G. H. (1963) EEG study of methysergide in migraine, *Electroenceph. clin. Neurophysiol.*, **15**, 699–701.
47. FLECKENSTEIN, A., and BURN, J. H. (1953) The effect of denervation on the action of sympathomimetic amines on the nictitating membrane, *Brit. J. Pharmacol.*, **8**, 69–78.
48. GADDUM, J. H. (1961) Antagonism between drugs, in *Neuropsychopharmacology*, Vol. 2, ed. Rothlin, E., pp. 19–24, Amsterdam.
49. GJESSING, L. R. (1965) Studies on urinary phenolic compounds in man. II. Phenolic acids and -amines during a load of α-methyldopa and disulfiram in periodic catatonia, *Scand. J. clin. Lab. Invest.*, **17**, 549–57.
50. GJESSING, R. (1938) Disturbances of somatic functions in catatonia with a periodic course, and their compensation, *J. ment. Sci.*, **84**, 608–21.
51. GLOWINSKI, J., KOPIN, I. J., and AXELROD, J. (1965) Metabolism of ^{3}H-norepinephrine in rat brain, *J. Neurochem.*, **12**, 23–30.
52. GREEN, H., and SAWYER, J. L. (1960) Correlation of tryptamine-induced convulsions in rats with brain tryptamine concentration, *Proc. Soc. exp. Biol.*, (*N.Y.*), **104**, 153–5.
53. HALEY, T. J., and MCCORMICK, W. G. (1957) Pharmacological effects produced by intracerebral injections of drugs in the conscious mouse, *Brit. J. Pharmacol.*, **12**, 12–15.
54. HESS, S. M., CONNAMACHER, R. H., OZAKI, M., and UDENFRIEND, S. (1961) The effects of alpha-methyl-dopa and alpha-methyl-tyrosine on the metabolism of normetanephrine and serotonin in vivo, *J. Pharmacol. exp. Ther.*, **134**, 129–38.
55. HESS, S. M., REDFIELD, B. G., and UDENFRIEND, S. (1959) The effect of monoamine oxidase inhibitors and tryptophan on the tryptamine content of animal tissues and urine, *J. Pharmacol. exp. Ther.*, **127**, 178–81.

56. Hess, W. R. (1954) *Diencephalon: Autonomic and Extrapyramidal Function*, New York.
57. Huxley, J., Mayr, E., Osmond, H., and Hoffer, A. (1964) Schizophrenia as a genetic morphism, *Nature* (*Lond.*), **204**, 220–1.
58. Jouvet, M., Michel, F., and Courjon, J. (1959) Sur un stade d'activité électrique cérébrale rapide au cours du sommeil physiologique, *C.R. Soc. Biol.* (*Paris.*), **153**, 1024–8.
59. Kety, S. S. (1959) Biochemical theories of schizophrenia; a two-part critical review of current theories and of the evidence used to support them. Part I, *Science*, **129**, 1528–32.
60. Kety, S. S. (1959) Biochemical theories of schizophrenia; a two-part critical review of current theories and of the evidence used to support them. Part II, *Science*, **129**, 1590–6.
61. Key, B. J., and Marley, E. (1962) The effect of sympathomimetic amines on behaviour and electrocortical activity of the chicken, *Electroenceph. clin. Neurophysiol.*, **14**, 90–105.
62. Krnjevic, K., Laverty, R., and Sharman, D. F. (1963) Iontophoretic release of adrenaline, noradrenaline and 5-hydroxytryptamine from micropipettes, *Electroenceph. clin. Neurophysiol*, **20**, 491.
63. Krnjevic, K., and Phillis, J. W. (1961) The action of certain amino acids on cortical neurones, *J. Physiol.* (*Lond.*), **159**, 62P.
64. Krnjevic, K., and Phillis, J. W. (1963) Action of certain amines on cerebral cortical neurones, *Brit. J. Pharmacol.*, **20**, 471–90.
65. Leimdorfer, A. (1950) The action of sympathomimetic amines on the central nervous system and the blood sugar. Mechanism of action, *J. Pharmacol. exp. Ther.*, **98**, 62–71.
66. Leimdorfer, A., and Metzner, W. R. T. (1949) Analgesia and anaesthesia induced by epinephrine, *Amer. J. Physiol.*, **157**, 116–21.
67. Levine, R., and Sjoerdsma, A. (1963) Estimation of monoamine oxidase activity in man: techniques and applications, *Ann. N.Y. Acad. Sci.*, **107**, 966–74.
68. Lewis, A. J. (1934) Melancholia: A historical review, *J. ment. Sci.*, **80**, 1–42.
69. Lewis, A. J. (1934) Melancholia: A clinical survey of depressive states, *J. ment. Sci.*, **80**, 277–378.
70. Ljungberg, von E. (1961) Die 5-HIES-Bestimmungen in Urin als wertvolle klinische-chemische Methode in der psychiatrischen Klinik, *Schweiz. Arch. Neurol. Neurochir. Psychiat.*, **87**, 351–64.
71. Marley, E. (1962) Action of some sympathomimetic amines on the cat's iris, in situ or isolated, *J. Physiol.* (*Lond.*), **162**, 193–211.
72. Marley, E. (1963) Brain-stem receptors for sympathomimetic amines in the chicken, *J. Physiol.* (*Lond.*), **165**, 24–25P.
73. Marley, E., and Payne, J. P. (1962) A method of anaesthesia with halothane suitable for newborn animals, *Brit. J. Anaesth.*, **34**, 776–84.
74. Marley, E., and Vane, J. R. (1963) Tryptamine receptors in the central nervous system: effects of anaesthetics, *Nature* (*Lond.*), **198**, 441–4.

75. Mayer, S., Maickel, R. P., and Brodie, B. B. (1959) Kinetics of penetration of drugs and other foreign compounds into cerebrospinal fluid and brain, *J. Pharmacol. exp. Ther.*, **127**, 205–11.
76. Milne, M. D., Crawford, M. A., Girao, C. B., and Loughridge, L. (1960) The excretion of indolylacetic acid and related indolic acids in man and rat, *Clin. Sci.*, **19**, 165–79.
77. Montagu, K. A. (1957) Catechol compounds in rat tissues and in brains of different animals, *Nature* (*Lond.*), **180**, 244–5.
78. Osmond, H., and Smythies, J. (1952) Schizophrenia: a new approach, *J. ment. Sci.*, **98**, 309–15.
79. Palmer, A. C. (1959) Injection of drugs into the central ventricle of sheep, *J. Physiol.* (*Lond.*), **149**, 209–14.
80. Paton, W. D. M. (1960) The principles of drug action, *Proc. roy. Soc. Med.*, **53**, 815–20.
81. Peart, W. S., Porter, K. A., Robertson, J. I. S., Sandler, M., and Baldock, E. (1963) Carcinoid syndrome due to pancreatic duct neoplasm secreting 5-hydroxytryptophan and 5-hydroxytryptamine, *Lancet*, i, 239–43.
82. Purpura, D. F., Girado, M., Smith, T. G., Gallen, D. A., and Grundfest, H. (1959) Structure-activity determinants of pharmacological effects of amino acids and related compounds on central synapses, *J. Neurochem.*, **3**, 238–68.
83. Rojas, J. H. P., and Zeidenweber, J. (1963) Local and EEG effects of adrenaline and acetylcholine application within the olfactory bulb, *Electroenceph. clin. Neurophysiol.*, **19**, 88–90.
84. Rothballer, A. B. (1956) Studies on the adrenaline-sensitive component of the reticular activating system, *Electroenceph. clin. Neurophysiol.*, **8**, 603–21.
85. Rothballer, A. B. (1957) EEG activation from microinjections of adrenaline into the brain-stem of the cat, *Anat. Rec.*, **127**, 359.
86. Rothballer, A. B. (1959) The effects of catecholamines on the central nervous system, *Pharmacol. Rev.*, **11**, 494–547.
87. Sandler, M., Scheuer, P. J., and Watt, P. J. (1961) 5-hydroxytryptophan secreting bronchial carcinoid tumour, *Lancet*, ii, 1067–9.
88. Sandler, M., and Snow, P. J. D. (1958) An atypical carcinoid tumour secreting 5-hydroxytryptophan, *Lancet*, i, 137–9.
89. Schanberg, S. M. (1963) A study of the transport of 5-hydroxytryptophan and 5-hydroxytryptamine (serotonin) into brain, *J. Pharmacol. exp. Ther.*, **139**, 191–200.
90. Scherbel, A., and Schmidt, E. A. (1962) Effect of serotonin inhibitors on connective tissue disease, *Cleveland Clin. Quart.*, **29**, 1–15.
91. Schildkraut, J. J. (1965) The catecholamine hypothesis of affective disorders: a review of supporting evidence, *Amer. J. Psychiat.*, **122**, 509–22.
92. Scott, J. A. (1962) 3-, 4-Dihydroxyphenylalanine (dopa) excretion in patients with malignant melanoma, *Lancet*, ii, 861–2.
93. Selle, R. M. (1940) An effect of benzedrine sulfate on chicks, *Science*, **91**, 95.

94. SHERWOOD, S. L. (1955) The responses of psychotic patients to intraventricular injections, *Proc. roy. Soc. Med.*, **48**, 855–64.
95. SJOERDSMA, A., LOVENBERG, W., GATES, J. A., GROUT, J. R., and UDENFRIEND, S. (1959) Alterations in the pattern of amino excretion in man produced by a monoamine oxidase inhibitor, *Science*, **130**, 225.
96. SOURKES, T. L. (1954) Inhibition of dihydroxyphenylalanine decarboxylase by derivatives of phenylalanine, *Arch. Biochem.*, **51**, 444–56.
97. VANE, J. R. (1960) The actions of sympathomimetic amines on tryptamine receptors, in *Ciba Foundation Symposium on Adrenergic Mechanisms*, ed. Vane, J. R., Wolstenholme, G. E. W., and O'Connor, M., pp. 356–72, London.
98. VOGT, M. (1954) The concentration of sympathin in different parts of the central nervous system under normal conditions and after administration of drugs, *J. Physiol.* (*Lond.*), **123**, 451–81.
99. VOGT, M. (1960) Central adrenergic mechanisms; chairman's opening remarks, in *Ciba Foundation Symposium on Adrenergic Mechanisms*, ed. Vane, J. R., Wolstenholme, G. E. W., and O'Connor, M., pp. 382–5, London.
100. WEBER, H. (1904) Uber Anästhesie durch Adrenalin, *Verh. dtsch. Ges. inn. Med.*, **21**, 616–19.
101. WEIL-MALHERBE, H. (1956) Phaeochromocytoma catechols in urine and tumour tissue, *Lancet*, ii, 282–4.
102. WEIL-MALHERBE, H. (1960) The passage of catechol amines through the blood-brain barrier, in *Ciba Foundation Symposium on Adrenergic Mechanisms*, ed. Vane, J. R., Wolstenholme, G. E. W., and O'Connor, M., pp. 421–3, London.
103. WEIL-MALHERBE, H. (1960) Synthesis of catecholamines in the depleted brain, in *Ciba Foundation Symposium on Adrenergic Mechanisms*, ed. Vane, J. R., Wolstenholme, G. E. W., and O'Connor, M., pp. 544–8, London.
104. WOOLF, L. I. (1963) Inherited metabolic disorders: errors of phenylalanine and tyrosine metabolism, in *Advances in Clinical Chemistry*, Vol. 6, ed. Bobotka, H., and Stuart, C. P., New York.
105. WOOLLEY, D. W. (1962) *The Biochemical Bases of Psychoses*, New York.
106. WOOLLEY, D. W., and SHAW, E. (1954) A biochemical and pharmacological suggestion about certain mental disorders, *Proc. nat. Acad. Sci.* (*Wash.*), **40**, 228–31.

15

Neuroendocrine Studies on Instinctual Behaviour

RICHARD P. MICHAEL

INTRODUCTION

THE work of my Unit has been coloured by the highly divergent sources from which my interests in behavioural mechanisms have sprung: namely, on the one hand, from clinical psychiatry and, in particular, from psychoanalysis: on the other hand, from an interest in the chemical control of behaviour and, in particular, in the neuroendocrine mechanisms by which hormones influence the activity of the brain. It always seemed highly improbable that such disparate interests could possibly find a way of coming together in any real sense until it became possible to take advantage of a Medical Research Council Fellowship in Clinical Research. This created an opportunity for a period of study in the laboratory of Professor Geoffrey Harris, F.R.S., who had, then, only recently been persuaded by Sir Aubrey Lewis to establish the Department of Neuroendocrinology at the Institute. A vista seemed to open up in which the possibility of studying 'id' or instinctual drive mechanisms in physiological terms became a reality. In 1954 it was too early to wonder whether such studies might eventually have a useful bearing upon the human situation; it was enough to have the chance to get to grips with these problems.

The study of the expression of emotions in animals and man has received the sporadic attention of scientists since the time of Darwin. The approach has been essentially observational, often anecdotal, and tinged with Cartesian dualism: this situation has only recently given place to more systematic psychological and psychiatric studies. The study of the instinctual drives or needs, in my view, falls into two primary categories: first, factors concerned in the expression of such basic emotional reactions as anxiety, fear, threat and rage (the agonistic responses) and secondly, factors concerned in the expression of a set of reactions leading to the development of consort bonds, to courtship, mating and parental behaviour (the affectional responses). These emotional reactions are not only important to the individual in diadic relations but also to the relations of the individual within its society or group. The very important instinctual mechanisms concerned in the relation between mother and infant and the development of the feeding responses are, regrettably, outside my scope.

CONTROL OF SEXUAL RECEPTIVITY IN THE FEMALE CAT BY HYPOTHALAMIC IMPLANTS

Our earlier studies, conducted in collaboration with Geoffrey Harris, were with the domestic cat, a readily available laboratory mammal, particularly suited for the investigations we had in mind because, except during its well-defined periods of heat (oestrus), the female ferociously rebuffs any male that shows sexual interest, often with a display of considerable aggression. This aggressive, refusal reaction of the anoestrous female changes, however, to the stereotyped sequence of receptive, oestrous behaviour when oestrogens are present in the circulation [8, 9]. This hormone can be supplied either naturally, by the secretory activity of the ovaries, or artificially, in ovariectomized animals, by oestrogen administration [18]. The particular aim of these studies was to administer an oestrogen directly to the substance of the brains of ovariectomized cats in such a manner that it would change the behaviour of females from the non-receptive to the receptive state, and that it would act locally in the brain and not generally in the body via the systemic circulation. It was first of all established that when oestrogens were administered subcutaneously, the vaginal smears became cornified and the uterus became fleshy and oestrous with dosages that were insufficient to evoke the mating responses: that is, with the systemic administration of hormone, the threshold for vaginal cornification was shown to be lower than the threshold for mating behaviour. Our aim, then, was to attempt to create a state of 'local oestrus' in the brain and thereby activate the behavioural pattern without producing any oestrous changes in the genital tract. It proved to be possible to do exactly this by developing a stereotaxic technique [Plate 3] for implanting in the brain very small amounts of a solid oestrogen-ester carried on the tip of a needle [6]. These needles were introduced into certain areas within the pre-optic region and hypothalamus of ovariectomized cats under conditions which resulted in the hormone acting locally and directly upon a neurological mechanism. Females bearing such implants of hormone in the hypothalamus and related areas, but not in other sites in the brain, became continuously receptive to males for periods of many weeks while their genital tracts remained in an anoestrous or atrophic condition [Plate 4]. Because of this latter observation it became obvious that the effect of the brain implant was being exerted locally upon a neural mechanism, and not generally via the systemic circulation [5, 10]. Numerous control procedures were undertaken to exclude the possibility of a non-specific, irritative effect of the implant in the brain. Thus, the introduction of implants of paraffin wax, cholesterol or progesterone into the hypothalamus in combination with oestrogen implants placed subcutaneously invariably failed to evoke any behavioural changes. Further, the introduction of higher (less active) esters of stilboestrol into the hypothalamus itself or the introduction of implants, identical to effective hypothalamic ones, into other cerebral sites, such as cerebellum, cerebral cortex, thalamus, caudate nucleus or amygdala, were in general without effect upon behaviour. It appeared to be essential to have an *oestrogenic* action in the pre-optic region or hypothalamus [12] [Fig. 19].

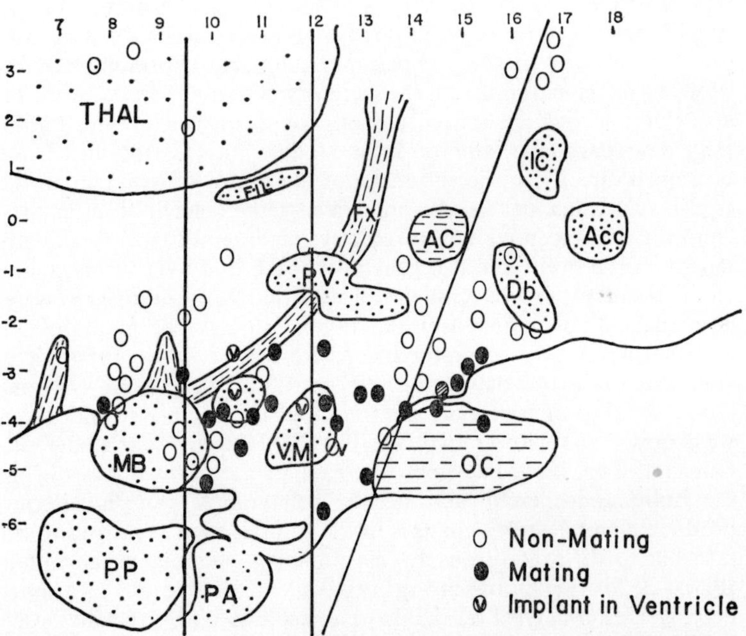

Fig. 19. Illustrating the distribution, on a lateral projection of the brain, of implants which both evoked and failed to evoke oestrous behaviour in ovariectomized cats without producing any genital tract changes (65 experiments). Sagittal section 1 mm. lateral to midline. OC, optic chiasma: IC, island of Calleja: Db, diagonal band: Acc, nucleus accumbens: AC, anterior commissure: Fx, fornix: PV, nucleus paraventricularis: VM, nucleus ventromedialis: MB, mammillary body: PA, anterior pituitary: PP, posterior pituitary: THAL, thalamus: FIL, nucleus filiformis.

THE ENTRY OF OESTROGENS INTO THE CENTRAL NERVOUS SYSTEM

Although it had been established that sexual receptivity could be induced by placing oestrogen implants directly in the hypothalamus, many problems remained. It could be argued that this observation was without true physiological significance until it had been demonstrated that oestrogen could pass the blood-brain barrier from the systemic circulation and reach these same neural regions in physiological, rather than pharmacological, amounts. To study this problem, in collaboration with Dr. Raymond Glascock, use has been made of ^{3}H-hexoestrol of high specific activity (150 μc./μg.) in conjunction with both isotopic gas analysis of small tissue samples and autoradiography [2]. Fifty-six mature, female cats were ovariectomized up to 6 months before the subcutaneous administration in oil of either 1μg. or 20 μg. per kg. body weight ^{3}H-hexoestrol and animals were killed at different intervals from 20 min. to 48 hr. after injection. Samples were taken from various endocrine glands and from the genital tracts, but particular attention was given to the following areas of brain: medulla, midbrain, thalamus, hypothalamus, pre-optic region, caudate nucleus, temporal lobes, cerebral cortex and cerebellum. Experiments were also carried out with ^{131}I-labelled human serum albumin from which the blood content of the various tissues was calculated and, from the measurement of the levels of radioactivity in blood, the radioactivity due to the blood content in the sample was calculated and a suitable correction made. Further, extraction procedures and isotope dilution studies showed that the radioactivity in brain followed the chemistry of unchanged hexoestrol or a simple conjugate and that there had been no prior metabolic modification [11]. Results, expressed as mμg. hexoestrol per kg. dry weight of tissue, are shown in FIGURE 20. It emerged that hexoestrol entered brain more rapidly even than a classical target tissue such as uterus: at 20 min. the level in cortex ($665 \pm 34{\cdot}8$ mμg,/kg.) was nearly five times that in uterus ($143 \pm 14{\cdot}9$ mμg./kg.), and considerably above that in blood ($403 \pm 78{\cdot}4$ mμg./kg.). However, while tissues such as uterus continued to accumulate radioactivity, after 20 min. all brain sites rapidly lost it. It was the manner in which activity was lost by different neural regions that distinguished them. Between 2 hr. and 5 hr. after injection, the hypothalamus lost activity less rapidly than all other brain regions, so that it came to have the highest concentration of any brain area studied. Analysis of variance showed the hypothalamic value at 5 hr. to be significantly higher ($P < 0{\cdot}05$) than those for medulla, midbrain, thalamus, caudate nucleus, cerebral cortex and cerebellum,

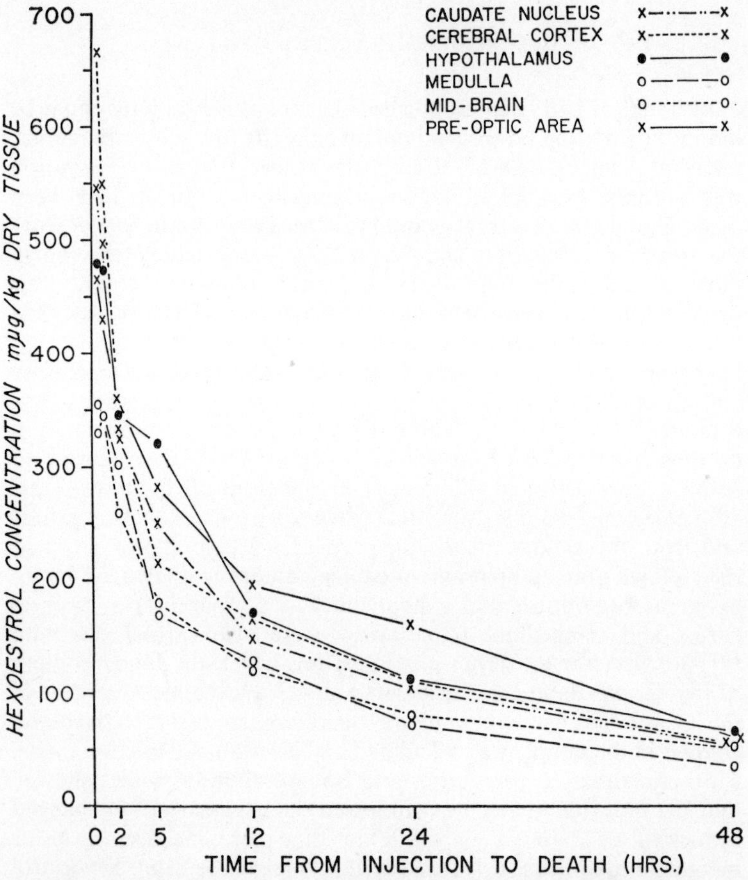

FIG. 20. Concentrations of hexoestrol reach maxima in brain 20 min. after subcutaneous injection in oil (1 μg./kg.). Showing marked retention by hypothalamus at 5hr, and retention by pre-optic area thereafter. (Michael and Glascock, unpublished results.)

but not significantly higher than pre-optic region or temporal lobe. After 5 hr., the pre-optic region retained activity in significantly greater concentrations ($P < 0{\cdot}05$) than all other neural tissues including hypothalamus. Owing to the great variability between cats it would, however, be dangerous on this evidence alone to assume that the hypothalamus and related areas have a special capacity for retaining hexoestrol. More weight can be placed upon these results when considered in combination with those obtained by autoradiography.

The best autoradiographic results were obtained at 5 hr. after the subcutaneous administration of tritiated hexoestrol to ovariectomized animals at a dose rate of 20 μg./kg. Following the administration of intraperitoneal pentobarbitone, animals were killed by exsanguination, the brains were rapidly removed and immediately fixed by immersion in liquid nitrogen. Serial frozen sections at 7–10 μ were prepared in the cryostat at $-18°$C. To minimize leaching and movement of labelled material, sections were picked up on specially prepared, dried slides while still frozen and coated with photographic emulsion in layers 5 μ thick. After their development weeks or months later, brain sections were stained with buffered cresyl violet acetate, and grain counts were carried out to establish background activities and activities within the various neural areas concerned. The autoradiographic data revealed a well-defined, bilaterally symmetrical neurological system involving the lateral septal region, the pre-optic area and hypothalamus; in these zones grain counts were significantly above the levels in adjacent tissues [13, 16] [PLATE 5].

It was demonstrated by these studies: (1) that oestrogens could enter the brain from the systemic circulation; (2) that they could then localize in a neurological system involving the septum, pre-optic area and hypothalamus without undergoing any previous metabolic modification other than conjugation; and (3) that this system corresponded, in part, with the demonstrated neurological site of action. Nevertheless, these studies were, in one sense, disappointing. It was not possible to demonstrate by radioactivity counting techniques, the very clear differences in the uptake of radioactivity by different areas of brain that were obtained by the more sensitive but, unfortunately, less specific autoradiographic methods. The probable explanation lay in the difficulty of dissecting out very small brain areas under the stereomicroscope and the consequent dilution of areas containing radioactivity when taking samples of a size that could be easily handled. It seemed worthwhile, therefore, to pursue these studies further in the rat.

^{3}H-testosterone (specific activity 41·8 c./mM.) and ^{3}H-oestradiol (specific activity 20·8 c./mM.) were administered as a single subcutaneous injection in oil (100 μc. or 1·3 μg. oestradiol, and 100 μc. or 10 mg. testosterone) to adult rats of both sexes. Animals were killed in groups of six at different time intervals from 20 min. to 24 hr. after injection. The brains were immediately removed, the hypothalamus and pituitary glands were dissected out, and samples were taken from cerebral cortex, uterus, testis, seminal vesicle, skin, muscle and blood. Samples were dried *in vacuo* and dissolved in hydroxide of hyamine, phosphor was added and an aliquot was counted in a Packard scintillation spectrometer. ^{3}H-hexadecane was used as an internal standard to correct for quenching and data were calculated to give counts per min. per mg. of wet tissue. The results indicated that for those tissues in common to both sexes there was a close similarity in; (1) the values for different tissues; (2) the relative concentrations in different tissues; and (3) the time-course for the accumulation and loss of radioactivity. Certain tissues were exceptional: following the administration of oestradiol, in both male and female at 20 min., radioactivity measured in the hypothalamus was greater than in plasma or cortex [FIGS. 21, 22]. Both male and

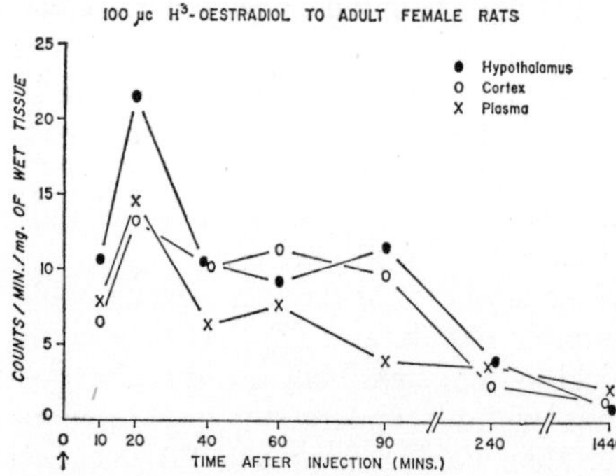

FIG. 21. In the female, greater amounts of radioactivity were found in the hypothalamus compared with cortex and plasma 20 min. after s.c. injection of ^{3}H-oestradiol in oil. Each point mean of 6 animals. (Green and Michael, unpublished results.)

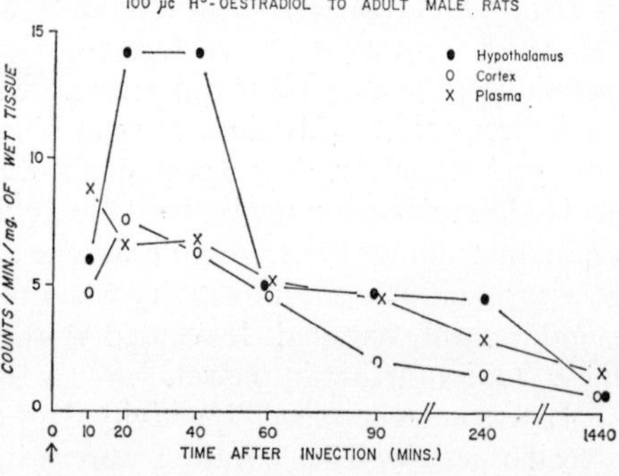

FIG. 22. In the male, greater amounts of radioactivity were found in the hypothalamus compared with cortex and plasma 20–40 min. after s.c. injection of ^{3}H-oestradiol in oil. Each point mean of 6 animals. (Michael and Green, unpublished results.)

female pituitary glands had a closely similar pattern of accumulation and loss of radioactivity derived from injected oestradiol; in each case pituitary values greatly exceeded the corresponding plasma values [FIG. 23]. Following the administration of testosterone, however, there was a marked difference between the pattern of uptake by the pituitary glands of the male (low) and female (high), but in each case they followed the corresponding values in plasma [FIG. 24]. It appeared that the pituitary mechanism depended more

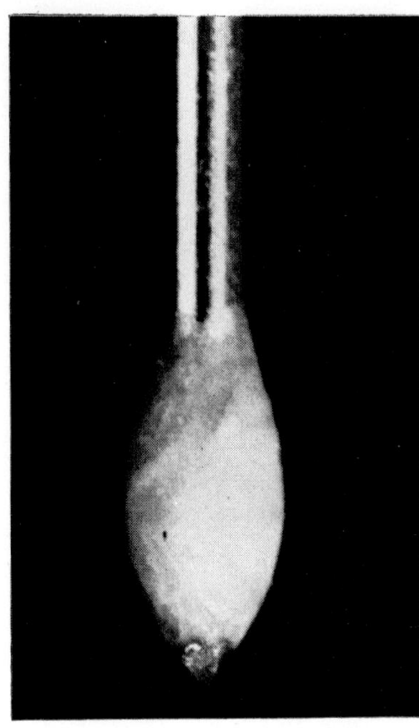

Small amount of solid oestrogen (about 0·15 mg.) attached to the tip of a stainless steel brain needle.

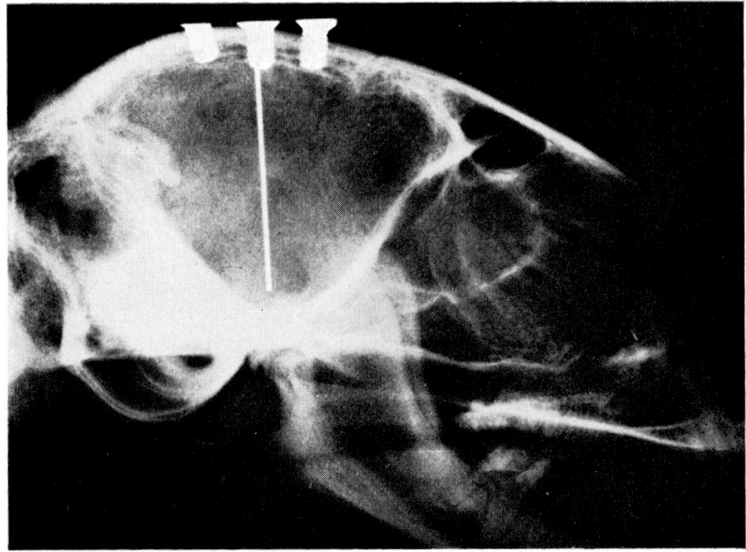

Lateral radiograph of cat head with needle in position; the tip is located in the hypothalamus.

PLATE 4

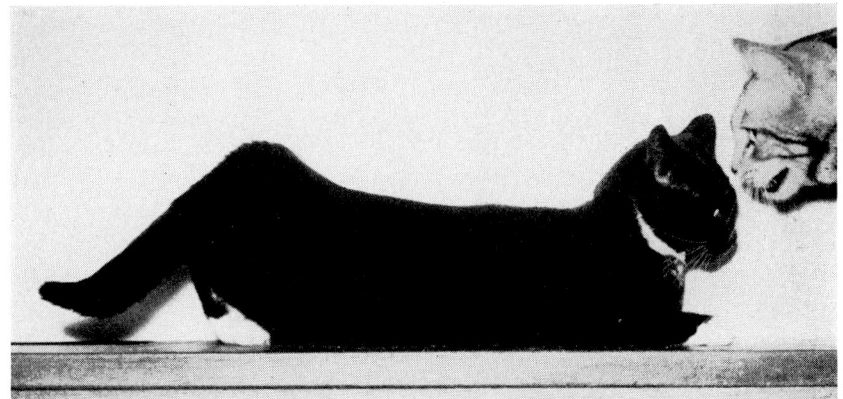

Continuously receptive oestrous behaviour can be produced by hypothalamic implants of oestrogen while the genital tracts remain anoestrous.

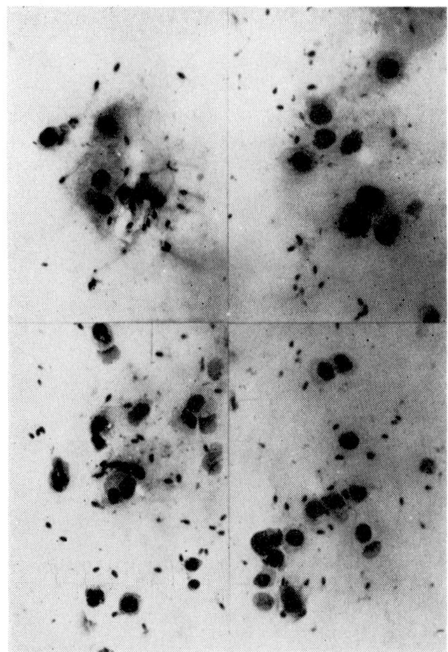

Anoestrous vaginal smear from receptive, ovariectomized cat with a hypothalamic implant of oestrogen. Sperm indicate that mating has occurred (4 fields).

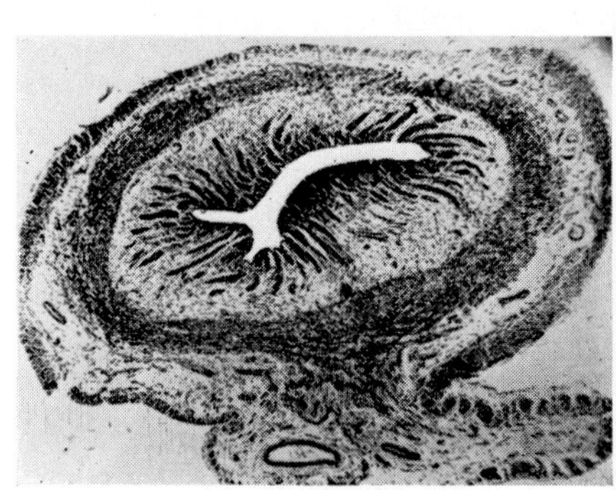

Cross-section of atrophic uterine horn from receptive, ovariectomized cat with a hypothalamic implant of oestrogen. (Scale = 1 mm.)

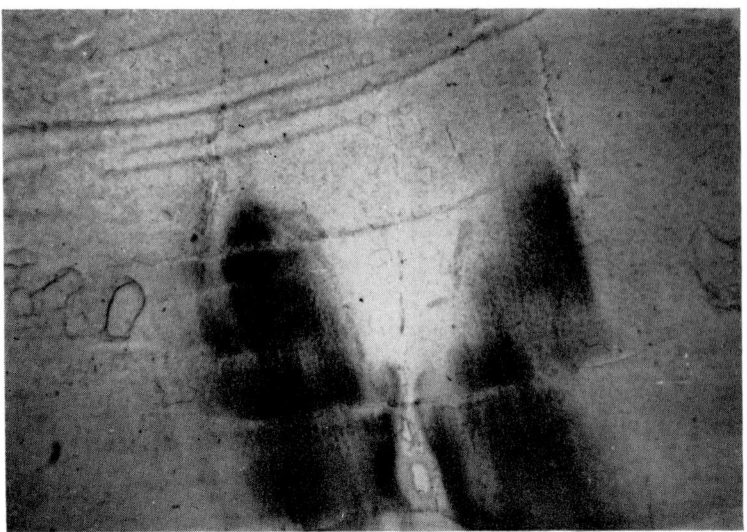

Autoradiograph of frontal section (7μ) through the septal region of the cat brain 5 hours after subcutaneous injection of ^{3}H-hexoestrol in oil. A well circumscribed, bilaterally symmetrical area of blackening occupies the lateral septum and the region of the nucleus of the diagonal band of Broca. ($\times$ 14.)

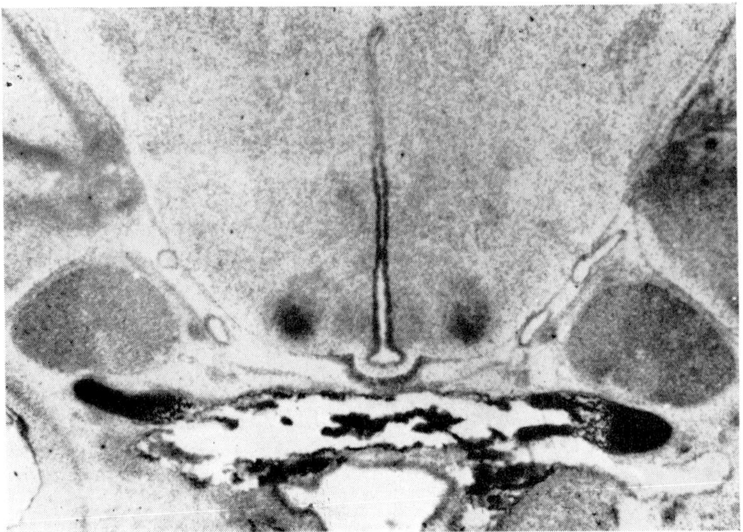

Low power photomicrograph of autoradiograph of section (7μ) of brain of 3-day-old female rat 1 hour after subcutaneous injection (0·05μg.) ^{3}H-hexoestrol in oil. The symmetrical blackening in the basal half of the ventromedial nucleus of the hypothalamus is clearly visible.

PLATE 6

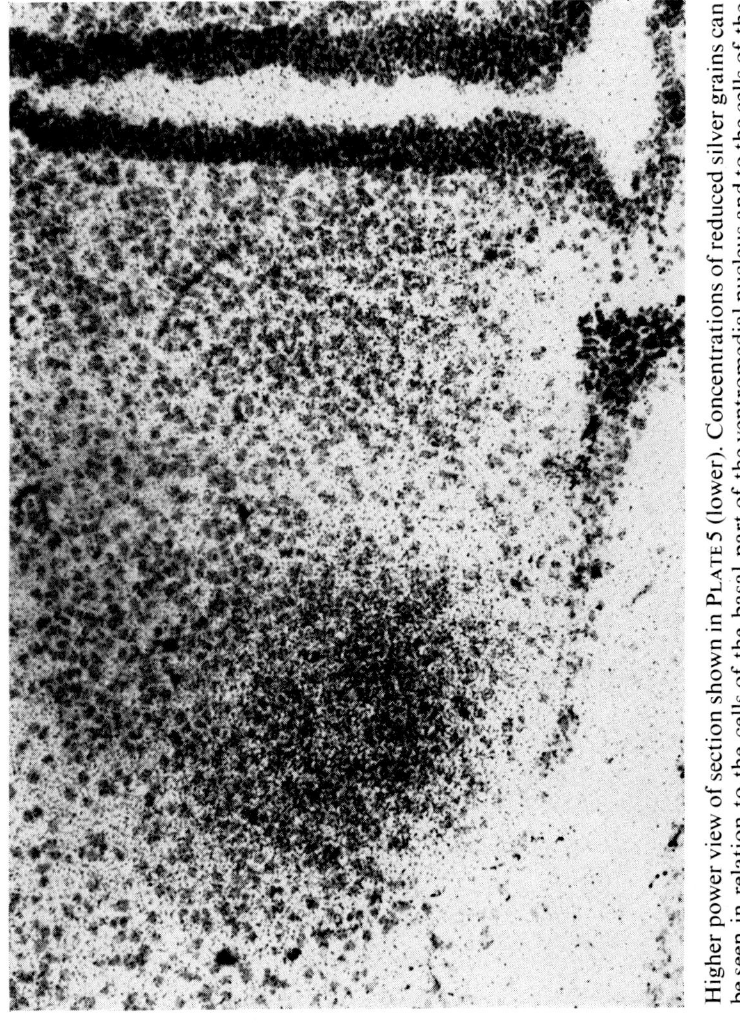

Higher power view of section shown in PLATE 5 (lower). Concentrations of reduced silver grains can be seen in relation to the cells of the basal part of the ventromedial nucleus and to the cells of the arcuate nucleus. Background can be assessed from the grain density overlying the third ventricle.

upon the chemistry of the hormone reaching the gland than upon the sex of the pituitary gland responsible for its metabolism. Since, following the administration of oestradiol, radioactivity in the hypothalamus was at all times higher than the corresponding values

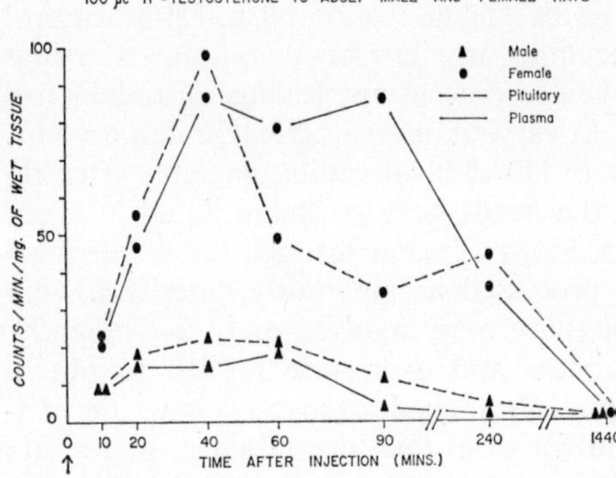

FIG. 23. Radioactivity in both male and female pituitary glands follows plasma values after s.c. administration of ^{3}H-testosterone. (Plasma values in females are very high.) (Green and Michael, unpublished results.)

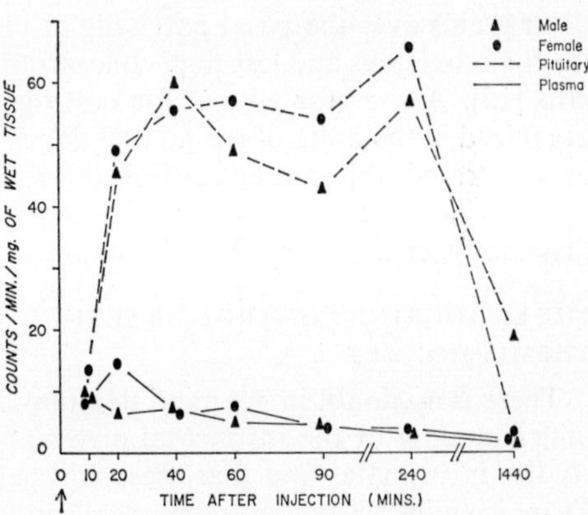

FIG. 24. Radioactivity in both male and female pituitary glands reaches high levels independently of plasma values after s.c. administration of ^{3}H-oestradiol. (Michael and Green, unpublished results.)

in cortex, the results in the rat were in good accord with the notion of a selective uptake of hormone by hypothalamus which originated in the studies with cats.

OESTROGENS IN THE BRAIN OF THE NEWBORN RAT

Attention has recently been re-directed [4] to the role played by hormones during the embryonic or early neonatal period as organizers of the sexual differentiation of the brain into male and female types. It is known that the administration of progestational agents with androgenic activity to pregnant women for threatened abortion has resulted in some degree of masculinization of the genotypically female infant [22]. It became important to ascertain whether or not these steroidal substances could gain access to the rapidly developing central nervous system of the neonatal animal, and use was again made of autoradiography to investigate this problem. ^{3}H-hexoestrol (0·05 μg.) was injected subcutaneously into female rat pups at 3 days of age, great care being taken to prevent any leakage of radioactive oil from the injection site. At varying intervals from 30 min. to 5 hr. after injection, animals were killed by decapitation and, after removal of the lower jaws, the heads were placed in liquid nitrogen for rapid fixation. Frozen sections were cut through the whole head (including the skull) and processed as previously described. Very minute amounts of radioactivity were involved and, consequently, exposure periods of 6 months and over were needed to obtain satisfactory autoradiographs. Prolonged exposures have the disadvantage that background activities due to random radiation are high; nevertheless, very clear evidence of specific uptake of radioactivity by certain nuclear groups within the hypothalamus was obtained. PLATES 5 and 6 show very high concentrations of reduced silver grains over the basal part only of the ventromedial nucleus of the hypothalamus and less high concentrations in the arcuate nucleus also [15]. A receptor system for oestrogens appears to be already organized in the brain of the rat at 3 days of age and could be clearly demonstrated: this finding confirmed for the first time the possibility that hormones could directly influence neural mechanisms during these early, critical periods in development.

THE ENDOCRINE CONTROL OF SEXUAL ACTIVITY IN THE RHESUS MONKEY

There is no doubt in my mind that important contributions to our understanding of the instinctual drives and needs will be made by studies in primates and that these will help us in the clinical field. There is an increasing awareness that certain phenomena, previously regarded as virtually inaccessible, are now becoming amenable to scientific scrutiny; this is so for both intrapsychic and interpersonal events. There is a strong argument for using primates when investigating behavioural mechanisms relevant to psychiatry: this is particularly the case when conditioning and training is involved, because of the great development of the primate neocortex: also in the field of reproductive physiology and behaviour, because the catarrhine (Old World) monkeys alone have a true menstruation and a cycle of about 30 days. Again, because of their complex organization, certain primate societies are especially useful when the interaction of individuals within the social group is being studied. With the establishment of the Primate Behaviour Research Unit in the Department of Psychiatry in 1966, long-term investigations along these lines became possible.

The rhesus monkey, like the woman, has a 28-day menstrual cycle and mating is not confined to those well-defined periods of oestrus that are so characteristic of lower mammals. The factors which determine sexual behaviour, whether they be genetic, developmental, neural or hormonal, are multiple and complex, and the sexual behaviour of laboratory primates reminds one of the human situation in another way also: very striking individual variations and partner preferences exist that are not encountered to anything like the same extent in lower mammals. For these reasons, it is always necessary to work with specific pairs of animals, to use them as their own controls, and not to extrapolate data between pairs.

When a female rhesus monkey is introduced into the cage of a male, unless aggression occurs, two main types of behaviour take place: namely, sexual activity and grooming behaviour. Although grooming was originally regarded simply as serving the needs of hygiene, it is now apparent that it has a wider, social significance. By this behaviour an individual's position within the highly organized primate society is defined [1, 21] and it is related to the establishment of hierarchies of dominance and submission between animals which help to maintain the stability of the group [7]. Changes in mutual grooming behaviour between pairs of monkeys of opposite sex also result from alterations in the reproductive condition in the female baboon [3] and in the chimpanzee [23, 24]. Thus, grooming behaviour occupies a position intermediate between a specifically sexual and a more generally social type of behaviour [17].

If mature, intact male and female rhesus monkeys are paired together daily for hourly test periods and observed behind a one-way vision mirror, it is possible to measure the changes in the patterns of grooming and of sexual behaviour that occur with the phases of the female's menstrual cycle [14, 19]. Well-marked rhythms of male mounting activity (changes in the number of mounts per test) and equally well-marked rhythms of grooming activity (changes in the time spent by each animal grooming its partner) were observed [Fig. 25]. Since these rhythms were abolished by bilateral ovariectomy of the female of the pair, there could be no doubt that they possessed an endocrine basis. It would appear, then, that the view that sexual activity in the primate has been emancipated from endocrine control has been over-stressed. If one considers the pattern of mounting behaviour in specific pairs of animals in more detail

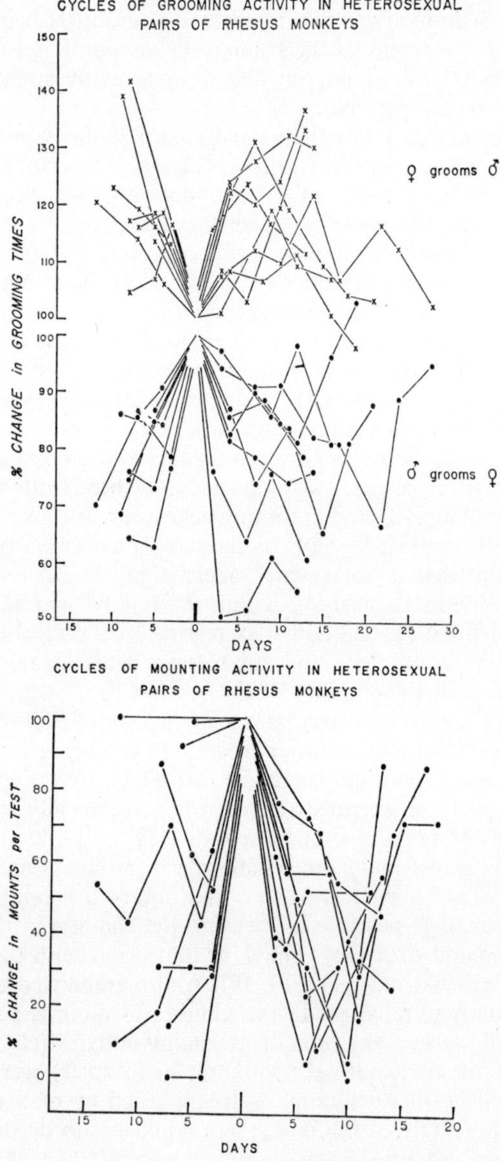

FIG. 25. Rhythms of mounting and of grooming activity that occur in relation to the menstrual cycles of female rhesus monkeys.

[FIG. 26], they fall into three main types: (1) those with well-defined maxima near mid-cycle, sharp decreases early in the luteal phase and secondary increases immediately before menstruation; (2) those with sustained high levels of activity during the follicular phase, again sharp decreases early in the luteal phase and with low levels persisting until menstruation; and (3) those pairs without rhythmic

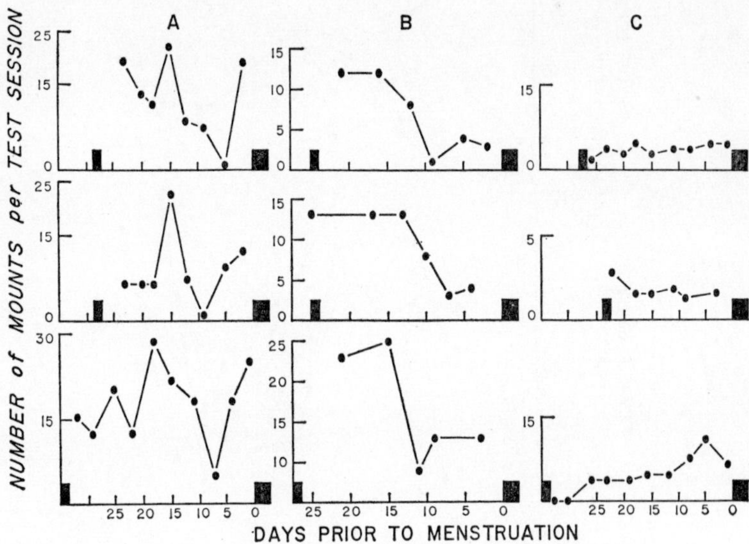

FIG. 26. Rhythmic changes in the mounting activity of male rhesus monkeys during the menstrual cycles of female partners (9 pairs). A, maxima near mid-cycle and secondary rises before menstruation: B, high levels during follicular phase and low levels during luteal phase: C, no rhythmic changes. Solid rectangles indicate menstruation. [*Journal of Endocrinology* (1967) **39**, 81.]

changes in mounting activity in relation to the menstrual cycle.The latter situation was encountered in about 50 per cent. of the pairs studied. It was of interest to attempt to account for these rhythmic changes and, in particular, for the marked decline in mounting activity that was so characteristic of the early part of the luteal phase. In order to do so a more detailed analysis of the behavioural and endocrine factors was necessary. Copulation in the rhesus monkey consists of a series of sexual mounts by the male upon the female, each with an intromission and thrusting, the series being terminated by a final, ejaculatory mount. This mounting sequence is not haphazard, but results from initiating movements by the male (courtship postures, mounting attempts or clasping), and from initiating movements by the female (sexual presentations and various invitational gestures). Endocrine-dependent changes in the mounting activity of

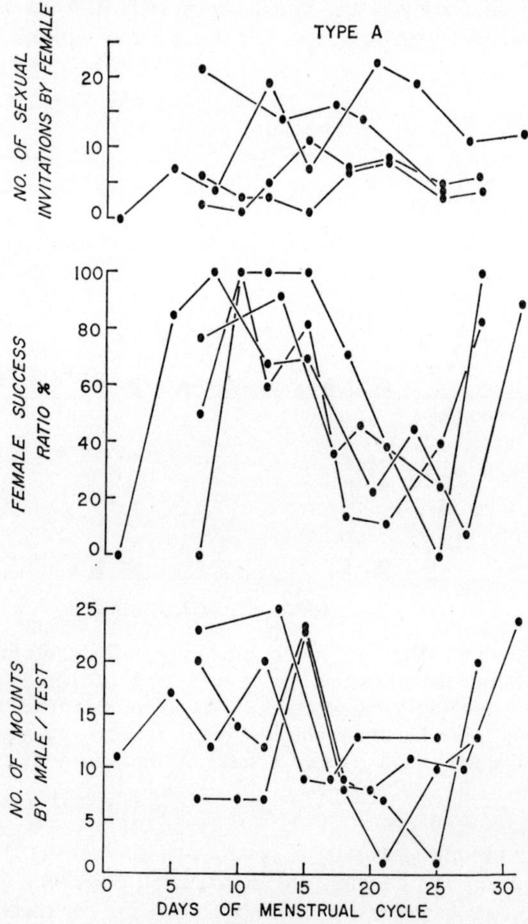

FIG. 27. Illustrating the decline in the female success ratio and her loss of attractiveness during the luteal phase of the cycle when her mounting invitations lose their effectiveness. This coincides with a decline in the number of mounts made by the male.

the males might therefore be mediated by changes in this initiating behaviour. FIGURE 27 shows the changes per test during the four menstrual cycles: (1) in the number of mounts made by the male upon the female; (2) in the number of sexual invitations made by the female to the male; and (3) in the proportion of these invitations that stimulate the male to mount. The latter is termed the Female Success Ratio—successful mounting invitations (those followed by a mount) expressed as a percentage of total mounting invitations made by the female. Although rhythmic changes in the number of mounts per test were observed in relation to the menstrual cycle, with a well-marked decline early in the luteal phase, the number of female sexual invitations remained at about the same level throughout the cycle, and did not decline when male mounting activity did so. However, the proportion of these invitations that were accepted by the male and that were followed by a mount (the female success ratio) diminished markedly during the luteal phase when male mounting activity declined. In such cases as these, the decrease in mounting activity of males was clearly related to the diminished effectiveness of the female sexual invitations and reflected her diminished value as a sexual stimulus during this part of the luteal phase [20]. However, this 'loss of attractiveness' appears not to be the only mechanism responsible for the decline in male sexual activity in the luteal part of the cycle. FIGURE 28 shows the changes per test during three further menstrual cycles in different pairs of monkeys: (1) in the number of mounts made by the male upon the female; (2) in the number of mounting attempts made by the male; and (3) in the proportion of these attempts accepted by the female and followed by a mount. The latter is termed the Male Success Ratio—successful mounting attempts (those followed by a mount) expressed as a percentage of the total mounting attempts made by the male. Although the number of mounts declined in the luteal phase of these cycles also, this was not associated with any corresponding decline in the number of male mounting attempts. However, the proportion accepted by the female (the male success ratio) conspicuously declined when the number of mounts declined. This was seen to be due to a corresponding increase in the number of active *refusals* of male mounting attempts made by these females. In these cases, the female retained her attractiveness, since the male continued to attempt to mount, but it became apparent that a female refusal mechanism was being brought into play during the luteal phase. Ample confirmation of this finding was obtained by studying the effects of progesterone in ovariectomized, oestrogen-treated females. FIGURE 29 shows the highly significant ($P < 0{\cdot}001$) decrease in the mean number of mounts per test made by males when their female partners were receiving 25 mg. progesterone s.c. per day. This decline in mounting by males was associated with a highly significant ($P < 0{\cdot}001$) increase in the mean number of refusals made by

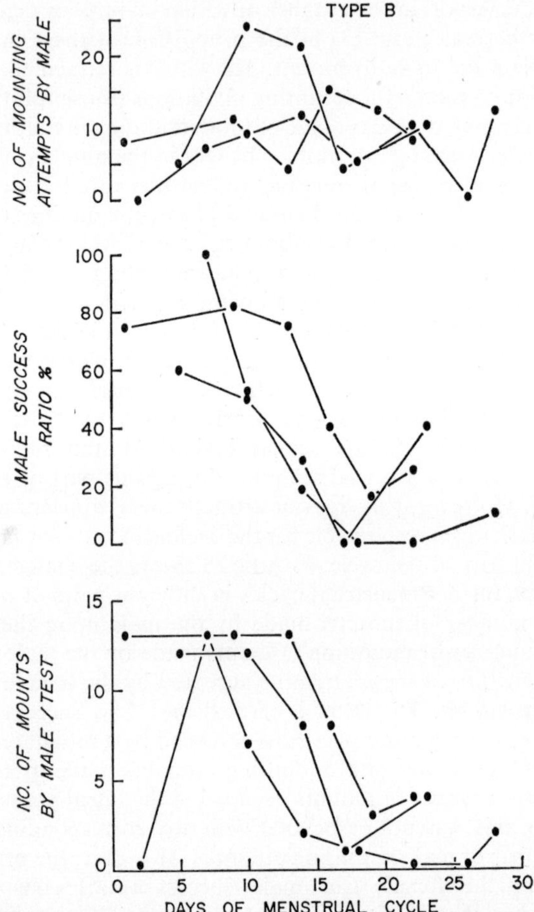

FIG. 28. Other females do not lose attractiveness during the luteal phase and male mounting attempts are met by refusals. This accounts for the decline in the male success ratio at this time.

females in these same tests; the effect was reversed when progesterone was withdrawn.

The studies outlined here represent an attempt, using reproductive behaviour as a model, to unravel some of the mechanisms by which hormones influence the brain and, hence, the behavioural interactions between animals. Although rapid technical advances will soon make studies such as these appear crude indeed, I believe that the principles that have emerged may help in our understanding of the nature of some of the instinctive interactions that occur between people.

Lastly, for this is in a sense a farewell to a man who has been an important influence in my life, a word about psychoanalysis.

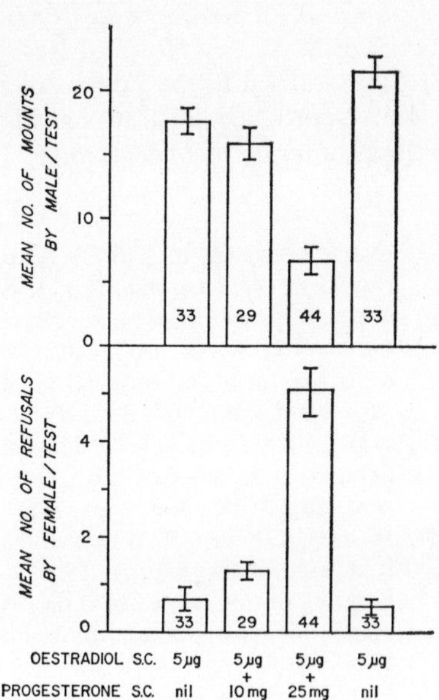

FIG. 29. When ovariectomized female rhesus monkeys receive subcutaneous injections of progesterone in addition to oestradiol, the number of refusals by the females increase and, in the same tests, the number of mounts by the male decreases (4 pairs).

These observations can come more easily from one whose psychoanalytic training was in the British Psychoanalytical Institute during a period when its relations with academic psychiatry were strained. It would be a mistake for psychoanalysts to confuse healthy criticism and scientific scepticism with unhealthy antipathy and prejudice. We have less to fear from the former than from a self-imposed isolation from the great body of medical knowledge by which we are surrounded. There must obviously be a two-way process of continuous cross-fertilization with mutual respect for the complexities of the tasks with which all of us are confronted. During the past 12 years in Aubrey Lewis' department, I only encountered a deep awareness of these needs and a clear recognition that, whatever the language in which we communicate, we are all studying different facets of a single problem—the advancement of the dignity and happiness of our patients.

ACKNOWLEDGEMENTS

The original work reported here has received sustained support over several years from the Medical Research Council, the National Institute of Mental Health, U.S. Public Health Service, the Foundations Fund for Research in Psychiatry, the Wellcome Trust and the Bethlem-Maudsley Hospital Research Fund.

I am grateful to the Editors of the following Journals for permission to reproduce illustrations: Fig. 19, *British Medical Bulletin* [16]; Fig. 25, *Journal of Endocrinology* [19]; Figs. 27 and 28, *Nature* [20].

REFERENCES

1. Carpenter, C. R. (1942) Sexual behavior of free-ranging rhesus monkeys (*Macaca mulatta*). I. Specimen procedures and behavioral characteristics of estrus, *J. comp. Psychol.*, **33**, 113–42.
2. Glascock, R. F., and Michael, R. P. (1962) The localisation of oestrogen in a neurological system in the brain of the female cat, *J. Physiol.* (*Lond.*), **163**, 38–39P.
3. Hall, K. R. L. (1962) The sexual, agonistic, and derived social behaviour patterns of the wild Chacma baboon *Papio ursinus*, *Proc. zool. Soc. Lond.*, **138**, 283–327.
4. Harris, G. W. (1964) Sex hormones, brain development and brain function, *Endrocrinology*, **75**, 627–48.
5. Harris, G. W., and Michael, R. P. (1964) The activation of sexual behaviour by hypothalamic implants of oestrogen, *J. Physiol.* (*Lond.*), **171**, 275–301.
6. Harris, G. W., Michael, R. P., and Scott, P. P. (1958) in *Ciba Foundation Symposium on the Neurological Basis of Behaviour*, pp. 236–51, London.
7. Maslow, A. H., and Flanzbaum, S. (1936) Role of dominance in the social and sexual behavior of infra-human primates. II. An experimental determination of the behavior syndrome of dominance, *J. genet. Psychol.*, **48**, 278–309.
8. Michael, R. P. (1958) Sexual behaviour and the vaginal cycle in the cat, *Nature* (*Lond.*), **181**, 567–8.
9. Michael, R. P. (1961) Observations upon the sexual behaviour of the domestic cat (Felis Catus L.) under laboratory conditions, *Behaviour*, **18**, 1–24.
10. Michael, R. P. (1961) in *Regional Neurochemistry*, ed. Kety, S. S., and Elkes, J., pp. 465–80, Oxford.
11. Michael, R. P. (1962) Oestrogen-sensitive systems in mammalian brains, in *International Congress on Physiological Sciences*, Series No. 47, pp. 650–2.
12. Michael, R. P. (1965) in *The Scientific Basis of Medicine: Annual Reviews*, pp. 316–33, London.
13. Michael, R. P. (1965) in *Hormonal Steroids*, Vol. 2, ed. Martin, L., and Pecile, A., pp. 469–81, New York.

14. MICHAEL, R. P. (1965) Some aspects of the endocrine control of sexual activity in primates, *Proc. roy. Soc. Med.*, **48**, 595–8.
15. MICHAEL, R. P. (1965) The entry of oestrogen into the brain of the neonatal rat, in *Proceedings of the 2nd International Congress on Endocrinology*, Series No. 83, p. 1278, Amsterdam.
16. MICHAEL, R. P. (1965) Oestrogens in the central nervous system, *Brit. med. Bull.*, **21**, 87–90.
17. MICHAEL, R. P., and HERBERT, J. (1963) Menstrual cycle influences grooming behaviour and sexual activity in rhesus monkeys, *Science*, **140**, 500–1.
18. MICHAEL, R. P., and SCOTT, P. P. (1964) The activation of sexual behaviour in cats by the subcutaneous administration of oestrogen, *J. Physiol.* (*Lond.*), **171**, 254–74.
19. MICHAEL, R. P., HERBERT, J., and WELEGALLA, J. (1966) Ovarian hormones and grooming behaviour in the rhesus monkey (*Macaca mulatta*) under laboratory conditions, *J. Endocr.*, **36**, 263–79.
20. MICHAEL, R. P., SAAYMAN, G., and ZUMPE, D. (1967) Sexual attractiveness and receptivity in rhesus monkeys, *Nature* (*Lond.*), **215**, 554–6.
21. WASHBURN, S. L., and DEVORE, I. (1961) The social life of baboons, *Scient. Am.*, **204**, 62–71.
22. WILKINS, L., JONES, H. W., HOLMAN, G. H., and STEMPEL, R. S. (1958) Masculinization of the female fetus associated with administration of oral and intramuscular progestins during gestation: nonadrenal female pseudohermaphrodism, *J. clin. Endocr.*, **18**, 559–85.
23. YERKES, R. M. (1933) Genetic aspects of grooming, a socially important primate behavior pattern, *J. soc. Psychol.*, **4**, 3–25.
24. YOUNG, W. C., and ORBISON, W. D. (1944) Changes in selected features of behaviour in pairs of oppositely sexed chimpanzees during the sexual cycle and after ovariectomy, *J. comp. physiol. Psychol.*, **37**, 107–43.

Index of Names

Anthony, E. J., 147, 148, 152

Baan, P., xi, (Introduction, 6–10)
Barber, L., 11
Bates, S., 123
Beck, A., 194
Bernard, C., x
Binet, A., 65, 66
Birch, H. G., 149
Brengelmann, J. C., 118
Brierley, J. B., 4
Brodie, B. B., 292, 294, 296, 298
Brown, G. W., 12
Bryant, P. E., 65, 74, 78, 79
Burt, C., 51, 66 , 148

Carstairs, G. M., 12
Chess, S., 149
Chrusciel, T. L., 298
Cobb, S., 3
Cochrane, A. L., 35
Connell, P. H., 5
Cooper, J. E., 112
Coppen, A. J., 243, 307
Cowie, V., 168, 182, 184

Davies, D. L., xi, (Ch. 10, 192–206)
Dawson, G. D., 4
Dewhurst, W. G., xi, (Ch. 14, 289–317)
Diggins, F. L., 289

East, N., 122, 123, 129
Eayrs, J. T., 4
Edwards, G., 110, 111, 117
Eysenck, H. J., 66

Fraser, R., 11
Freud, S., 147
Fry, M., 124

Galton, F., 184
Gelder, M. G., x, (Ch. 6, 106–21)
Gibbens, T. C. N., x, (Ch. 7, 122–43)
Gibbons, J. L., 240
Gibson, J. G., 209, 240
Gillies, C., 229
Gjessing, R., 226
Glascock, R. F., 321, 322
Glover, E., 125
Glueck, E., 132
Glueck, S., 132
Goldman-Eisler, F., 11, 107
Golla, F. L., 192
Graham, P., 150, 152, 162
Grant, G., 36
Guttmann, E., 194

Harris, G. W., 4, 318, 319
Helmholtz, H. von, 218
Hermelin, B., 65, 74
Heron, A., 11
Hilliard, L. T., 51, 52
Hinton, J. M., 244

Jackson, H., 114
Jaspers, K., 226

Kety, S. S., xi, (Introduction, 3–5)
King, R. D., 60
King, W. G., 289
Kraepelin, E., 86
Kushlick, A., 57, 62

Lader, M. H., 115
Lewis, A. J., 5, 6, 8, 10, 11, 193, 194, 195, 227, 233, 304
  and child psychiatry, 147, 156
  and clinical research, 107, 195, 226, 227, 228, 233
  and forensic psychiatry, 122
  and mental subnormality, 50, 51, 65
  and metabolic research, 225, 233, 248
  and neuroendocrinology, 318
  and psychiatric education, 8, 196, 197, 198, 202, 205
  and psychiatric genetics, 168, 169
  and psychoanalysis, 333
  and psychological treatment, 107, 111

Lewis, A. J.—*contd.*
  and psychopharmacology, 253
  and psychophysical research, 211
  and psychosomatic medicine, 225, 226
  and the department of psychiatry of the Institute of Psychiatry, ix–xi
  and the Institute of Psychiatry, ix, 4, 5, 227
  and the Medical Research Council Social Psychiatry Unit, 11–12, 83
  and the World Health Organization, 6, 8, 10
Lewis, E. O., 52, 56–57
Loudon, J. B., 12, 36, 41

Malherbe, M., 174
Mapother, E., 192, 193, 194, 195, 201, 205
Markowe, M., 11
Marks, I., 116
Marley, E., xi, (Ch. 13, 253–88), 289, 301
Maudsley, H., 3, 4, 5
Mayer-Gross, W., 194
McHugh, P. R., 233
McIlwain, H., 4
McKissock, W., 114
Meyer, Adolf, 3
Meyer, Alfred, 4, 194
Miall, W. E., 47
Michael, R. P., xi, (Ch. 15, 318–35)
Moncrieff, J., 58
Morse, W. H., 266
Mott, F., 192

Norris, H., 219
Norris, V., 5

O'Connor, N., x, (Introduction, 11–13; Ch. 4, 65–82)

Palmai, G., 136
Piaget, J., 148
Pless, I. B., 162
Price, J. S., 184
Prince, J., 127
Prince, M., 3
Pritchard, M., 152

Rashbass, C., xi, (Ch. 11, 209–24)
Rawnsley, K., x, 12, (Ch. 2, 32–49)
Rey, J. H., 233
Robinson, J. O., 47
Rodnight, R., 4, 289
Russell, G. F. M., xi, 203, (Ch. 12, 225–52)
Rutter, M., xi, (Ch. 8, 147–67)

Sainsbury, P., 107, 209, 210, 211
Sakinofsky, I., 108
Sargant, W., 114
Scott, P. D., 122
Shepherd, M., (Preface, ix–xi), 5, 36, 201
Sherrington, C. S., 218
Shields, J., xi, 4, (Ch. 9, 168–91)
Silverman, M., 140
Slater, E. T. O., 4, 168, 173, 175, 177

Tennent, T., 193, 195
Thomas, A., 149
Tizard, J., x, 11, 17, (Ch. 3, 50–64), 65, 162

Venables, P. H., x, (Ch. 5, 83–105)

Walter, W. G., 194
Whitmore, K., 160
Willcox, D. R. C., 233
Wing, J. K., x, 12, (Ch. 1, 17–31)
Withers, M., 11
Wootton, B., 133

Yarbus, A. L., 217
Yule, W., 162

Index of Subjects

Adrenaline, 291, 292, 293, 295, 297, 298, 299, 300, 301, 302, 304
See also Amines, biogenic
Affective illness, genetic aspects of, 174, 180, 185
Age, maternal, of psychiatric patients, 169, 181–2
Agoraphobia, 112, 114, 115
  and prefrontal leucotomy, 114, 115
Alerting, 293, 295, 302, 303, 309
Amenorrhoea, 234, 236, 239
Amines, biogenic
  amphetamine-like, central actions, 265–70
  and cerebral receptors, 302–4
  and mood, 304
  catecholamines, central actions, 264–5
  central depressant, 264–5, 274–7
    functions in disease, 304 *et seq.*
  in health, 292 *et seq.*
  hypotheses of central action, 292–302, 305–9
  sources of error in study of, 290–2
  sympathomimetic, central actions, 254–70, 276–81
    peripheral actions, 253–4
  See also Adrenaline, Amphetamine, Dopa, 5-Hydroxytryptamine, Noradrenaline, Phenylethylamine, Tryptamines
Amphetamine, 293, 297, 301, 306, 308, 310. *See also* Amines, biogenic
Anorexia nervosa, 233–40
  and appetite disorder, 239–40
  attitudes to feeding in, 239
  criteria for diagnosis of, 233–4
  malnutrition in, 234–6
  possible hypothalamic basis of, 236–9
  psychopathology of, 233, 239
Antidepressants, 305, 306, 307
Approved schools, 128, 138
Arousal, 89–92, 101
Association for the Aid of Crippled Children, 59
Assortative mating, 184
Attitudes to mental disorder
  of general practitioners, 35, 36
  of the general public, 39
  of medical and other university students, 36–9
  of mental welfare officers, 39–40
  of parents, 150
  of patients' relatives, 33–35
Autism, early childhood, 27, 147, 153, 154
  and severe mental subnormality, 79
Automatism, 138
Autonomic activation, 92
Aversion therapy, 115–17
  and patients' attitudes, 117
  and suppression of fantasies, 116
  for sexual disorders, 116, 117
  See also Behaviour therapy

Behaviour therapy, 111–17
  desensitization, 112–15
  See also Aversion therapy
Bereavement, 157–8
Bethlem Royal Hospital, The, 151, 184, 196, 203, 283. *See also* Maudsley Hospital
Birth-order and psychiatric illness, 169, 181–2
Blood-brain barrier, 257, 291, 293, 297, 299, 301, 305, 306, 321
Blood pressure and emotional disorder, 47
Body weight, in depression, 241–2
  in premenstrual tension, 244
Borstal boys, 131
  homosexuality, 134
  mental abnormality, 131
  outcome, 131, 141
  parental relations, 134
  personality, 131, 132, 141
  recidivism, 131, 132, 134, 139

Borstal boys—*contd.*
  sexual behaviour, 133
  See also Delinquency
'Brain damage' in childhood, 154, 163, 164
British Broadcasting Corporation, The, 39, 171
British Council, The, 204
British Postgraduate Medical Federation, The, ix, 195
Brixton Prison, 123, 137, 140
Brooklands experiment, the, 59

Camberwell psychiatric register, 26, 27, 162
Cat, sexual behaviour of, 319–20
  brain implantation of hormone, 320
  oestrous behaviour, 319
  refusal reaction, 319
  stereotaxic techniques, 319
  stilboestrol esters, 320
  vaginal cornification, 319
Child victims of sex offences, 137
  welfare project, 59–62
Childhood, behaviour disorders of
  antisocial behaviour. *See* Delinquency
  encopresis, 148, 155
  enuresis, 163
  fidgetiness, 161
  hyperkinesis, 156, 163
  micropsia, 148–9
  nail-biting, 163
  nightmares, night terrors, 149, 155
  reading, difficulty in, 163
  school phobia, 155
  sleep disturbance, 149, 151, 155
  temper tantrums, 161
  truancy, 155
  See also Childhood, development of behaviour in
Childhood, development of behaviour in
  and age, 151, 156
  and sex, 151, 156
  disorders of, 148–9, 151
  See also Childhood, behaviour disorders of
Children's homes, 59, 60, 61
Chromosomal abnormalities, 182–3, 185
Classification in child psychiatry, 155–6
Clinical research, 227
  education and training for, 194, 195, 200, 203, 227, 228
  moral aspects of, 230–3
  See also Metabolic Unit
Community care, 23, 24, 26, 27
Congenital malformations, 183, 185
Cornell Medical Index Health Questionnaire, 43–5
Cortical activation, 92
Creatinine, urinary output, 230
Criminal careers, 139–41
  responsibility, 138
Cruelty to children, 125

Delinquency
  and antisocial behaviour, 148, 151, 152, 158, 163
  and family background, 133, 134
  and genetic factors, 177
  in girls, 184
  social aspects of, 135, 136
  See also Borstal boys
Depression, 304–7
  metabolic studies of, 240–4
    adrenocortical function in, 240–1
    body weight, water and electrolytes in, 241–2
    endocrine studies in, 240–1
    plasma cortisol in, 240–1
    sleep disturbances in, 244
    thyroid function in, 240
Desensitization, 112–15
  and anxiety, 114, 115
Diagnostic process, the, 28
  in child psychiatry, 160–2
Diploma in Psychological Medicine, 193, 196, 197, 200, 201, 203
  dissertations for, 203, 228
Dopa, 294, 298, 299, 305. *See also* Amines, biogenic
Down's syndrome. *See* Mongolism

Education and training in psychiatry, 7, 8, 9, 10, 192 *et seq.*
  of junior hospital staff (registrars), 192, 193, 198, 203
  of postgraduate students, 193, 194, 204, 205
  See also Clinical research
Educational retardation, 158, 163
Electro-convulsive treatment
  electrolyte changes and, 243

metabolic consequences of, 242
'mock' treatments, 242
psychological effects of, 118
Electroencephalogram, 102
and psychopathy, 129
in Huntington's chorea, 181
quantification of, 90, 102
Electromyogram, 209, 210, 211
and anxiety, 210
and depression, 210
and leucotomy, 210
and restlessness, 210
Epidemiology
of childhood behaviour, 162–4
of early childhood autism, 27
of mental disorders, 32, 47
of mental subnormality, 52
Eye movements, 211 *et seq.*, 232
effects of barbiturates on, 215, 216, 217, 218, 247
vergent, 217
vestibular, 218

Family, the, 156–60
and the mentally subnormal, 57–59
care of discharged psychiatric patients, 21
epidemiological studies of, 169, 185
relationships and problems, 23, 25, 26, 27
See also Parents
Fertility of the mentally ill, 169
Fountain Hospital, The, 51, 182

Galvanic skin response, 108, 115
General practitioners, referral of psychiatric patients by, 35, 36
Goodenough Committee, Report of, 195, 203

Hallucinogens, 308–9
Homicide Act (1957), 138
Huntington's chorea, 169, 181
5-Hydroxytryptamine (serotonin), 289, 292, 293, 294, 296, 297, 298, 299, 300, 301, 302, 308. *See also* Amines, biogenic
Hypnosis, 109–11
in treatment of alcoholism, 111
in treatment of smoking, 111
post-hypnotic effect, 110

Immature animals, behaviour, 259–61
cerebral electrical activity, 257–9
Industrial Rehabilitation Units, 20, 21
Institute for the Study and Treatment of Delinquency, 127
Institute of Psychiatry, The, ix, x, xi, 4, 5, 6, 11, 50, 168, 169, 182, 185, 200, 205, 227, 318
Institutionalism, 17, 18, 24
Intelligence, 65, 66, 118, 148, 163
and cross-modal coding, 73, 74, 75
and infantile psychosis, 153, 154
and mental subnormality, 66
and recidivism, 132
and scholastic function, 79
defects of, 73–77
functional subdivisions of, 72, 73
generality of, 79
See also Mental subnormality; Mental subnormality, severe
Interaction chronograph, 107
Interview
in child psychiatry, 160–2
investigations of, 107–9
standard, of 'family functioning', 28
of 'present mental state', 28
Isle of Wight, epidemiological and experimental research in, 63, 163
Isotopes, application of methods using, 228, 241, 242, 243, 247

King's College Hospital, 192
Kleine-Levin syndrome, 310, 311

London County Council, The, 57, 192, 193, 194

Mania, 305, 306, 308
Marital relationships, 157, 159–60, 162
Maudsley, Hospital, The, ix, 4, 5, 6, 11, 122, 151, 154, 156, 157, 168, 172, 173, 174, 175, 177, 178, 181, 185, 192–6, 198, 199, 203, 205, 283
junior staff, careers of, 203–4, 225
See also Bethlem Royal Hospital
McNaughten Rules, 138
Measurement of family life and relationships, 159–60
of 'mental state', 28
of psychiatric morbidity, 43, 44, 45, 46
Medical Research Council, The, 59, 60, 231, 232, 283, 318

Medical Research Council, The—*contd.*
  Epidemiological Research Unit, 35, 42
  Pneumoconiosis Research Unit, 47
  Psychiatric Genetics Research Unit, 168, 169, 170, 173, 180, 182, 184, 185
  Social Psychiatry Unit, 11–13, 32, 39, 42, 50, 52, 65, 66, 83, 107
Mental Deficiency Act (1913), 52, 122
Mental disorders, links between childhood and adult life, 151–2
Mental Health Act (1959), 33, 39, 54, 72, 136, 231
Mental Health Research Fund, 59
Mental hospitals
  admission rates to, 22
  bed-occupancy in, 17, 22
  comparison of social environments, 18, 19
  discharge rates from, 22
  readmission rates to, 22
Mental subnormality
  and childhood psychosis, 79
  and genetic counselling, 184
  epidemiological studies of, 52–54
  experiments in residential care, 62–63
  genetic aspects of, 182–4
  incentives and learning of skills, 66, 67, 68
  personality and work adjustment, 69–70
  psychotherapy of, 71
  services and institutional care, 51, 57–62
  social competence of, 72
  workshop studies, 54–55
  See also Intelligence; Mental subnormality, severe; Mongolism; Phenylketonuria
Mental subnormality, severe
  and childhood psychosis, 79
  and perception, 74–75
  language and transfer, 78–79
  memory, immediate, 77–78
  memory, long-term, 77–78
  reading and coding, 77
  reading skill, 77
  recall, 77–78
  speech and thinking processes, 74–78
  studies of trainable imbeciles, 55–56
  verbal inefficiency, 76
  vocabulary of, 76
  See also Intelligence, Mental subnormality, Phenylketonuria
Metabolic balances
  calorie, 235
  difficulties in psychiatric patients, 229
  in depression, 242
  in premenstrual tension, 247
  nitrogen, 235, 236
  potassium, sodium, water, 235, 241–2, 244, 247
  principles of, 229 *et seq.*
Metabolic Unit for Psychiatric Research, 225, 228–30, 232, 233, 235, 236, 239, 240, 243, 248, 289
Methysergide, 295, 296, 303, 304, 308
Ministry of Health, The, 26
Mongolism, 56, 57, 182–4
  and maternal health, 182–3
Morbid jealousy, 124
Murder and murderers, 123–4, 138

National Health Service, 196
National Health Service Act (1946), 51
National Institute of Mental Health, 5
Neurosis, genetic aspects of, 174–7, 180
  in childhood, 151, 152, 155, 156, 163
Noradrenaline, 289, 291, 292, 293, 294, 296, 297, 298, 299, 300, 304, 305, 306, 309. *See also* Amines, biogenic
Nystagmus, barbiturate-induced, 247
  physiological, 213

Oestrogens and sexual behaviour of cat, 319
  entry into the central nervous system, 321–5
  in the neonatal rat brain, 325–6
Offenders
  attitude to courts, 128
  cultural factors, 136
  educationally maladjusted, 138
  female, 126
  homosexual, 128
  intelligence, 129
  male and female, 133

neurotic, 130
psychological types, 128–32
psychopathic, 129, 130
remand in custody, 137
social class, 136

'Paradoxical' and 'ultraparadoxical' phenomena, 84–86
Parents
and children, psychiatric illness in, 158, 159
both mentally ill, 168–9
consanguinity of, 179
death of, 157, 158
effects of mental illness on children, 150, 156–9
physical disorders in, 157, 159
See also Family
Pathography, 184
Pedigree studies, 169
Personality and declaration of illness, 46
genetic aspects of, 170–2, 175, 184–5
psychopathic, 129–31, 156
Phenylethylamine, 291, 295, 306, 307. *See also* Amines, biogenic
Phenylketonuria, 169, 181, 182
Phobic disorders, 112, 113
Premenstrual tension, 244–6
Prevalence of mental disorders, 40, 45, 46
of mental subnormality, 56–57
in London, 56
in Middlesex, 56
in Wessex, 57, 62
Primate Behaviour Research Unit, 327
Prostitutes
clients of, 135
prognosis, 126
psychopathology, 125
Psychiatric ailments, detection of, 40
Psychoanalysis, 333
Psychosis
adult and childhood disorders, 151
in adolescence, 151
infantile, 151, 152–4, 156, 163
manic-depressive, in childhood, 152
prison, 124
'Psychosomatic' illness, 225, 226
asthma, in childhood, 155
peptic ulcer, 155
Psychotherapy
and deconditioning therapies, 111–15
and verbal conditioning 108, 109
evaluation of, 112, 113
group, 113, 114
individual, 113, 114
research in, 106, 107, 109, 110, 119

Questionnaires, children's, 160–1

Radioactivity in blood, brain, uterus, 321
in hypothalamus of rat, 324
in nucleus ventromedialis of rat, 326
in pituitary of rat, 324
Rating scales, 28, 88, 100, 112, 113
Register of contacts with psychiatrist, 26
Rehabilitation, 19
Reserpine, 291, 298, 305, 306, 308
Reticular activating system, 89 *et seq.*
inhibitory functions of, 98
Rhesus monkey
dominance and submission, 327
endocrine control of sexual activity, 326 *et seq.*
grooming rhythms, 327
individual rhythms, 327
luteal phase of menstrual cycle, 321
mounting rhythms, 327
progesterone and sexual activity, 331, 332, 333
Rockefeller Foundation, The, 194

Saccadic eye movements, 213, 214, 215, 217, 218
St. Francis' Hospital, 194, 199
Schizophrenia
and body build, 179
and epilepsy, 179
biochemical studies of, 308–10
course of, 21, 23, 24, 25
genetics and, 170
in childhood, 152, 154, 156, 157
mode of inheritance, 178–80
periodic catatonia, 225
possible heterogeneity, 179–80
relation to other disorders, 180–1
social crises in course of, 24
social precipitants of, 23, 27
study of adopted children, 181
twin studies, 177–9
Schizophrenia, chronic, 83
and arousal, 101
coherent delusions in, 91, 99

Schizophrenia, chronic—*contd.*
  incoherence of speech and, 100
  internal inhibition and, 87
  paranoid and non-paranoid, 91, 100
  protective inhibition, 85
  reaction time, 83, 84, 85, 101
  reactive inhibition, 86, 87
  reminiscence, 86
  set, 84
  slowness, 83, 87, 102
  withdrawal, 88, 89, 99
Schizophrenic patients
  age of parents, 26
  attitudes of hospital staff, 21
  attitudes of relatives, 21, 23, 25, 26, 27
  attitudes to discharge, 18, 20, 35
  attitudes to work, 20
  community care, 23, 24, 26
  handicaps of, 20, 25
  learning curve, 19
  length of stay in hospital, 18, 22, 23, 24, 25, 34
  marital status, 26, 34
  motivation, 19
  readmission to hospital, 22, 24
  rehabilitation, 19, 20, 21, 25
  secondary handicaps, 18, 25
  symptomatology, 18, 23, 24, 25, 28
Seeing, probability of, 222
Serotonin. *See* 5-Hydroxytryptamine
Services for offenders, 136–9
  for the mentally subnormal, 57–62
  for schizophrenics, 19–21, 24, 26
Servo-mechanism, 98
Sex, nuclear or chromosomal, 169, 179
Sexual deviations
  exhibitionism, 123
  homosexuality, 128, 133, 134, 169, 176, 181–2
  transvestism, 116, 117, 139
Sheltered work, 20, 21
Shoplifting, 126–8
Sibling studies, 169, 184
Skin potential
  and epidermal membrane, 96
  level, 90 *et seq.*
  response, 88
  spontaneous fluctuations, 94
Sleep, 244, 292, 293, 295, 298, 302
Social anthropology, 33, 42
Social attitudes and mental disorder, 40, 42, 43, 45, 46
South Wales, 32, 33, 34, 35, 42
  detachment of M.R.C. Social Psychiatry Unit, 32
  private population census in, 42
  social groupings in, 42, 43
Symptom scales, 43, 44

Temperament, 162
  development of, 149–50
Thefts
  of motor cars, 126
  psychological types of, 126, 128
Threshold, two-click, 100
  two-flash, 90 *et seq.*
    effect of drugs on, 97
Tristan da Cunha—community characteristics, 40
  epidemic of hysteria, 40, 41
  headaches in the population, 41
  Norwegian expedition to (1937), 41, 42
  socio-medical survey (1962), 41
Tryptamines, 289, 290, 291, 293, 295, 297, 298, 300, 301, 303, 305, 306, 309, 310
  central actions, 271–6
  See also Amines, biogenic
Twin studies
  and fingerprints, 174
  and temperament, 150
  diagnostic resemblance in, 175–6
  methodology of, 170
  of affective illness, 174, 185
  of anxiety, 169, 175
  of childhood behaviour disorder, 177
  of discordant pairs, 169, 185
  of homosexuality, 176
  of hysteria, 174
  of intelligence, 172
  of neurosis and personality disorder, 174–6
  of normal personality, 169, 170–3
  of response to drugs, 169
  of schizophrenia, 177–9
  zygosity determination in, 174
Twins
  brought up apart, 171–3
  in mental hospitals, 173
  Maudsley Hospital Register of, 173–9
  normal children, 170–1

University of London, 194, 200, 201

Venereal disease, 135
Visual localization, 218
system, temporal summation in, 221
threshold, 220, 221, 222
Weight loss, insensible, 230
White noise, 86, 92, 93
Wood Report (1929), 52
World Health Organization, The, 6, 8, 10, 136, 185, 204